Art is Work

Milton Glaser

PHOTOGRAPH: STEPHEN GREEN ARMITAGE

Milton Glaser

Art is Work

THE OVERLOOK PRESS, WOODSTOCK & NEW YORK

Dedication

For Shirley, Annie, Willy, Mimi, Ollie, and Mookie

Acknowledgements

This book would still be a proposal if not for the enthusiastic and intelligent efforts of Katja Maas and the consistent support and guidance of Peter Mayer.

Also my thanks to my friend, the ever resourceful photographer Matthew Klein, who has, as this volume documents, helped me create many of my projects over the last 30 years.

Every effort has been made to correctly attribute work mentioned in this book that was of a collaborative nature. Any errors or omissions will be corrected in future editions.

First published in the United States in 2000 by
The Overlook Press, Peter Mayer Publishers, Inc.
Lewis Hollow Road Woodstock, NY 12498
www.overlookpress.com

Library of Congress Cataloging-in-Publication Data

Glaser, Milton, 1929-
Art is work : graphic design, interiors, objects, and illustrations / Milton Glaser.
p. cm.
Includes index.
1. Glaser, Milton—Themes, motives. 2. Glaser, Milton—Sources.
I. Title.
NC999.4.G55 A4 2000 741.6"092—dc21 00-057986

Book design by Milton Glaser and Katja Maas
Manufactured in Hong Kong
First Edition
9 8 7 6 5 4 3 2 1
ISBN 1-58567-069-3
ISBN 1-58567-071-5 (deluxe ed.)

Introduction

If one of the definitions we have concerning art is that it serves its public by reflecting and explaining the world at a particular moment in history, it is hard to believe that design does not serve in a similar way. In any case, the issue has become blurred since art currently seems mostly about money, and designers seem to be increasingly concerned about ethics, the environment, and their effect on the world. There seems to be much confusion about what we mean when we use the word *art*. I have a recommendation. We eliminate the word *art* and replace it with *work* and develop the following descriptions:

1. Work that goes beyond its functional intention and moves us in deep and mysterious ways we call *great work*.

2. Work that is conceived and executed with elegance and rigor we call *good work*.

3. Work that meets its intended need honestly and without pretense we call simply *work*.

4. Everything else, the sad and shoddy stuff of daily life, can come under the heading of *bad work*.

This simple change could eliminate anxiety for thousands of people who worry about whether they are artists or not, but this would not be its most significant consequence. More important, it could restore art to a central, useful activity in daily life – something for which we have been waiting for a very long while.

Interview with Peter Mayer, twenty five years after the first book, MILTON GLASER GRAPHIC DESIGN. Mayer's questions are printed in bold.

What is design?

What is design?

Obviously I have given this issue a lot of thought over the years. In teaching, you have to be clear about what you tell your students, so I developed a set of definitions about what design could be. One definition is that design is the intervention in the flow of events to produce a desired effect; another is that design is the introduction of intention in human affairs. A third and a rather elegant definition is that design moves things from an existing condition to a preferred one. This last one reduces the complexity of the idea, but I like all three definitions. Design doesn't have to have a visual component. Ultimately, anything purposeful can be called an act of design.

The title of this book is *Art is Work*. Do you ascribe any social, moral, or professional attributes to the word "work" when it is applied to design?

Work is essential to people's lives. To do work that is meaningful and excellent seems a fundamental desire of the best human beings. If we assume that art is a form of work, it becomes more related to our daily life. The disassociation of art from other human activities has impoverished our lives. When art is defined as an activity driven entirely by the needs of self-expression, I become very nervous. The overwhelming history of art, in fact, has been the history of people doing work for a specific purpose; in other words, commissioned works with specific intentions. After all, Michelangelo did not paint the "Last Judgement" to express himself. He painted it because the Pope wanted to scare the bejeesus out of the congregation. The idea that art is primarily an expressive medium is a recent invention not more than two hundred years old. This notion is supported by individuals like Vincent van Gogh, who couldn't work for anybody because he was so emotionally incapacitated; he has assumed heroic status as a result. One quickly realizes that Van Gogh is an aberration in the history of art. It is more instructive to look at another genius like Rubens, who organized painting workshops, executed innumerable commissions, and whose life was spent responding to other people's needs. Art is not only a vehicle for self-expression or exclusively for the pursuit of the spiritual. From the very beginning, drawing an animal on the wall of a cave had a purpose—you would more easily be able to control the animal and this magic would help the tribe. In a most fundamental way work that was socially productive was very often combined with personal expressiveness to define the nature of art. If the word "fine" means to purify, when used to explain the difference between fine and applied art, one has to ask what is the impure in the latter. The lack of a spiritual intention seems to be the answer. However, we come across very few works created exclusively for a spiritual purpose. Throughout history, art has been purposeful and, almost without exception, has had a directive.

Can the commissioning of Piero della Francesca by the Duke of Urbino for his portrait really be compared to a record company commissioning you to do that famous head of Bob Dylan for a poster sleeve insert? [p. 60]

It is difficult to compare them because there is so little agreement about what art is. One could take the point of view that art is whatever you point at and call art, the judgement of the art world at a particular moment in time. At this postmodern moment, another view is that artistic standards are a conspiracy of history to be viewed with scepticism. Or we can believe that art has standards that derive from historical comparisons. We know that in the presence of certain works we feel transformed. In our minds we establish a threshold at which we are metaphysically transformed. For me, art is anything above that threshold, whatever the category. We discover that a Persian rug or a work of Chinese pottery can be more transforming than an oil painting. It's not the category that seems to matter, but the effect the work produces in us.

Yes, but aren't rugs and pottery squarely within the tradition of artistic workmanship, and isn't that something different altogether?

During her graduate studies my wife Shirley reintroduced me to African sculpture. These works were never intended to be "art"—in fact the construct doesn't even exist in the culture—yet they are incredibly powerful in their effect on our consciousness. Few cultures—including that of Hellenistic Greece—have produced an idiom so moving. Its expressive power cannot be denied. But it was also created for reasons other than making art.

Illustration has been central to your design. It is one example of your elusiveness regarding a particular artistic niche. During your first quarter century as a central figure within Pushpin Studios, there was an attempt by the studio to break down many distinctions in professional practice. Why was that important to you?

I was always personally interested in the idea that you could draw, you could design, you could do three-dimensional work, and so on. At Pushpin we viewed ourselves to some degree as generalists, not specialists. It really emerged from the Western tradition. Artists like Giotto, Michelangelo, and Leonardo were also architects, designed uniforms, and did lettering. In their day there was no need for the extraordinary specialization that our culture seems to value. Specialization comes out of the needs of commerce. From a professional point of view, typecasting is a more efficient way of using people. It seemed to me that one could practice a broad spectrum of activities and learn from those activities so that one informed the other. This is not necessarily true for everyone, nor should it be. I'm not even suggesting this is a desirable aim. I wanted to do different things that interested me. I was interested in interiors. I was interested then, as now, in color and the relationship between space and light. I was interested in drawing. I was interested in typography and letterforms. I was interested in the intersection of design and illustration. It seemed to me that rich results could emerge from the hands of somebody with a variety of interests. I always thought that drawing and illustration established my sense of scale and proportion, which in turn could be applied to a page of typography. I did not see these categories as being unrelated. I thought each supported and broadened the possibilities of the other. One of the things that may make my work distinctive is that I see no difference between drawing and designing. To some degree, designers think I'm an illustrator and illustrators think I'm a designer. If you cannot draw, you must draw on the image of others.

Intention and change are integral in your approach to work. Where do you begin?

The first question to be asked about any design problem is: who is it for? This is a question that obviously relates to the nature of the audience. Who are the people in that audience? What do they know? What do they desire? The job is empathizing sufficiently with them in order to shape the message to accommodate their nature. It is not all quantifiable and is partly intuitive. You then have to ask yourself, what do I tell them and what do I want them to do? That links the message to the audience's response. In all cases you want the audience to do something, to buy something, to go to a concert, to become informed about a subject, to vote for a particular politician. Finally, the question emerges: how can I express that message most forcefully and most appropriately? Here, for the first time, aesthetics, organization, and appearance come to the fore. In the first two phases questions of beauty are not part of the thought process. Only in the third phase do I choose a particular form to express the message. That is informed by my own sense of style, by the vernacular language surrounding me, by the zeitgeist, and by the other factors that shape our ideas of beauty and appropriateness.

You've been doing this for a long time, but you still like to draw, create, print, design, and paste.

I'm never happier than when I'm making things or thinking about making things. I have not lost the passion or the satisfaction of working. When I was doing the Dante monoprints last year, I would go to the studio at nine a.m. and before I knew it, it was twelve o'clock at night. I felt the same way when I was a student. It's an experience I cannot imagine living without.

How do you keep your ideas fresh?

Without generalizing too much, at a certain point we all lose the capacity to accept the new. For instance, the music you grew up with becomes your identity, and it becomes very hard to listen to new music with the same level of interest or appreciation. Then you discover that you haven't heard of the musician that has the country's number one hit. Finally it all begins to sound strange and uninteresting. We have preferences that we develop throughout a lifetime, and there is no eliminating those preferences. We can only hope to keep an open mind and recognize that these new forms have vitality even if we don't like them.

Do the ideas always have to be new?

Our culture is obsessed with the new. This obsession is driven by economic interests. Magazines, for instance, have to celebrate the new because they are based on the idea of what's new, what's hot, and not necessarily what's good. The new is energizing and essential to our economic system. Things occur that are fresh and represent an opening for the imagination. So as a teacher, I can say you must remain open to fresh possibilities. At the same time, you must be critical, not simply accept what is new without a historical frame of reference.

You are a designer who comes out of a classic tradition -- your studies in Bologna with Morandi, your interest in Piero, Monet, and many other artists. What is there in that tradition that can find a platform in today's environment?

You have to be aware that we're not talking about art now. Much of what is produced, driven by advertising and fashion, is basically ephemeral and concerned with novelty. It is work that exists for two, three, or five years. We've just gone through what I think is a misunderstood period of typographical design. Type was used expressively at the expense of understanding.

Yet some people really liked that work and thought it was some new beginning.

If you are in the design field you have to understand this ephemeral characteristic. There is a lot of work that signals the moment and has no other ambition. It doesn't aspire to become a permanent part of human history. Novelty has always been and will continue to be an aspect of work—short-term, opportunistic work that takes advantage of a shift in language signals something to people, particularly when you are selling products to them.

Does this kind of work have any lasting influence?

It has opened the way for more expressive ideas in the area of typography. It was integral to the work of the Futurists and the Dadaists and their typography. But, fortunately, disregarding the meaning of words was something that could not persist. It has finally become less interesting and everybody has moved along.

A lot of life consists of walking by things. How do you arrest the viewer? You have often said that the goal of posters is to sell something and the job is to stop the viewer for a second. Which is more important, the message or the image?

Which is more integral in a pop song, the words or the music? Obviously they are both important, although in certain cases the music is much better than the words, and in others the words are better than the tune. Ultimately, we hope they are two of a piece, that they no longer can be thought of separately.

To what extent do clients impose their will on your work?

The nature of the professional life means you are constantly working with people you don't know. As in all relationships, there are good ones and bad ones. Through the years I've come to believe the personal relationship with a client is central to the quality of the work produced.

When does the designer/client relationship work best?

A good brief expresses the objectives. A bad brief says, "Do anything you want." Then, when you bring in the solution, the client says, "You missed the point." (Incidentally, it is usually done this way to suggest some vague idea of artistic freedom, but that is nonsense.) Uncontrolled egocentricity, on the part of either the client or designer, is counterproductive. Getting your own way is usually less desirable than solving the problem. The good brief does not offer freedom; it establishes boundaries. Incidentally, the brief can be challenged. A designer can say, "I don't think this is the most important aspect in terms of what needs to be communicated." The best jobs I've done in my life came about because I had a great relationship with somebody who trusted me and my judgement. I wanted to do the best work I could for that client. Not to express myself, not to impose my vision, but to do work that would solve the problem because we were in the same boat and we were trying to achieve the same thing. Usually, because of my relationship with my clients, I show them one solution. If they're unconvinced, I'll do something else. The process of showing endless variations usually is exhausting and also counterproductive. An editor once complained that he needed some guidance in selecting a magazine cover. The art director had submitted two hundred alternatives. I told him it wasn't possible to make a selection from two hundred alternatives.

What about the budget?

The budget is not a significant factor, although it has some effect. It all relates to creating an environment in which people feel they want to do their best work. In my mind, an art director's major role is to make people do their best work.

And also pick the right designer for the project?

First, you have to find somebody who is intrinsically interested in the job. Second, you have to shape the problem so that the person feels they have a contribution to make. It is devastating for anyone to feel that they are just another cog, and that things have already been figured out. "Give me something by Monday and make sure you make the type big." That guarantees a mediocre product because the designer has been reduced to an anonymous vendor. You're saying, in effect, "Give me a pound of bologna and make sure that it's not too expensive." This approach robs people of their emotional and intellectual energy. In certain circumstances you find small organizations paying very little money for designers' services but somehow managing to maintain a wonderful level of quality because people feel their work is respected. Of course, the financial constraint should be real, not a device to rip someone off.

What about pressures of time?

A friend once told me: "Fast, cheap, and good—you can have two out of three." Time constraints very often generate quality. I don't try to do a two-week job in one day. I transform it into a one-day job. I know what is attainable within a day, and I know how to marshal my resources so I can most effectively do something within that amount of time. If someone commissions a drawing and it's due in four hours, I'm not going to do cross-hatching.

You have talked about dignity and the loss of dignity in the design community. How do you reconcile this idea of dignity with concepts of business in which the bottom line is everything?

Ultimately, I can't believe that the species can ignore the fact that there are other things in life besides money. My fundamental belief is that form-making is essential to a culture and those who make form to communicate ideas have a very important responsibility. Since the dawn of history, those involved in transferring ideas from one place to another have had an important role in shaping the value system of our culture. Today designers take ideas that generally don't originate with them and transfer them to the culture at large in some way. Sometimes this activity has been so compromised that those involved don't want to examine the nature of the message they are transferring. In the advertising field the central issue is not whether you are harming your culture; it is how effectively you are communicating your client's desires. I've always found this an ethical problem — not from a position of self-righteousness but from a position of self-questioning. What is my responsibility to others, what can I do in the course of my daily work that won't make me ashamed of what I do? What I'm interested in from that point of view are decisions that come out of another historical model, which is the culture of art, the theory of beauty, and the well-made object; other important values don't always have to be trumped by economic considerations. I believe well-made things have a beneficial social effect.

It would seem with you to come down to personal decisions about how people want to live their lives. But I'm not sure too many people ask the questions you do.

Everybody has the notion of doing the right thing, wherever that comes from. When you violate your own belief something happens to the personality and to the self—something is damaged.

Is there something about living in New York that exacerbates this factor?

I spent several years in Bologna, and Shirley and I spent a year in Rome, and we've gone back for extended stays. Those were important experiences. But New York has always been a driving force in my life. I've received a tremendous education here. I've had access to things that I would never have had access to any place else. The challenge of competition, the high levels of expectation and many of the best and most interesting people in this field make New York irresistible as a place to accomplish things. Of course there are many reasons for living elsewhere, too.

Do you think it really matters where designers are based now? After all, is there really much difference today between the American design community and, say, the European one?

Less and less. It has become one vernacular language. Globalism in advertising and communications has little respect for local peculiarities.

Is this the inevitable consequence of the advances in communication, especially the Internet?

The Internet erodes culture. It destroys the prohibitions about what you can and can't do. And since culture is largely defined by what you can't do, the Internet is post-cultural.

A new format and a new world has emerged with the development of web page design. How is that affecting the design community?

Many aspects of electronic media have become big economic forces in the culture. The same design issues still hold true whether we are talking of web pages or other things. It's still the same question of understanding how to convince an audience of something.

Is there a different kind of client today? Perhaps there is a different set of needs. Does that require a different vocabulary from the designer?

It is a learning process and mistakes are made. But everybody is beginning to coalesce around a set of principles, some of which are already useless. We're at a point where people are trying to understand what is effective and what is not. That is always true of new categories of work. Some succeed, and those that do are copied. We are in a field where imitation and plagiarism are rampant and accepted.

In a wider context, has technology fundamentally changed the role of the designer?

The computer and devaluation of drawing skills have undoubtedly changed things. We are living in a "collage" world. The extraordinary reservoir of available historical and contemporary imagery means designers can find and assemble anything on screen. It can be called electronic surrealism. You can take images from any moment in history, assemble them electronically, distort them, shift them, stretch them, color them, and make them your own to some degree. But you're not starting with material that you have invented.

Doesn't all art play on previous ideas?

Of course. I wasn't saying that collage is not an imaginative approach. After all, since Max Ernst and Kurt Schwitters invented collage, it has been a fundamental tool of artists. In fact, it is hard to understand how we lived without it. The work we see now all tends to be assembled of existing materials — combined, distorted, recontextualized. The process has changed.

Are skills and talents being lost because of these changes?

Certain skills have become irreparably lost. People have lost the motivation to draw because drawing seems unrelated to their vocational life. The Chinese have a quote that has always given me comfort: "When things are at their fullest they are already in decline." Basically the act of drawing has nothing to do with being an illustrator. We draw because it enables us to see. The act of drawing is perhaps the only time you pay attention to what is in front of you. For instance, if I decided to draw you, I would pay attention to how much gray there is in your beard and how wrinkled your shirt is and what kind of shadow is falling across your face. I wouldn't pay attention to that otherwise. I am immune to experience the same way that most people are. Drawing is the path to observation and attentiveness. Technology makes old standards irrelevant and creates its own aesthetic.

So observation and attentiveness are lost?

Yes, but the form-making impulse is so powerful in human behavior that even the most incomprehensible technology eventually becomes usable as an instrument of the imagination. One has to remain optimistic about this and not simply deplore changes. Some older practitioners view these changes as both dangerous and a reduction of artistic quality and basically say that this new stuff is all trash. Many young people feel they are being criticized and held in contempt. This separation hurts the field and the sense of generosity and professional friendliness that should characterize our practice.

We've been talking mostly of two-dimensional work, but in fact in your career you have always done work in which drawing perhaps was only a starting point. What is the effect of technology, if any, on three-dimensional work?

Well, I refer to a recent quote by the well-known architect, Charles Gwathmey: "The worst thing that has happened to the field of architecture is that people don't draw anymore." He thinks a lack of drawing skill is a tremendous limitation for an architect. The computer is not useful as a conceptual instrument. It crystallizes an idea too quickly, before that idea has had a chance to develop conceptually. There isn't anything more powerful in learning than the interrelationship of eyes, hand, and brain. When you're thinking, you do a sketch and it's fuzzy. You have to keep it fuzzy so that the brain looks at it and imagines another iteration that is clearer. Then you do another sketch that advances it again. It may take a number of these intermediate solutions before you arrive. Sadly, the computer bypasses this dialectic between the hand and the brain.

But architects continue to design buildings with the help of computers and some of them are very good.

Yes, but something is lost. If you get on the computer right away you are immediately subjected to the will of the computer. What people don't understand (I use this analogy frequently) is that the computer, which seems like a willing servant — at first an empowering servant — turns out to be like the servant in the famous film with Dirk Bogarde in which, by the end, the servant has become the master and the master the servant. It changes your value system, it changes the way you think and it is an encumbrance to certain kinds of thought. This needs to be put alongside the advantages. My wife wanted to buy me a good turntable on which to play our old LPs. She went to a store and asked for the best turntable. She bought a turntable called "The Well Tempered." It was a primitive looking wooden box consisting of a tone arm stuck in a tube of silicon, a thick plastic base, an elastic cord that moved the turntable and nothing else. In order to make it work, you had to lift the arm onto the record. It was like the first Victrola. This new one cost one thousand dollars and it looked like nothing. So I went to the store and I said, "What is this dinky thing you sold my wife for a thousand dollars?" He asked, "Did you play it?" I said, "No." He said, "Go home and play it." I went home and put the arm on the record, and I heard the most extraordinarily glorious music. I went back and said, "What's that about?" He said, "Every time there is a piece of convenient technology added to the record player, we lose musical quality. What you want is an uninterrupted relationship between the needle, the arm, and the speaker. If you put a spring in there that brings the arm back, you lose fidelity. If you put a button in there that starts it at the right spot, you lose some more. It is only in this direct relationship between the needle, the arm, and the speaker that you get the sound that is better than any CD."

There is no instrument more direct than a pencil and a piece of paper for the expression of ideas. Everything else that interferes with that direct relationship between the eyes, the mind, the arm, and the hand causes a loss of fidelity, if I can use that word this way. I like the idea that this ultimate reductive simplicity is the way to elicit the most extraordinary functions of the brain.

So we are losing something important with technology?

Technology has a price, like everything else. It can be used well or badly, and it changes forms. I mean it changes our perceptions of form, and we're at a point where we're going to have to deal with it. You lose some things and you gain others.

You're of a certain age; what are your personal goals?

I don't think I have any new personal goals. Two years ago I bought a black and white houndstooth jacket, something I had wanted since I was a teenager. After I bought it, I suddenly realized that I no longer had any aspirations.

Would you like to do any other kind of work?

It's not the categories of work. Let me try to be clear on that. It is people I work with, the nature of clients and the shared objectives.

You said that twenty-five years ago.

It's all still true. On the other hand, the idea of sitting down and drawing something, whatever it is, has not lost its importance in my life. It's not what you do; it's the way you do it. Even though you may have done something a thousand times, the issue still is how do you make it extraordinary?

Design and Language

While driving in the country with my wife, Shirley, we passed the undistinguished sign depicted below. "That's a fantastically designed sign," I said. My wife, as straight man, said, "What makes you say that?" "Well," I replied, "if the purpose of the sign is to get you to go to this garage to get your car fixed, it uses language brilliantly." Then, slipping into my most pedagogical tone, I continued. "Why doesn't someone go to a strange garage to have his car repaired? Because he's afraid of being ripped off." To reassure the customer, garages frequently use the word "reliable" in their self-description. Because it is used so often (frequently by scoundrels), it has lost credibility. The genius in this sign is the use of the word "Dutchman." Incidentally, no one uses this archaic term any longer—"he's Dutch" having replaced "he's a Dutchman"—but it serves the mood of the sign and conjures visions of hard-working, honest workmen and small boys with fingers in the dike that we all remember from childhood. The word "Dutchman" makes "reliable" believable. Of course, here we have entered the realm of stereotypes. If you think I'm making this up, try substituting "French" or "Indonesian" for "Dutchman" and see how completely unconvincing the sign becomes. All of this may have to do with our preexisting preferences, but that's one of the things that design and persuasion depend on. "Uh huh," said my wife.

RELIABLE DUTCHMAN
AUTO REPAIR

The Role of the Poster

An interview with *Commercial Art* from 1989.

What is the commercial / artistic / social role of the poster?

If by "role" we mean a pre-existing, intrinsic function, then the poster is to convey information from a source to an audience in order to move that audience to an amplification or change of perception that produces an awareness or an action.

When a poster has a commercial intention it is obviously to convince an audience to buy goods or services. The artistic role of any poster is more complicated. Depending on your definition, posters do not have to be "artistic" to be effective—i.e., be successful in their "roles." It is far more important for posters to be effective than artistic. The aesthetic part of poster making has more to do with the objectives of its maker than the requirements of its form. Because of the poster's historical relationship to the world of painting, and by virtue of its physical size, the poster seems to offer more opportunities for the designer to do artistic or imaginative work than many of the other areas in which he may be working.

In addition to the significant function of informing and motivating a public audience, the question of the poster's social role is a more subtle one. Does society benefit from works that have "artistic" merit and are well-made? Without beginning to define those evasive terms I would say yes, although I would be hard-pressed to prove a case. To add to the ambiguity, it should be noted that a well-made object may have little artistic merit, and an artistic object does not have to be well made.

What do you think of the old-fashioned term "commercial art" (vis-à-vis "graphic design")? Design seems to occupy the place between fine art and craft, between aesthetics and commerce, beauty and persuasion, novelty and familiarity, and so on. Obviously, the emphasis between the polarities changes in response to the specific problem, and the intention and talent of the designer. The term "commercial art" is a simplification and seems to eliminate the inherent conflict. For this reason I prefer the more ambiguous term "graphic design."

Is money a corrupting influence in poster design? Perhaps in one sense: When financial risks are greatest, clients tend to be most conservative. The fear of losing a significant amount of money can have a chilling effect on one's sense of adventure and imagination.

What is your view of the poster and its relation to "high art"? When does "high art" meet "low art"? Is everything above this demarcation "art" and everything below "non-art"? Shall we call the material below the line craft, applied art, commercial art, decoration? Who invented this question? Who is served by the distinction? Does it matter? The search for "high art" is a theological issue, like the search for the true cross. The culture priests attempt to protect the world from false religion or faith, a never ending task. I'm encouraged by one simple fact: We value a good rug, a beautiful book, or a good poster over any bad painting.

Does mass reproduction diminish the value of posters—i.e., does the value in visual matters depend on the uniqueness of the masterpieces? I seem to be getting terribly Talmudic, but it depends on one's definition of value; the most significant value of any work of art or design is in its effect on the world. Mass reproduction is one way for these works to be seen and experienced. Of course, this has nothing to do with the selling price of art objects. In the first case we are talking about the value of art in a cultural and historical sense, in the second we're talking about the manipulations and illusions of the marketplace.

I was asked to create a poster for the School of Visual Arts (SVA) interpreting a text by Alexander Pope that deals with the relationship between the old and the new. The school wanted to be seen as a serious educational institution to attract students interested in the subject of style and art.

RIGHT My fuzzy original thoughts had to do with playing with the words in some way, emphasizing some, diminishing others, to create a provocative sentence. The color forms are a substitution for an idea I hoped would follow. Clearly there was much work to do. I began with this sketch on the back of a pad as a first response to the words themselves:

In words as fashions the same rule will hold,
Alike fantastic if too new or old.
Be not the first by whom new are tried,
Nor yet the last to lay old aside.

On the following pages I've documented the convoluted path from this sketch to the finished poster. For one reason or another it was more difficult than usual. Perhaps because I found the poem itself resistant.

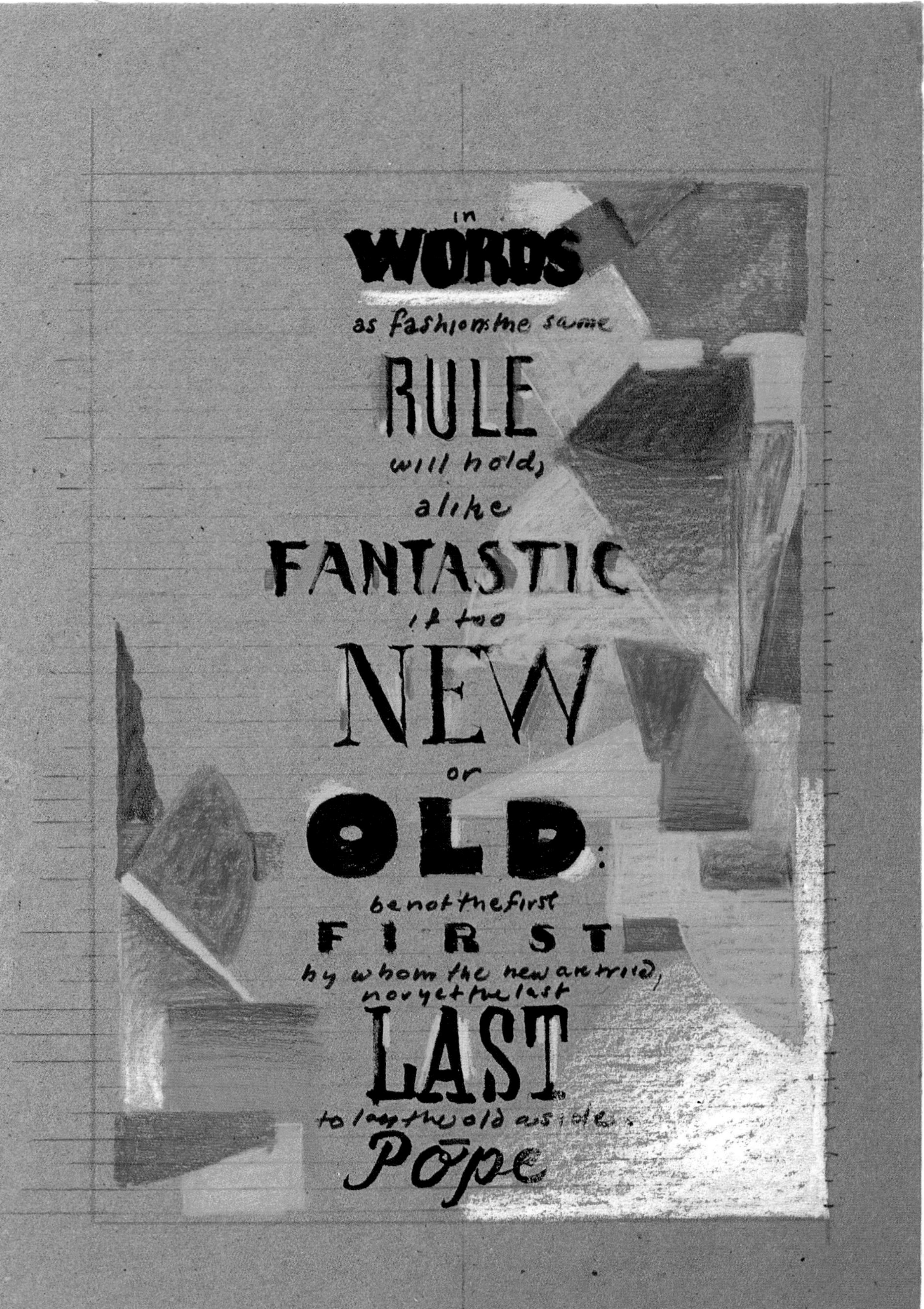

1

2

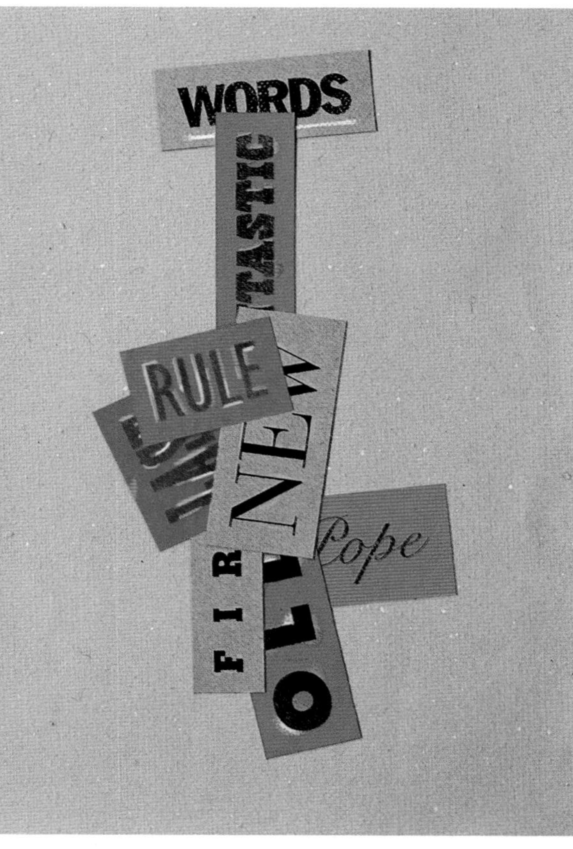

3

TOP LEFT I printed some of the words on scraps of colored paper, hoping that it would lead to a solution.

TOP RIGHT When that didn't work, I collapsed the fragments, with the idea of running the actual poem alongside the visual.

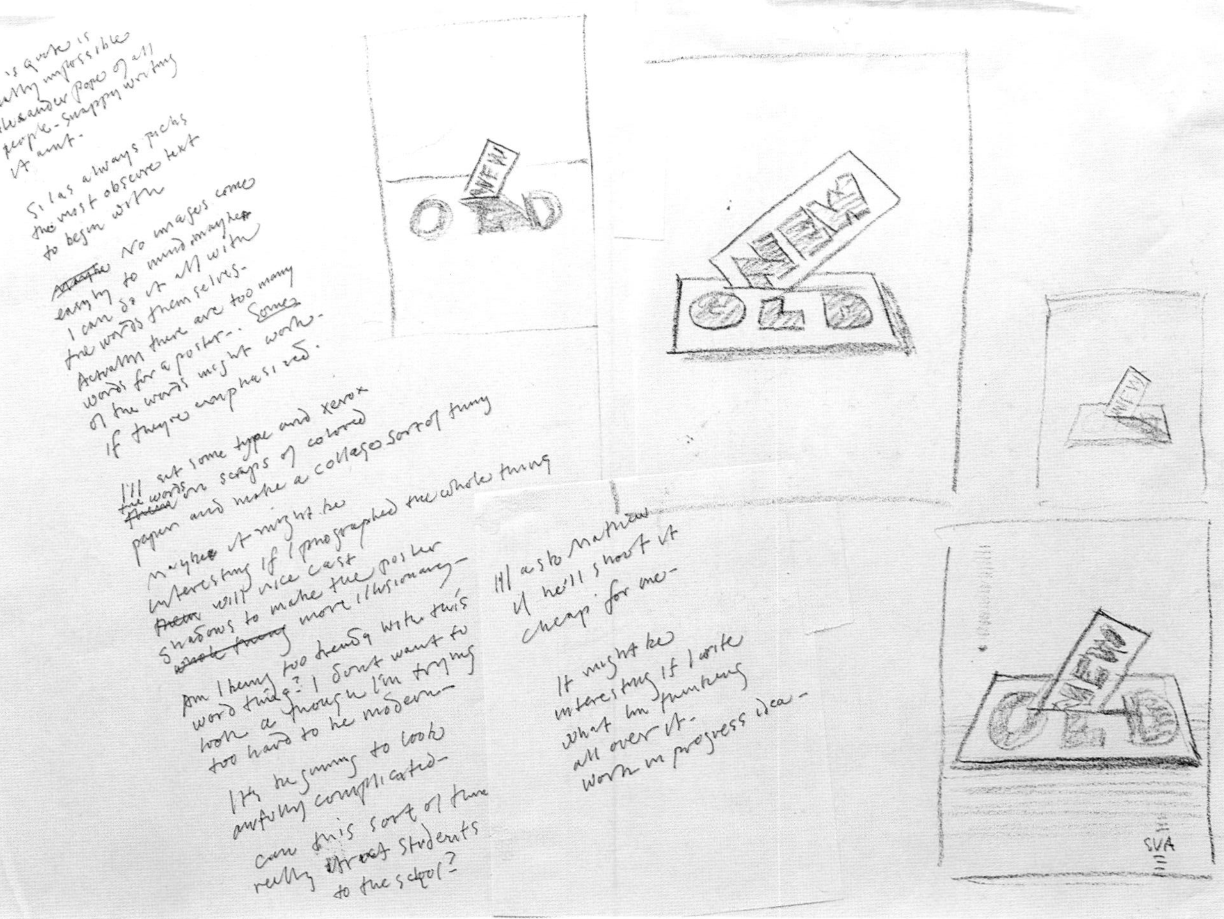

4

LEFT This seemed to be going nowhere, so I began to record my thoughts about making the poster on a sheet of paper, as I frequently do when I'm stuck in the middle of a project. You can see that what develops is the idea of the word "new" penetrating through or emerging from the word "old." This became the basis for a series of studies and variations—none of which ultimately turned out to be quite right. There was, however, the remnant of an idea in example number six, which I used as part of the finished poster.

RIGHT In stages five and six of the development I played around with the idea of the new coming out of the old.

BELOW RIGHT Then I lost my train of thought again. This time I chose a rather traditional and somewhat clichéd approach. Fortunately I saw the error of my ways and quickly returned to the previous thread.

BELOW Along the way, I thought to start afresh, discarding the poem itself and using two drawings I had of sleeping people. I thought of referring instead to an idea about dreams and dreaming, or perhaps making your dreams come true. I quickly recovered and was profoundly embarrassed that I had even thought of changing the ground rules. I never showed it to the client.

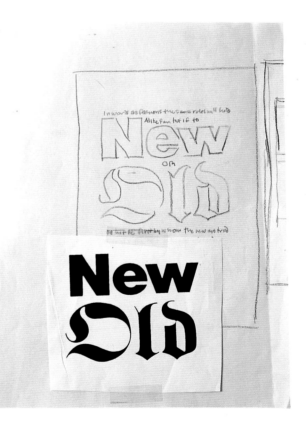

5

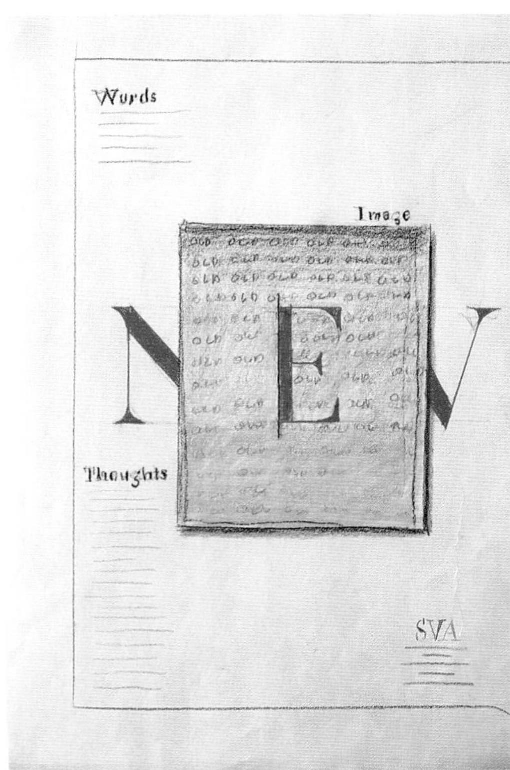
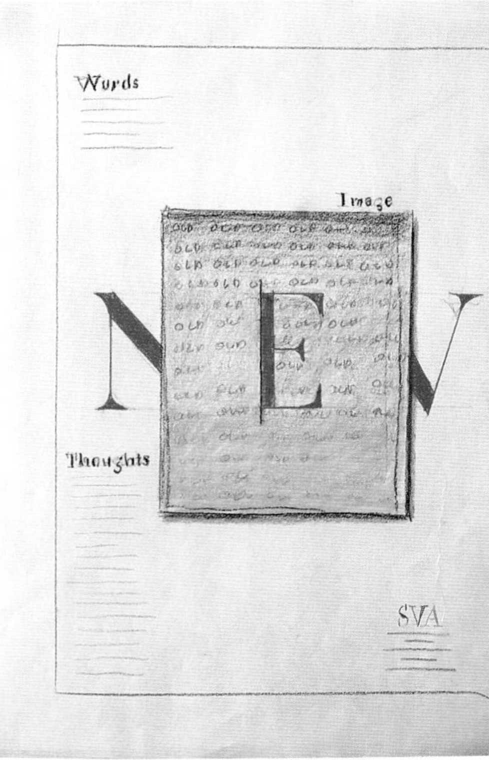

6

7

8

Words

In words as fashions the same rule will hold,
Alike fantastic if too new or old.
Be not the first by whom the new are tried,
Nor yet the last to lay the old aside.

Alexander Pope

Image

Thoughts

This poem is impossible. Silas usually has a better touch with his choice of quotations. This one generates no imagery at all. Maybe the words can make the image without anything else happening. What's the heart of this poem? Don't be trendy if you want to be serious. (Isn't doing the poster this way trendy in itself?) I guess one could reduce the idea further by suggesting that the new emerges behind and through the old, like this.

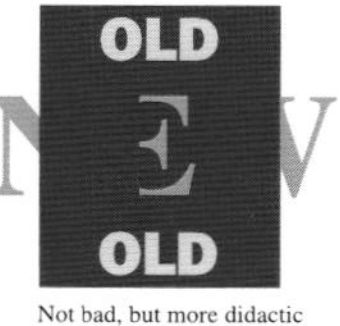

Not bad, but more didactic than visual. Maybe what wants to be said is that the old and the new are locked in a dialectical embrace–a kind of dance where each defines the other.

Am I being simple-minded? Is it the kind of simple that looks obvious or the kind that looks profound? There is a significant difference. This could be embarrassing. Actually, I realize fear of embarrassment drives me as much as any other ambition.

Do you think this sort of thing could really attract a student to the school?

Milton Glaser

School of Visual Arts

A COLLEGE OF THE ARTS

B.F.A. Programs in Advertising, Animation, Art Education, Art Therapy, Cartooning, Computer Art, Film and Video, Fine Arts, Graphic Design, Illustration, Interior Design, Photography. M.F.A. Programs in Computer Art, Fine Arts, Illustration, Photography and Continuing Education Programs.

209 E. 23 ST., N.Y.C., 10010-3994 1-800-366-7820 FAX: 212-725-3587

LEFT The final poster is basically divided into three components—words, images and thoughts—where the "thoughts" explain the process of making the poster. This is rare in the graphic arts and in other forms of performance, since concealing the methodology is very often linked to its effectiveness. It also seemed appropriate at the time to introduce the idea of *doubt* to graphic design (even if it was merely a tool for generating interest), by providing a second graphic solution in the left hand margin. Because a lack of conviction is considered a sign of weakness, introducing a second solution (in the event that the first one is not acceptable) threatens the basic assumptions of communication. The graphic problem actually was the integration of the words "old" and "new" so that neither was dominant and so that the poster could be read easily as one or the other.

ART IS... This recent poster began with an assignment from Silas Rhodes, the chairman of the School of Visual Arts. Ten designers were asked to interpret the phrase "Art is." The results were distributed simultaneously throughout the city in the subways and at bus shelters. Trying to define art is perhaps impossible, but the variety and range of the responses made for a lively series of public announcements. In my own case the accompanying text attempts to extend the visual message. A point that the text omits, I realize, is that some forms are intrinsically and mysteriously more satisfying than others. I am convinced the form of the bowler hat is—sculpturally speaking—one of the most elegant and aesthetically pleasing objects ever made. Can we call it art if that was not the maker's intent? That question will require more than a poster to answer.

Art is...
WHATEVER
School of VISUAL ARTS
SVA 50

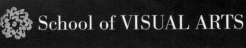

Note To the Viewer:

I thought I might use a visual cliché of our time, Magritte's Everyman, to express the idea that art has mystery, continuity and history. I am also convinced that in an era of computer manipulation, surrealism has become banal, a shadow of its former self. The phrase "Art is WHATEVER" expresses the current inclusiveness that surrounds art making; a sort of "it ain't whatcha do, its the way thatcha do it" notion. The shadow of Magritte's man falls across the central part of the poster, a poetic event that occurs as the shadow man isolates the word "hat" hidden in the word "whatever." The four hats shown in the poster suggest how art might be defined: as the thing itself, the word for the thing, the shadow of the thing and the shape of the thing. . . . Whatever.

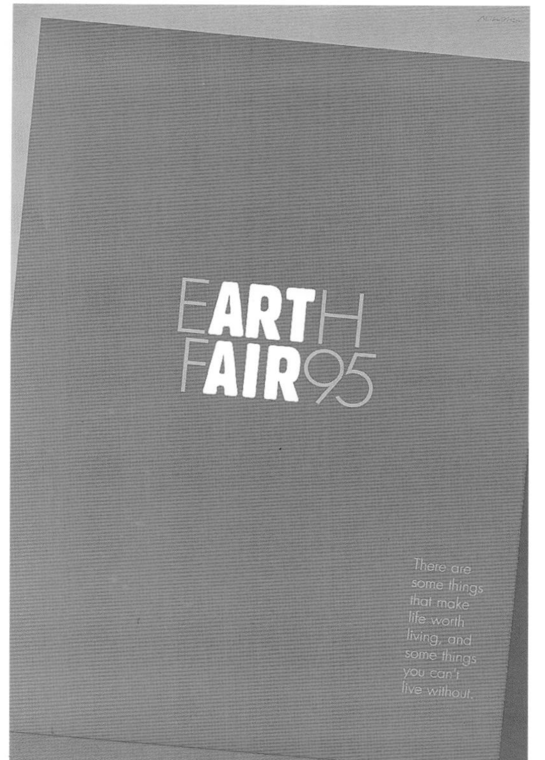

Copy in poster reads: "There are some things that make life worth living, and some things you can't live without."

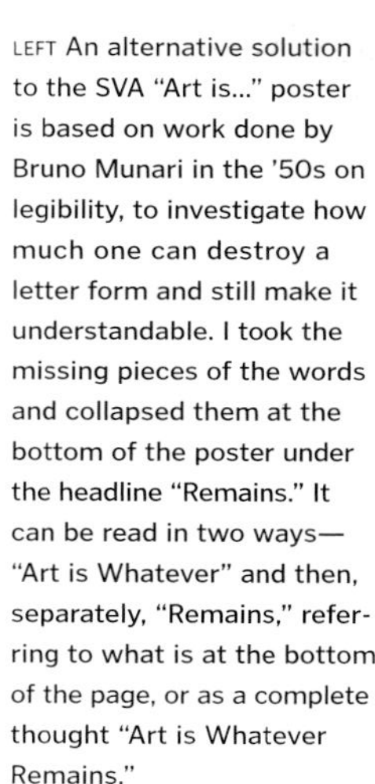

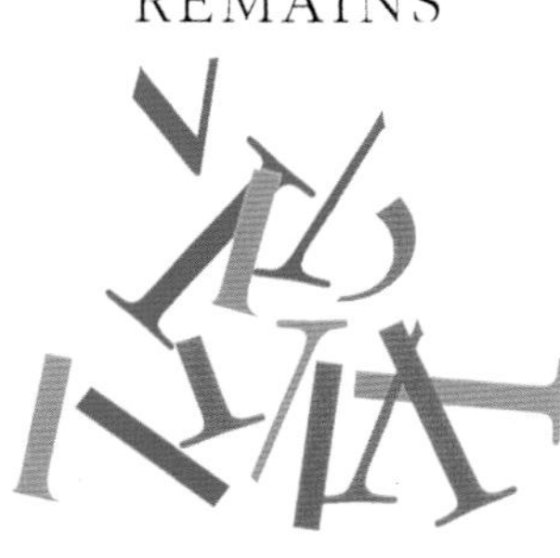

LEFT An alternative solution to the SVA "Art is…" poster is based on work done by Bruno Munari in the '50s on legibility, to investigate how much one can destroy a letter form and still make it understandable. I took the missing pieces of the words and collapsed them at the bottom of the poster under the headline "Remains." It can be read in two ways—"Art is Whatever" and then, separately, "Remains," referring to what is at the bottom of the page, or as a complete thought "Art is Whatever Remains."

Breaking Rules

The earliest rule I remember about posters (in my first year of high school fifty years ago) was that they were made for people on the run. Consequently, the ideal poster should be simple in form, reductive in content, and easily understood. By and large, these seemed to be useful if not obvious assumptions.

In recent years, however, I've found myself modifying these beliefs in a variety of ways—partially from my desire to investigate alternative visual and philosophical possibilities, and also in an attempt to recognize the changes that have occurred in the last half-century regarding the public's ability to respond to ambiguity and complexity. Film, computers, and television have helped create a visual environment that scarcely resembles the one I knew as a student. In addition, designers have become increasingly interested in thinking of design as a tool for philosophical and social inquiry—to some extent replicating the role that painting traditionally assumed. At the moment such issues as "what is real," "what is beautiful," or "what is socially responsible" can engage a designer's interest as much as the more traditional questions of effective communication.

Both the Earth Fair and the Coexistence poster also depend on the discovery of words hidden within words, which, when discovered, illuminate a concealed relationship. In one case the search for a healthy ecology requires the pursuit of those aspects of life that are both desirable and essential and in the other the need for one side to listen to the other in order to survive.

RIGHT I wanted to find out if it was possible for a poster to teach something instead of simply motivating action or generating desire. It is important to know that this poster, and the other SVA posters, are subway posters. The audience is momentarily captive between trains and usually keen to find something to read.

The original sketch had a drawing by Matisse, to complete the idea of Matisse drawing the swan. We could not get the rights to reproduce the Matisse drawing so I had to rethink the poster. The swan bones at the bottom are actually goose bones (you can't kill a swan legally in the United States and consequently swan bones are not easily found). I bought a goose, my wife cooked it, and we had it for dinner. I then soaked the bones in lye for a week to turn them white (they are in fact a dark gray).

A Drawing Lesson

The difficulty in drawing from a photograph is knowing what to omit. The photograph contains too much information and generally too many contrary sources of light. Drawing from a photograph is a matter of selection and editing. Degas used photographs in an appropriate way. That is to say, he was not dominated by the material contained in the photo, and felt free to depart from it at will.

Illustration of Matisse sketching a swan at Bois de Bologne

I have often wondered about the distinction between drawing and illustration, and, as usual, the difference is contained within the words themselves. 'Illustration', which comes from the root 'lustrare' means to shed light on, or to make clear. It suggests the idea of a surface of an object interrupting the flow of light. 'Drawing' comes from the root 'trahere', meaning to draw forth, like water from a well or blood from a stone. It suggests the idea of revealing something that is contained within an object and can be drawn out, rather than something that is on the surface. This may explain why those who begin to draw often start with the bones. Both activities require intelligence, perseverance, and talent.

Milton Glaser

Photo of Matisse sketching a swan at the Bois de Bologne

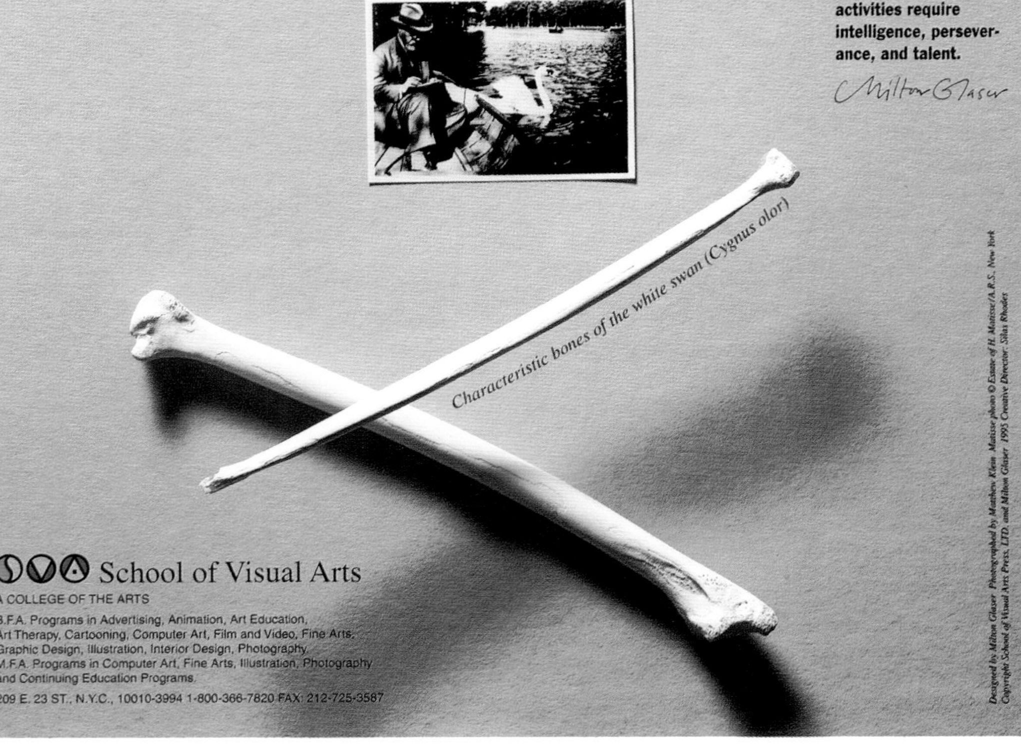

Characteristic bones of the white swan (Cygnus olor)

School of Visual Arts
A COLLEGE OF THE ARTS
B.F.A. Programs in Advertising, Animation, Art Education, Art Therapy, Cartooning, Computer Art, Film and Video, Fine Arts, Graphic Design, Illustration, Interior Design, Photography.
M.F.A. Programs in Computer Art, Fine Arts, Illustration, Photography and Continuing Education Programs.
209 E. 23 ST., N.Y.C., 10010-3994 1-800-366-7820 FAX: 212-725-3587

Designed by Milton Glaser Photographed by Matthew Klein Matisse photo © Estate of H. Matisse/A.R.S., New York
Copyright School of Visual Arts Press, LTD. and Milton Glaser 1995 Creative Director: Silas Rhodes

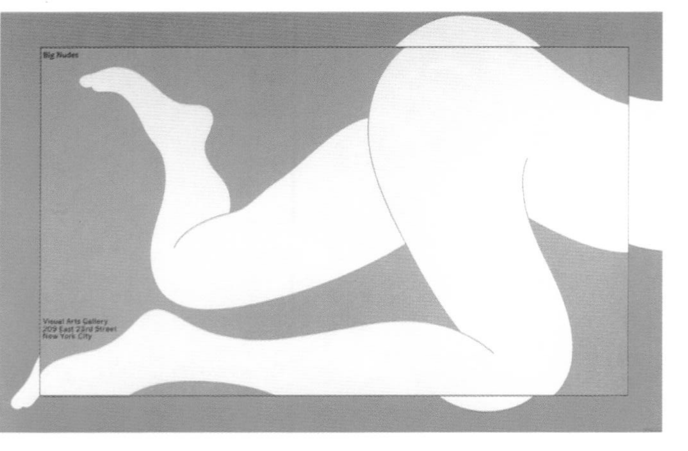

LEFT *Big Nudes*, 1967.
An early poster that explored the idea of transgressing the boundaries of the poster graphically.

BELOW A non-rectilinear poster done in the '60s for Utopia, a record company from the days when records were twelve inches and made out of vinyl. The label, which represents the idea of Utopia in an abstract way, was the source of this design. It replicates the typical Utopia record in an enlarged 24 inch version.

Shaped Posters

The standard shape of a poster is rectangular, principally because the manufacture of posters is driven by economic and convenience issues. But once one becomes interested in transgression, the idea of violating the rectangle becomes very attractive. Throughout the years, I have done numerous posters that deviate from the rectilinear form to produce interesting and arresting effects.

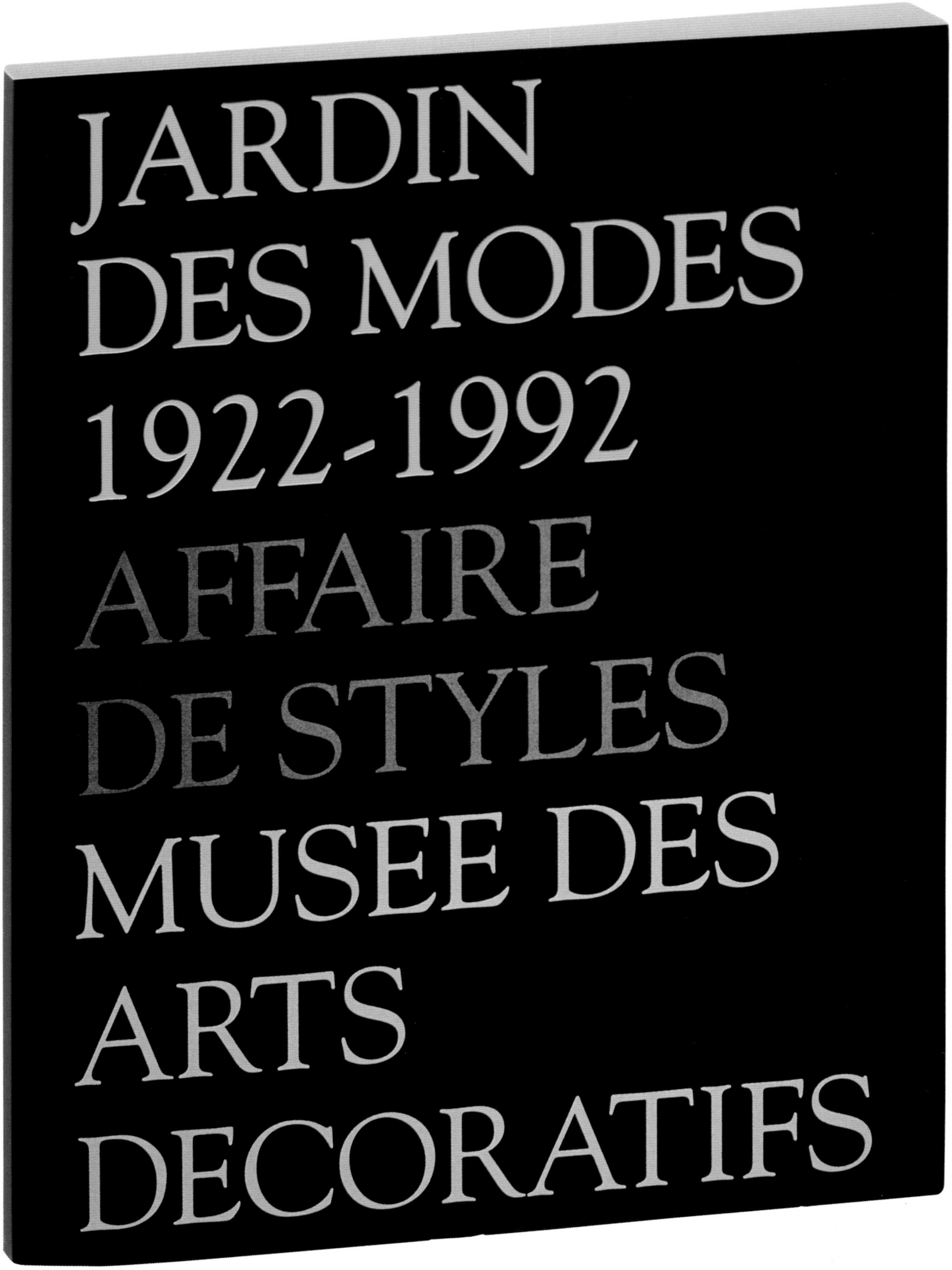

JARDIN
DES MODES
1922-1992
AFFAIRE
DE STYLES
MUSEE DES
ARTS
DECORATIFS

LEFT A poster for a French magazine I redesigned called *Jardin des Modes*. The Musée des Arts Décoratifs celebrated the magazine's long history with an exhibition. The effect of the poster depends almost entirely on a slight modification of the rectangle to make it look as though it is in perspective. When it was posted around Paris and seen at an angle, it looked strange until you stood directly in front of it and realized it wasn't a rectangle.

BELOW This is typical of the sketchbooks that I carry with me whenever I travel. I tend to fill these books with innumerable drawings of meals and details of the landscape. They really serve, more than anything else, as a prod to my memory. Otherwise I'd have virtually no past at all.

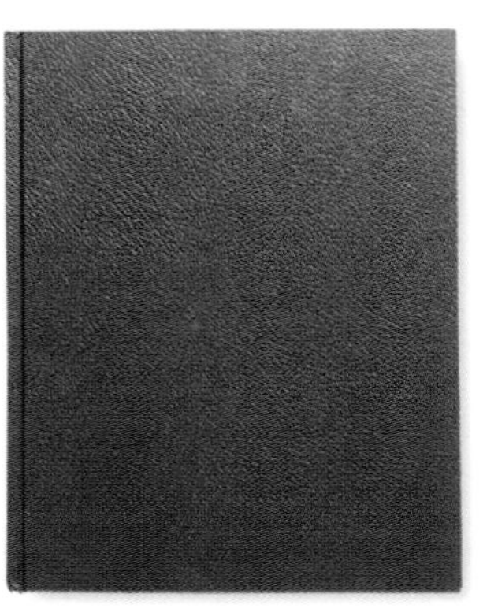

RIGHT This is an announcement of a show at the School of Visual Arts in which I used a page of my Tuscany sketchbook as a representation of my work. What interested me more than anything else about this piece was the extraordinary sense of volume of the empty left-hand page—its voluptuousness and almost baroque quality—created by only a slight shading of form, and the curve of the top and bottom. I saved that observation for a future application. (opposite page)

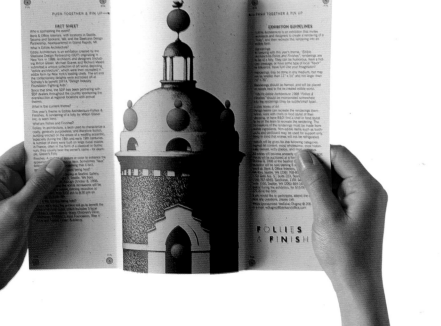

RIGHT In this brochure I thought it would be amusing if, when the brochure is pinned to a wall, it emphasized the round form of the tower, actually a Folly.

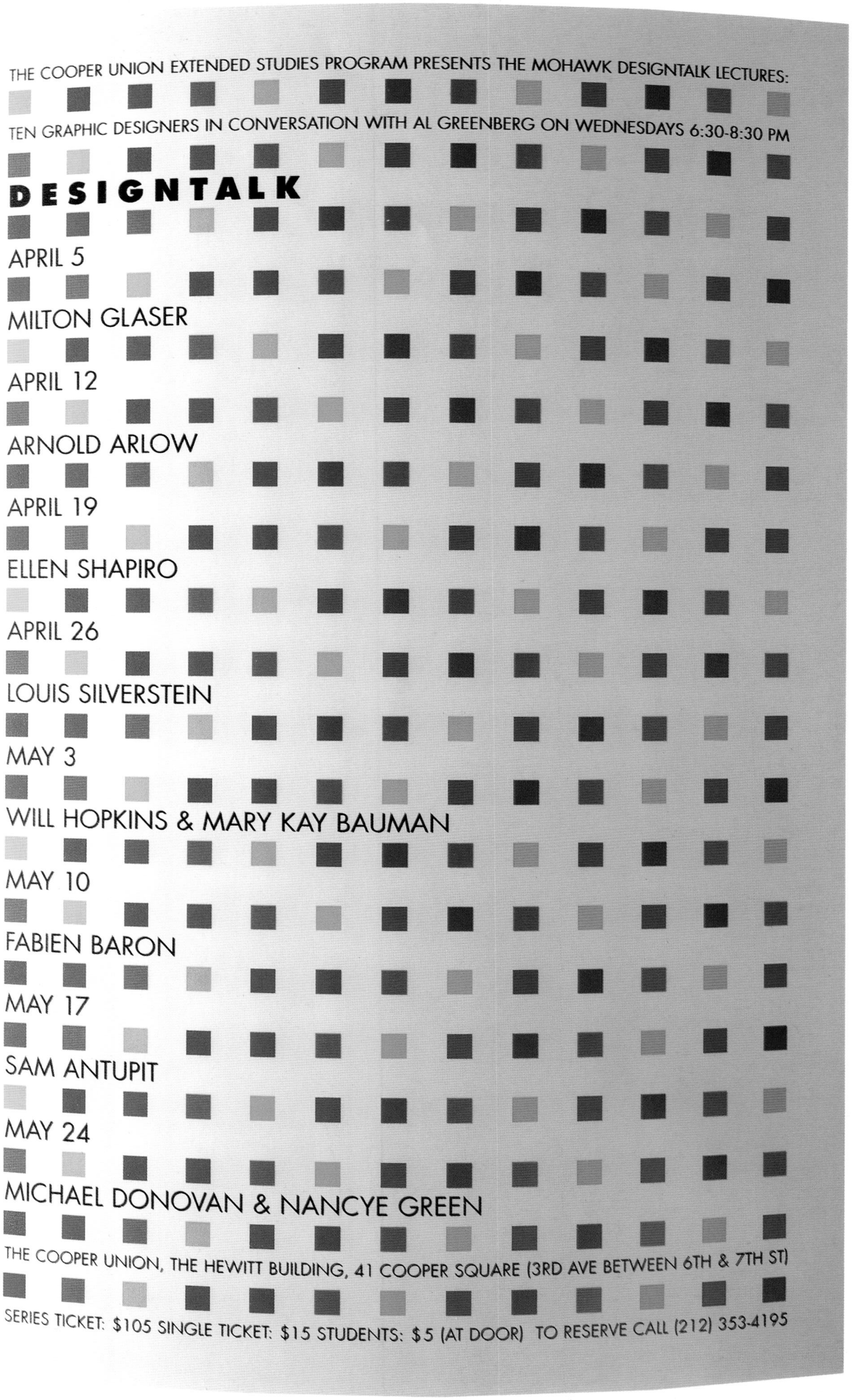

THE COOPER UNION EXTENDED STUDIES PROGRAM PRESENTS THE MOHAWK DESIGNTALK LECTURES:

TEN GRAPHIC DESIGNERS IN CONVERSATION WITH AL GREENBERG ON WEDNESDAYS 6:30-8:30 PM

DESIGNTALK

APRIL 5

MILTON GLASER

APRIL 12

ARNOLD ARLOW

APRIL 19

ELLEN SHAPIRO

APRIL 26

LOUIS SILVERSTEIN

MAY 3

WILL HOPKINS & MARY KAY BAUMAN

MAY 10

FABIEN BARON

MAY 17

SAM ANTUPIT

MAY 24

MICHAEL DONOVAN & NANCYE GREEN

THE COOPER UNION, THE HEWITT BUILDING, 41 COOPER SQUARE (3RD AVE BETWEEN 6TH & 7TH ST)

SERIES TICKET: $105 SINGLE TICKET: $15 STUDENTS: $5 (AT DOOR) TO RESERVE CALL (212) 353-4195

LEFT When an announcement was needed for a series of lectures on design at Cooper Union, I began a series of sketches based on the idea of a curved surface. The poster was produced as a flat artwork, which then was wrapped around a column and photographed with a light source on the left. The idea of introducing light as an element in graphics is unusual; what I found interesting was how the illusion of form was amplified by cutting the poster in a curve at the top and bottom. Under the right circumstances, the wall seemed to be bulging behind the poster.

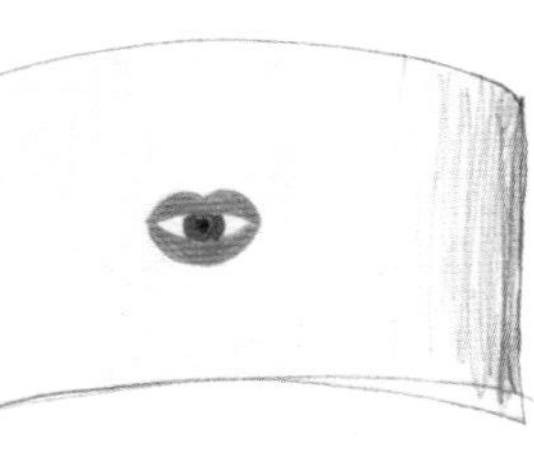

The announcement for the Art Directors Hall of Fame, whose practitioners are elevated to a position of eminence by the award. The idea started with the notion that these are people who cast long shadows. The poster was cut in perspective with the initials of the Art Director's Club and the symbolic representation of the personalities casting long shadows on the page. The problem, of course, was how to fold it.

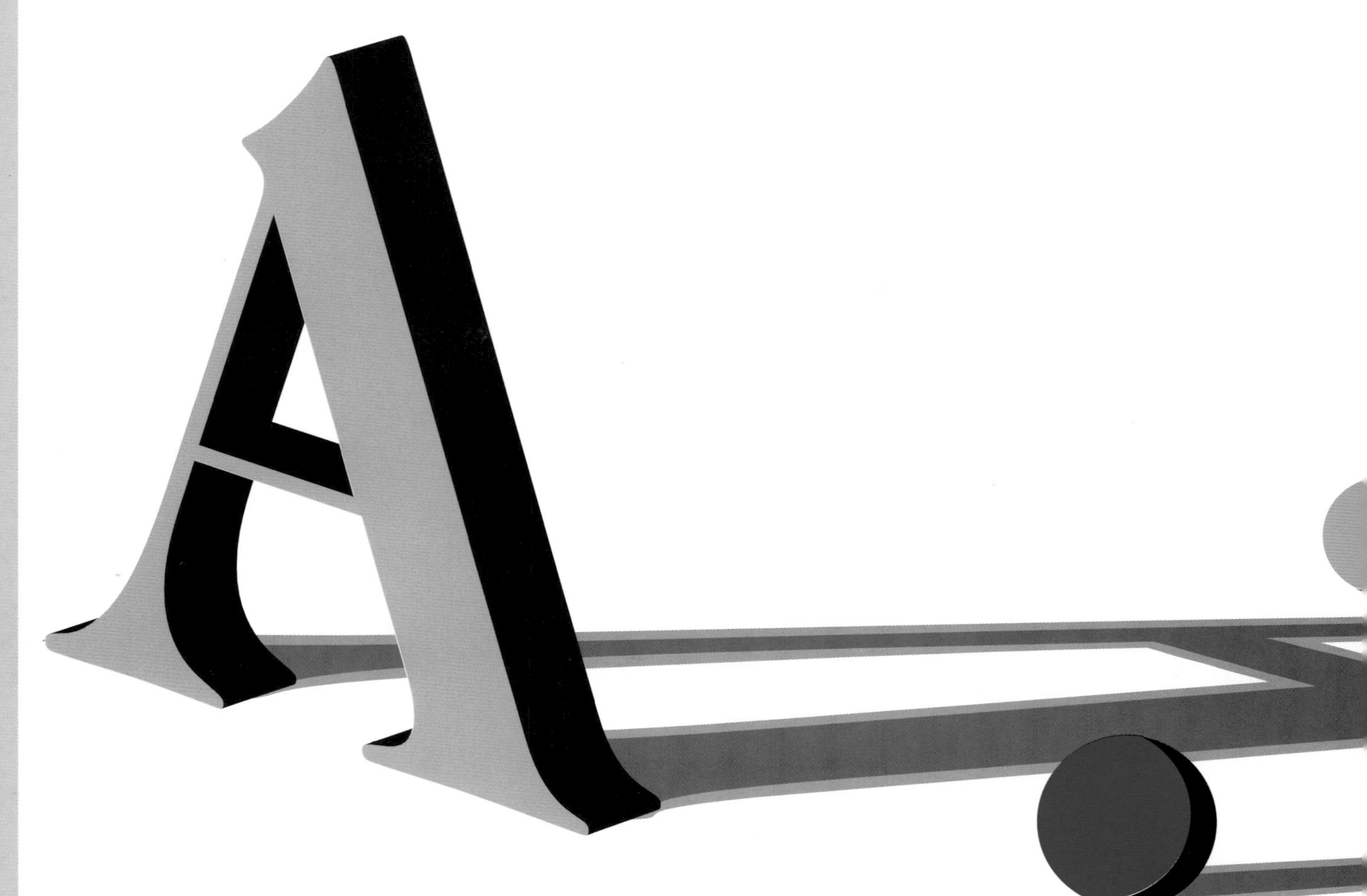
You are cordially invited to the 1997 Hall of Fame
Honoring laureates Allan Beaver, Sheila
The Art Directors Club 250 Park Avenue South at 20th St
Black tie. RSVP early
Special thanks to Color by Pergament for initial sponsorship of the Hall of Fame Video Project. This year's Hall of Fame presentation is being

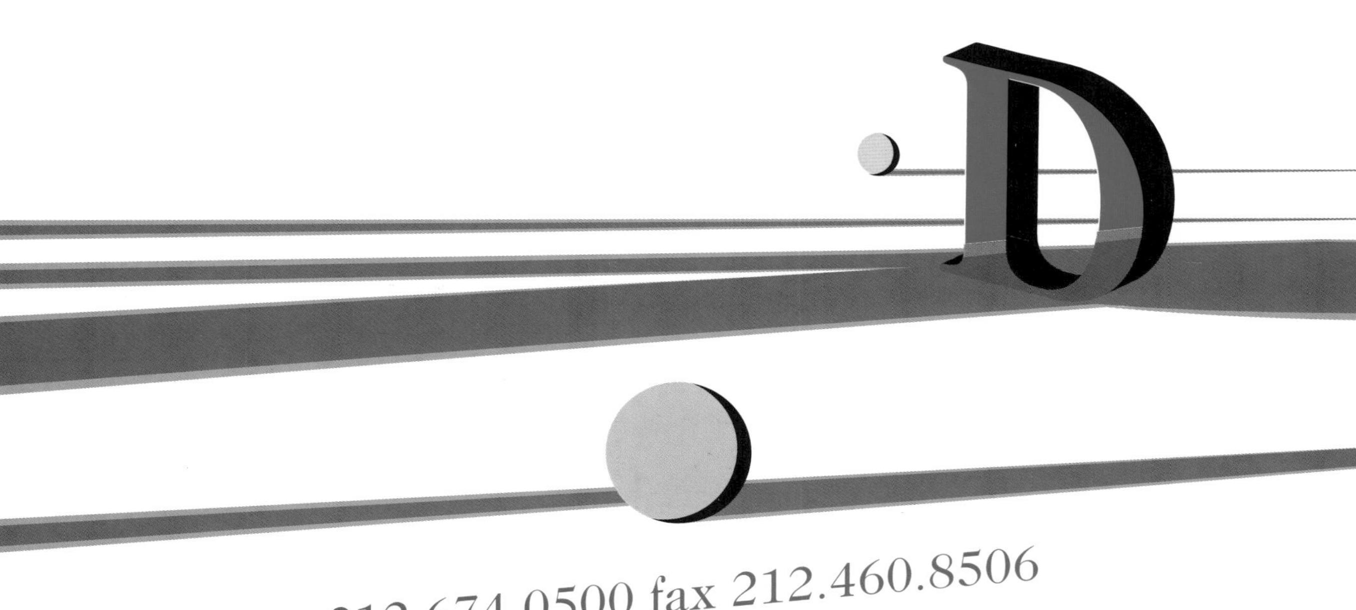
nner and Presentation
tzner, B. Martin Pedersen, George Tscherny
hursday, November 6, 1997 at six o'clock in the evening
D
New York City 212.674.0500 fax 212.460.8506
eating is limited. Reply card enclosed.
ssible in part by Daniels Printing, New York. Design by Milton Glaser. Paper by Mohawk.

BELOW I tried to create a spatial illusion here by cutting off the corners of the poster to suggest the corner of a room. The admiring "Q" and the Olivetti power book called "Quaderno" cast shadows that add to the dimensionality. The floating book is executed in isometric (like a Japanese woodcut) rather than one-point perspective. The effect is that as you observe it, the back end of the Quaderno seems to become wider than the front, a destabilizing event that compels the viewer to take a second look.

OPPOSITE When an element breaks the rectangular boundary of a poster we are surprised. In this case the bubbles contain the range of colors available in the client's paper stock. The die-cutting required to achieve this effect was both expensive and impractical. However, the client was convinced that the result was worth the extra effort.

BELOW An earlier experiment combining the idea of illusion with isometric perspective.

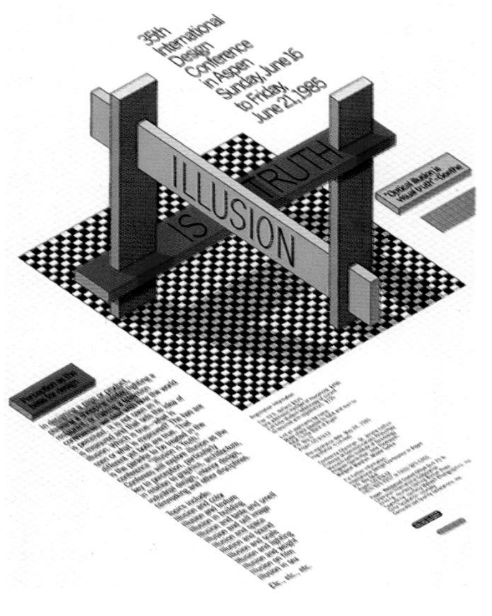

EXPERIENCE
UNCOATED

Milton Glaser

FraserPapers

Designed for Fraser Papers by Milton Glaser. Printed on Passport Tale, 80 lb. Text, Smooth Finish

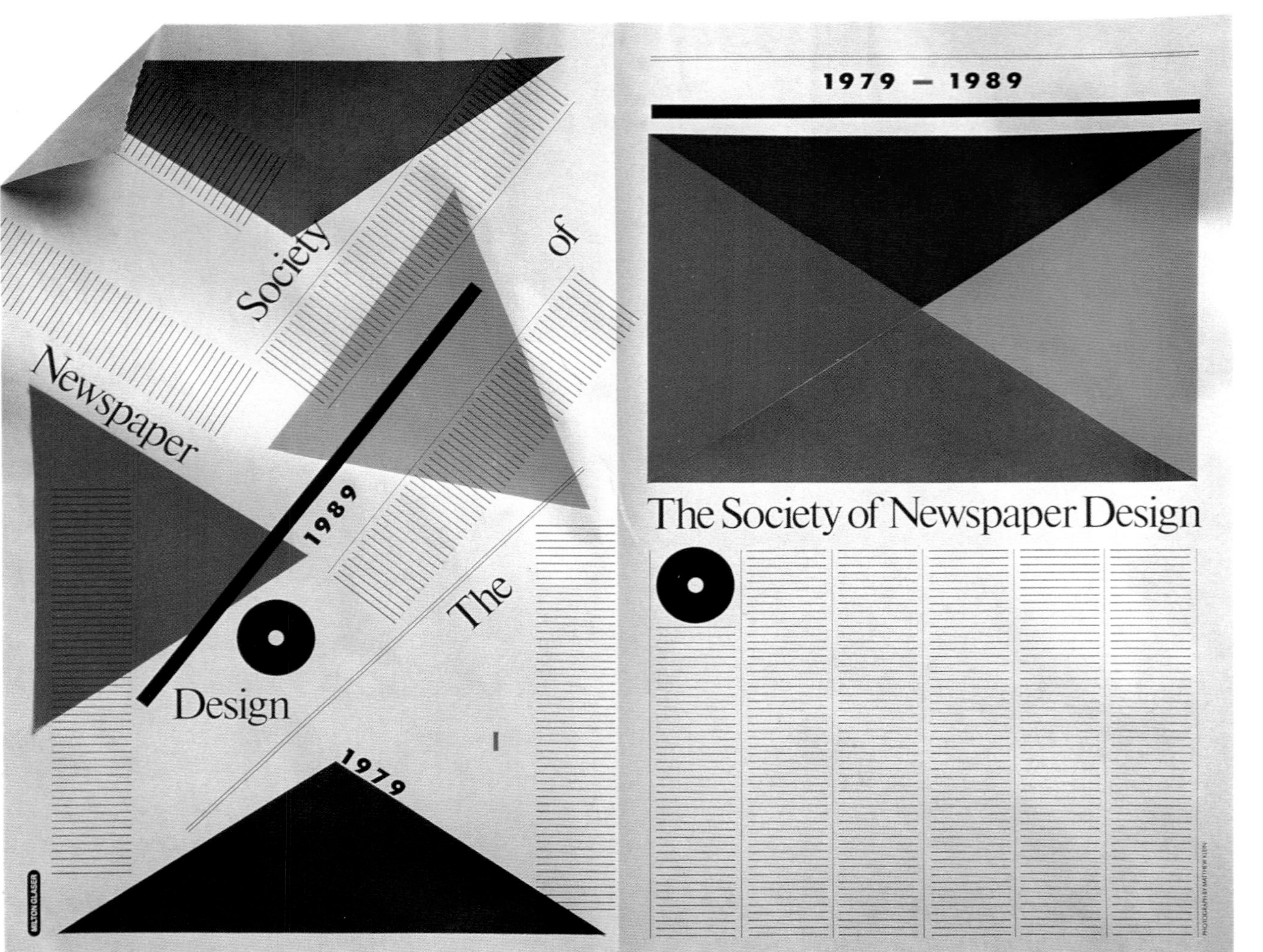

LEFT A poster for the Society of Newspaper Design's 10th Anniversary. The corner of the newspaper design poster is not folded, but merely cut diagonally. The basic idea was to show that what newspaper designers do is make order out of chaos. All the elements of the left-hand page are exactly the same as the elements on the right-hand page. Nothing has been added or subtracted. It is also a demonstration of why chaos is often more interesting than order.

Illusion and Reality

Artists have always been concerned with the representation of the "real." How to represent reality convincingly is one of the central themes in the history of art. What convinces us that an object actually exists or did exist is one of the most complex questions in the visual arts. Although historically, painting has been the appropriate place to explore these ideas, they are equally interesting as subject for exploration in the graphic arts. There are devices that one employs to create this sense of believable illusion. One of them is the use of shallow space. American artists William Harnett and John F. Peto explored this approach by creating paintings that involved the flat surfaces of cards, newspaper clippings, ribbons, and so on. Because we see stereoscopically, paintings that represent objects in a very shallow space are more convincing illusionistically than paintings that attempt to represent greater depth. I've tried to take advantage of this fact from time to time.

JOHN F. PETO "REMINISCENCES OF 1865"

DEADLINE: 4 DECEMBER 1987

The Art Directors Club Inc.

SECOND INTERNATIONAL EXHIBITION

CALL FOR ENTRIES

NEW YORK, NY 10003 U.S.A.

The Art Directors Club of New York is extending its prestigious annual awards program to the international design and advertising community. The 2nd International Exhibition, a juried competition for excellence in print, television and film art direction, will be judged by a distinguished panel of ADC Hall of Fame laureates and designers of international stature.

MILTON GLASER

LEFT The illusion of this folded poster was so convincing that everyone who came into my office and saw it hanging on the wall tried to lift the flap. The effect is achieved entirely through photography and cutting the top of the poster at a diagonal.

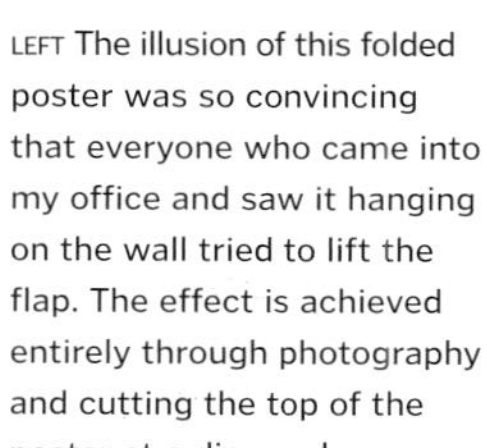

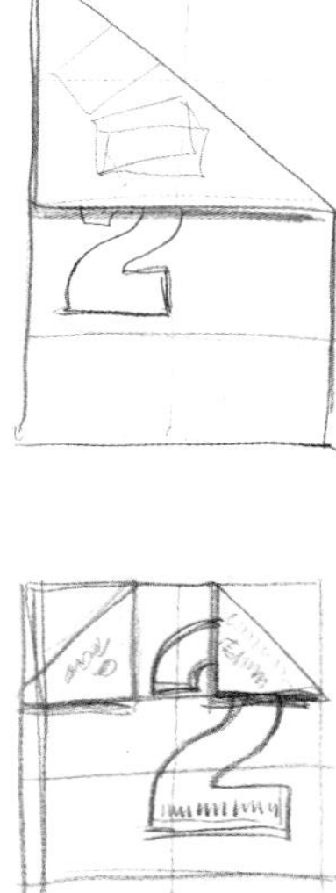

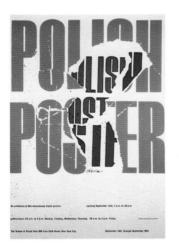

ABOVE *Polish Poster*, 1966. An early example of graphic illusion.

RIGHT In this poster for The School of Visual Arts, I originally intended the pieces of cut paper to be glued down, but when I looked at my mechanical I decided that it was improved by the little pieces of masking tape. I asked Matthew Klein, the photographer, to light the art so that the masking tape would appear believably dimensional. Several times, while the poster was displayed in the subway, I observed people trying to lift the masking tape.

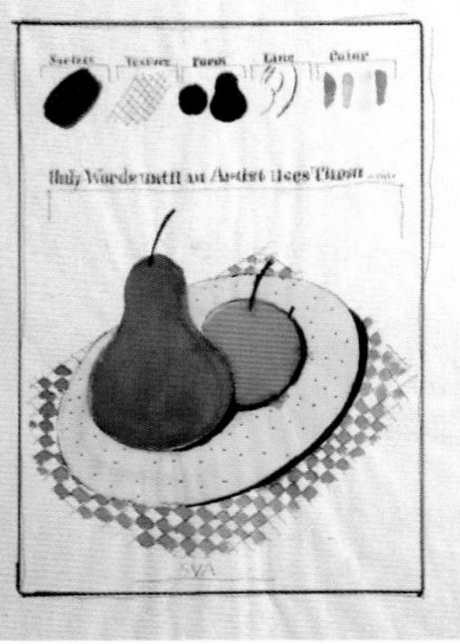

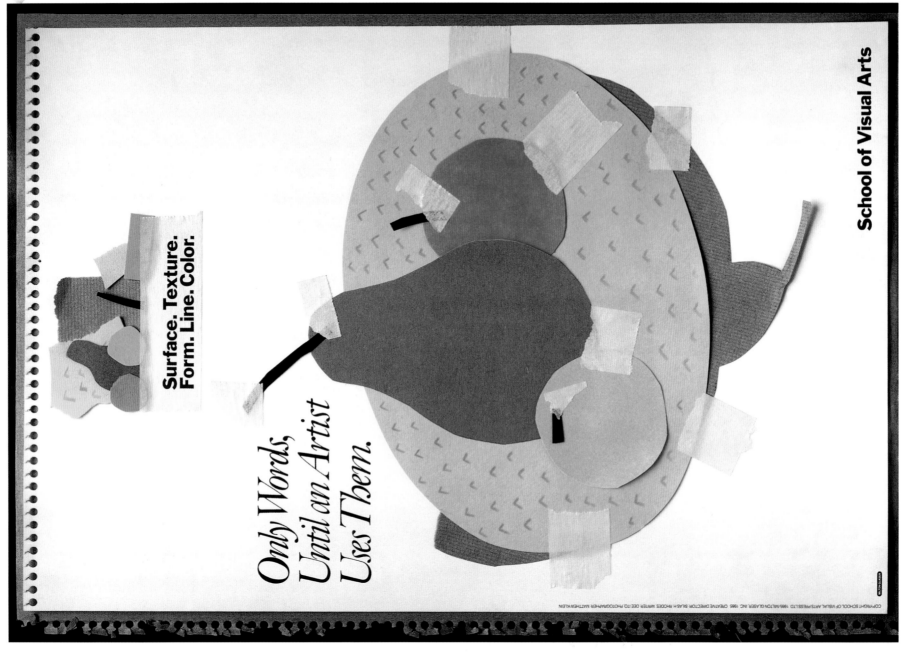

Surface. Texture.
Form. Line. Color.

Only Words,
Until an Artist
Uses Them.

School of Visual Arts

ABOVE What is real? In this case neither the drawing of the flowers nor the clay models. However, one perceives the clay models as being *more* real than the drawing.

LEFT The idea for the vase on the beach came from a drawing I made several years earlier.

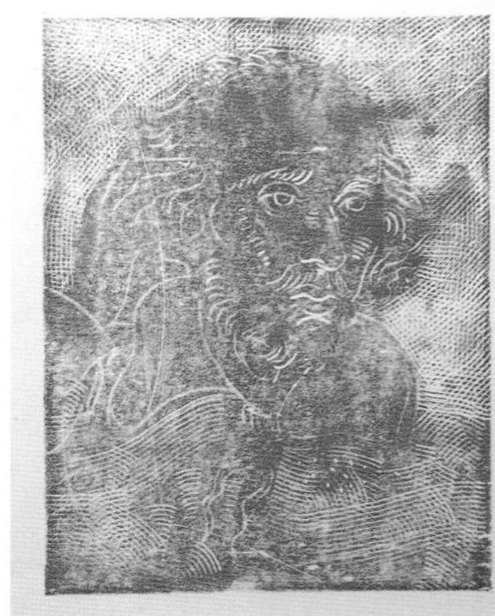

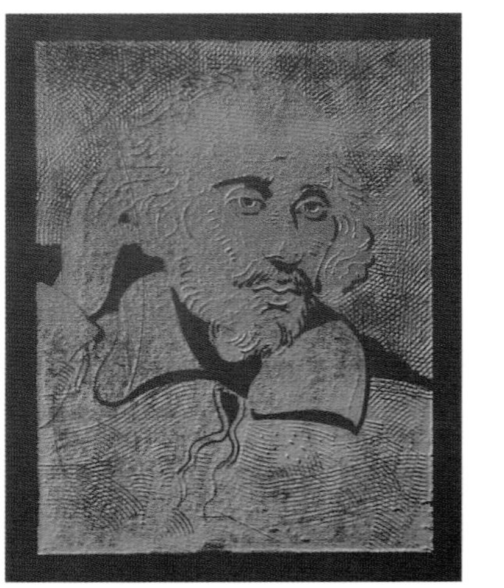

A lively man named Jeffrey Horowitz runs a theatrical company that produces modern, adventurous versions of classic and contemporary theatrical works. He asked me to design a twentieth-anniversary poster for the group. A portrait of William Shakespeare seemed appropriate. All Shakespeare portraits derive from two or three original sources that are not in agreement with one another. The only agreement seems to be a high-domed forehead, a beard, mustache, and a wide, white collar. This opens the portrait to numerous possibilities. After a few false starts, I arrived at the drawing used on the poster on the OPPOSITE PAGE—more like a non-white actor playing Shakespeare than a portrait of Shakespeare. It still looked a bit conventional for the spirit of the theater, so I cut it into overlapping shapes to suggest a more modern spirit. The lettering amplifies the same idea by alternating a classic and a modern font.

THEATRE FOR A NEW AUDIENCE
TWENTIETH ANNIVERSARY
Milton Glaser
Photo by Matthew Klein

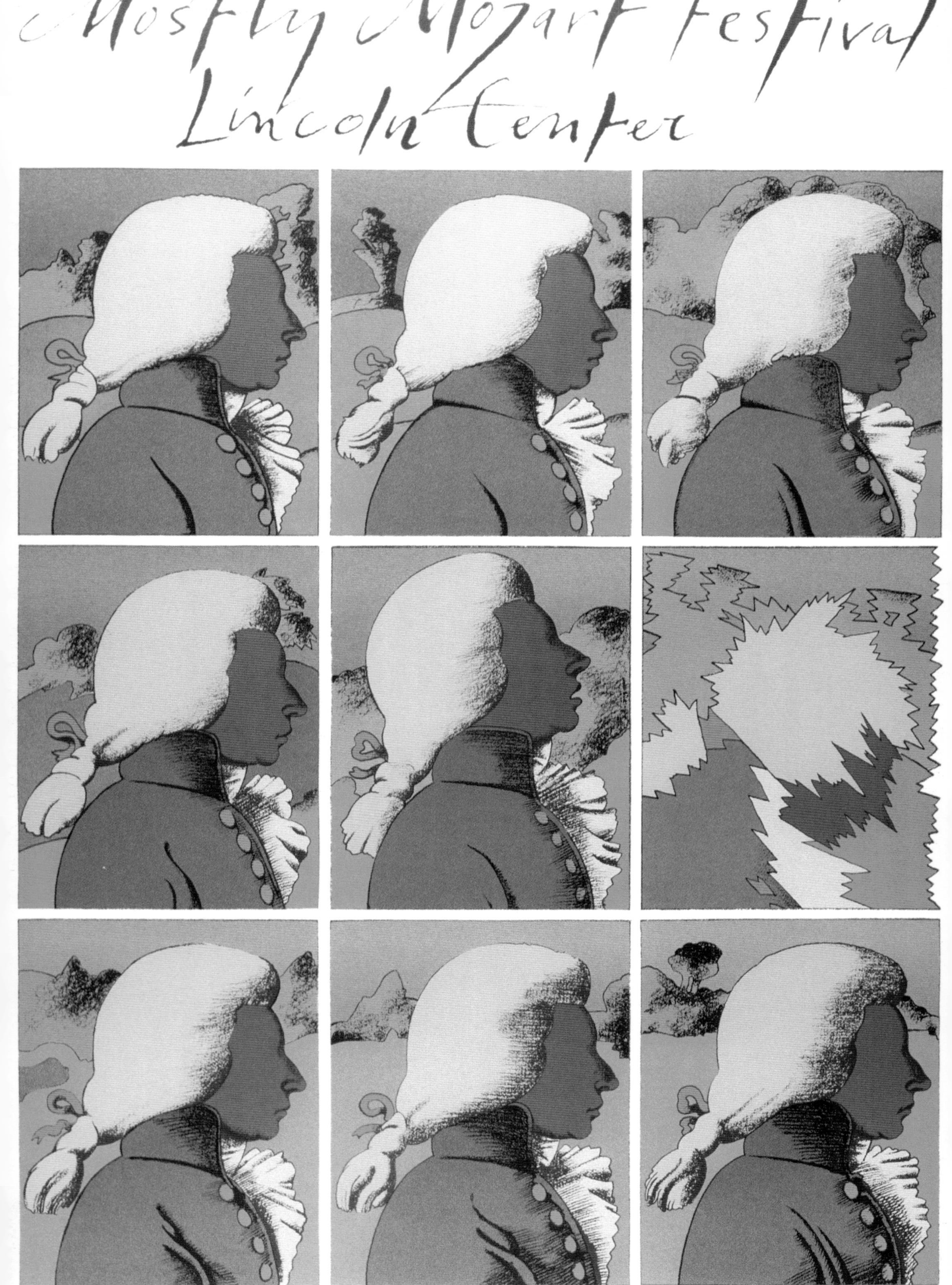
Mostly Mozart Festival
Lincoln Center
Mozart Sneezes
Milton Glaser

For as long as I can remember, music has been central to my life and it is no coincidence that much of my work has involved musical subjects. On this page are two posters that respond to the wonderfully evocative phrase, "Full Color Sound," invented by the Waring La Rosa agency.

BELOW The Magritte man in black profile has had his ear metaphorically replaced by a brightly colored shell.

RIGHT The score of a Beethoven symphony is visually enhanced by tiny watercolor landscapes. As so often is the case, the words drove the imagery.

OPPOSITE PAGE An early poster for a series of musical events that uses the most basic form of visual narrative, the comic strip, as a device to engage the viewer. A disruption of expectation, or challenging the public's sense of appropriateness, is a fundamental device of the arts in our time. Here, the sublime Mozart has a human moment.

Juilliard is one of the world's great schools of the arts. Although predominately known for its music studies, it also excels in the theatrical arts. These three posters are part of a series that attempts to represent the general idea of aspiration and achievement.

BELOW These two studies did not seem quite right until I remembered a Miro painting of a dog baying at the moon and appropriated it.

OPPOSITE PAGE The combination of a fragment of a Chinese textile with a strong black and white drawing created a series of pleasing visual accidents.

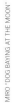

MIRO "DOG BAYING AT THE MOON"

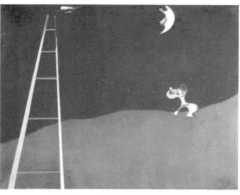

JUILLIARD
This poster made possible by a grant from TDK.

Although there are an infinite number of ideas in the world of graphic design, I frequently find myself returning to an earlier idea. In this case, two posters are strikingly similar in style and idea even though they were done three years apart for very diverse musical organizations. I like the way the drapery in the Newport poster has been stylized. Incidentally, the erotic implications of this piece were inadvertent.

SAN FRANCISCO OPERA

Kurt Herbert Adler, General Director

59TH SEASON
1981

Two very different approaches to posters using cellos.

RIGHT A cubist version influenced by a painting by Picasso. My client was concerned that musicians would be horrified by the image of a cello cut in half, but the poster became quite popular with the students and the teachers at the school.

PICASSO "THREE MUSICIANS" 1921

PICASSO "VIOLIN AND SHEET MUSIC" 1912

ABOVE An earlier cubist-derived record album for Columbia Records.

JUILLIARD

Milton Glaser

This poster, fifth in a series made possible by a grant from TDK.

THIRD AMERICAN
CELLO CONGRESS

JUNE 3-7, 1986
INDIANA UNIVERSITY SCHOOL OF MUSIC
BLOOMINGTON, INDIANA

Among the most persistent influences on my work have been the prints and paintings of the idiosyncratic turn-of-the-century artist, Félix Vallotton. He himself was profoundly influenced by the wave of Japanese woodcuts that flooded Paris at that time and aroused the interest of the French avant-garde. Vallotton's reductive woodcuts, in sharp black and white, contain an enormous amount of compressed visual and psychological energy. His use of limited means to suggest a narrative is unexcelled. In the arts, one has many mentors, including those one has never met. Thanks, Félix.

FÉLIX VALLOTTON "GETTING READY FOR A VISIT"

Tomato Records

In 1966, I met a baby-faced Irish record entrepreneur named Kevin Eggers, who was starting a new label named Poppy—a name in keeping with the psychedelic, stoned-out zeitgeist of rock in the '60s. He produced numerous records, and his heart and energy were in the right place. He wanted to produce good music and was willing to get the details right. I designed all the albums and promotional material, as well as the logo for the company. As is frequently the case, work that offers the most creative opportunity generally pays badly, but the reward of being able to do one's best work was significant compensation. The protean Mr. Eggers reinvented himself and his company through the years, changing from Poppy to Utopia to Atlantic Deluxe and, finally, to Tomato, his most ambitious statement. Here, he produced Mozart, Bach, John Cage, Philip Glass, Townes Van Zandt, Harry Partch, Albert King, and others—a collection that reflected his personal musical interests. I don't believe Tomato was a great business success, but in terms of musical and aesthetic accomplishments, it set the standard for the industry.

ABOVE This image of a tomato in a chair depends on one's sense of the discomfort with the up-tight armchair encountering the erotic intentions of the tomato. Sometimes the effectiveness of a piece is more related to its detail, in this case the choice of the chair, than to the generality of the idea.

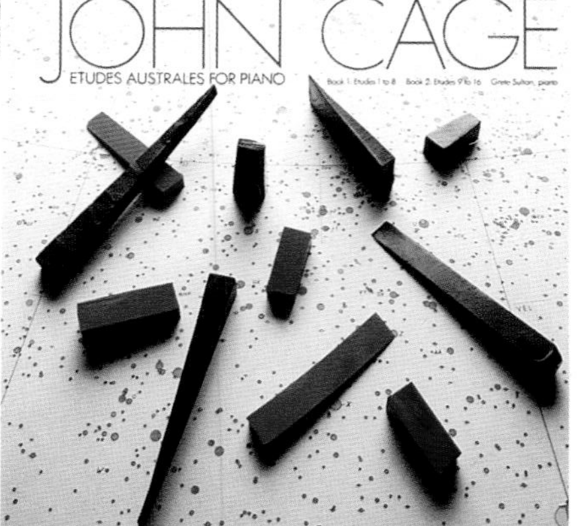

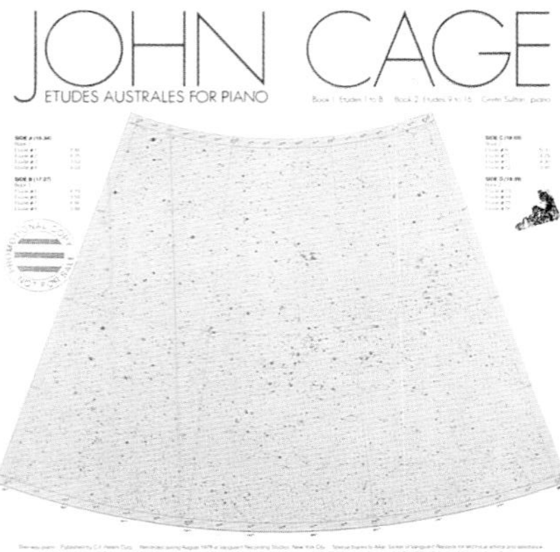

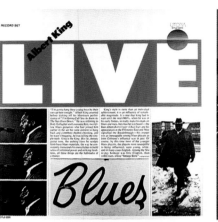

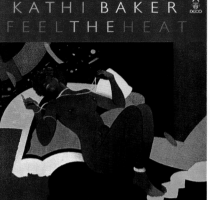

LEFT A variety of album covers. In those days they were twelve-by-twelve inches, which afforded the designer a larger canvas. These examples show the variety and range of albums. On the bottom left is a lovely photo of Townes Van Zandt taken by Saul Mednick in my kitchen in Woodstock, New York. Sadly both artists have passed on.

BELOW For a while the Tomato album liner used craft paper reminiscent of the brown bags used by green grocers rather than the usual plastic sleeve.

Albert King LIVE Blues

KATHI BAKER FEEL THE HEAT

The American Music Theater Festival Production of HARRY PARTCH'S Revelation in the Courthouse Park

BELOW More covers for Tomato. I am particularly fond of the image of Chopin looking over the shoulders of Bach.

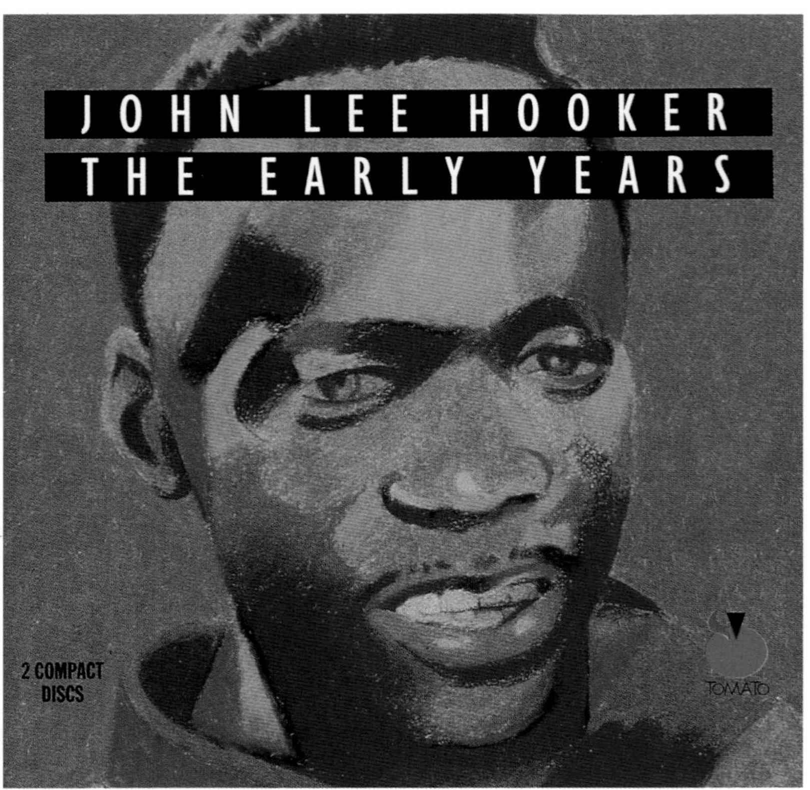

OPPOSITE PAGE Arthur Crudup. Early in my life I was a printmaker and did etchings—a medium I loved. The technique of etching requires building up tone through the use of cross-hatching. The form of this drawing relates to these earlier experiments, although in this case the hatching is achieved by strong brush strokes instead of the more subtle use of a pen or burin.

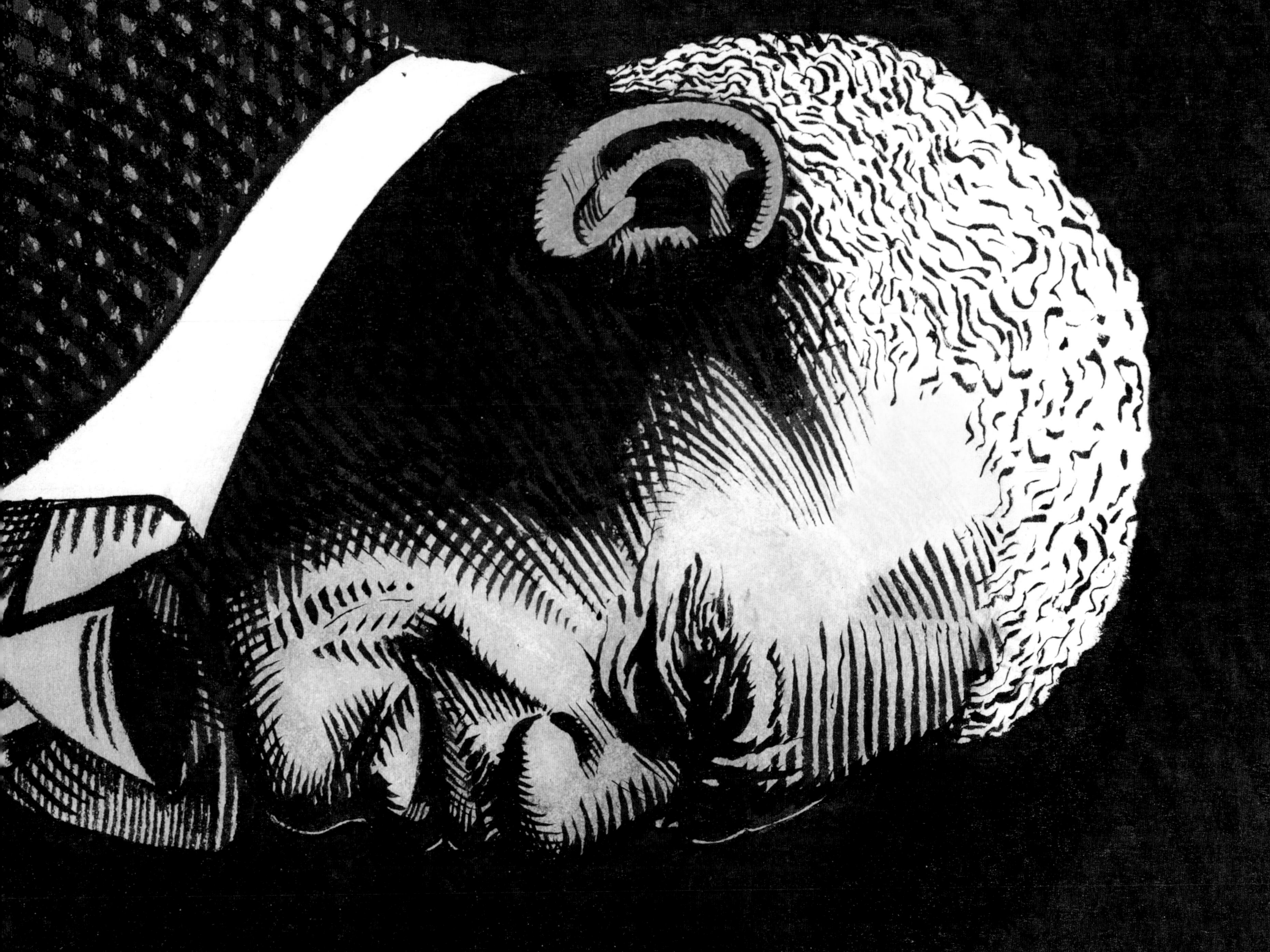

I still am overcome after all these years by the knowledge that I can manipulate the characters in my drawings. Doing that convincingly is another matter. In this case, one great blues musician plays while the other dances to the music. An invented moment, but it could have happened.

Album cover illustration for Chuck Jackson.

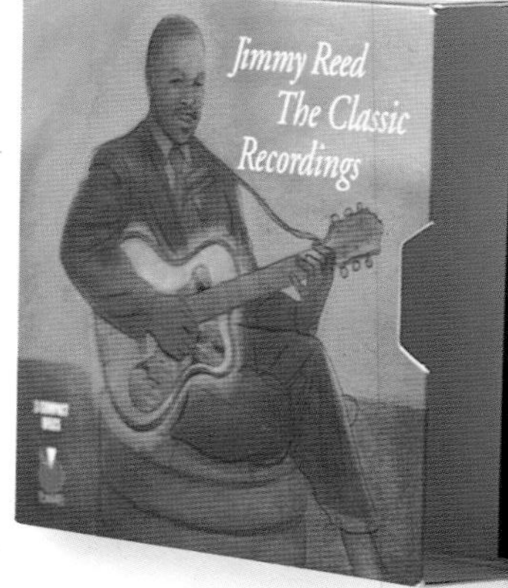

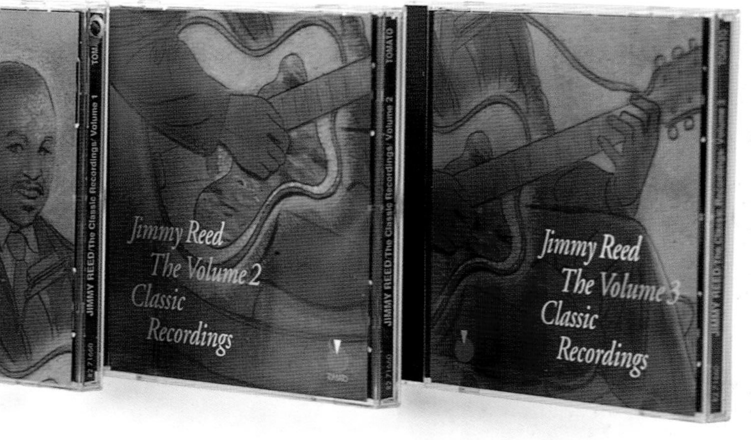

ABOVE For Jimmy Reed's *The Classic Album*, I used a colored pencil drawing for the outside box, which I then cannibalized for the three CDs inside. The parts make the whole—not profound, but less costly for the client than doing four original drawings.

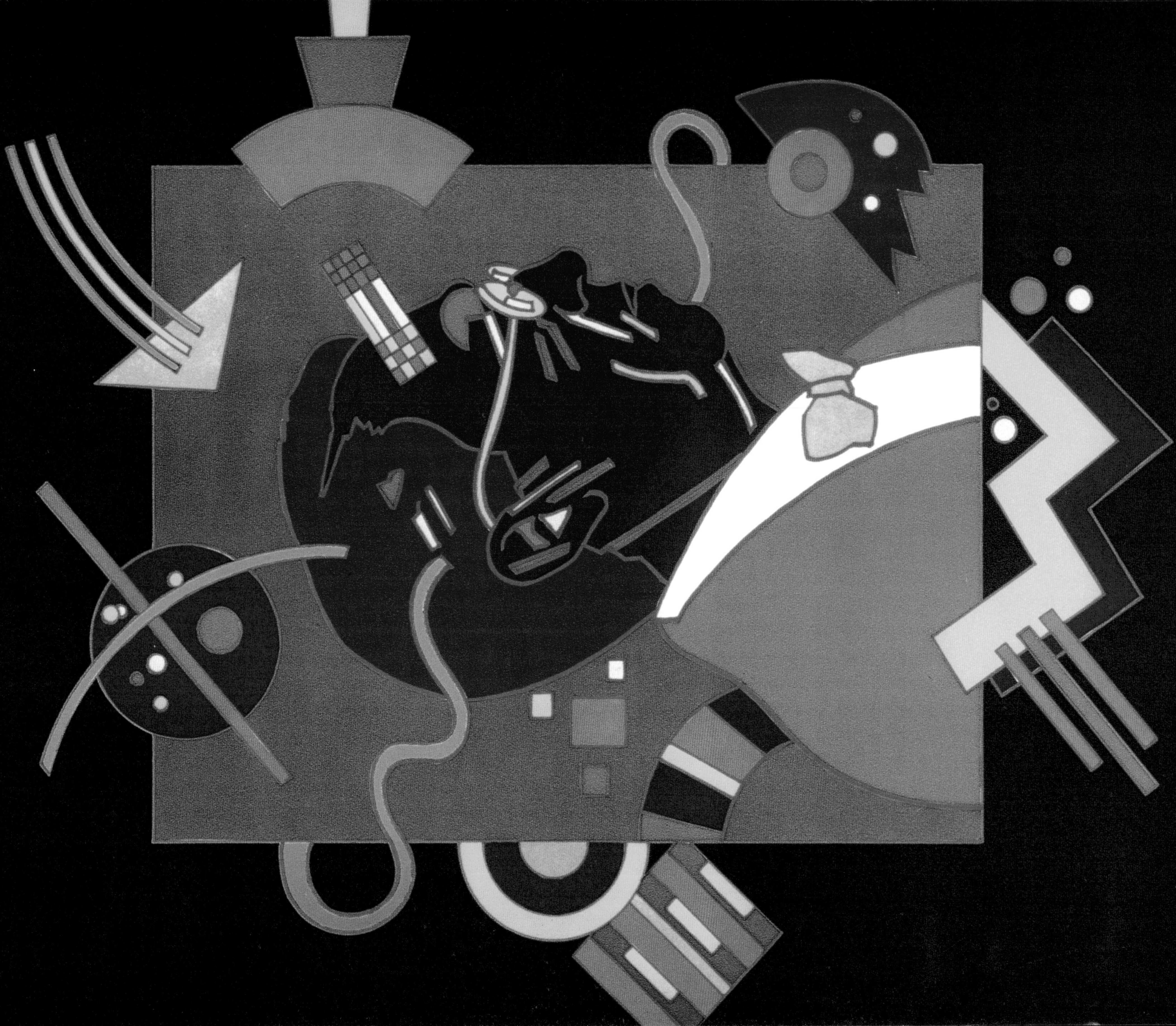

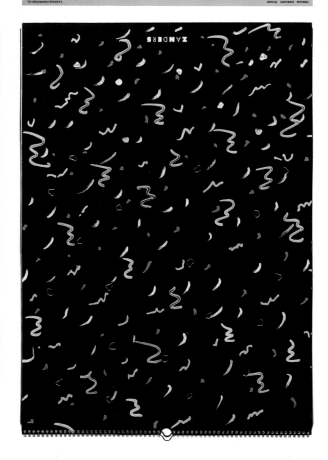

The Zanders paper company has a long tradition of producing impressive annual calendars to demonstrate the quality of its product. They approached me with the idea for a calendar on the theme of color (perhaps because their paper is particularly good for color printing). A dream assignment. I proposed a series of portraits of artists whose works were notable for their color. I attempted to execute each portrait in a manner that would reflect some aspect of their work.

There also is a thematic "frame" around each portrait to create an additional narrative. I might have been inspired by a show of Seurat paintings in which he frequently continued his painting on to the frame.

OPPOSITE PAGE A detail from the April page of the Zanders 1984 calendar features Wassily Kandinsky.

LEFT Zanders Calendar
Front cover

RIGHT Claude Monet
January

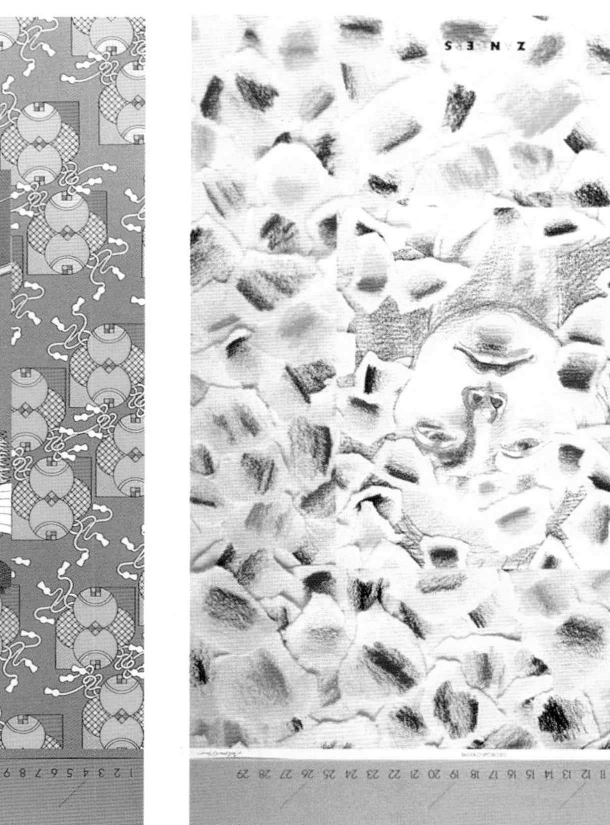

LEFT Georgia O'Keeffe
February

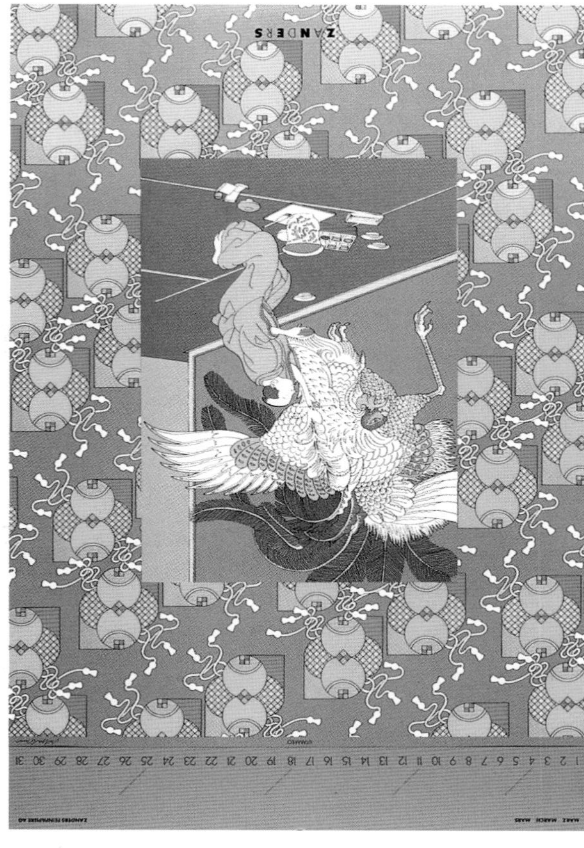

LEFT Utamaro
March

LEFT Edvard Munch
May

RIGHT Paul Klee
June

LEFT Odilon Redon
July

RIGHT Piet Mondrian
August

LEFT Sonia Terk Delaunay
September

RIGHT Max Ernst
October

LEFT Gustav Klimt
November

RIGHT Giorgio de Chirico
December

BELOW This calendar preceded the one for Zanders by nine years. It has the same basic idea, although the stylistic variations occur to emphasize the changing character of a single personality, Hermann Hesse. Fortunately for the project, Hesse's appearance went through dramatic changes throughout his life.

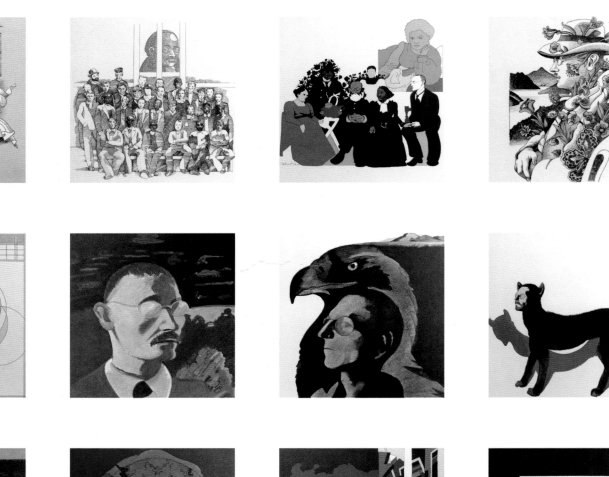

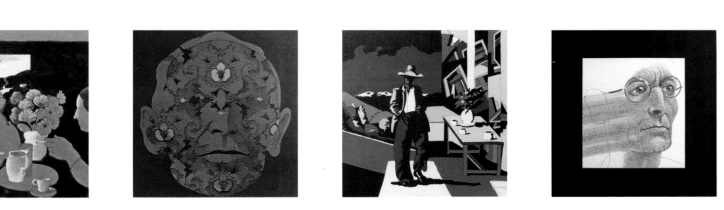

Hermann Hesse 1975 Calendar Illustrated by Milton Glaser

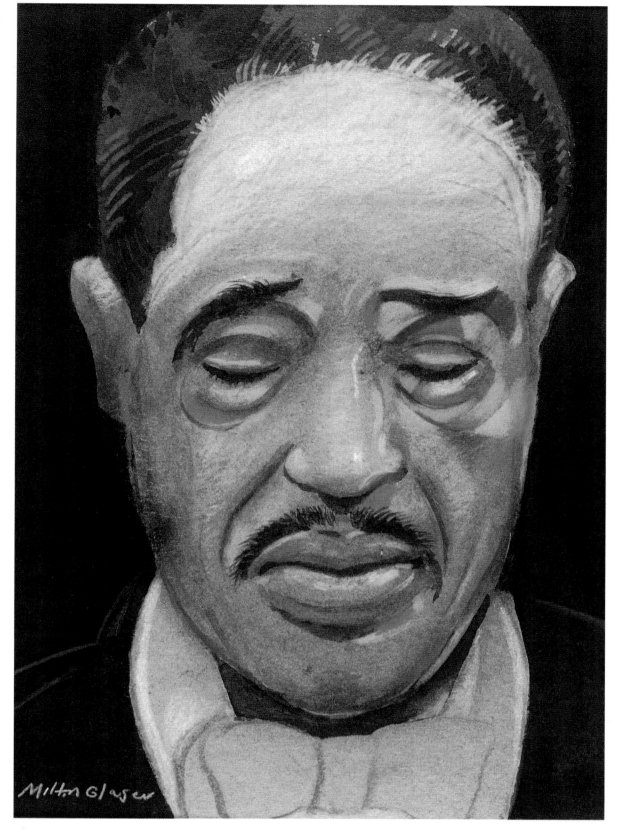

THIS PAGE Duke Ellington as a young man, a grown man and a poet.

FÉLIX VALLOTTON "PORTRAIT OF GERTRUDE STEIN" 1907

PICASSO "PORTRAIT OF GERTRUDE STEIN" 1906

Likeness

The ability to create likeness seems innate among artists, although some struggle with it. Occasionally, when I see a sidewalk artist making a portrait that captures the appearance of its subject in a few strokes, I am filled with envy. Curiously, likeness is not dependent on accuracy, as many of us who have traced photographs of people have discovered. In fact, distortion or caricature are more likely to produce a resemblance. The reasons for this phenomenon remain obscure.

To further complicate the issue, let us consider two portraits of Gertrude Stein—one by Félix Vallotton, the other by the consummate visual genius of the twentieth century, Picasso. On the one hand, you have a portrait of Ms. Stein in all her corporeal reality. One can easily imagine sitting across a table from this woman. On the other hand, we have a painting to which Ms. Stein was moved to say, "But Pablo, honey, I don't look like this." To which Picasso, not known for his modesty, replied, "You will, Gertrude. You will." There is no doubt as to which is the greater painting.

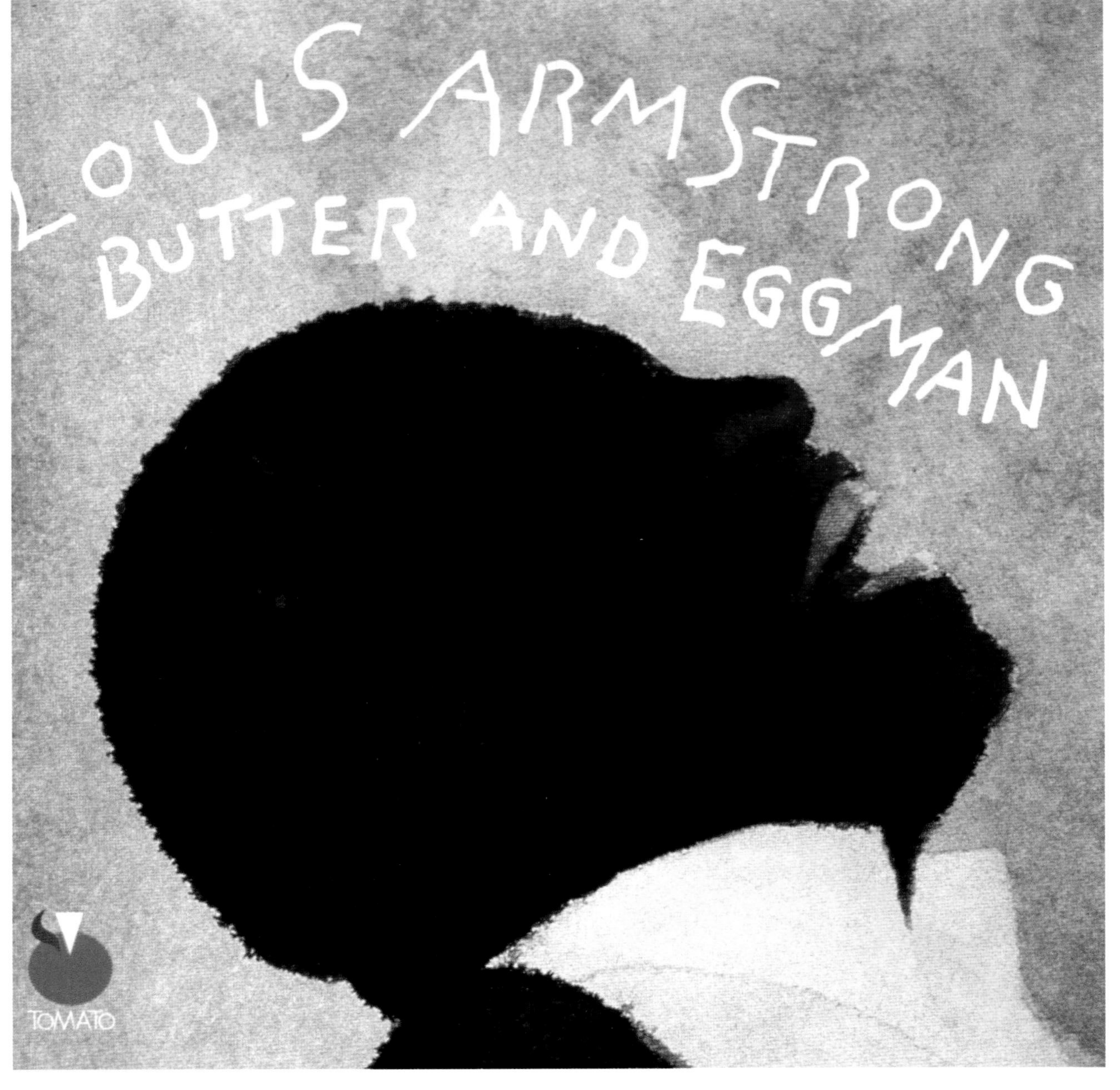
LOUIS ARMSTRONG
BUTTER AND EGG MAN
TOMATO

It's always interesting to make more than one portrait of a person over a period of time and then compare what you have (or have not) learned. In this case two interpretations of Louis Armstrong and Albert King. I can't say which version I prefer.

ALBERT KING MASTERWORKS
(or, The Velvet Bulldozer)
When Albert King hooked up with Memphis, Tennessee's super-hot Stax label in 1966 and began making singles with backing by Booker T. and the MG's and the Memphis Horns, fortune began to smile on him. He was not a youngster. He was born near Indianola, Mississippi, which is the heart of the Delta, blues country, in either 1923 or 1924, and he made his first records in Chicago in 1953, thirteen years before the beginning of his fortuitous association with Stax. But it was at Stax that his mature playing and singing and the definitive soul rhythm section of the sixties clicked together to produce music that would fundamentally alter the mainstream of white rock as well as the sound of commercial blues within a few years' time. In 1968, Stax collected King's best singles of the preceding two years on an album, *Born Under A Bad Sign*. It was the most influential blues album of its era. Within months, Eric Clapton and Cream were regurgitating chunks of it whole (e.g. "Strange Brew" and their own "Born Under A Bad Sign") and rockers everywhere were scurrying into their woodsheds to learn King's songs and his signature guitar licks.
Seven selections from the *Born Under A Bad Sign* album are reissued in this collection: "Personal Manager," "The Very Thought of You," "Born Under A Bad Sign" itself, "Laundromat Blues," "Kansas City," "Cross-cut Saw," and "As The Years Go Passing By." Since *Born Under A Bad Sign* hasn't been available in this country for a number of years, these tracks, the backbone of any good modern blues collection, are worth the price of admission all by themselves. But there is more here, lots more—Albert King with the great Allen Toussaint's New Orleans band ("Angel of Mercy" and Toussaint's "We All Wanna Boogie,") King with several other groupings of musicians, updating his backdrops, as he always has, while playing the natural blues.
The development of King Albert's music, and especially of his recordings, is the ultimate case study in the continuing relevance of the blues, which keeps hanging in there with an almost uncanny tenacity as changing fashions swirl around it. To begin with,
(Continued on inside)

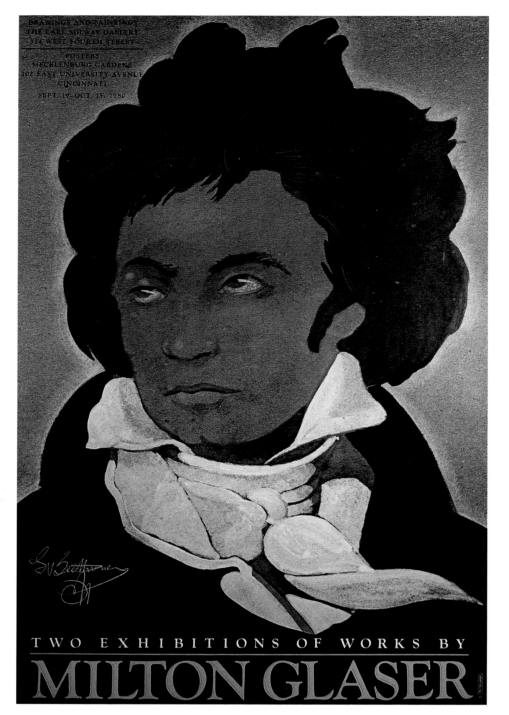

RIGHT A heroic portrait of Beethoven I used for a show of my work in 1980.

BELOW RIGHT I used the same pictorial reference for Beethoven, somewhat reduced in visual content, in this later print (1985), called "White Eggplants and Beethoven."

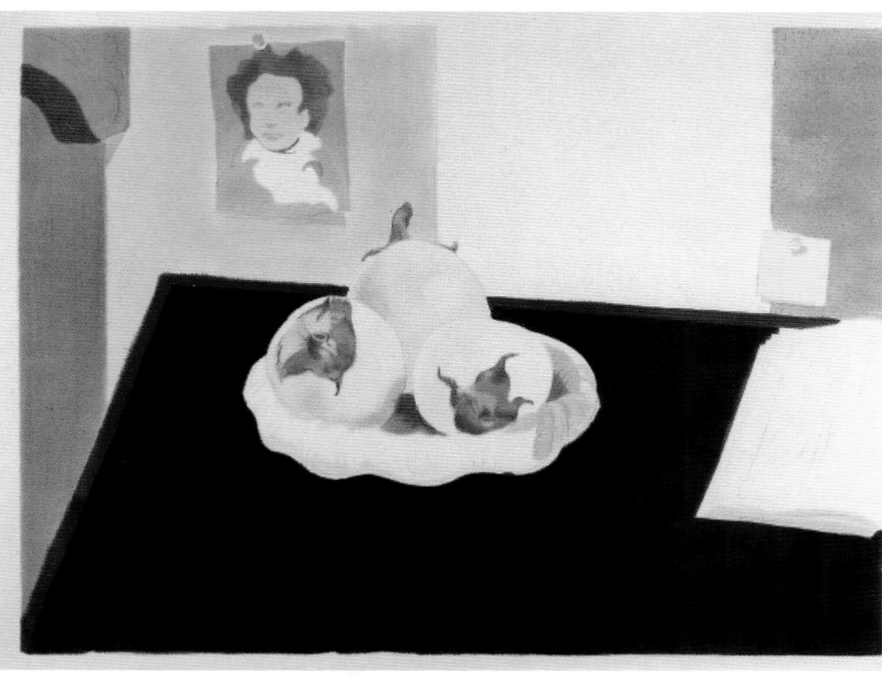

BELOW A series of Beethoven portraits for album covers.

These twelve drawings of Bach derived from a single line drawing I made and then photocopied on a variety of papers. I proceeded to color each one differently. It was interesting for me to discover how much the portraits differ based on the way they were colored. These all appeared on a poster entitled "Bach Variations"—a small inside joke, since these are not musical variations but variations on the head of Bach. Matthew Klein photographed them cleverly to create slight differences in their depth, which created some additional surface interest.

I've made several other portraits of Bach—one for Columbia in 1967, the other more recently for Tomato. In the latter, I've dressed him in what I call a "fugueing suit." A small geometric pattern appears on his vest, gets larger on his jacket and pants, and finally spills over onto the wall itself in an enlarged and expanded form. This is my attempt to visually represent the form of the fugue, a musical expression so identified with this great Baroque master. Whether the viewer gets all this is open to discussion.

BELOW This Dylan poster of 1966 remains one of my most iconic works. I have mixed feelings about this. I don't like being entirely identified with a moment that has clearly passed, with the inevitable suggestion that I have as well. It's difficult, in that sense, to overcome your past, but that seems to be a recurring problem for many who have become well known. Most of my later work bears little resemblance to this style.

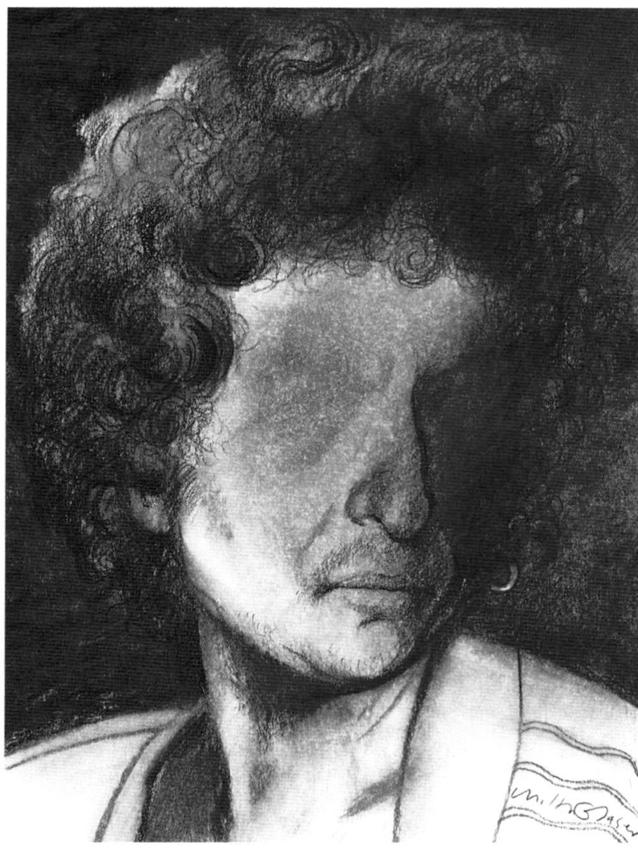

Creation
INTERNATIONAL GRAPHIC DESIGN, ART & ILLUSTRATION — Number 10

RIGHT In a later portrait of Dylan, I used a more naturalistic approach for a magazine piece that asked whether Dylan had lost his way musically.

RIGHT This Stevie Wonder poster, from the same period as the early Dylan, demonstrates a similar graphic intensity, although it never became well known.

Produced by Gary Keys
STEVIE WONDER
STEVIE WONDER
Friday September 26, 8:30 p.m.
Lincoln Center Philharmonic Hall

THE DAVID BOWIE STORY
STARDUST
HENRY EDWARDS AND TONY ZANETTA

Mick Jagger

This portrait of Jerry Garcia was done for *Time Magazine* the week he died. It was rejected, then published by *Rolling Stone*. My idea was to show him fading away. The bones are a reference to an image frequently used by his band, The Grateful Dead.

Many have observed the eerie resemblance of Elvis to Greek and Roman ideals of beauty. In this colored drawing, I was attempting to show his androgynous beauty as well as a quality of benign innocence that seemed present in his early years. Later, that quality was replaced in our minds by another, sadder image of a life that had come undone.

The Imaginary Life of Claude Monet *by Shirley Glaser*

Text that accompanied my studies of Claude Monet. Exhibited at the Nuages Galleries, Milano and the Creation Gallery, Tokyo

Monet wakes up.

The first time he woke up he didn't know where he was for a minute or two, then as his eyes moved around, recognizing the familiar objects of his bedroom, he took a deep breath and slowly exhaled. He lay there in his bed, warm and comfortable under the feather comforter made from the tiny soft down of his very own geese. The dogs sensed his awakening and began the rhythmic slapping of their tails on the Oriental rugs which overlapped each other on the floor. The big brown bitch approached the bed first, nuzzling her large wet nose against his cheek, followed by the smaller dogs trying to leap up, their claws slipping and sliding against the comforter as they tried to get into position to lick his face with their drooling tongues.

He pushed them away with his arm, calling out "down." He moved very carefully, made a slight groan and began to catalog his various aches and pains, testing each limb gingerly and then rolling over to test his back. Each morning he vowed to order a new and softer mattress, or should it be a new and harder mattress? Most people would think that someone with his soft, round, (let's face it) fat body type wouldn't need a mattress at all, that he should just be able to curl up on the floor with the dogs. He hadn't done that in fifty years but, it was true, he didn't remember wake-up aches and pains.

Choosing a comfortable position for his back and placing another pillow under his head, he looked around the room, checking all the familiar cracks and bumps in the walls and ceiling. He noticed that one of the cracks had extended. That worried him for a moment. Then he began looking for the familiar images the bumps and cracks made. He looked at the slightly raised surface that in the morning light looked like a peach with a broken stem; today it looked like a melon, one of those small ones, or perhaps a dumpling squash. He became displeased by the wall color. Perhaps it should be repainted, perhaps a warmer ivory with just a touch of ochre, or a pale banana color.

Lifting his head very, very carefully, he stretched to look at the voluptuous Renoir hanging over his bed. Yes, it was still there. His dear friend, he sighed, remembering when they left old Gleyre's art school and took rooms together. Everyone thought that he was the very antithesis of Renoir. Someone wrote that the life that Renoir infused into people, Monet infused into things. What do critics know?

His eyes glanced around the room, touching on the portrait of a young woman by Manet, then Cezanne's Negre. His eyes stopped on the blue trousers in the painting. Maybe I should paint the room that blue, no I can't do that, I would have nightmares. He looked at the other paintings by Cezanne, well, not really looking—more like counting them. Fourteen in all. His glance went back to Cezanne's Apples and then he noticed how hungry he was.

He wondered what he would eat today. For breakfast, sausages and bacon as well as cheese of course; he wondered if there was any good strawberry jam. For lunch, he would like wild mushrooms, baked with *crème fraîche* and cognac, followed by chicken in white wine sauce or perhaps oxtail stew, baby carrots and a green salad, just something simple.

On the other hand, he thought that he might have some of yesterday's ratatouille. It was not just some gross vegetable stew, but made according to his very specific instructions. What is the point, after all, of growing your own vegetables and paying huge salaries to kitchen and garden staff if you couldn't eat well? He breathed deeply and relived sitting on a rocking chair in the blue and white kitchen directing the preparation of the ratatouille. Spread out on the table were round white eggplants, slim long lavender eggplants, yellow and green zucchini, shiny red, green and yellow peppers, yellow and red tomatoes, fresh red Italian onions, tight heads of garlic and bouquets of lemon thyme, sweet marjoram and basil. He instructed them to cook each vegetable separately in Tuscan olive oil, then add some good white wine and the fresh herbs to cook slowly together for forty-five minutes. The perfumes from the memory of the stewed vegetables reminded him of his gardens. It was a very quick leap in his mind from the vegetable garden to the flower gardens. He turned his head to gaze out of the window alongside of his bed.

As he moved, his leg grazed something soft, furry and very warm. Once again he wondered how that cat could breathe, sleeping under the quilt all night and anyway weren't cats supposed to prowl around at night looking for little rodents? Mimi was always unusual; she didn't even look like a cat. Her face divided in half: one side orange the other side black. Her tiny cobby body hid her strong muscled frame. The messages to her brain that controlled her tail were working overtime, the tail swishing back and forth constantly, but not ever to indicate irritation, as with most cats. Unless of course she was *constantly* irritated—a feline virago. Could be. Maybe it isn't fun to go through life looking like a tiny primitive painting of a cat. *Ma Jolie*, that's what he called her.

A movement outside caught his eye, a flash of red. It was a cardinal. He never understood cardinals. Was there anything less adaptive than a cardinal in a winter landscape? Most creatures, when still, are colored to be camouflaged by their environment, but when still, a cardinal screams "catch me if you can." That might be very interesting: to plant something scarlet red in the middle of the white gardens. Just a touch of red. Of course it had to be the right red and it couldn't be anything invasive; I don't want red and white gardens. It can't be a daylily even if I could find one in the right red, too domineering. Perhaps Lobelia cardinals: right color, blooms in the summer, but just slightly untidy looking, not quite the right form. Tall and elegant when not in bloom, it has lovely narrow spear-shaped leaves, and, in the late summer, a lovely arching stem of cardinal red small tubular flowers. Crocosmia, of course. It's easy to control. Probably the wrong weather conditions—well, he thought, I'll try it, I can replace it every year.

His thoughts drifted through the seasons of his flower garden, so distinct from his vegetable garden and his water garden. He followed it in his mind's eye from the earliest spring with a dazzling show of narcissus: large yellow, emperor, and poets. Two weeks later the tulips arrive, rows and rows of all hues. Then violet borders of aubretias, yellow rows of tulips emerging from the pink and red clumps of leopard's bane with lace curtains of clematis resting on light trellises; under the clematis, white mullein and Oriental poppies. Then in June, roses of all shapes and colors, but not long-stemmed florist roses. Irises are in bloom at the same time. Imagine thousands of a single color in long wide beds. Elsewhere hollyhocks, digitalis, phlox, flame-colored nasturtiums and his favorite penstemons. At the end of September, sunflowers, goldenrod, and Japanese anemones compete with the sun in their dazzling yellow. People told him it was the most dazzling estate in France. It only proved to his satisfaction that he didn't have to be English to create a garden.

Well, he thought, looking through his bedroom window, it's time to get up and see what happened overnight, what started and what finished. My garden has to work month after month: it's a working garden, not a frivolous garden that declines after June. He sat at the edge of his bed and reached for a cigarette. With the cigarette clamped between his lips, he shuffled towards the bath.

Dear Monet
Over the last year I have been working on a series of drawings based more or less on your life. I say more or less because some of the events I have depicted are based on actual photographs of you, your garden, and your contemporaries. Other scenes are completely made up. There is a sense that all history is a series of opportunistic lies, in the air right now, that makes it quite possible for me to invent your life to suit my own needs. Curiously I've never felt drawn to your work because I related it to my own. Actually I embarked on the series because I felt it might move me in a direction that was unfamiliar. The attempt to transform solid intractable paint into mutable light has never been a concern of mine. I realize that as much as anything, the way you looked, portly, solid, earthy, bearded, with a cigarette dangling from your lip, and a wide brimmed hat on your head make you eminently drawable. I also recall the pleasure of a visit to your home and garden at Giverny, some years ago. The scope of your ambition in creating an earthly paradise was what impressed me most.

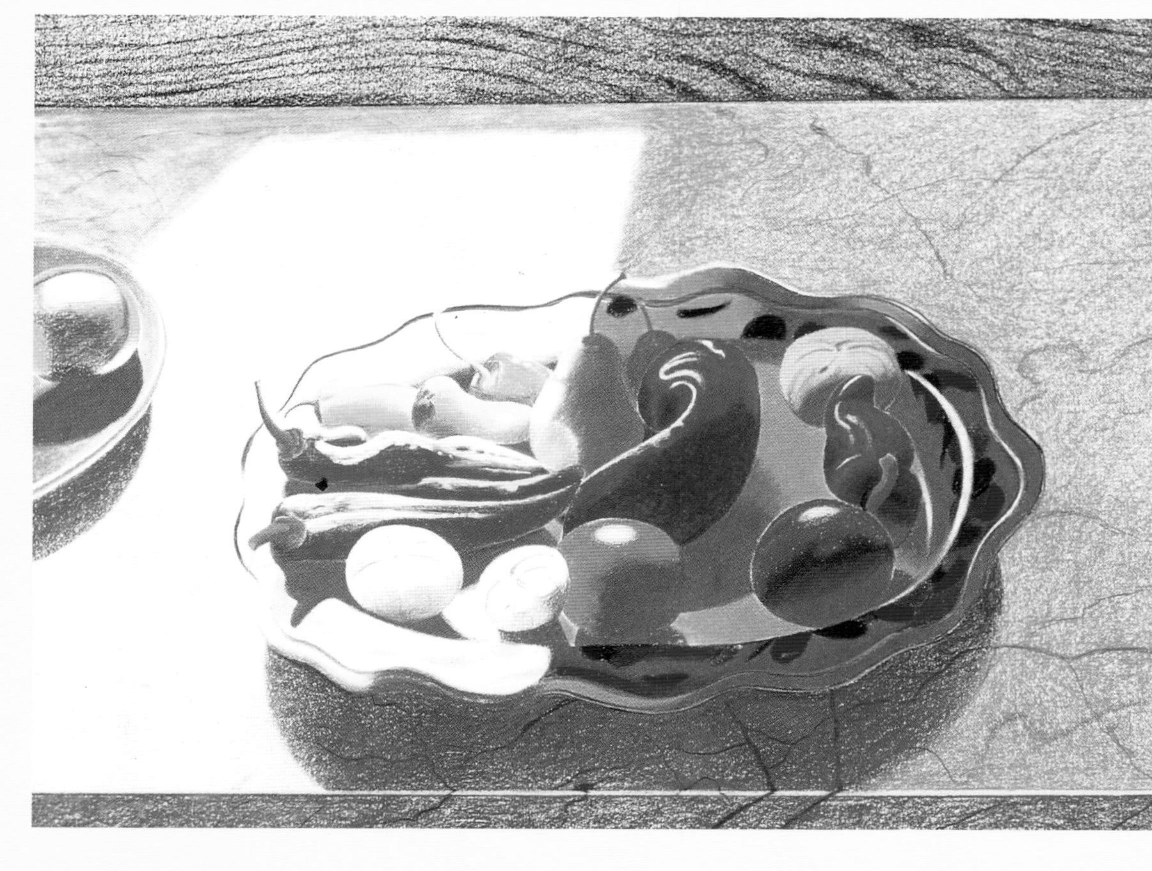

The restored gardens, the lilypond, the wisteria that covered the Japanese bridge all exceeded my expectations, but it was your yellow dining room and blue tiled kitchen that delighted me most - Years later I designed a restaurant for the Barbazon Hotel called 'Monets dining room', based on your remarkable interiors - Sadly the project was never implimented. Perhaps, on the other hand it is better for some ideas to remain unexploited. It is the harmony and totality of your life and vision I find most compelling. The yellow dining room with its Japanese prints, painted chairs and specially designed yellow plates create an atmosphere as pleasurable and life enhancing as any of your paintings -

I suspect that you wer not an easy man to be with - No one with your immense will and appetite could be. As for me, holding you in my mind and entering your luminous world this past year, has been a source of profound pleasure - Thank you for all that -

Milton Glaser

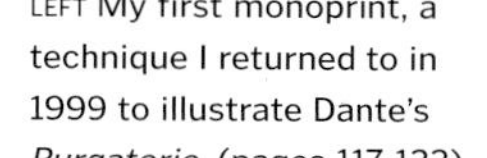

LEFT My first monoprint, a technique I returned to in 1999 to illustrate Dante's *Purgatorio.* (pages 117-122)

I now realize that, collectively, these drawings could have made an excellent comic strip entitled "A Week in the Life of Monet."

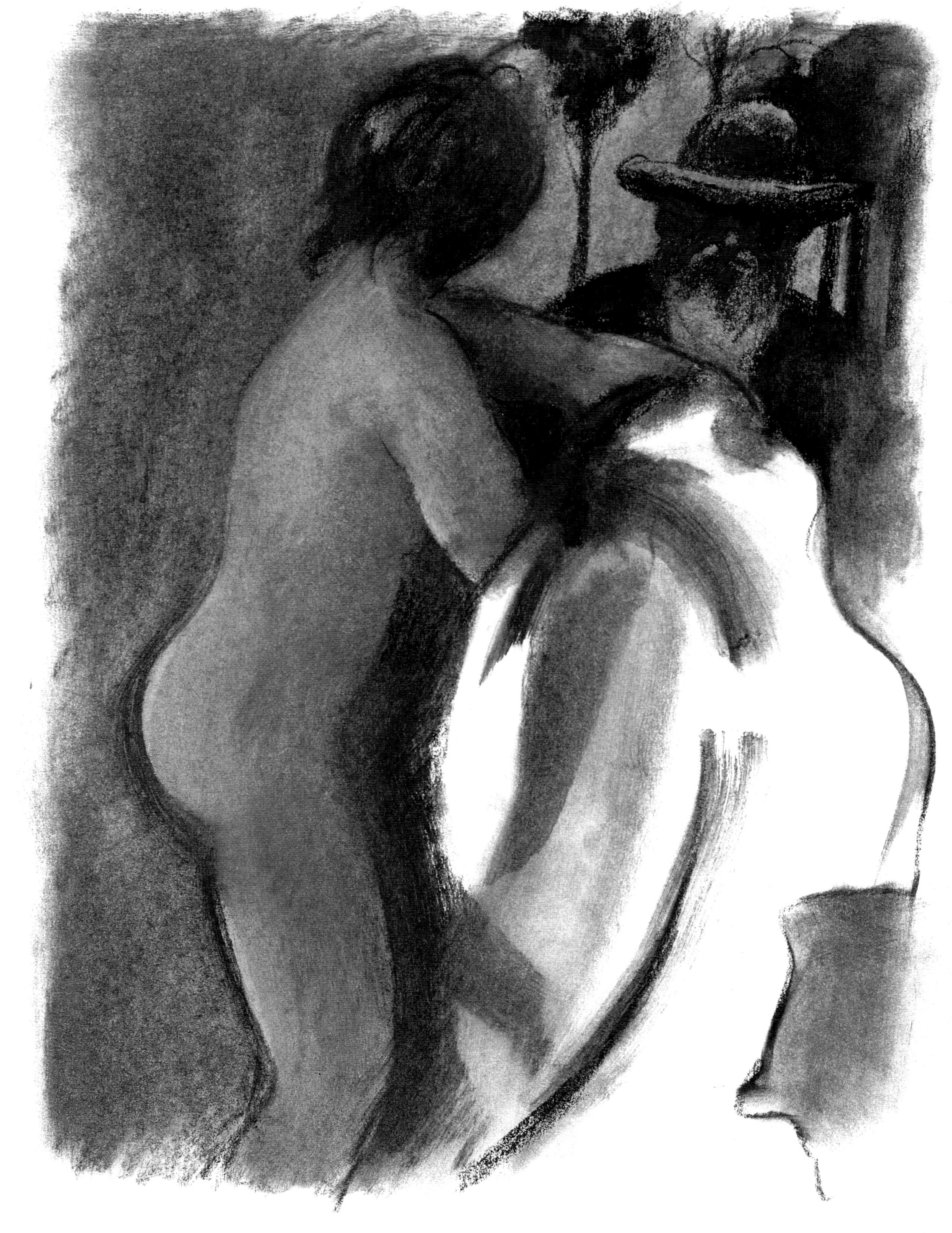

September, 1987

Milan, 1989

Drawing

I don't consider myself an illustrator, although I love to illustrate. Like Hokusai, I am one of those individuals "mad about drawing." In his ninetieth year, shortly before he died, Hokusai was reported to have said, "If I only had ten more years, I could really learn how to draw." Ingres said, "Drawing is the probidity of art." (Probidity being "proof" for all of you, like myself, who never knew the meaning of the word before.) For me, the principal reason for drawing is that it is unparalleled as a means of making you pay attention to whatever you are looking at. Paying attention, as any Buddhist will tell you, is extremely difficult—which is why we mostly avoid doing it.

When you draw something, your mind shifts into another gear. Ideally, you approach the subject with a sense of reverence or humility as you acknowledge its extraordinary nature and attempt to describe it. Of course, it's possible to draw without paying attention by imposing your will or style upon the subject; but that is, I believe, another kind of activity.

For me, drawing is only partially an end in itself. The Italians, as usual, have it right when they use the word "design" to describe both drawing and design, recognizing the inevitable relationship between the two. The work I have done in design, posters, supermarkets, trademarks, interiors, and so on, has been informed by my enthusiasm for drawing. I cannot imagine how it could be otherwise.

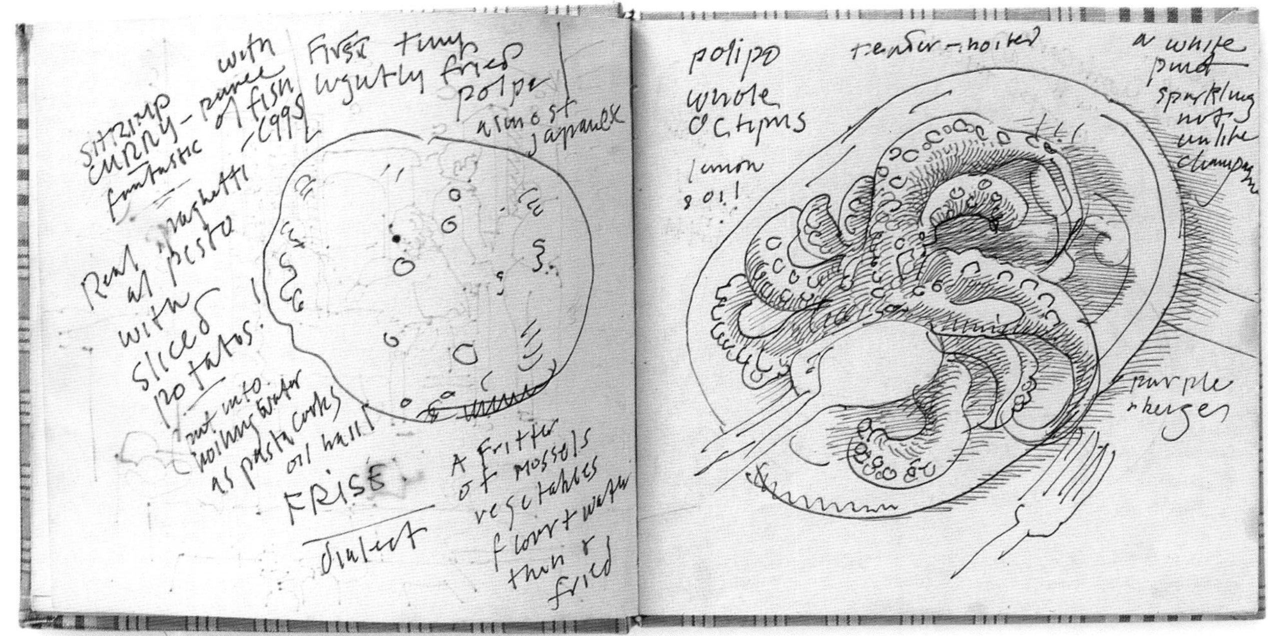

Tuscany, April 1978

Paris, July 1979

Studies of Richard Meier, New York, 1995

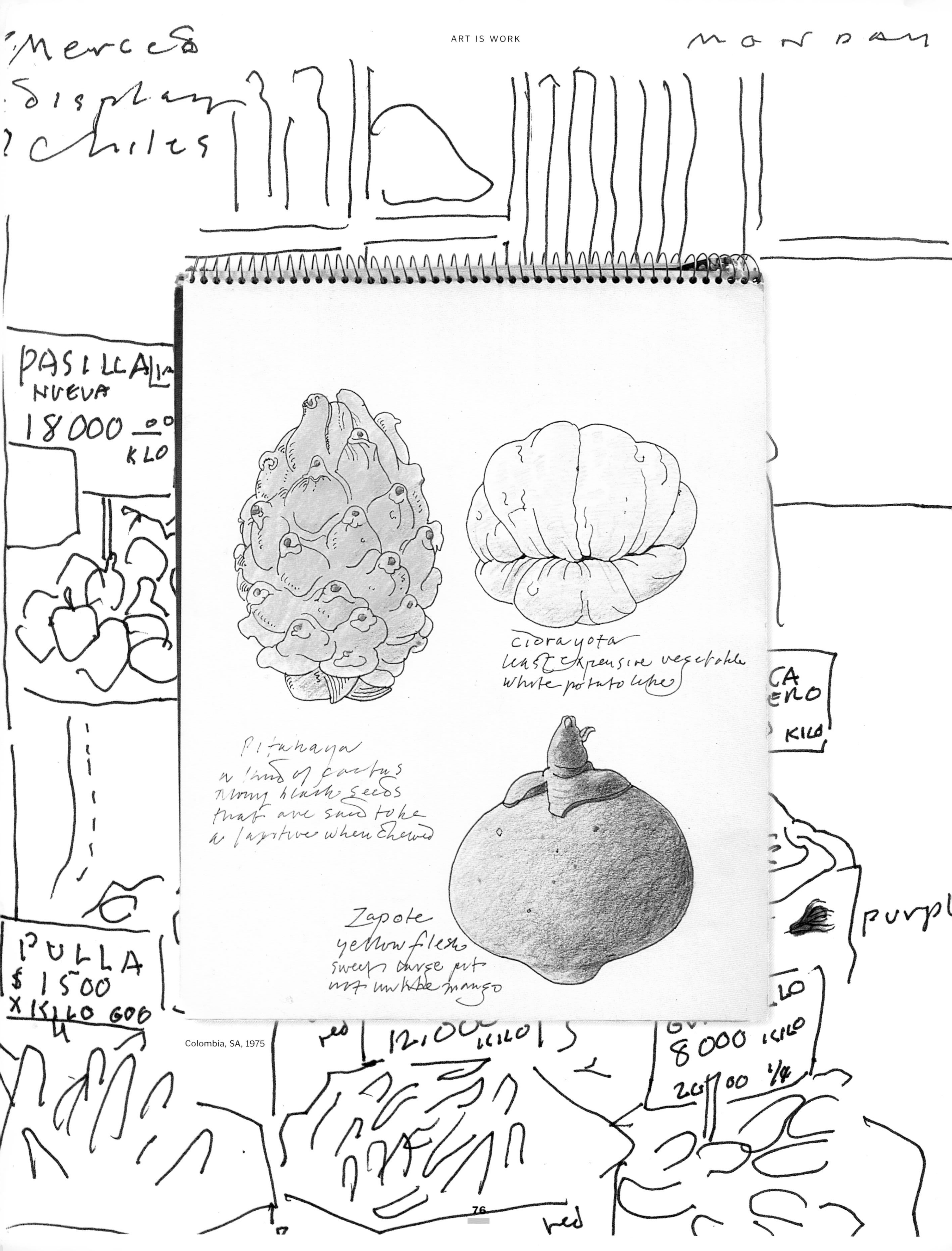

Colombia, SA, 1975

OPPOSITE PAGE A notebook from a trip to South America in which I drew exotic fruits that I had never seen before —many of which now are available in our supermarkets.

BELOW A record of a wonderful dinner in Morocco and a drawing of Evelyn Menasche, my agent in Paris, but more important, a dear friend who died some years ago.

Morocco, 1983

Venice, 1991

I frequently work on assignments when I travel, especially on long flights or during evenings in hotel rooms. This sketchbook shows the development of some ideas for an exhibit of Leonardo in Venice. I had a number of ideas but, ultimately, the image of a young da Vinci seeing Venice for the first time seemed the most evocative—perhaps because I remember my own entreé into Venice.

When I was growing up in the Bronx, there was only one work of art in the house, aside from the coal company calendar in the kitchen. That was an enormous brown tapestry of a Venetian lagoon with a gondola in the foreground. Behind the jaunty gondolier was the Piazza San Marco revealing the Doges Palace, the Basilica, and the Campanile. This incomprehensible scene hung above a red convertible sofa in our living room where the entire family spent every evening—my mother darning socks, my father reading the newspaper while listening to the radio, and my sister and I doing our homework. I must have studied that tapestry five thousand times. When I first arrived in Venice in 1952, I came in by way of vaporetto on the canal. We turned a corner and there before me was an exact replica of my childhood memory—including the jaunty gondolier—only now in full and glorious color. The effect was very much like one of those films where a sepia engraving gets transformed into a full-color movie.

This sketchbook is the result of a three-month stay in Tuscany in 1989. The drawings are somewhat more finished than usual because a friend, Pamela Fiori, then editor of *Travel + Leisure,* suggested that she would like to run a Tuscan notebook in her pages. I also used this sketchbook as the basis for a poster (page 24).

BELOW RIGHT I'm still hoping to find the strange and delicious vegetable called agretti in a New York market. It seems to grow only in Tuscany and only for two weeks in the early spring. It tastes like a cross between seaweed and asparagus.

The legendary San Marzano tomatoes.

The sabbatical in Tuscany also resulted in a series of landscape drawings and water colors that I translated into three prints. These silk screens originated as black and white brush drawings done on the spot.

Poems by
Conrad Aiken
Cats and
Bats and Things
with Wings
Drawings by
Milton Glaser

ABOVE *Cats and Bats and Things With Wings* was a book I designed with the famous American author, Conrad Aiken. We approached the project in reverse. First I did the illustrations, then Conrad wrote the poems.

BUFFALO ZOOLOGICAL GARDENS

OPPOSITE PAGE A watercolor of a snow leopard that takes considerable liberties with its coloring. Although snow leopards are mostly white, I thought that using intense color would attract the viewer's attention. What surprised me was that the client, The Bronx Zoo, accepted the premise and suspended its usual concern for scientific accuracy. I explained that since the color white contained all other colors, we were on defensible ground. Why they bought the argument, I'll never know.

LEFT On the other hand, the white tiger on this page shows a variation of the same idea but makes the color effect more suggestive.

BELOW This image is more complex than my usual posters because of the negative and positive drawing of the leopard and the large image of the leopard contained within the smaller one. In this case, the complexity resulted from trying to express the relationship between animals and their environments.

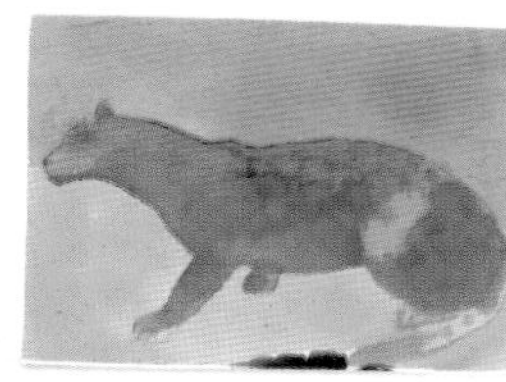

Cats and Bats

I don't know what it is about animals that I find so fascinating to observe and draw. Of course that they are beautiful and lively creatures is sufficient. I realize that what started me on my path in life was a drawing of a bird by my cousin Saul, on the side of a brown paper bag. I was five and, for some reason, had never watched an adult draw something. Watching the drawing take shape was miraculous. Then and there I decided to devote myself to making images.

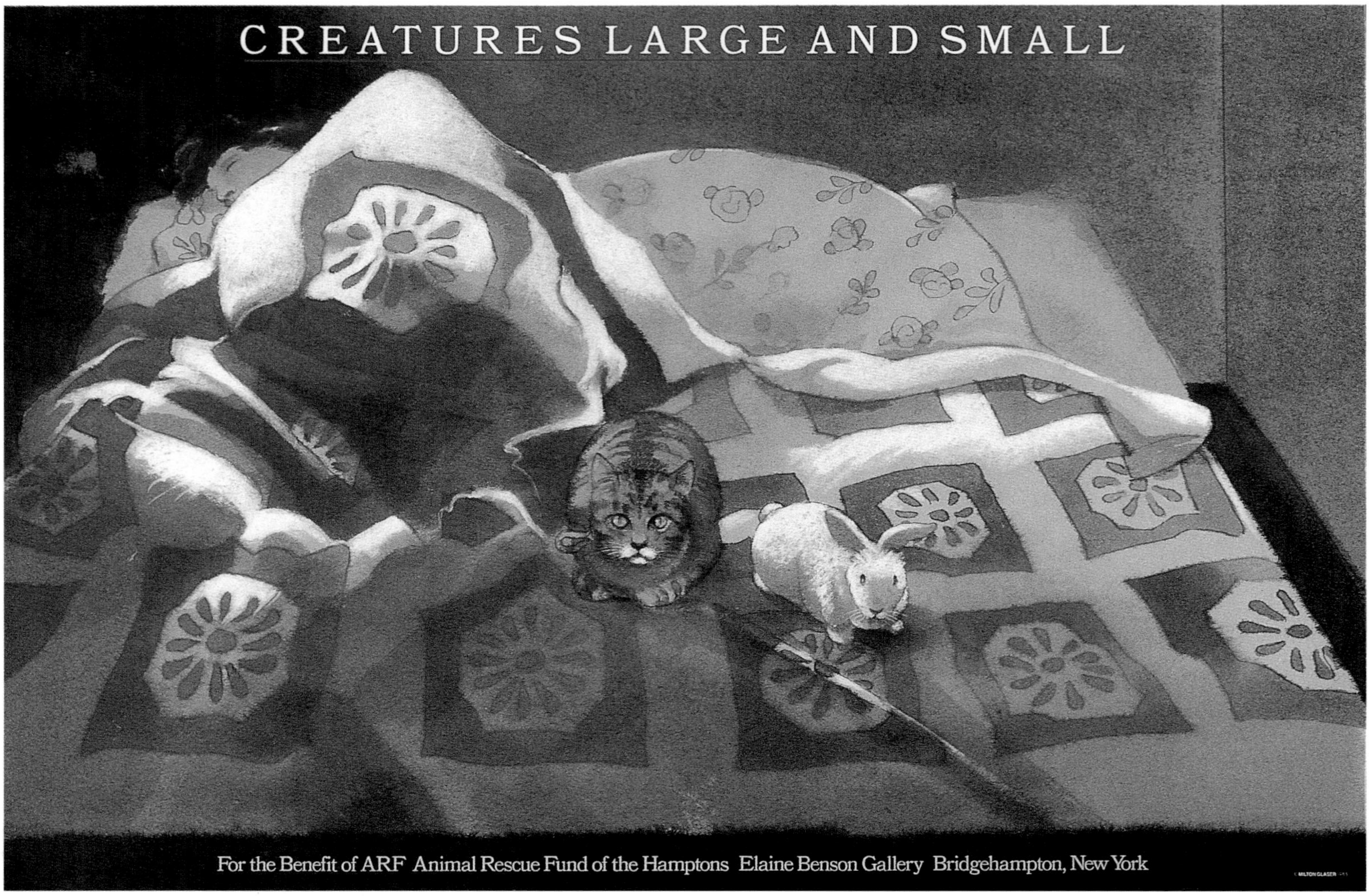

CREATURES LARGE AND SMALL
For the Benefit of ARF Animal Rescue Fund of the Hamptons Elaine Benson Gallery Bridgehampton, New York

Things More Personal

Work that involves personal aspects of your life has a different, sweeter meaning. On this page are two watercolors; one of our home in Woodstock that shows Shirley, our favorite cat, Annie, and a dwarf Polish rabbit named Mr. Hoffman. I particularly like the fact that you can see the difference in intelligence between the cat and the rabbit. The other, a portrait of Annie in a most endearing pose. Although I did these for myself, they each found their way into posters for the Animal Rescue Fund.

Creatures Large and Small
For the Benefit of ARF Animal Rescue fund of the Hamptons Elaine Benson Gallery Bridgehampton New York

One of any number of studies of our darling Annie.

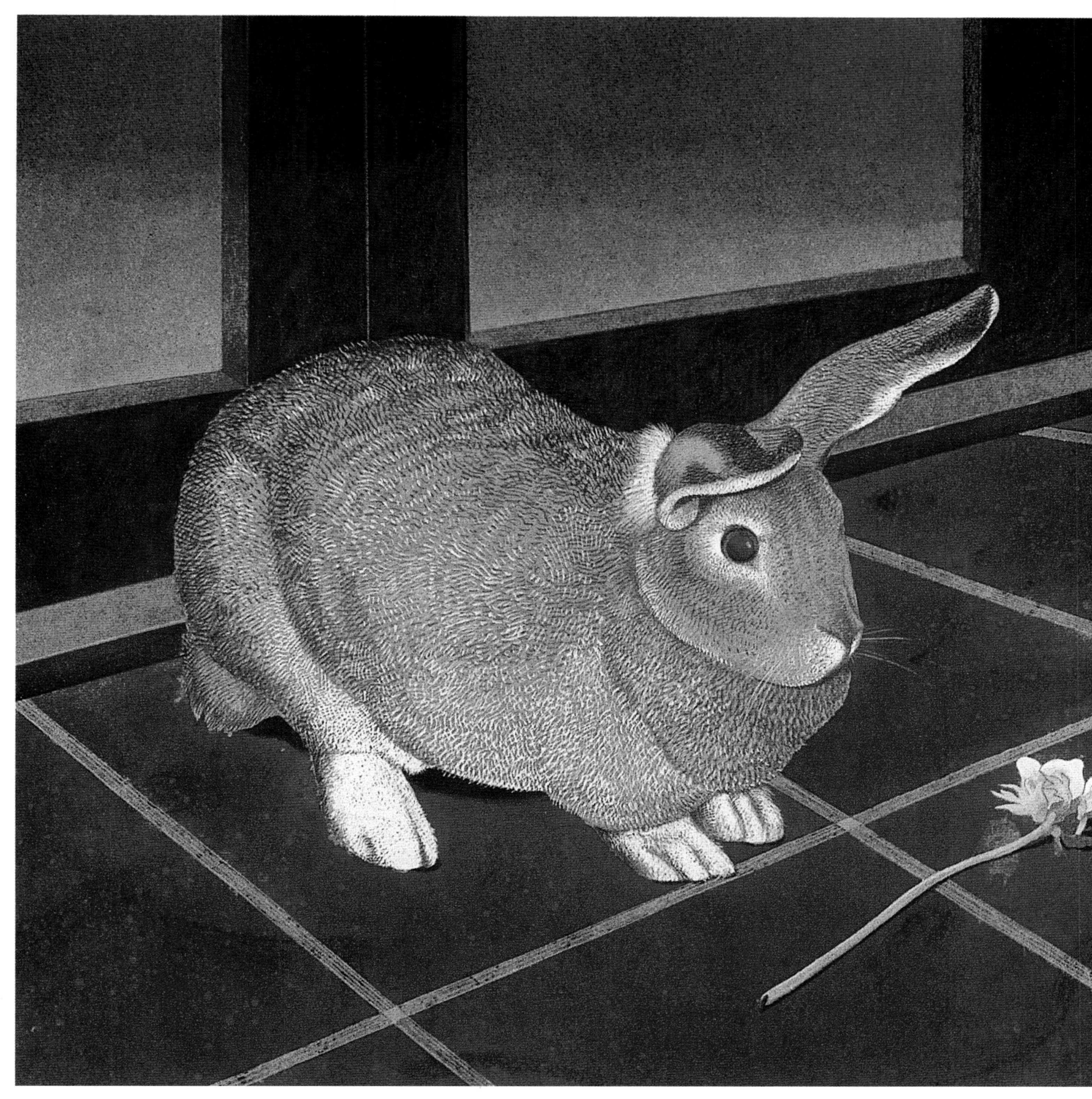

ABOVE Another pet rabbit, Mookie, who was part French Lop, part wild hare. We hated each other.

From time to time, Olivetti would assign me to produce a print edition as a gift (see pages 225-228). This one was for Olivetti Japan, celebrating the Year of the Cow. I thought it would be amusing to create a large silk screen out of four segments. When assembled, the print measured about 67" x 45." Some years later, I met the head of Olivetti Japan at an art opening. "Mr. Glaser," he said, "do you have any idea of the size of an average Japanese apartment?"
There is a modest graphic joke in the print: the crescent of the moon is echoed in the eye of the cow.

In 1980 I was asked by the committee to design a series of posters for a variety of events taking place in Venice. I chose a familiar symbol of the city, the lion of St. Marks. The notion of theme and variation is well entrenched in the arts—visually, musically, and in literature. The use of repetition and variety permits you to engage the listener or viewer in a game. The game consists of the viewer's remembering what he has already seen and, consequently, being pleased and delighted by each new iteration. These are three of the eight posters produced.

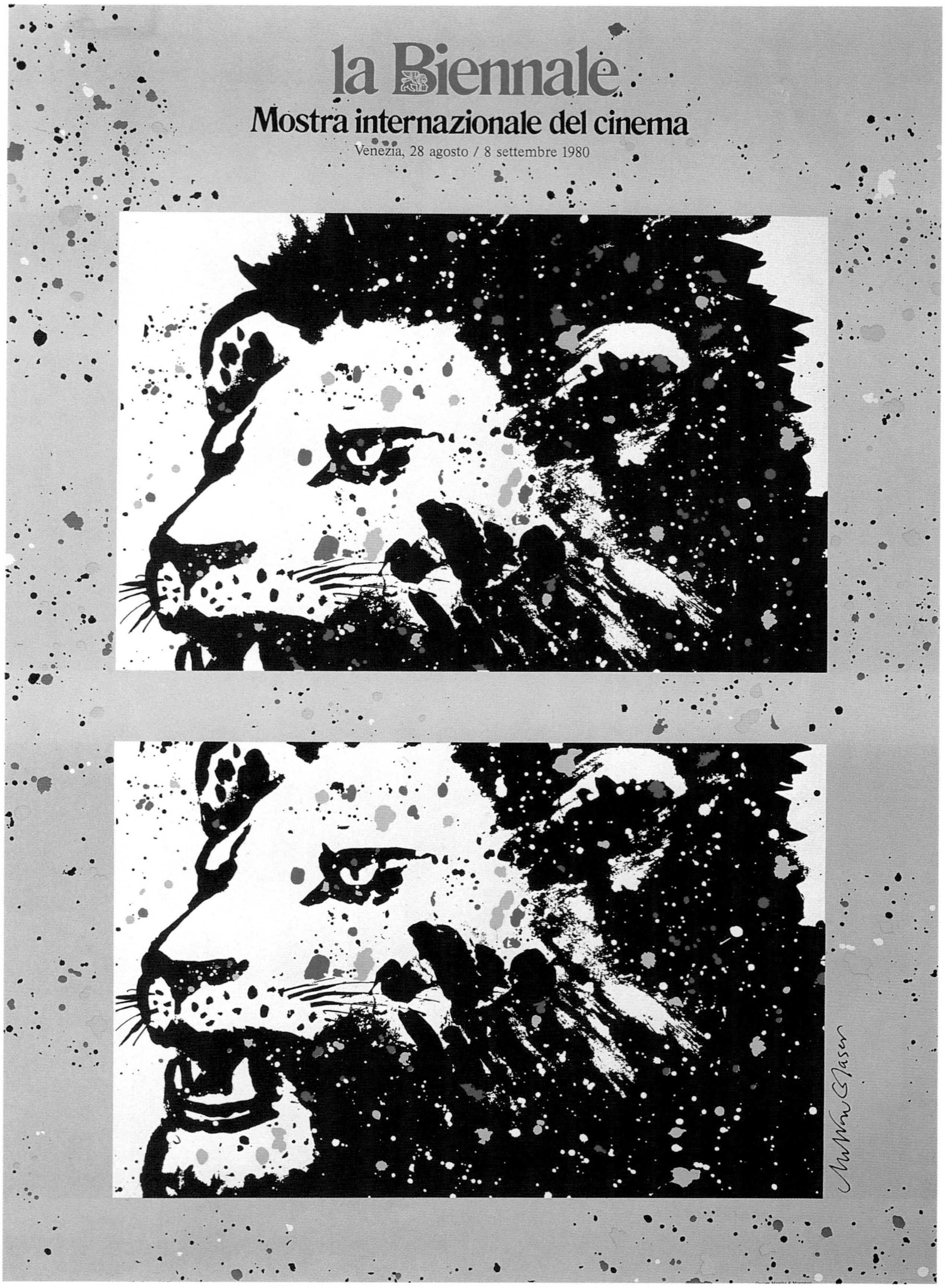

la Biennale
Mostra internazionale del cinema
Venezia, 28 agosto / 8 settembre 1980

The drawings were splashed with a variety of colors to make them more interesting texturally and to acknowledge the powerful influence of Jackson Pollack and abstract expressionism at that time.

Peter Mayer has been my friend and publisher for more than thirty years. Because he loves elephants, I thought that a flying elephant might be used as his logo to suggest the difficulty of making a publishing company take off.

RIGHT Three anniversary posters published at ten year intervals.

BELOW The original logo.

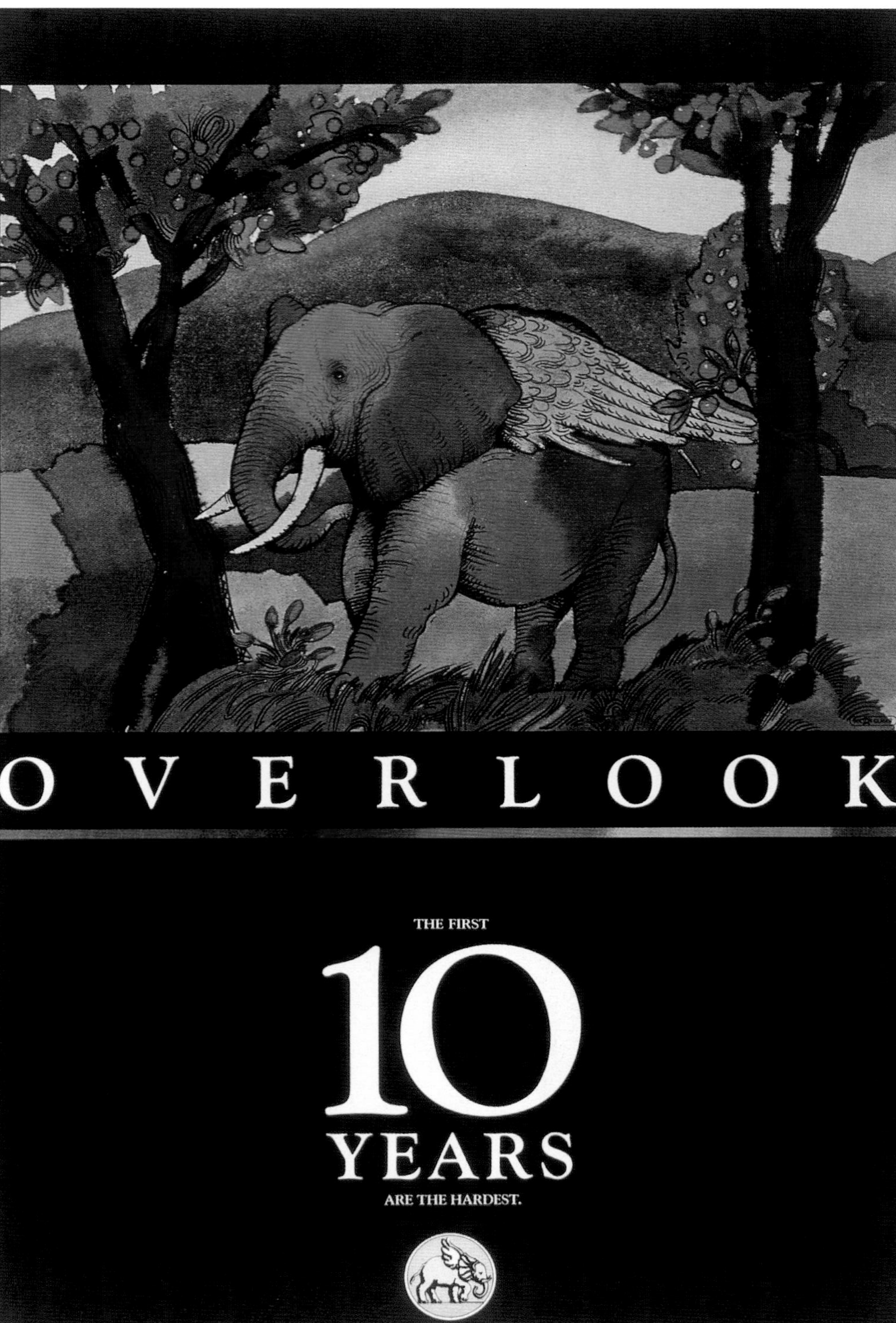

OVERLOOK
THE FIRST
10
YEARS
ARE THE HARDEST.

RIGHT Preliminary studies, one for Overlook at ten years and one for Overlook at thirty years.

BELOW The logo for visual books from Overlook.

OPPOSITE PAGE A rare view of an elephant seen from below.

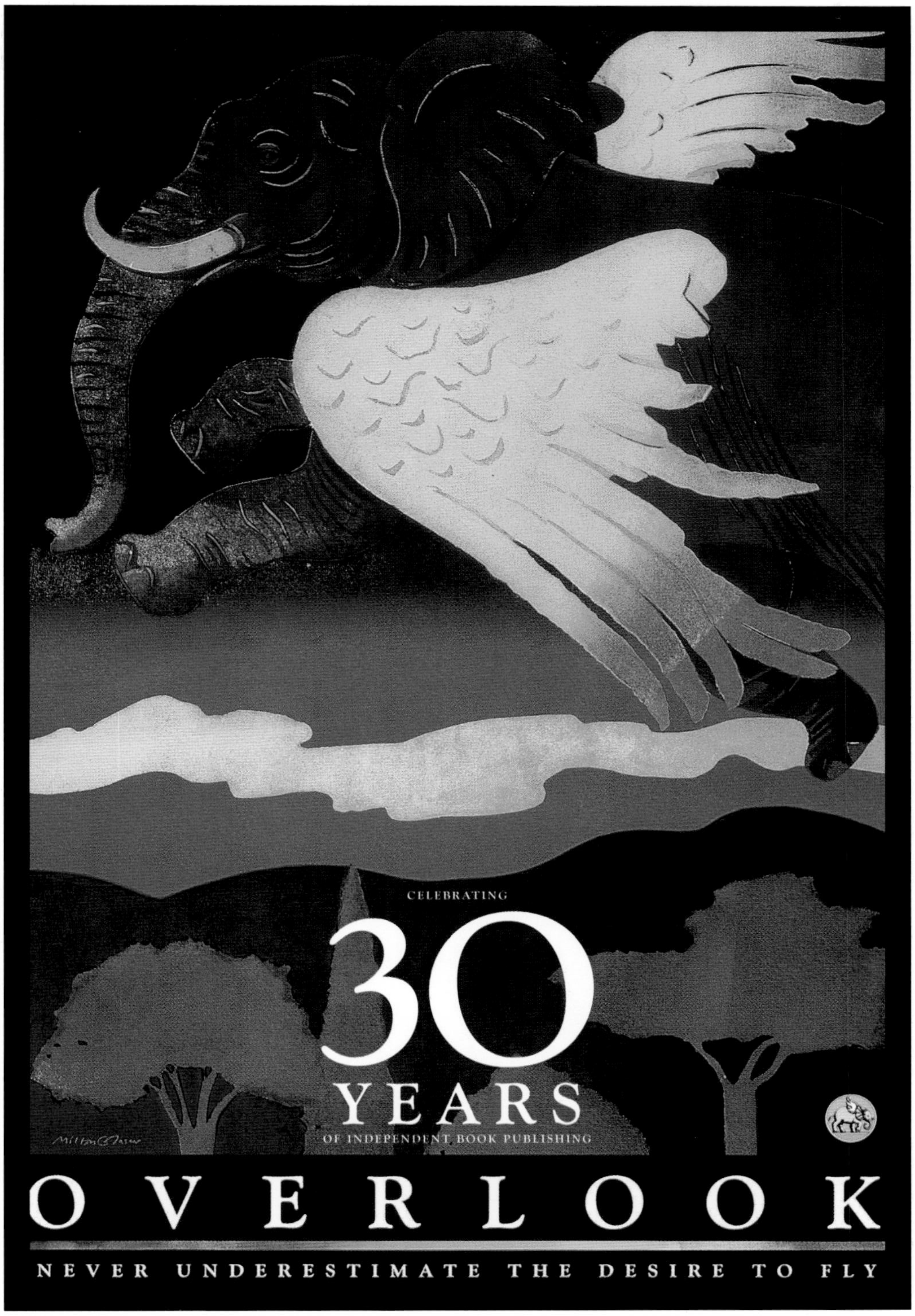

CELEBRATING
30
YEARS
OF INDEPENDENT BOOK PUBLISHING

OVERLOOK

NEVER UNDERESTIMATE THE DESIRE TO FLY

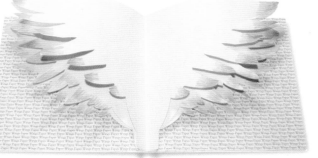

OPPOSITE PAGE. I've drawn any number of angels in my life, perhaps the best known being the one for Tony Kushner's play *Angels in America*. Here, the graphic idea was to contrast the dark despair of the angel's body with the luminous affirmation of the wing. As a reference, I used one of Dürer's most beautiful watercolors.

The Linda Cohen angel is strange for two reasons: Angels are rarely seen in the mud and probably don't have behinds.

DÜRER "LEFT WING OF A BIRD"

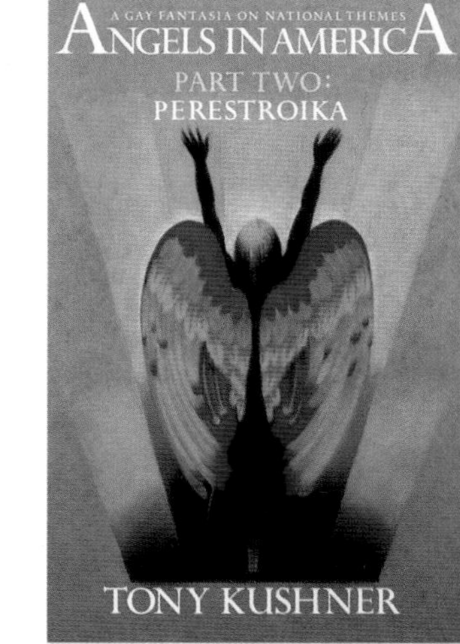

A GAY FANTASIA ON NATIONAL THEMES
ANGELS IN AMERICA
PART TWO:
PERESTROIKA
TONY KUSHNER

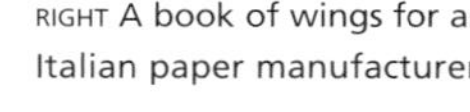

RIGHT A book of wings for an Italian paper manufacturer.

ABOVE This poster for LU Biscuits began with the scene on the left: a seated woman and our rabbit, Mookie, in his habitual spot on our couch (he had eaten half of it). The small box of biscuits on the table was the only reference to the client's product. I thought the somewhat surreal nature of the scene made an effective poster but, after a while, I thought it could be amusing to replicate the scene with the client's biscuits and place the two images side by side. This, of course, meant that the poster had to be a horizontal one, but that was not a problem. My surreal intention became more obvious as a result of the change.

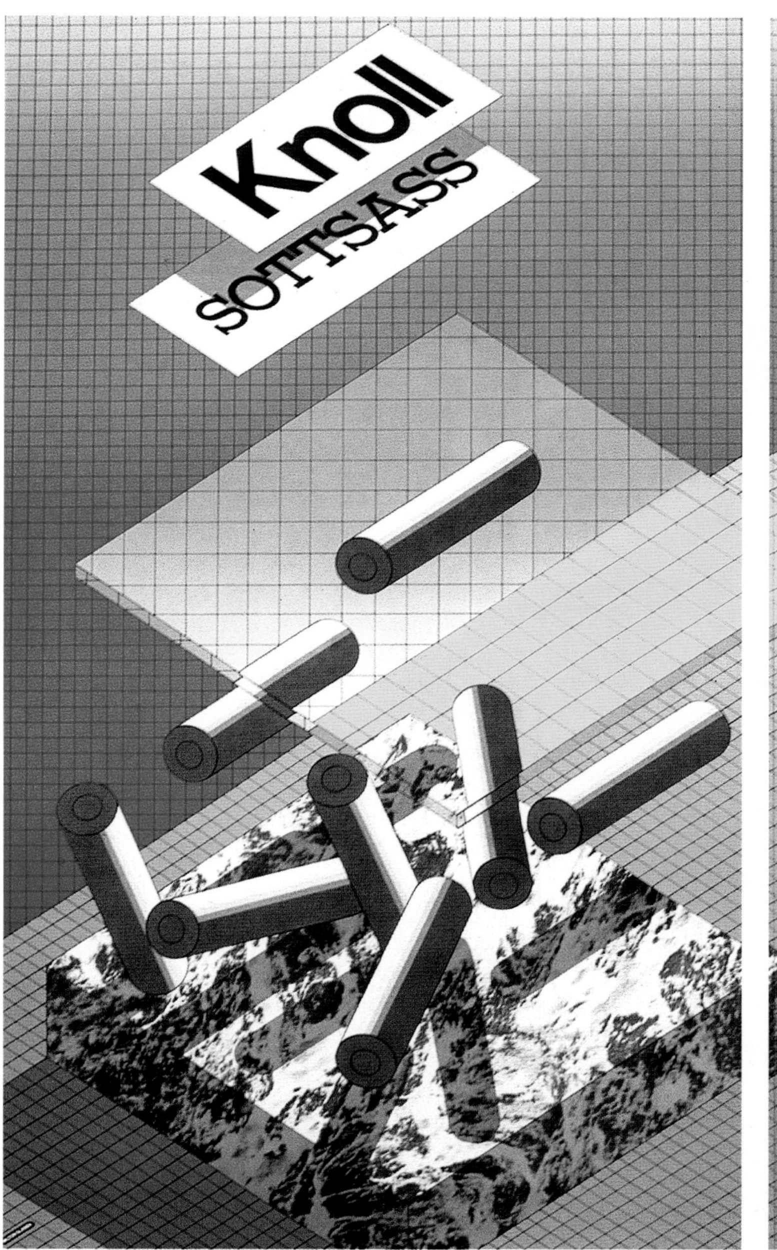

These examples also relate to a surrealistic vocabulary.

ABOVE In the two-sided poster for Knoll, a Sottsass table composed of tubular marble columns and plate glass is shown in a state of collapse. Surprisingly, neither the client nor Sottsass complained.

LEFT One can hardly think of two creatures that resemble each other less than a moth and a clam. One is the very essence of trembling fragility, the other of brittle resistance. Yet, open a clam and the resemblance becomes obvious. Surrealism has shown us the power of these hidden relationships.

BELOW This poster for an early show of mine was limited to two colors. I chose a red and green that, when printed over one another, produced a rich black. As is frequently observed, "Limitation stimulates the imagination."

OPPOSITE PAGE Twenty four years later, I designed this poster for the School of Visual Arts. The drawing is more fluid but has a similar sense of form. To produce the image, I combined two separate drawings that overlap to create a third area of color. In this case, the color created would not actually be the result of the colors used in the figures. It would be fair to say that in one case, two colors suggest three and in the other, three colors suggest two.

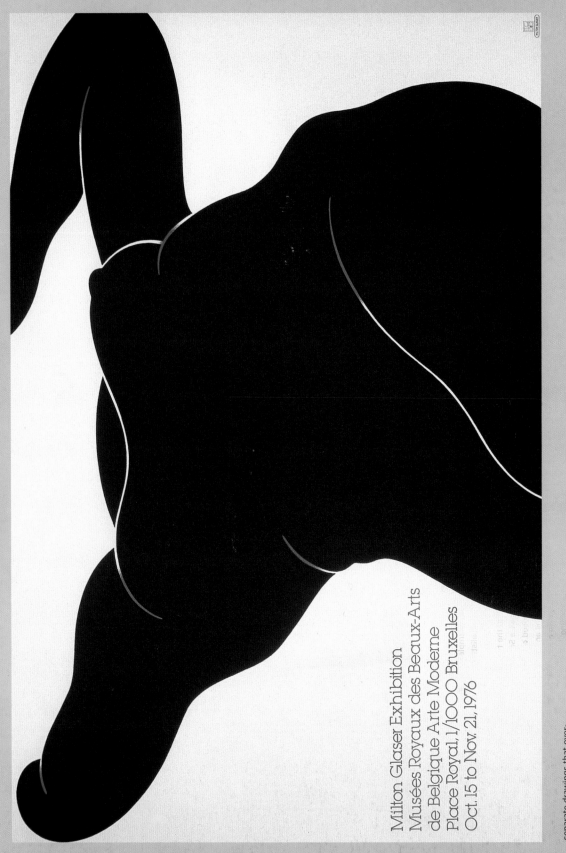

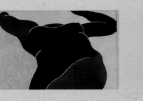

Milton Glaser Exhibition
Musées Royaux des Beaux-Arts
de Belgique Arte Moderne
Place Royal, 1/1000 Bruxelles
Oct. 15 to Nov. 21, 1976

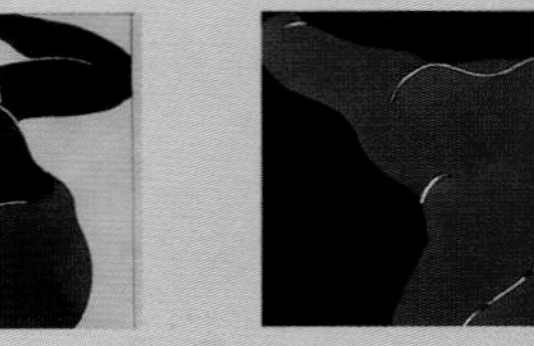

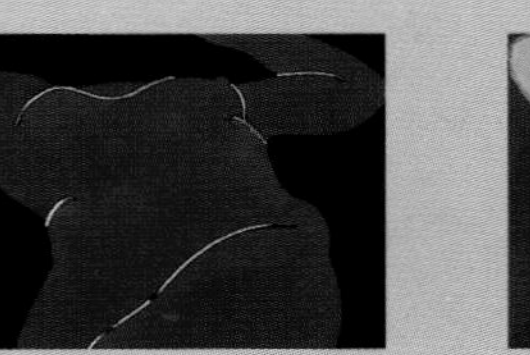

Art is...
Undergraduate Programs
Advertising
Animation
Art Education
Art History
Cartooning
Computer Art
Film & Video
Fine Arts
Graphic Design
Humanities and Sciences
Illustration
Interior Design
Photography
Graduate Programs
Art Therapy
Computer Art
Design
Fine Arts
Illustration
Photography
Continuing Education Division
S V A School of VISUAL ARTS
209 East 23 Street, New York, NY 10010-3994 Tel 800.366.7820 Fax 212.725.3587 www.schoolofvisualarts.edu
©2000, Visual Arts Press, Ltd. Creative Director: Silas H. Rhodes Designed by Milton Glaser

This kind of gestural drawing recurs regularly in my work. Its roots are in my admiration for Chinese brush drawings, as well as the spirited wash drawings of Picasso, Degas, Tiepolo, and Victor Hugo, among others. In this case, I was asked by Italo Lupi to illustrate the entire issue of an Italian literary periodical. Unfortunately, none of the manuscripts were available, and I was left to invent a generic solution in less than a week. The struggle between good and evil seemed as general as one could get for purposes of establishing a series of visual situations that could apply to any text. These lively angels and devils cavort throughout the magazine and manage to avoid the problem of specifically illustrating the individual articles. In many types of drawing, the lack of specificity creates the viewer's interest and involvement. When a drawing is suggestive rather than explicit, the opportunity to project meaning into it becomes intensified.

Aspenia

A cosa servono i giornali? di Umberto Eco. Indagine sulle nuove egemonie di Z. Brzezinski e J. LaPalombara. Mediterraneo un mare di culti di Andrea Riccardi. L'euro nel mercato mondiale di Paolo Savona. Le nuove frontiere dell'Europa centrale di Sergio Romano. Nomenklatura russa di Giulietto Chiesa. Atlante dell'economia post-sovietica di Gianluca Colombo. Balcani, etnie in guerra di Giuseppe Zaccaria. Geopolitica dell'oro nero di Sergio Minerbi. La giovinezza è nel dna di W. Haseltine.

This page shows the result of an unusual opportunity to illustrate a section for *The New York Times.* Since it was not in color I made the drawings rich in texture by varying the quality of line. Considering that newspaper reproduction is not of the highest quality, the results were quite nice.

ABOVE The original sketch, the finished drawing, the reproduction in the *Times,* and an application in color I made for another client.

RIGHT A drawing from inside the same section.

ABOVE Satyrs are a recurring theme in my work, perhaps because of Picasso's influence.

NYPC
March
6:30
Tom Allen
MONDAY
Sept
28
Oct
Nov 9
ARISTOTLE
7:30

OPPOSITE PAGE One of the discarded drawing-table tops I worked on demonstrates my compulsive drawing. It relates to a kind of visual annotation that I used to illustrate Asimov's annotated *Don Juan* some years ago. Asimov created this massive volume by tracing the references of almost every phrase and paragraph that Byron had written. I tried to create a visual equivalent by pursuing the same idea—using unrelated images piled on top of one another in a variety of styles and textures.

Words and Images

Like many American practitioners, I began my drawing career by copying comic strips. By the time I had defined myself as a *designer*, I was convinced that narration—and the dialectic between words and images—was central to all design problems.

The issue becomes more complex when one attempts to create narratives where words and images do not repeat one another. The most obvious and familiar way to illustrate a story is to render, in a recognizable way, the images described by the text. This didactic method is the one generally favored in journalism, since objective credibility is the sought-after heart of journalism. Up until our time, photographic illustration provided that credibility since photographs didn't lie—at least not often. Of course the history of journalism is full of photographic frauds, but that's not the issue; we still believed in photographs as a representation of reality. Today, the advent of the computer has virtually destroyed photographic credibility. Can anyone who watched Forrest Gump shake hands with John Kennedy ever believe in photography again?

How this fact affects journalists is interesting, since journalists are concerned with truth. We might be at a point where journalists can be more subjective, more symbolic, more metaphoric, and more poetic than ever before. This raises all sorts of difficult questions about the nature of what is real.

The greatest impediment to this development will not be the resistance of a new audience to such ideas, but the literal mind-set of journalists and editors who think of words and images as necessarily having conflicting objectives unless they are used in a literal way. Curiously, the road to truth and the understanding of reality may only be discovered through the poetic—not an easily defensible position when you're talking to a newspaper man. In the fifties, two linguists, Colomb and Williams, were interested in determining whether academic papers might be written in a more understandable way; they were convinced that it was faulty structure and not the complexity of ideas that made most academic writing incomprehensible. Through the use of a device they called the "geography of introductions," they demonstrated how a reader could become involved in any narrative process. The process begins with the creation of stability, then a disruption of that stability that causes the introduction of disorder, and finally the restoration of stability. This is not as complex as it seems; take *Little Red Riding Hood*. Little Red Riding Hood is walking down the lane (a stable world); suddenly, the Big Bad Wolf leaps out from behind a tree (destabilization). The story continues until the destruction of the wolf and the restoration of a stable world. This formula can be applied to any kind of writing and, according to Colomb and Williams, guarantees reader interest. The same practice occurs in most communication under the general heading of "disruption of expectation."

I would like to make another, perhaps obvious, point. For all their similarities, words and images act on the nervous system and brain in different ways. There is a wonderful quotation by T.S. Eliot (*The Use of Poetry and the Use of Criticism*, 1930) about the purpose of a poem. I quote:

"The chief use of the 'meaning' of a poem, in the ordinary sense, may be to satisfy one habit of the reader, to keep his mind diverted and quiet, while the poem does its work upon him: much as the imaginary burglar is always provided with a bit of nice meat for the house-dog."

It becomes clear that when the narrative and the poetic operate together, we can produce our most powerful and meaningful work.

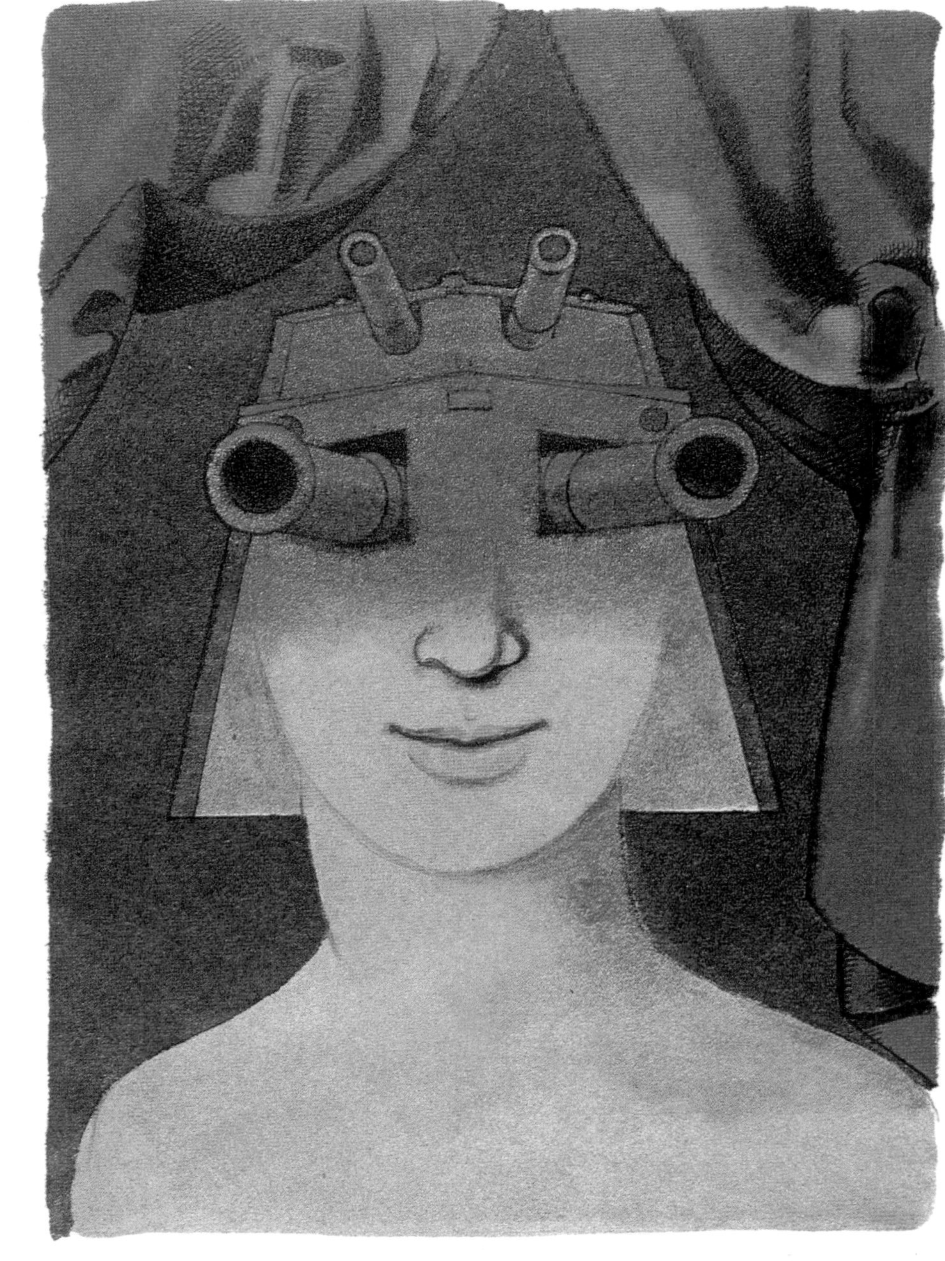

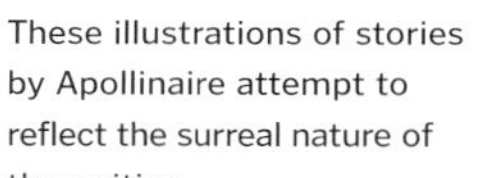

These illustrations of stories by Apollinaire attempt to reflect the surreal nature of the writing.

Boris Vian, a French author influenced by American detective fiction, produced novels that combined eroticism and violence in a powerful, albeit occasionally tacky, way.

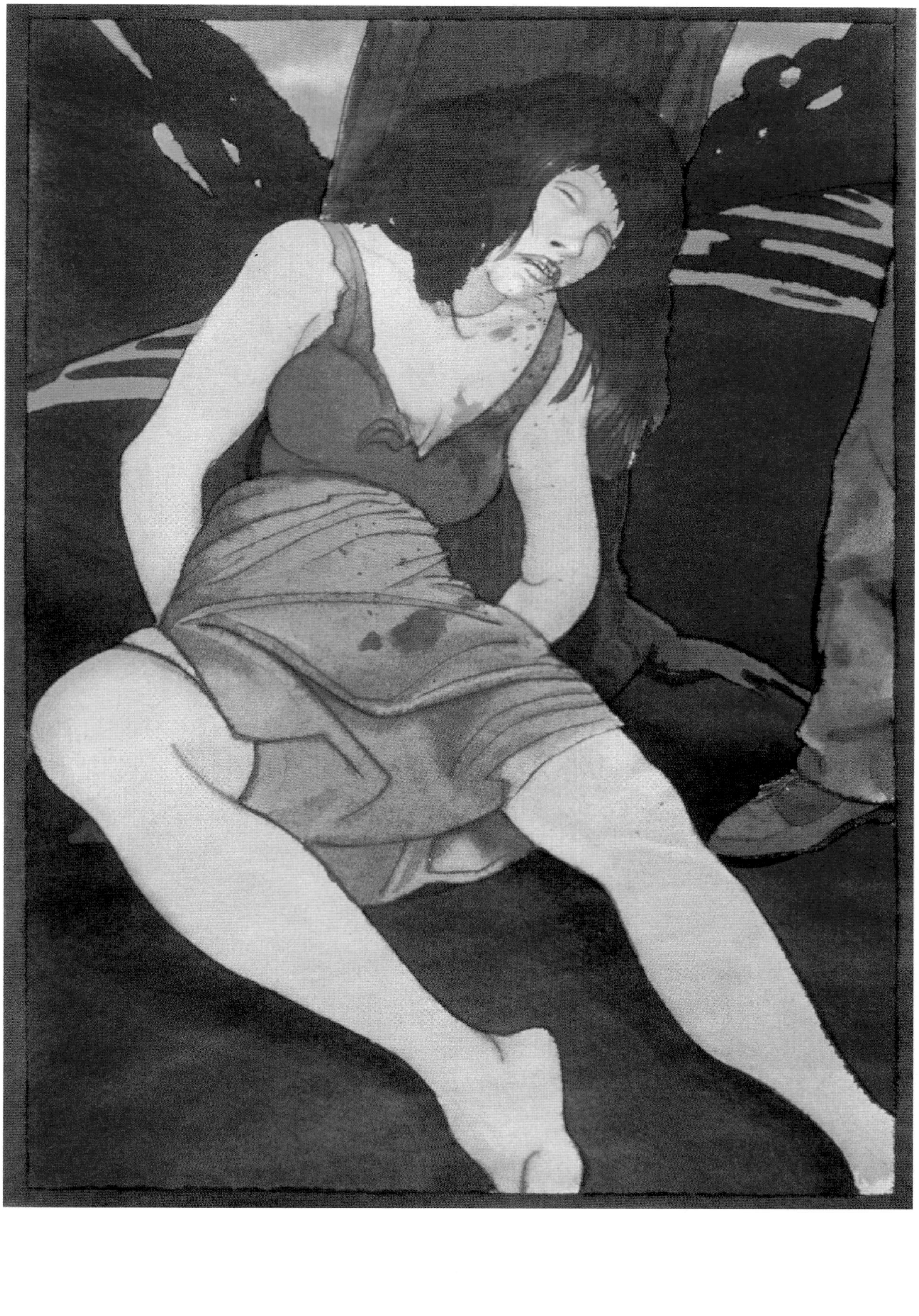

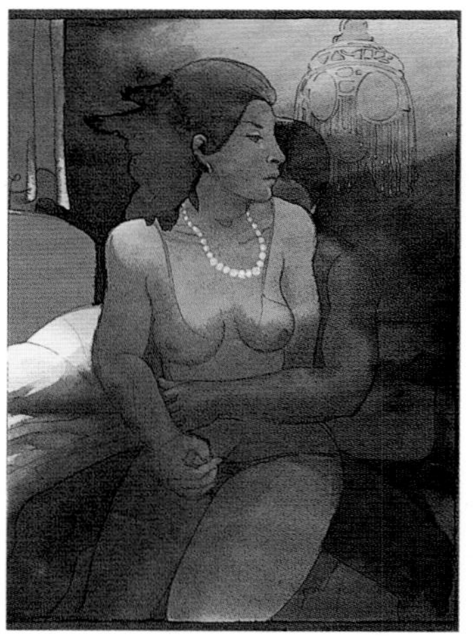

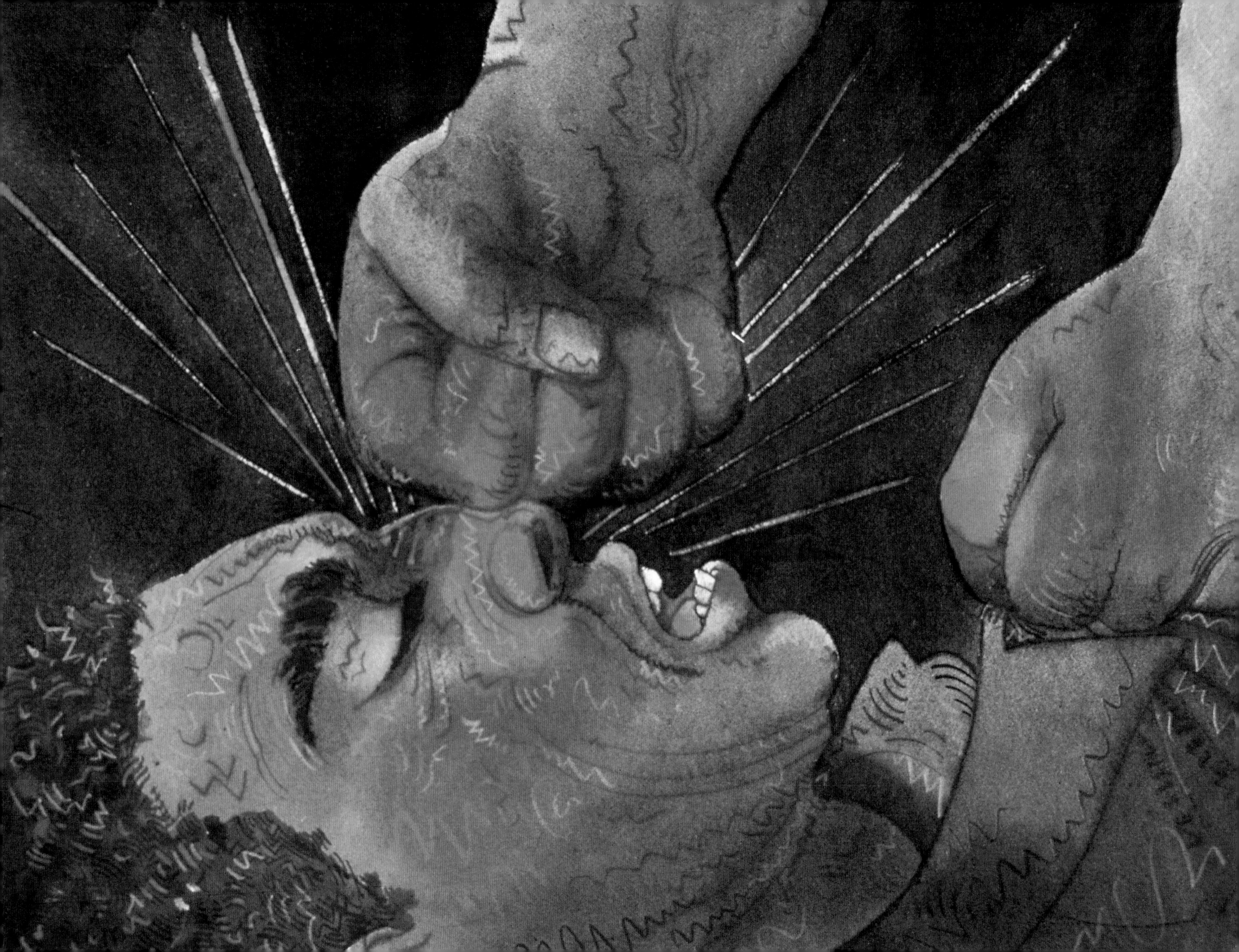

These illustrations from another one of Vian's works, *I Spit on Your Graves*, are the most violent I have ever done. I tried to use color expressionistically, as in the example on the opposite page, where the red travels from the fist to the face to suggest the shock and pain of the blow.

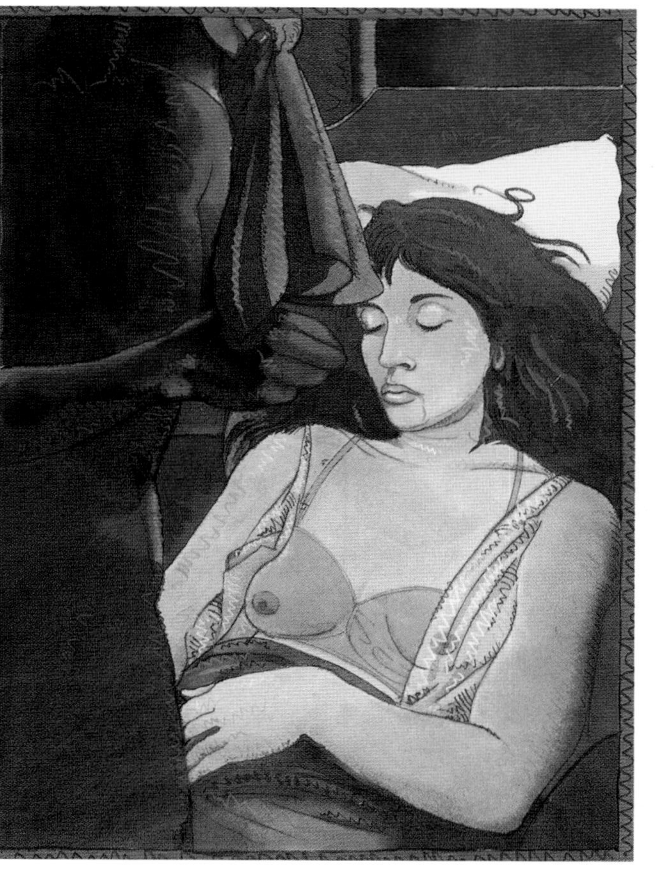

RIGHT In these drawings for Baudelaire's *Flowers of Evil*, I attempted to create a visual world that Baudelaire would have recognized, rather illustrate the poems. At the same time, I experimented with a different way of displaying the drawings by having them turn the page. The idea is to compel the reader to hold one part of the work in the mind as the page is turned; looking at the drawings becomes less of a passive act.

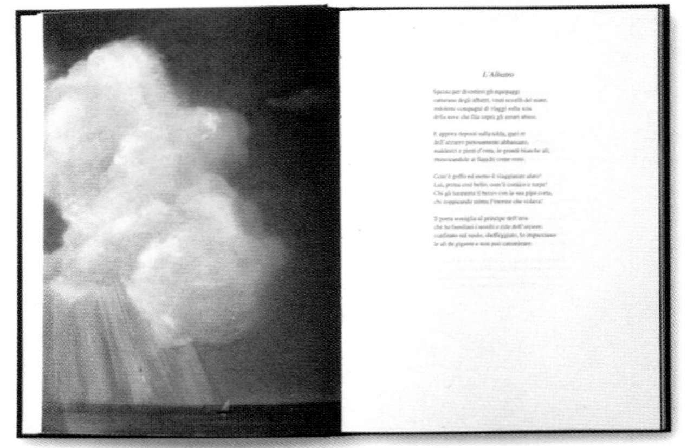

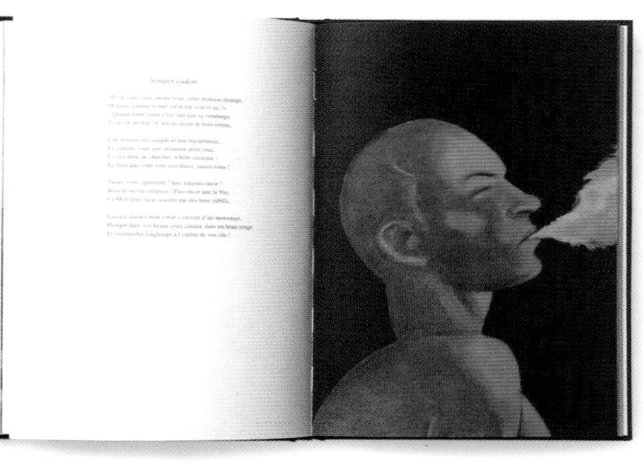

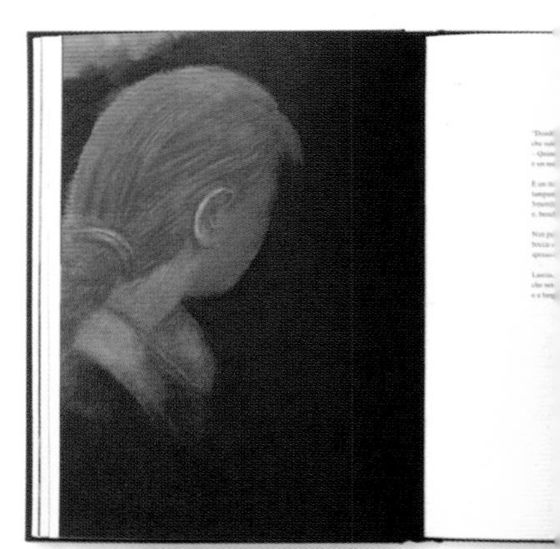

I actually began the drawings with this study of an orchid cactus blossom from a plant that has survived for twenty-five years in our home in Woodstock. It looks quite ominous to me. The drawing on the opposite page that relates to the title *Flowers of Evil* was intended to be used as an endpaper. I then took another path and made a series of dark drawings that ran parallel to the text. I called them "unnatural events."

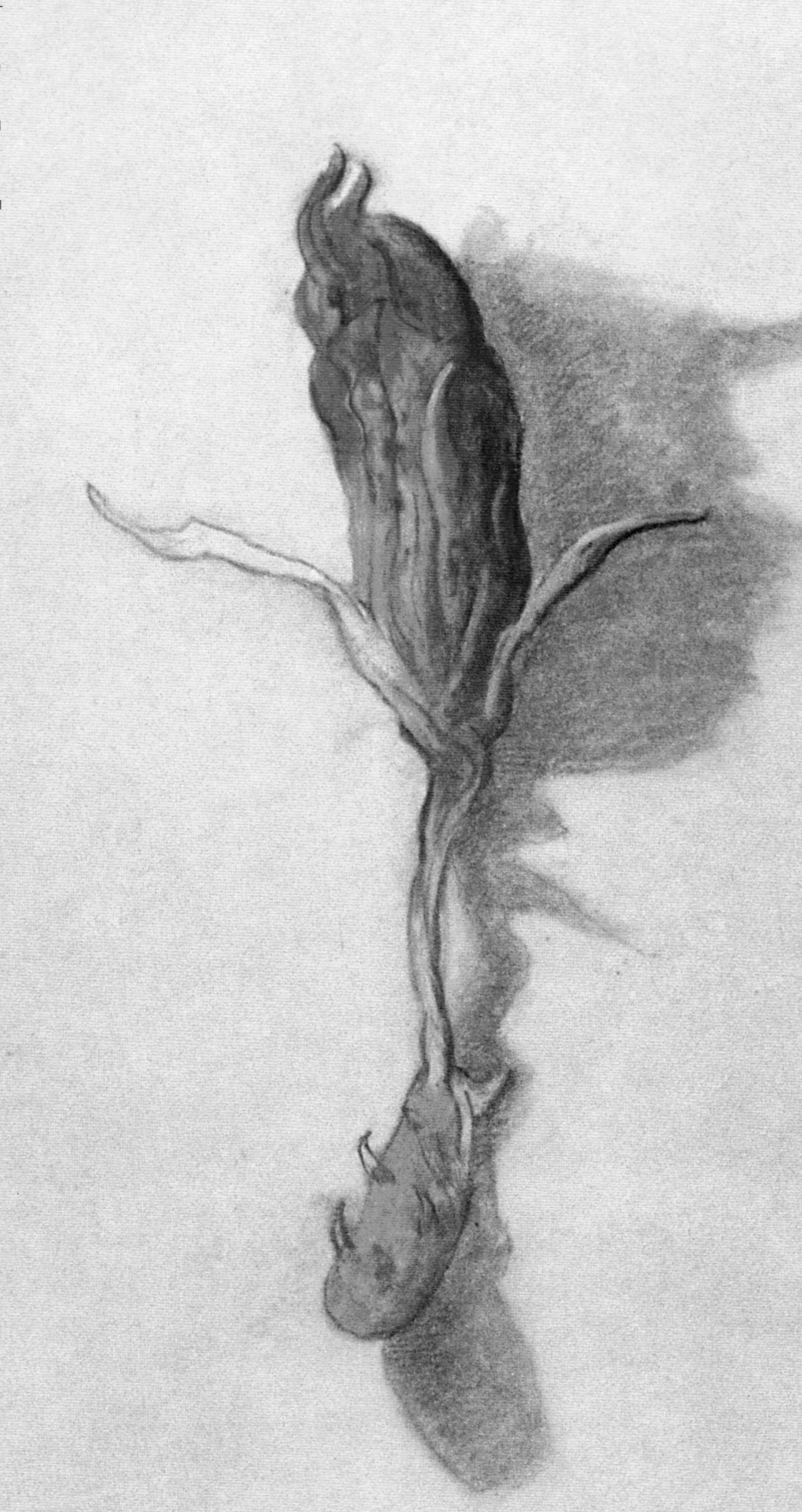

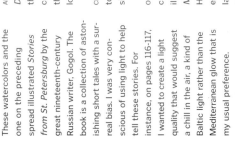

These watercolors and the one on the preceding spread illustrated *Stories from St. Petersburg* by the great nineteenth-century Russian writer, Gogol. The book is a collection of astonishing short tales with a surreal bias. I was very conscious of using light to help tell these stories. For instance, on pages 116-117, I wanted to create a light quality that would suggest a chill in the air, a kind of Baltic light rather than the Mediterranean glow that is my usual preference.

ABOVE An illustration from *Diary of a Madman*. I thought that a raking, diagonal light could be used to illuminate the face of the madman's love interest.

CENTER *The Portrait*. I wanted to suggest the dim, pervasive light just before dawn.

OPPOSITE PAGE I attempted to create the light in Hell when illustrating *Diary of a Madman*. I decided that Hell's light could be expressed by a swinging lantern that alternately lights up the table and then plunges it into darkness.

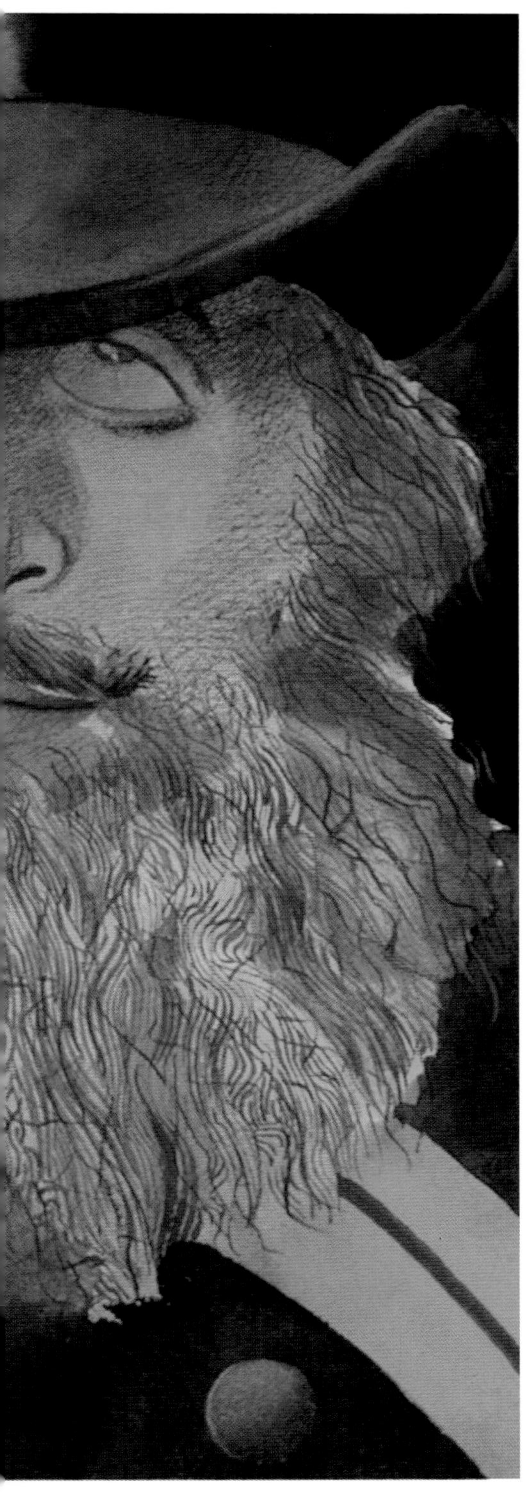

These examples continue to use light in a variety of ways to support the narrative.

TOP LLEFT A portrait of Gogol.

TOP RIGHT I'm fond of this example from *The Nose*—an alarming and hilarious story in which a nose disappears from someone's face and turns up all over town—in this case, in a breakfast roll. You can tell that it's early in the morning from the quality of the shadows and the light reflecting off the blade of the knife.

BOTTOM RIGHT *The Coat*—a sweet story about an old couple in which the wife dies and comes back to keep her husband company—it's not easy to draw an invisible person.

Painting, Light and Technology

The source and meaning of light in painting has changed throughout history. As early as 80 BC in Pompeii the wall paintings showed shadows created by sunlight. When the subject of painting changed to the depiction of the spiritual, shadows vanished. When painting a saint you wanted the light to emanate *from* the saint. The idea of light as an external force, as opposed to an internal manifestation, was reintroduced hundreds of years later during the Renaissance. At that moment one could say the death of God began.

The idea that you could interrupt the flow of light to create form was one of the profound rediscoveries of the Renaissance. Also, one might observe that the idea of fame itself was a product of Renaissance thinking. People could become famous for what they accomplished rather than for their affinity to God. By stopping light you also stopped the passage of time and this offered the possibility of immortality to the subject. These two ideas happening simultaneously—fame and immortality—subsequently becoming a primary motivation for portraiture. Eventually the association with art itself became the key to immortality, which may explain why the rich and powerful are interested in art.

Technology also produced changes. The move from painting in egg tempera to oil paint had an enormous effect on painting. Egg tempera has to be done on a solid ground because there is no elasticity in the medium. Also, when you paint a fresco, you have to do it on a solid wall.

Frescos and wall paintings in churches had to be done on the site from cartoons. When it was discovered that linseed oil could be used as a medium for paint, it meant that for the first time, because of oil's elasticity, painting on a flexible surface became possible. Painting on canvas, which could be rolled up and transported, gave the artist new freedoms.

I remember once painting in casein on canvas at school. On a damp day somebody walked by, tapped the canvas, and the entire painting fell off the canvas onto the floor. It was instructive. Never use an inelastic material on an elastic surface. The discovery of oil as a medium meant that painters could paint under controlled lighting conditions wherever they chose, instead of under the random lighting of the church. It became possible to paint directly from observation and from nature—all of which led inevitably to Impressionism. Who would have guessed that a shift in technology, in this case changing from egg tempera to an oil-based medium, would have produced such a profound change of vision?

In reading Dante this year I learned that the only differences between those unfortunates in Hell and those in Purgatory was that the former had no idea of how they had sinned. Those in Hell were there forever. Those in Purgatory knew what they had done and were waiting it out, with at least the possibility of redemption, thus establishing the differences between despair and hope.

Purgatory

I had a marvelous time illustrating Dante's *Purgatory* throughout the last year. I feel changed by this extraordinary work. In book illustration the question is always how to illustrate text without compromising it. The real issue becomes how metaphoric the images should be in relationship to the already metaphoric content. I carefully examined the interpretations of Botticelli, Doré, William Blake, and others, all of whom helped me find my way through Purgatory.

I chose to illustrate the text with a series of monotypes—perhaps the most primitive form of printmaking—I cut out paper shapes, inked them with oil paint and placed them onto a plexiglass plate. I then ran them through the press on a sheet of dampened, cream-colored stock. The results were somewhat unpredictable, so I would run off six to eight in a series and select one or two for further re-working. As a result, in several cases I had more than one version of the same scene. It occurred to me that in Purgatory, where passage of time is interminable, one could represent the same scene with two images a scant second apart.

This idea began to solve the difficult question I have always had about illustration—how can one illustrate a text that the reader might imagine more richly in his or her own mind?

By not creating a singular image and offering alternative variations, the reader might be encouraged to invent an image somewhere in between.

ABOVE My little etching press.

PIERO DELLA FRANCESCA, "NATIVITY," LONDON NATIONAL GALLERY

In 1991, I received an amazing assignment from an Italian group planning the events surrounding the 500th anniversary of Piero della Francesca's birth. Since I have always been passionate about Piero, along with Vermeer, the most Mozartian of painters, I was thrilled and intimidated.

Beginning in 1950, at the Frick Museum in New York, I followed Piero all over the world. I believe I have seen everything he ever painted. It occurred to me that the world did not need bad copies of Piero's paintings, yet the intent of the assignment was to create a homage.

One morning after a number of aborted starts, I realized that Piero could be thought of as nature. His paintings could be looked at as though one were looking at a landscape through a window. One could take any part of the view and interpret it freely, acknowledging, as we do with nature, that it would be impossible to replicate it.

This insight allowed me to develop a series of watercolors and drawings inspired by Piero that explored details from his works in a more analytical way. On this page, three works derived from the glorious *Nativity* at the National Gallery in London.

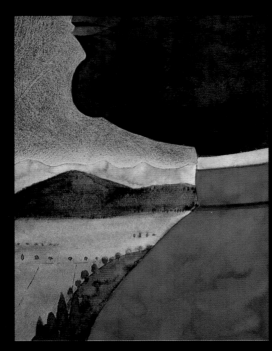

This painting of the Duke of Montefeltro is one of the greatest portraits of the Renaissance. It is small (47cm x 33cm) but overwhelmingly powerful. In the Uffizi in Florence, the Duke eternally faces his consort, Battista Sforza, whose portrait is equally brilliant but less fully realized.

DELLA FRANCESCA, "FEDERICO DA MONTEFELTRO" UFFIZI

OPPOSITE PAGE Frederico and Battista. I reunited the two in a lithograph.

DELLA FRANCESCA, "FBATTISTA SFORZA" UFFIZI

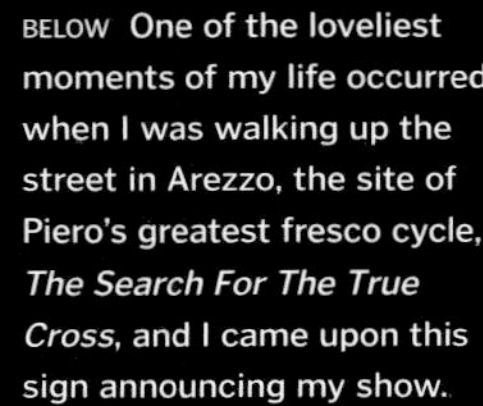

BELOW One of the loveliest moments of my life occurred when I was walking up the street in Arezzo, the site of Piero's greatest fresco cycle, *The Search For The True Cross*, and I came upon this sign announcing my show.

RIGHT The exhibition was beautifully designed and installed by Italo Lupi, a good friend and a wonderful designer.

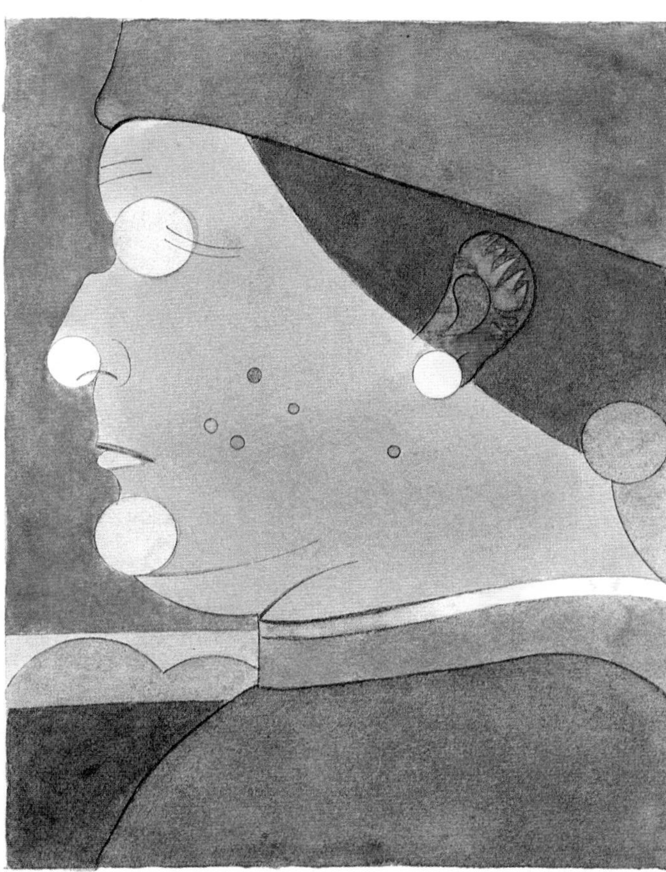

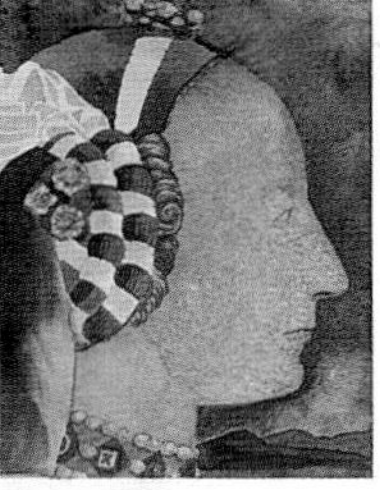

OPPOSITE PAGE Detail of the head of Christ from *The Resurrection* in Borgo San Sepolcro.

BELOW LEFT Study of a Roman soldier from *The Resurrection.*

LEFT A soldier from *The Legend of the True Cross.*

FAR LEFT Detail from *Constantine's Victory Over Maxentius* from *The Legend of the True Cross* in Arezzo.

BELOW Detail from *The Death of Adam* from *The Legend of the True Cross.*

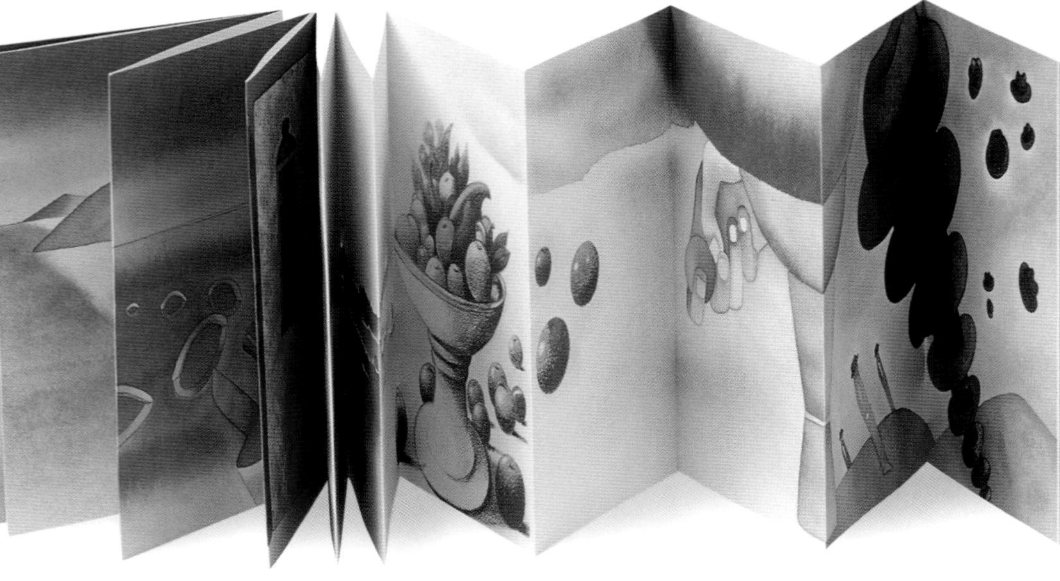

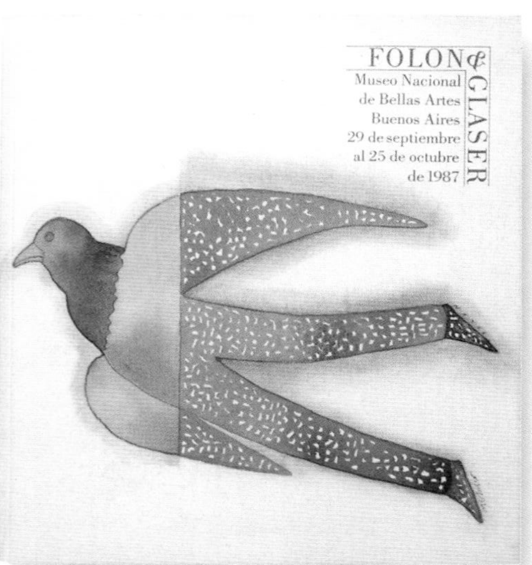

Ever since we were introduced by Giorgio Soavi (see essay, page 225), Jean Michel Folon and I have worked on projects and have had many exhibitions together. The sense of ego identification with works of art makes collaboration a relatively rare occurrence even though the benefits of creating something beyond one's own capacity are evident. Some years ago, my wife organized an exhibition of pairs of artists working together on single works. Afterwards, they all said the experience was marvelous and they had learned a lot. None of them, to my knowledge, ever did it again.

For many years Folon and I wanted to create a book that paralleled our friendship. He speaks no English, I speak no French. We realized that our entire relationship might be a series of misunderstandings. We celebrated that possibility with a folding (Japanese style) book in which one of us began an image and the other continued it. Nothing was planned in advance, we simply extemporaneously responded to whatever the other had started.

Folon and I also had shows together all over the world.

ABOVE The bird man for our show in Buenos Aires.

LEFT A poster printed by Blue Shadow Posters, owned by Paolina Girenghelli, Folon's admired companion.

Giorgio Soavi, Milton Glaser, and Jean-Michel Folon.

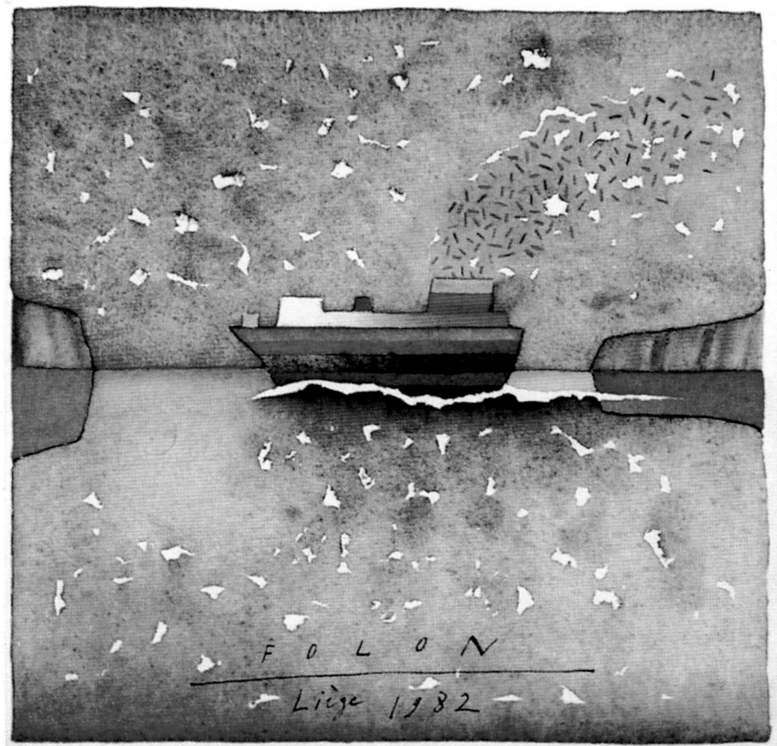

FRONT

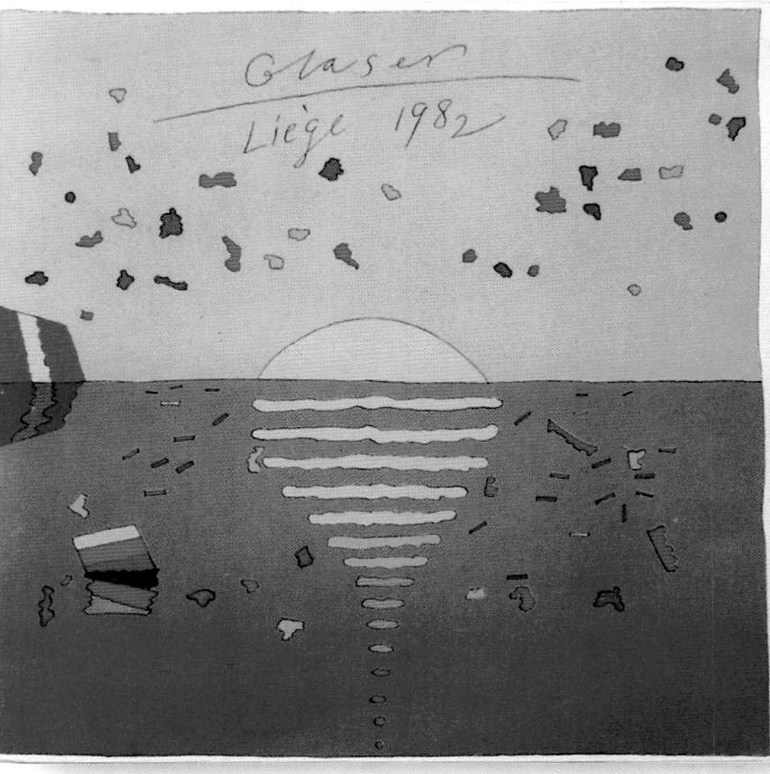

BACK

ABOVE The same scene minutes apart on the front and back covers of the catalog of our two man show in Leige, Belgium.

Paper companies often provide opportunities for graphic designers, generally motivated by the desire to demonstrate dramatic visual effects that highlight the printing qualities of their paper stock (see pp. 50-53). I was approached by Gilbert Paper to create a promotional piece with few requirements except the desire to make it collaborative and international. Together with David Freedman, I thought it might be interesting to create a visual questionnaire around the subject of beauty. The questionnaire on the right was the result. I sent 100 out to designers and received 82 answers. Not a bad ratio considering how much time had to be spent responding to it. I have found that unlike most fields, the best professional designers, illustrators and artists are willing to work for nothing if the project is interesting and challenging.

ABOVE Cover collage
Foreground: Isolde Monson-Baumgart
Midground: Hans Hillman
Background: Ken Cato

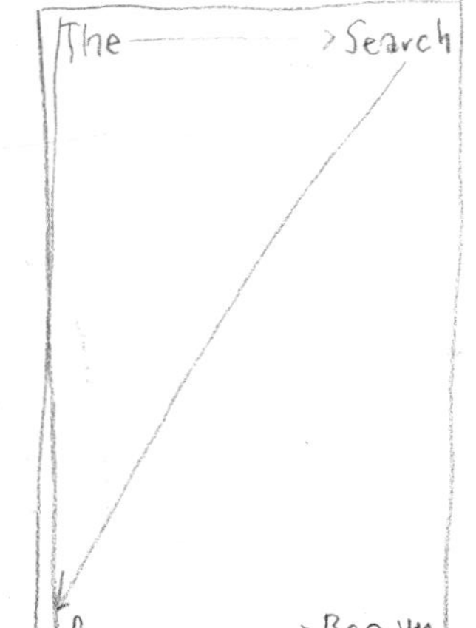

Sketch for envelope.

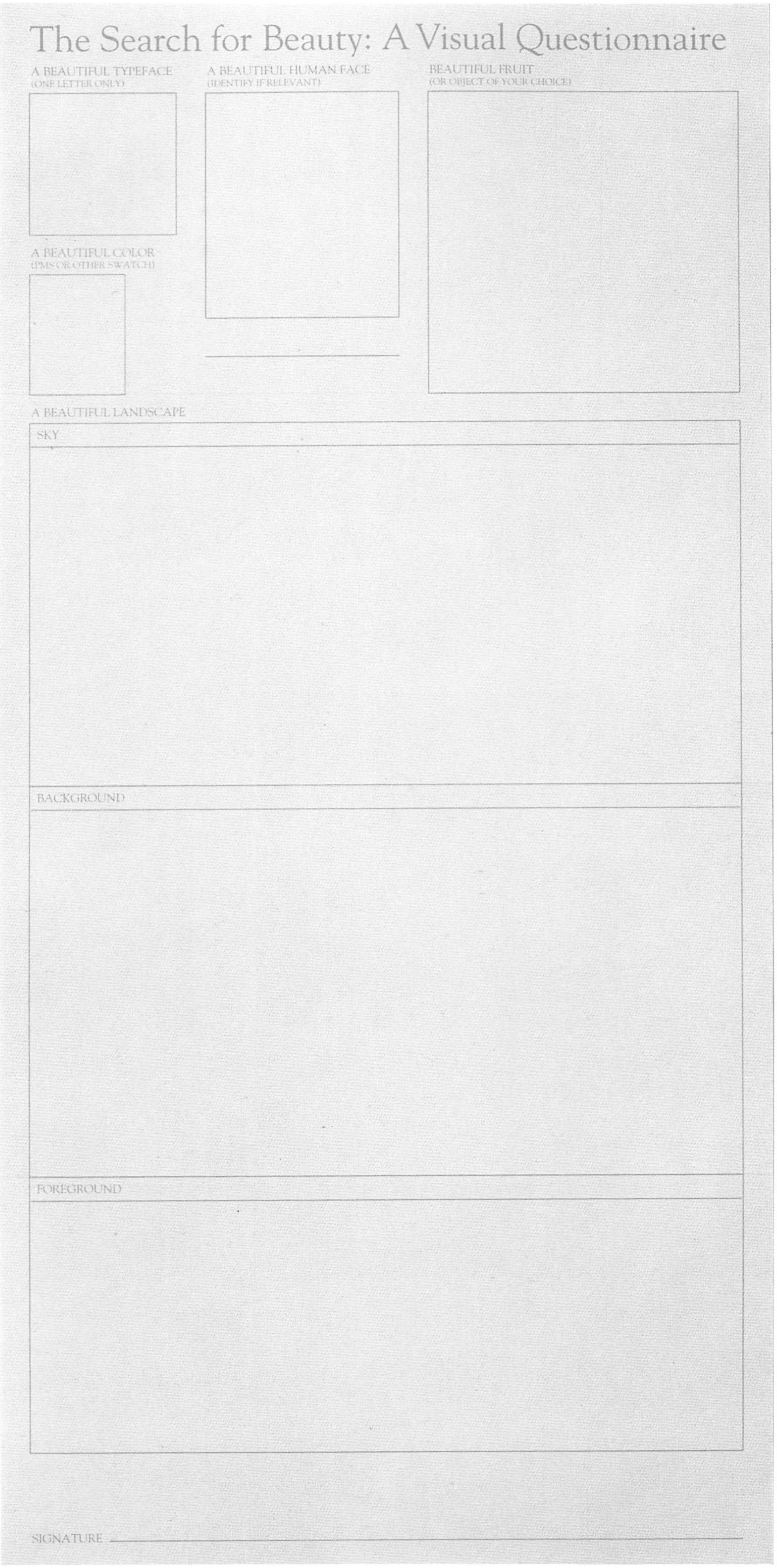

The Search for Beauty: A Visual Questionnaire

A BEAUTIFUL TYPEFACE
(ONE LETTER ONLY)

A BEAUTIFUL HUMAN FACE
(IDENTIFY IF RELEVANT)

BEAUTIFUL FRUIT
(OR OBJECT OF YOUR CHOICE)

A BEAUTIFUL COLOR
(PMS OR OTHER SWATCH)

A BEAUTIFUL LANDSCAPE

SKY

BACKGROUND

FOREGROUND

SIGNATURE

PARTICIPANTS:
KIYOSHI AWAZU
SAUL BASS
ANTHON BEEKE
FÉLIX BELTRÁN
WALTER BERNARD
R.O. BLECHMAN
WILBURN BONNEL
PIETER BRATTINGA
BORIS BUĆAN
KEN CATO
IVAN CHERMAYEFF
SEYMOUR CHWAST
HENRIETTA CONDAK
BRIAN CRONIN
WIM CROUWEL
MYRNA DAVIS
PAUL DAVIS
LOU DORFSMAN
STEPHEN DOYLE
OLLE EKSELL
GENE FEDERICO
LOUISE FILI
ALAN FLETCHER
JEAN MICHEL FOLON
COLIN FORBES
MICHAEL FOREMAN
DAVID FREEDMAN
SHIGEO FUKUDA
STEFF GEISSBUHLER
DAVID GENTLEMAN
MILTON GLASER
JOHN GORHAM
SUSAN GRAY
DAVID HILLMAN
HANS HILLMAN
MIRKO ILIĆ
ALEX JORDAN
CHI-MING KAN
MITSUO KATSUI
GÜNTHER KIESER
MATTHEW KLEIN
PETER KNAPP
MERVYN KURLANSKY
GEORGE LEAVITT
UWE LOESCH
ITALO LUPI
LES MASON
BROOKIE MAXWELL
JOHN McCONNELL
KATHERINE McCOY
JAMES McMULLAN
FERNANDO MEDINA
PIERRE MENDELL
ARMANDO MILANI
MORTEZA MOMAYEZ
BRUNO MONGUZZI
ISOLDE MONSON-BAUMGART
JOSEF MÜLLER-BROCKMANN
ANGELA PALLADINO
TONY PALLADINO
TULLIO PERICOLI
DUŠAN PETRIČIĆ
JOSEP PLA-NARBONA
ANDREA RAUCH
DANIELLE ROY
ROBERTO SAMBONET
GEORG SCHMID
HENRY STEINER
JAROSLAV SŮRA
DEBORAH SUSSMAN
WALDEMAR SWIERZY
NIKLAUS TROXLER
GEORGE TSCHERNY
BARRIE TUCKER
YAROM VARDIMON
TOMÁS VELLVÉ
JUGOSLAV VLAHOVIĆ
JEAN WIDMER
ANN WILLOUGHBY
KURT WIRTH
HENRY WOLF
MIRIAM WOSK

The Search for Beauty: A Visual Questionnaire

A BEAUTIFUL TYPEFACE

A BEAUTIFUL HUMAN FACE

BEAUTIFUL FRUIT

N

A BEAUTIFUL COLOR

my grandfather

A BEAUTIFUL LANDSCAPE

SKY

BACKGROUND

FOREGROUND

Paul Davis

SIGNATURE

Demonstrate your opinions on the subject of Beauty on the enclosed questionnaire and return by December 31, 1993. The collection will recycle as a travelling exhibit.

Send questionnaire to:

Gilbert Paper
The Search for Beauty
430 Ahnaip Street
P.O. Box 260
Menasha, WI 54952-0260

DAVID HILLMAN

MITSUO KATSUI

SUSAN GRAY

THIS PAGE Using the material provided by the questionnaire as a basis, we recomposed the contributions into new assemblies, creating juxtapositions that were never originally intended.

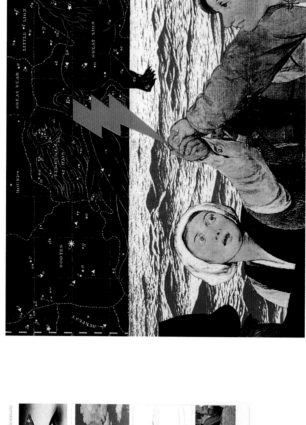

STEVEN DOYLE

FERNANDO MEDINA

ITALO LUPI

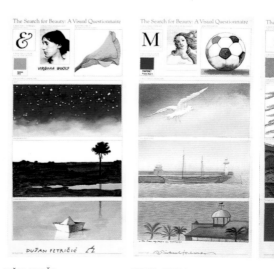

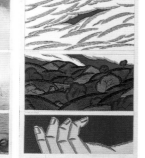

DUŠAN PETRIČIC

MICHAEL FOREMAN

BRIAN CRONIN

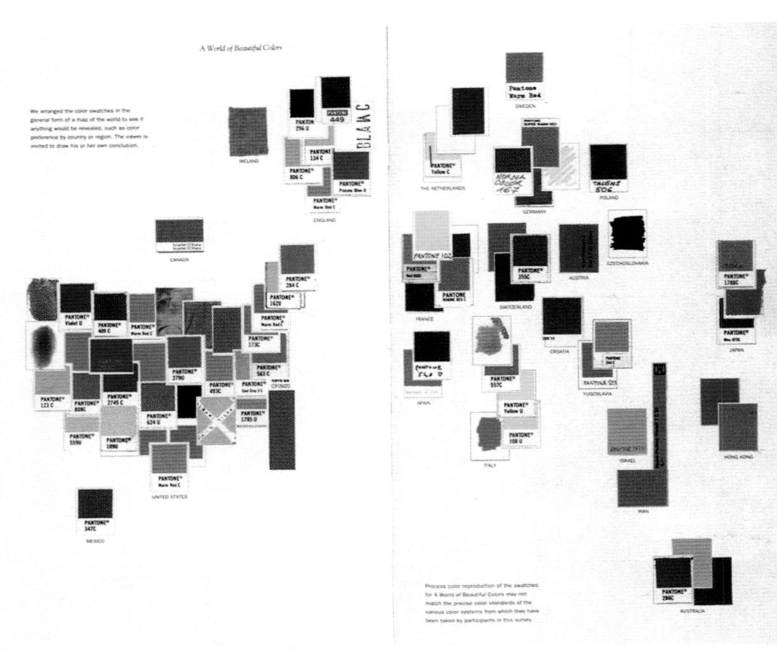

TOP We took all the beautiful objects suggested by the participants and arranged them together on a single surface to compose a still life.

LEFT The page of beautiful men as perceived by the respondents.

ABOVE A geographical distribution of color preferences.

LEFT The entrance to Aurora.

BELOW Since Aurora was "The Rosy Fingered Goddess of Dawn" I considered a hand showing rosy fingers.

OPPOSITE PAGE A section of the carpet design.

Aurora

After many years of inventing some of the world's most unique restaurants for a variety of clients, Joe Baum decided to open his own. I was thrilled when he asked me to design it even though I knew it would not be easy. Baum was my idea of the perfect client, sophisticated, demanding and obsessively concerned with quality, whether it was about the texture of the menus or the quality of the oysters. What was more important was the fact that he trusted me. If Joe ever felt that you were not up to the job you would be eaten alive. We started the project as though restaurants had never existed. Even professional assumptions were questioned. Could all the tableware go to the right of the plate? Should the napkins be rolled or folded? Is a cloakroom needed or would an armoire do? Joe brought over a chef who owned a two star restaurant in Paris to run the kitchen. For six months they travelled across the country eating at the best restaurants and checking out produce so the chef could become acquainted with America's culinary vocabulary. The view was that America had unsurpassed ingredients and enormously talented cooks but perhaps lacked the technical skill and training that characterized the best European restaurants. By combining American dishes with French technique, the best of both worlds could be achieved. Even the chairs were distinctive. We selected Eames office chairs designed in the fifties, upholstered in soft leather, that were seductively comfortable and, because they had wheels, made getting up from the table easier.

The early reviews were mixed, partly because expectations were so high. Over time the chef lost interest in American food and began cooking the French dishes he preferred. Joe became diverted by his new project at the Rainbow Room (page 162-167), and wasn't at Aurora every night greeting his loyal customers. The location was neither a trendy adventure downtown, nor an accessible spot midtown. Whatever the reasons after several years the restaurant closed. It was a sad day for all of us. Of course people now talk about how innovative and beautiful it was.

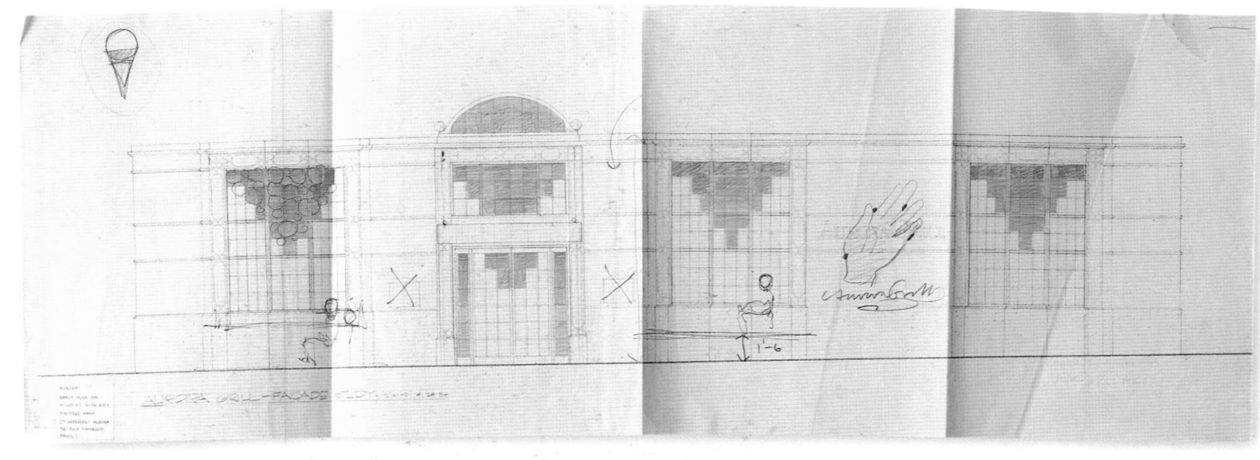

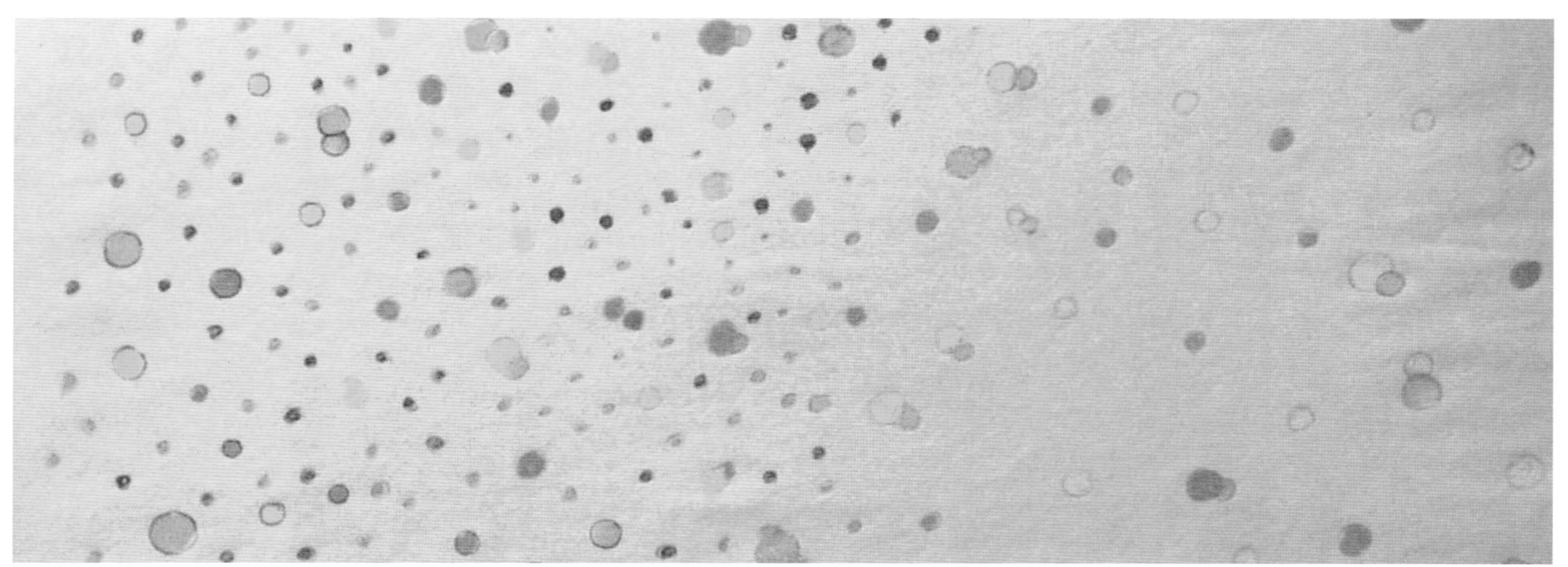

This doodle of circular dots actually initiated the entire design process for Aurora.

Some steps in the process of developing the logo.

An early portrait of the goddess.

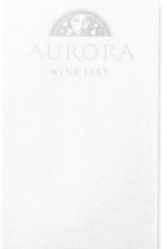

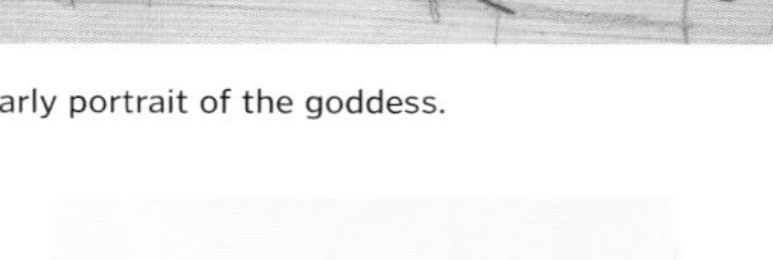

The wine list

The service plate.

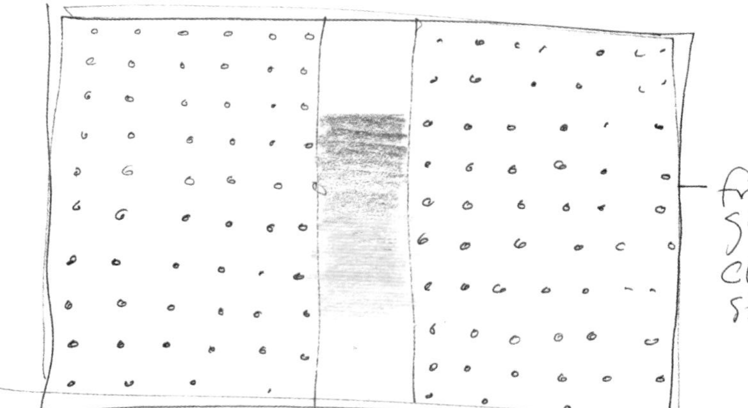

An early study for a colored window that later became a wooden lattice.

LEFT The bar was designed with the help of a good friend, Phil George, who designed the elegant back bar and Jordan Steckel who created the playful sculpture of Aurora submerged in a field of stylized clouds.

Together with Tim Higgins, I developed all the other elements of the room including rugs, lights, plates and printed materials.

BELOW LEFT A view of the front entry showing the "wardrobe" check-room, the window treatment, the rug, and the tiled area adjacent to the bar.

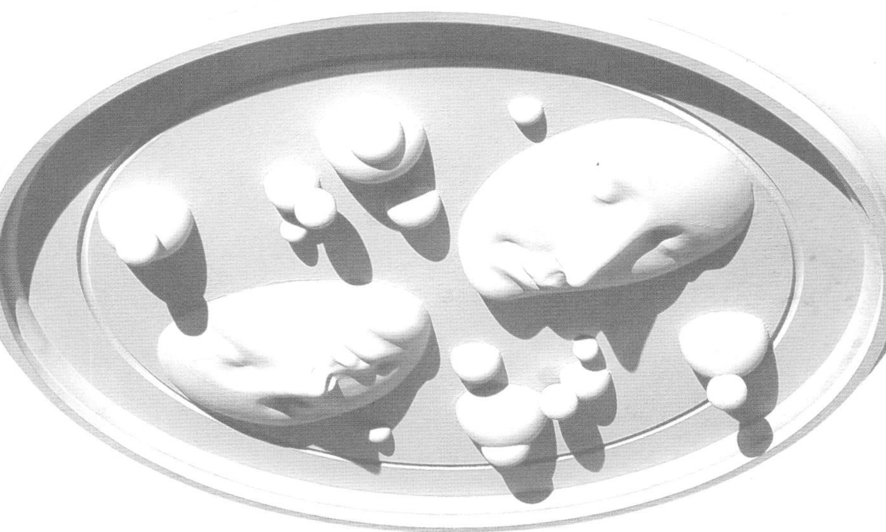

Ceiling detail in the ladies' room.

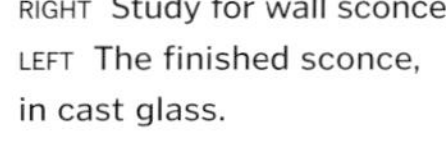

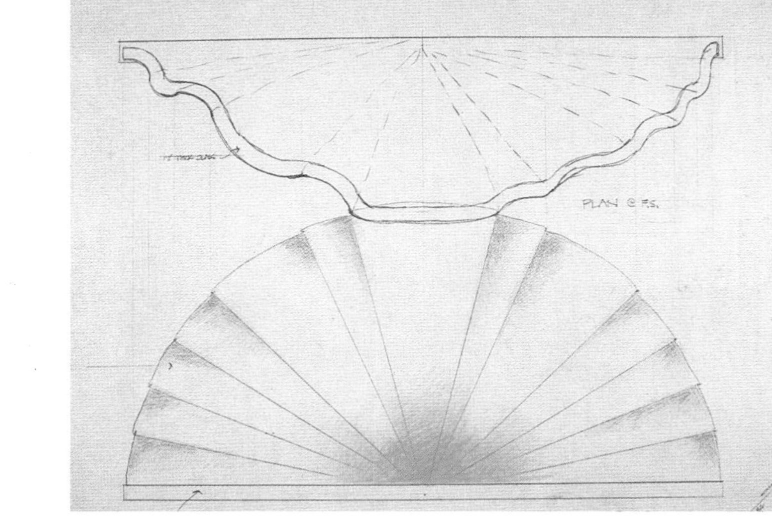

RIGHT Study for wall sconce.
LEFT The finished sconce, in cast glass.

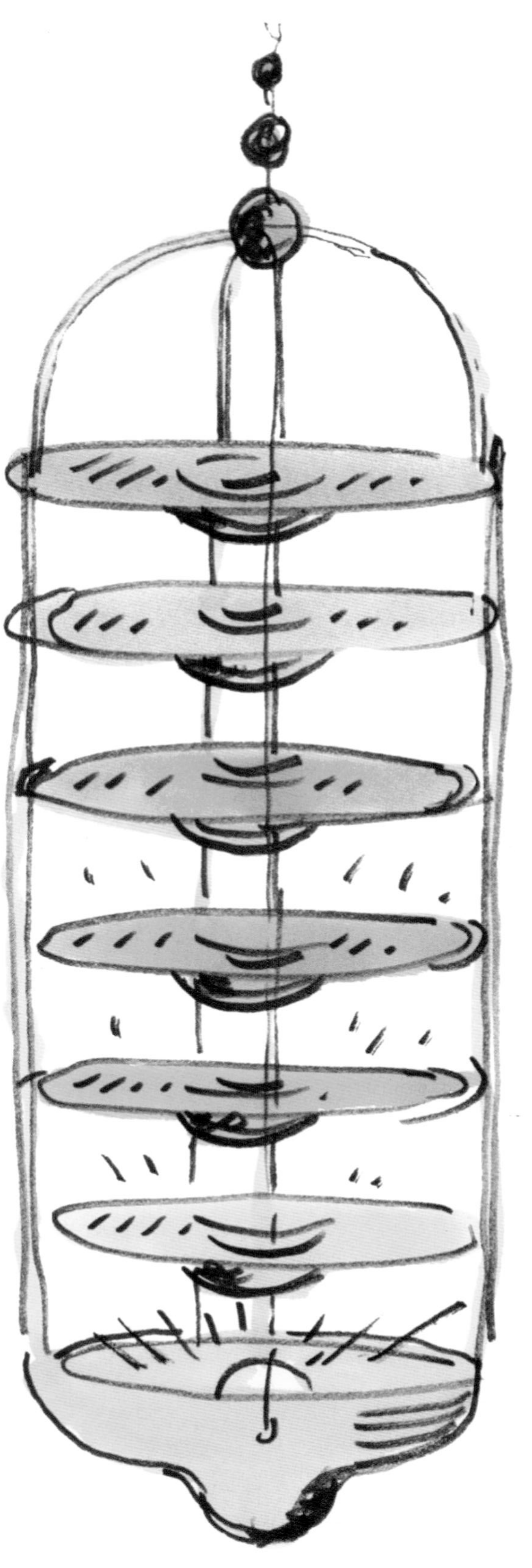

Joe Baum wanted to create a variety of moods for the restaurant. At lunch he wanted a kind of diffused, white light that would bathe the diners in a soft but clear atmosphere. In the evening, at bar time, he wanted a pinkish glow in which drinkers could feel relaxed. At dinner time he wanted to deepen the tonality to create a romantic mood, and late into the night there were other color adjustments. Aided by a talented lighting engineer, I invented a simple system for doing all of this by installing three banks of light bulbs in the large chandeliers; white, red, and blue, each on a separate dimmer system. By intensifying or dimming any of the colors one could achieve a remarkable range of color hues, from bright white to pale pinks to deep purples and everything in between. The effect was quite dramatic.

TOP LEFT An early study of lighting for Aurora in which I thought a variety of different shapes and sizes might be interesting. But soon I realized that it might look like a lamp store if designed this way, so I chose simpler forms that would create a cosmology of light.

OPPOSITE PAGE Another approach to the lighting that was never executed. It still strikes me as something that could look quite charming. I also designed a table light that repeats the form of the ceiling fixtures and provides a soft romantic glow (see page 183).

These drawings were used as the basis for the watercolors that surrounded the room at Aurora. Since they are involved with the idea of changing light they seem thematically right for Aurora. They were placed on a railing and leaned against the wall to create a casual effect. I originally made the drawings in Puerto Vallarta during a Christmas vacation. We were booked into the last available resort—it was a ghastly experience! I became ill shortly upon arrival and was confined to my room with nothing to do but read and look out the window. Fortunately the view across the bay was breathtaking. Something about the weather system created a constantly changing display of light and color. I drew these in my notebook over the course of a day or two. In addition to the watercolors I also transformed them into a print called "Mexican Skies."

Left to right:

Carol Anthony,
Emanuel Schongut,
Marc Rosenthal,
Dale Glasser,
Steven Alcorn.

Paul Davis,
J.C. Suarez,
Rafal Olbinski,
Barbara Nessim,
Jim McMullan.

Ivan Chermayeff,
Susan Stillman,
George Stavrinos,
Brookie Maxwell,
Stephen Guarnaccia.

Joan Hall,
Susan Gray,
Richard Hess,
Seymour Chwast,
George Leavitt.

Michelle Barnes,
Javier Romero,
Anna Walker,
Jack Tom,
Julian Allen.

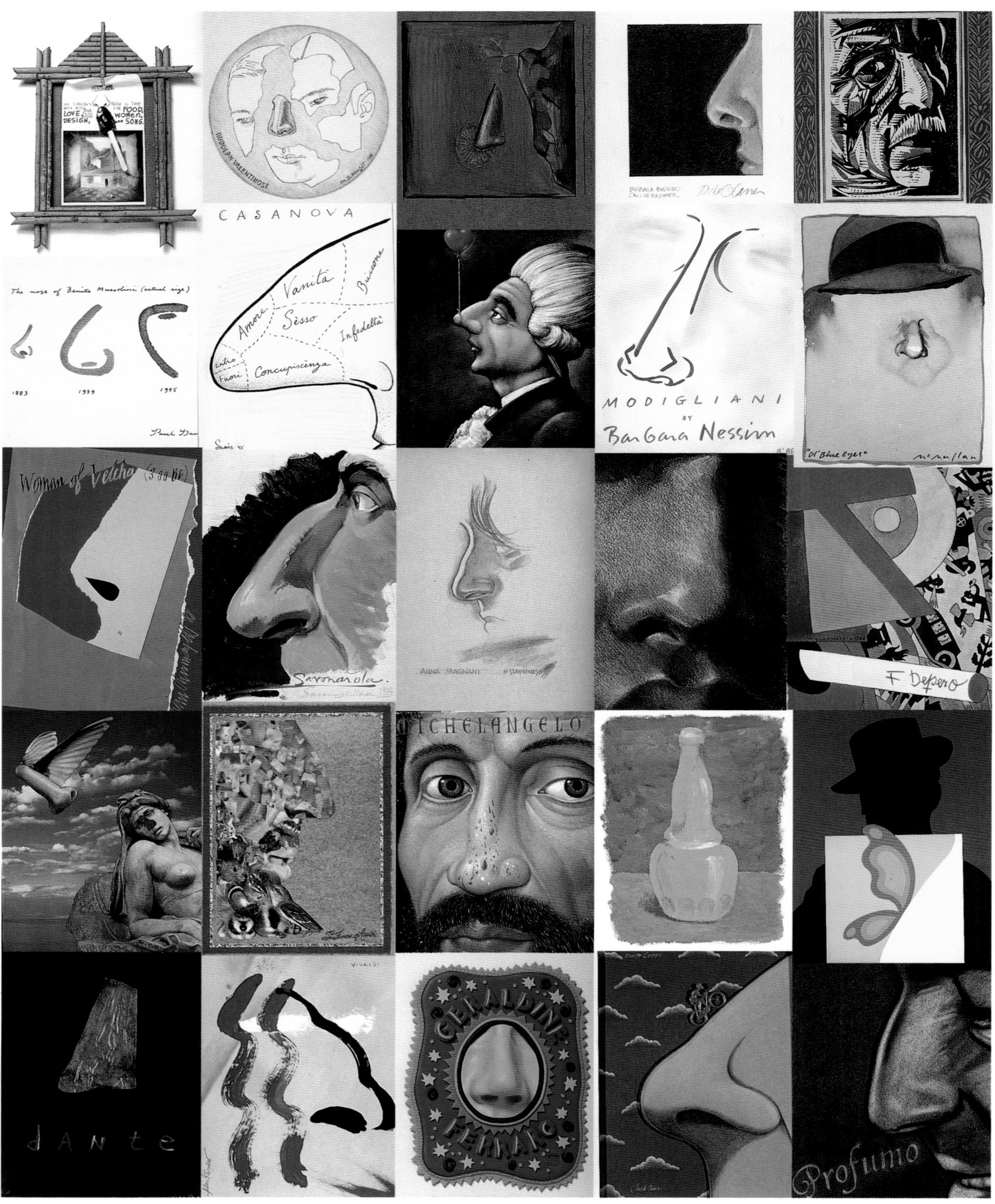

"Famous Italian Noses" was the theme that inspired the nose studies, which were created to decorate the walls of the upstairs dining room of the Trattoria Dell'Arte in New York City. Here are twenty-five of the forty contributions.

When I was approached to design an Italian restaurant on 56th Street and 7th Avenue, I thought of doing an homage to the time I spent in Italy in the early fifties, studying at the Academy of Fine Arts in Bologna. For whatever reason I thought of putting a large nose in the window (essential to our sense of taste) and calling the place "Il Naso," (The Nose). The owner, a cautious man, was concerned that his Jewish customers might be offended because it sounded too much like "The Nazi." He suggested "Trattoria Dell' Arte," less provocative and safer. In any event the giant nose remained.

LEFT The central, high-ceilinged yellow room is based on the studios at the Academia del Belle Arte, with paintings by Elliot Levine stacked against the wall and the simulated skylight. Adjacent to the studio is a more protected, less noisy green room that encourages quieter dining.

Designing Restaurants

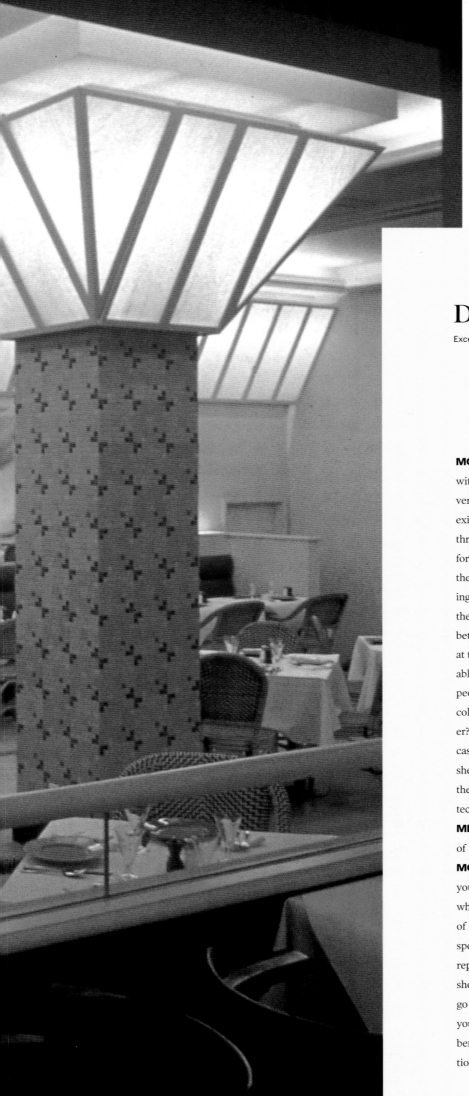

Excerpt from an interview with Marshall Blonsky, *Graphis 270* December, 1990

MG: I'll tell you why I love to design restaurants. It's because they deal with many elements of form that I'm interested in, including light. I'm very interested in the effect of light on color, in space issues that don't exist on a flat surface. I'm very interested in the fact that you can create, through the use of space, light, and color, a place where people are transformed emotionally. One of the things that happens when you come into the Trattoria [Dell'Arte] is you get a lift, you suddenly feel a little lightening of your spirit. It's created by the use of color, form, and shape. I love the social effect of restaurants: the fact that for a brief moment you feel better there than elsewhere. Listen to the conversation, the laughter, look at the physiognomies; people seem more sophisticated, more knowledgeable, more elegant—in the right restaurant, you feel enlarged. Why do people feel good in a space? How can you, through the use of light, space, color—transform the psychology of personality and make people happier? A restaurant can make you feel comfortable, agreeable. The light that's cast from the side on a woman's face makes her look more beautiful than she looks outdoors. I love the idea that people, through the intervention of these elements, are changed into another state of mind, that they're protected from the world for the brief moment of the meal.

MB: I listen to you and I think of your Trattoria, where you have the noses of famous Italians from Dante to Durante, as a "Paradiso" for today.

MG: It also can be an interpersonal "Inferno." The restaurant is where you tell your lover that you're breaking up. But it can also be the place where you first declare your love. Restaurants are now the social center of people's lives. You meet your friends in restaurants. Very often you spend the entire evening there. To some extent the restaurant has almost replaced the theater in New York. People used to eat out and then go to a show. Now it has become so expensive to do both that very often people go to dinner, have a conversation, and go home. To exchange intimacies if you aren't already living with someone—where do you do that? On a bench? In your apartment? No, you do it in a restaurant. Not enough attention has been paid to the real significance of restaurants in people's lives.

The “green” room.

The restaurant consists of a series of spaces, each with a clearly defined spirit. One enters an informal, low-ceilinged bar area distinguished by a large painting by Teresa Fasolino of famous Italian noses in history. The floor is enlivened by a series of tile “throw rugs.” At the end of the bar room, we designed an Italian sushi bar with the idea of serving single diners and those in a hurry in an effective and pleasant way. I asked a group of New York illustrators to do a portrait of a famous Italian nose for an intimate, almost residential room, one flight up. The splendid results are shown on page 150. Because they were amused by the idea and liked the company they were in, they were all willing to work in exchange for a dinner for two at the Trattoria, continuing an old European tradition of art-ists exchanging work for food.

All this visual activity proved to be attractive to a wide range of diners. Businessmen, musicians, students, tourists and concertgoers all feel at home here and continue to make the restaurant one of the city’s most popular. My conceptual model for the restaurant was the old La Coupole in Paris, where everyone felt they were in the right place regardless of where they came from. Tim Higgins, an architect who was working at the studio at the time, was immeasurably helpful in creating the restaurant.

A private dining room.

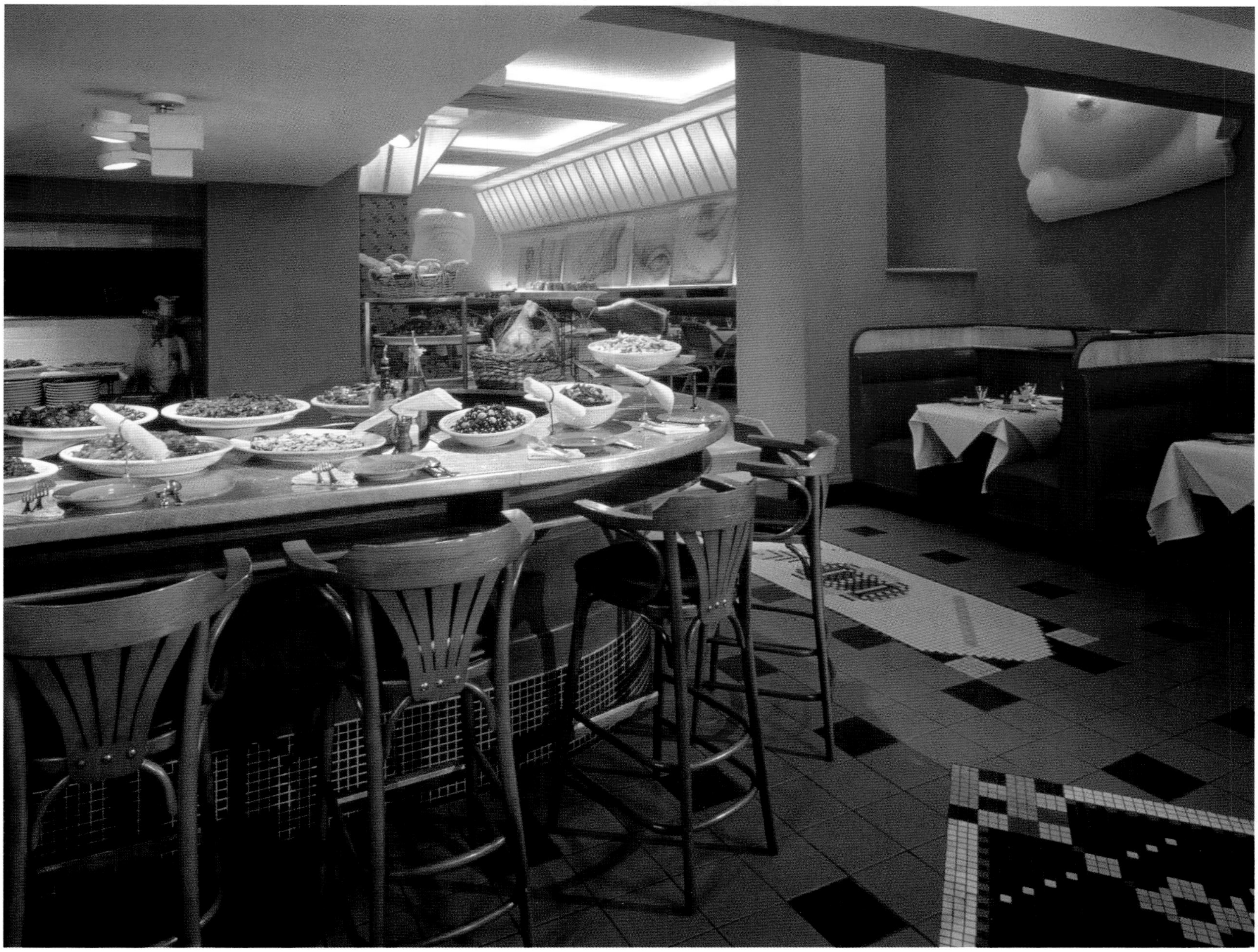

The Italian sushi bar

The Teresa Fasolino mural.

A series of other body parts—eye, ear, mouth, breasts etc.—formed a decorative theme inside the restaurant. These were enlarged versions of the plaster casts we worked from at the academy to develop our drawing skills. They were brilliantly sculpted by Jordan Steckel, an old high school friend. The references to art school were entirely misunderstood by the restaurant critics, who perceived them as some sort of perverse misogynist expression.

RIGHT An earlier use of a plaster cast was this splattered version that ended up as a cover for *Graphis* magazine.

Sesame Place was a project based on the popular characters created by Jim Hensen for public television. The idea was to create a theme park supported in part by an educational intention. Of course the educational part had to

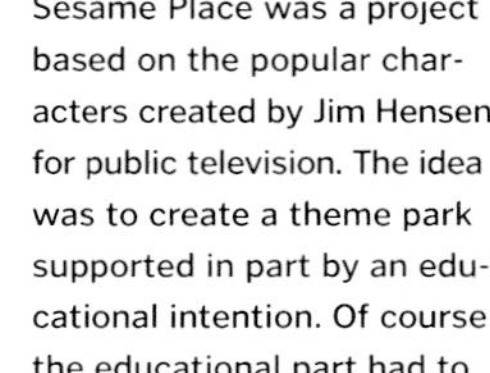

be experienced within context of play, or else neither parent nor child would ever return. Our first problem was creating a visual equivalent for the muppets, since there was no practical way of replicating them dimensionally from either an aesthetic or financial point of view. Our approach was to flatten them and make them more geometric. We used the "flat plane" aesthetic for all systems including the entrance gate BELOW, the signage system and a "joining" method (page 158) developed by Murry Gelberg and Larry Porcelli, that linked all sorts of things together. The architectural component was in the good hands of Cope Lindner, architects from Philadelphia. We were responsible for interiors, colors, signage, and other environmental issues.

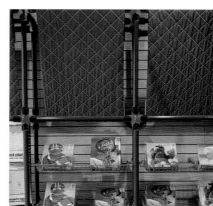

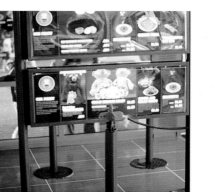

RIGHT The "joining system" used to build all of the structures shown here.

BELOW The Sesame Place alphabet was based on an earlier typeface I had designed called Houdini.

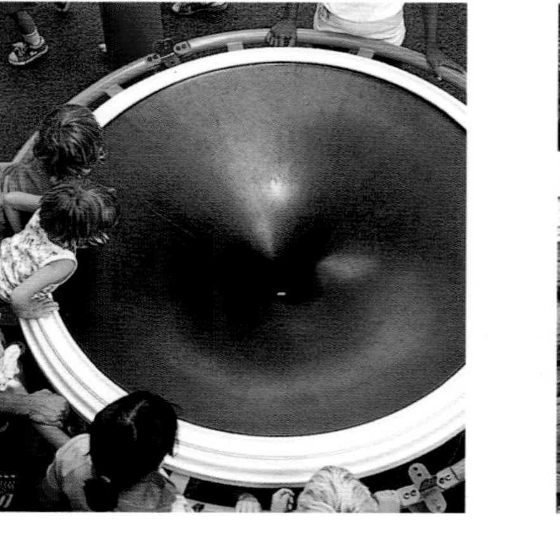

The entry gate, PREVIOUS PAGE, and the whirlygigs that respond to a breeze and the signage, RIGHT, were based on the
idea of intersecting planes. The signs permitted you to read instructions regardless of which direction you approached from.

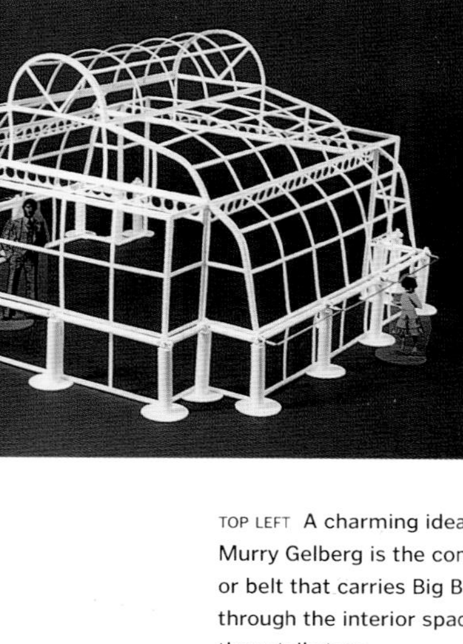

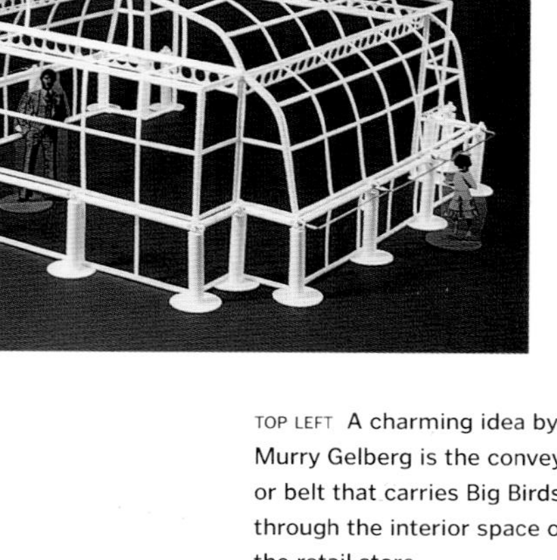

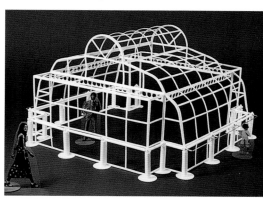

TOP LEFT A charming idea by Murry Gelberg is the convey- or belt that carries Big Birds through the interior space of the retail store.

LEFT The umbrella fixtures that created a soft and beau- tiful light in the restaurant interior.

ABOVE RIGHT A study for the greenhouse kitchen where customers could see all the activity (sometimes you really don't want to see what is going on in a restaurant kitchen).

RIGHT Franklin Mills is a large shopping mall in Pennsylvania. We worked together with the architects Cambridge Seven to develop a vernacular for the signage and interiors. Initially, we used cut paper to express some of these ideas which are reflected in the final results. The logo is based on Benjamin Franklin's kite with the famous lightening bolt now contained within it. The kite is shown flying in a variety of ways in relationship to the words "Franklin Mills," depending on the application.

RIGHT This enormous head of Benjamin Franklin is lowered from time to time to make announcements. His jaw moves up and down to complete the effect.

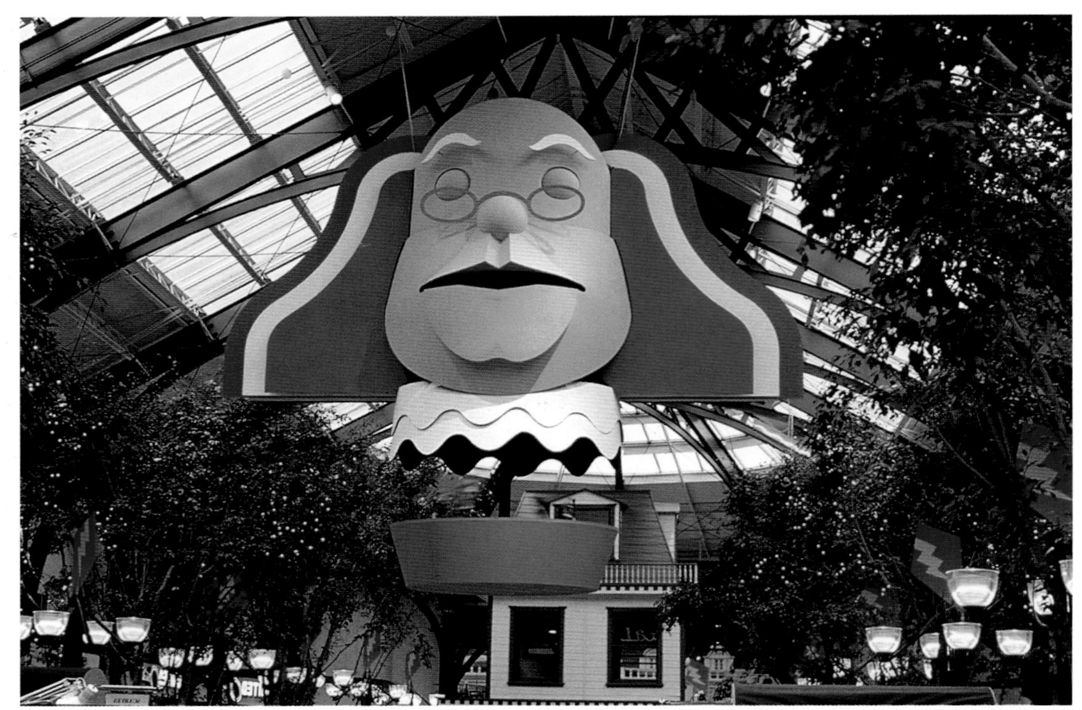

FRANKLIN MILLS
BED, BATH & BEYOND
MODELL'S SPORTING GOODS
FILENE'S BASEMENT

The Rainbow Room was the last major project I worked on with Joe Baum. He was one of the most extraordinary clients I've ever worked with (See page 141-149). It would be difficult to describe his particular genius, but I learned more about how to think about design from him than from anyone else in my adult life. During the course of more than thirty years, we worked on many projects, beginning with Windows on the World at the World Trade Center (see page 168) in 1975. In 1987 we started to work on the design restoration of the Rainbow Room complex, together with Hugh Hardy of Hardy Holzman and Pfeiffer Associates, a firm noted for its sensitivity in developing new ideas within the framework of an architectural restoration.

The work on the Rainbow Room itself was essentially an attempt to restore it to its original glory. In fact, the only new element was a glass wall (the rectangle at the top left in the picture above) by Dan Dailey, a superb designer in glass. It depicts the history of art from the "Venus of Willendorf" to Raymond Lowey's "20th Century Limited." The background colors diffused by the glass were supposed to change seasonally, but as so often happens when projects require ongoing maintenance, this idea eventually disappeared. There was much concern that the Rockefeller cousins (there are about eighty of them) would object to this new element that replaced a tacky maroon curtain. As it happened, on opening night, they all thought the glass wall had always been there. The rest of the complex was completely new and was created in the spirit of that wonderful expression of the twenties and thirties frequently called Art Deco, but in this case more accurately referred to as American Modernism. I was entrusted with developing the interior art program for the complex. After determining that a budget of one million dollars would not buy much in the painting market (in fact, when William Rubin, the curator of American painting at the Metropolitan Museum of Art, was asked by David Rockefeller how many quality paintings he might hope to buy for a million dollars, he replied wearily, "You might be able to get a third of a painting.") we shifted our attention to the world of crafts and sculpture. We hired such extraordinary designers as the aforementioned Dan Dailey, the prodigious father of the American Glass Movement, Dale Chihuly, Howard Ben Tre, Dan Dailey, Nancy Graves, Ray King, John McQueen, Arman, Ed Moulthrop, and Frank Roth. They all contributed specially designed pieces for the public and private dining rooms throughout the complex.

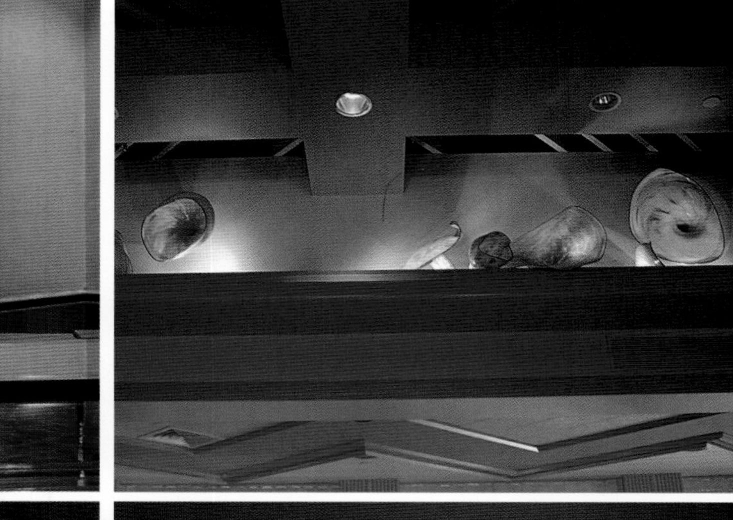

LEFT Front desk lamp by Ray King.

RIGHT Detail of the Dale Chihuly mural.

LEFT Entry to the Rainbow Room. Lamp design by Milton Glaser.

RIGHT Wall sconce by Ray King.

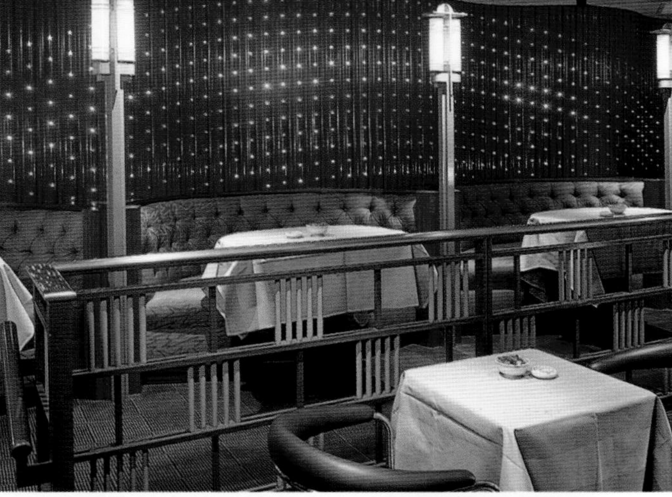

LEFT Floating ocean liner model discovered in California, originally designed by Norman Bel Geddes.

RIGHT Fiberoptic rainbow designed by Milton Glaser.

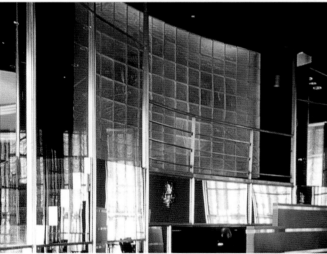

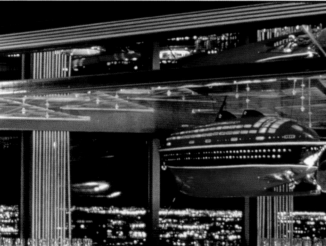

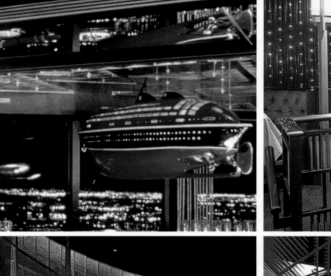

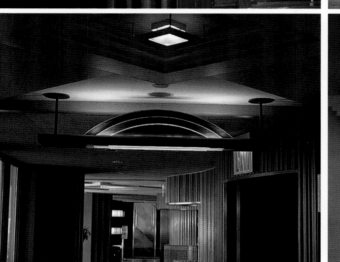

LEFT Detail of the Dan Dailey glass wall.

RIGHT Entry to the Radio City suite showing the bakelite radio collection.

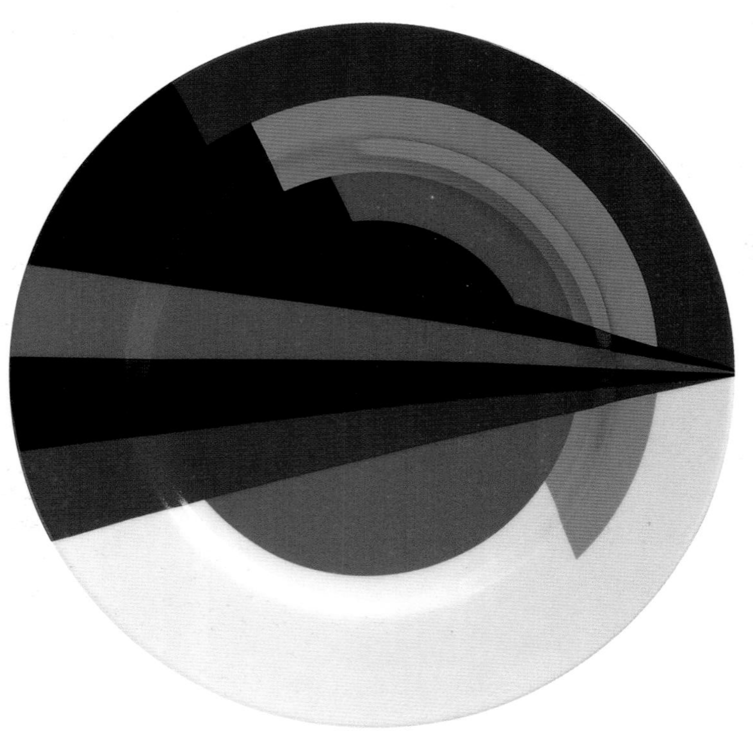

ABOVE An adaptation of the design theme for enamel jewelry.

LEFT The Rainbow umbrella, enormous and very decorative, with some early studies.

OPPOSITE PAGE Detail of a wall mural room divider, the uniforms by Carrie Robbins incorporating the theme of geometric modern design, and the service plate.

RAINBOW!

AABBCCDDEEFFGGHHII

RAINBOW REGULAR

RAINBOW HEAVY

RAINBOW EXTRA BOLD

We developed a proprietary alphabet for the Rainbow Room based on an amusing idea—two variations for every letter, a narrow one and a wide one. By combining the two forms, all sorts of visual possibilities occurred. For instance, if one wanted two words of unequal length to flush left and right, it could easily be achieved by varying the number of narrow and wide letters.

RAINBOW

EXPANDED LETTERS

RAINBOW

CONDENSED LETTERS

RAINBOW

COMBINATION

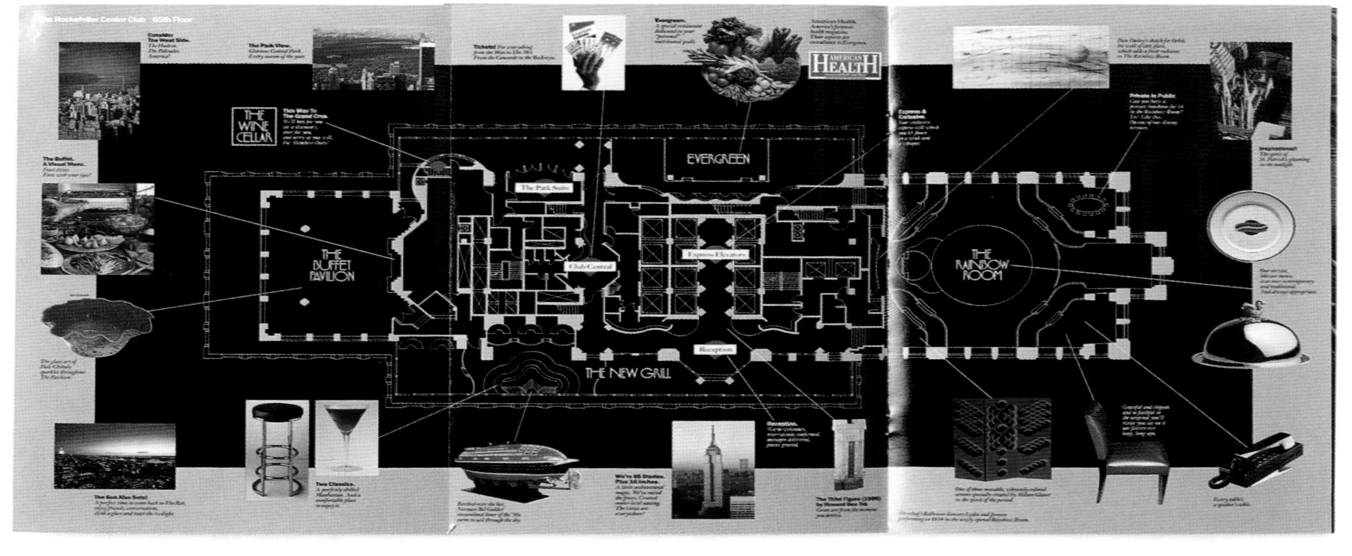

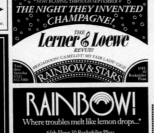

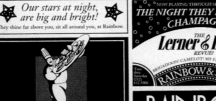

LEFT A promotional brochure showing the floor plan, to demonstrate the exciting offerings of the Rainbow Room complex in order to attract members to the club.

BELOW LEFT A full page newspaper ad treated as though it were a composite of small ads, again emphasizing the variety of possibilities that an afternoon or an evening might offer at Rainbow. It was an effective way to express an extremely complex series of messages without ending up with a page full of text. Only after a few moments does one realize that all these ads were for the same place.

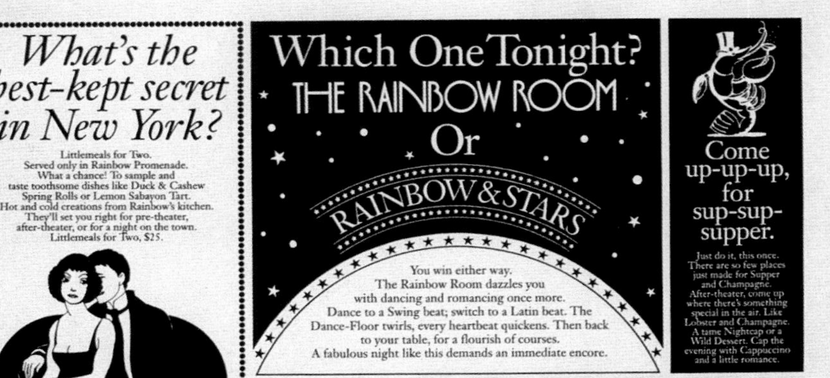
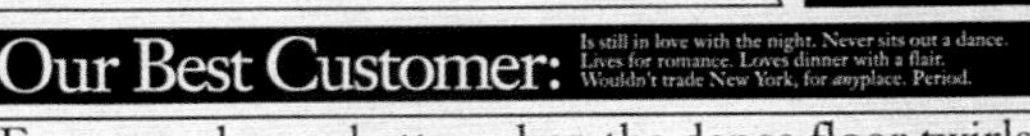

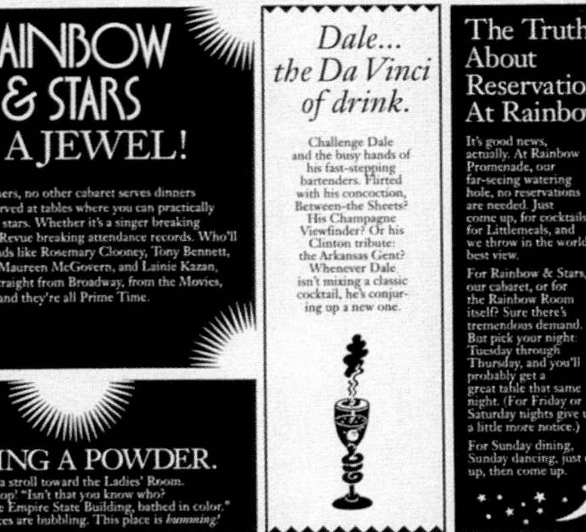

ABOVE *Overview.* Club members received these monthly mailings of upcoming events.

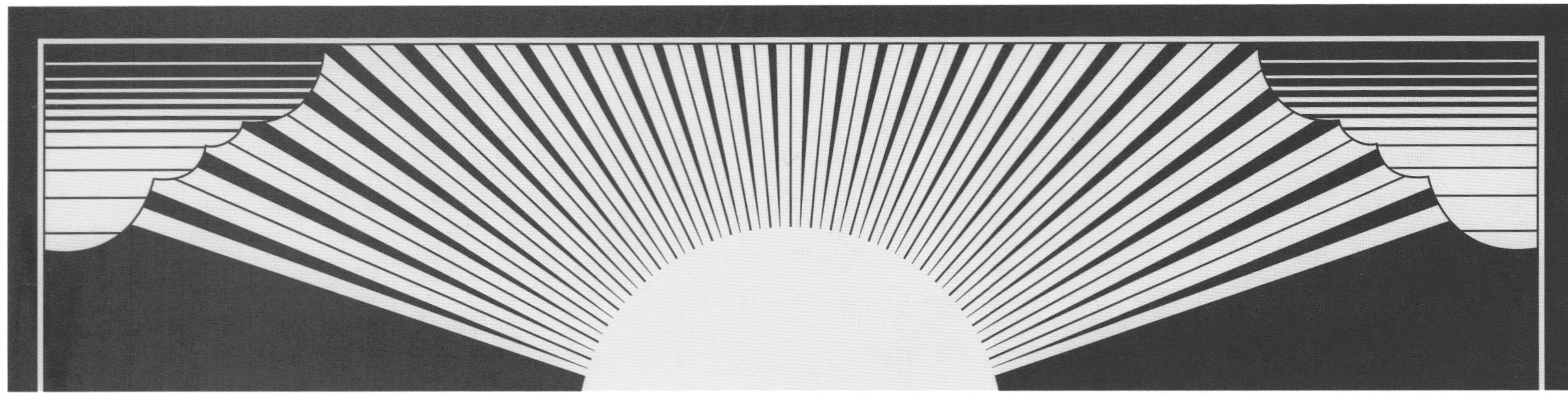

ABOVE Usually logos are simple and reductive. In this case we wanted the logo for Windows on the World to be expansive to create a sense of generosity.

LEFT The logo applied to a wine bottle and RIGHT, the basic stationery.

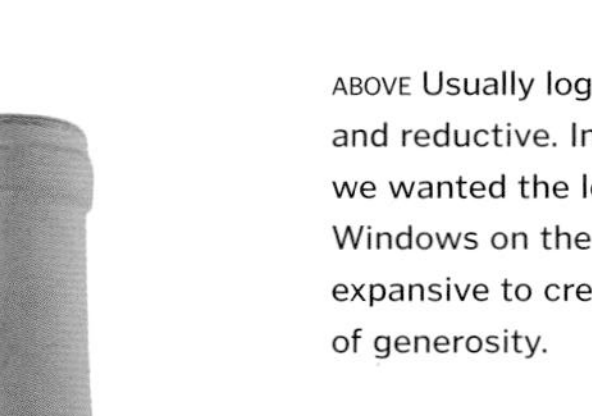

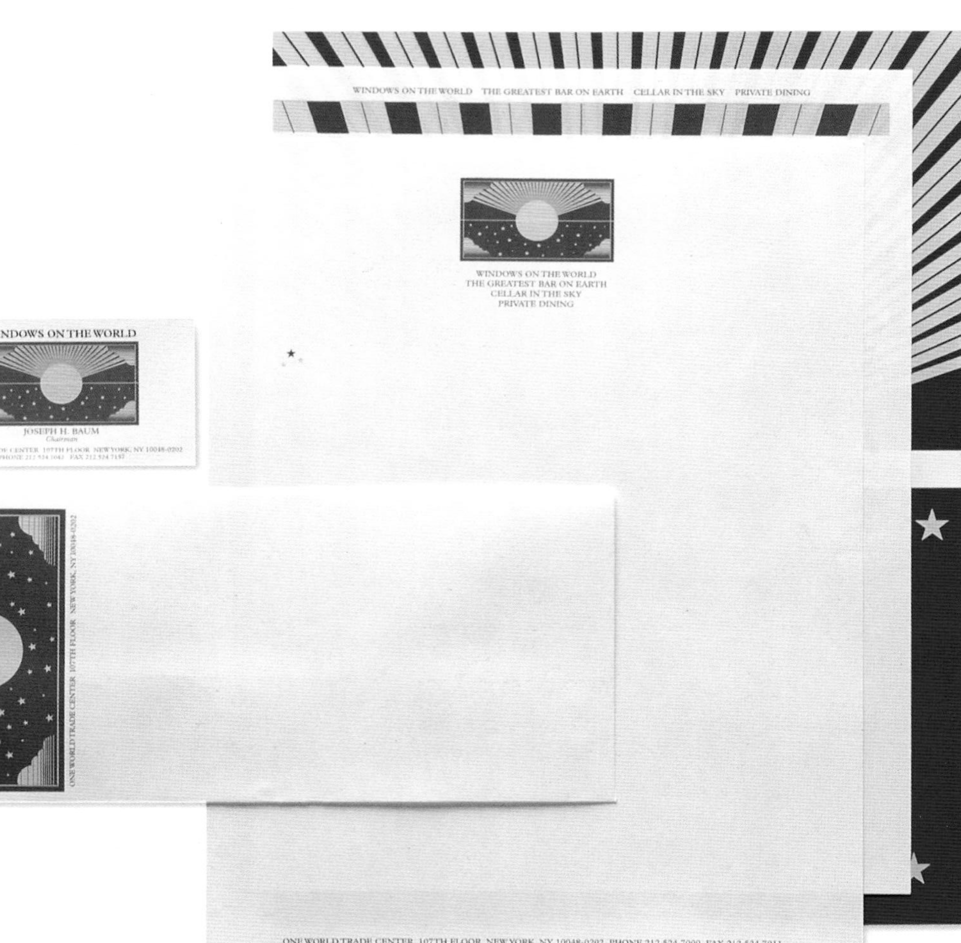

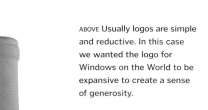

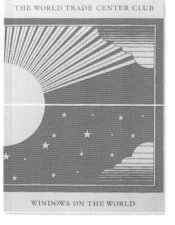

LEFT A variety of dishes designed to produce an interesting effect when piled upon one another. We took advantage of the opportunity created by the curved vegetable plate to make a crescent moon. The Bacchus plate is a service plate for Cellar in the Sky.

THE TOP CLUB IN NEW YORK, AGAIN.

At the foot of the Isle of the Manhattoes. On the top floor of New York's tallest building. Looking out on the world's most celebrated view.

The totally new World Trade Center Club. Open weekdays for members and their guests, for breakfast, lunch and after the New York financial markets close.

The sparkling new Windows on the World, for à la carte dining and the Grand Buffet. The Greatest Bar on Earth, less formal, more rollicking, for a quick lunch or a lingering carouse. The Skybox, your private luxury lounge.

The World Trade Center Club. The sum of what we know about what you need.

Business at a whole new level.

6

7

OUR THOUGHTS ON A FEW OTHER FAMOUS CLUBS: CLOSE BUT NO CIGAR

"...Skull and Bones members...need a place to practice the sacred male-bonding traditions, which reportedly included lying naked in a coffin while recounting one's sexual history..." —The New York Times

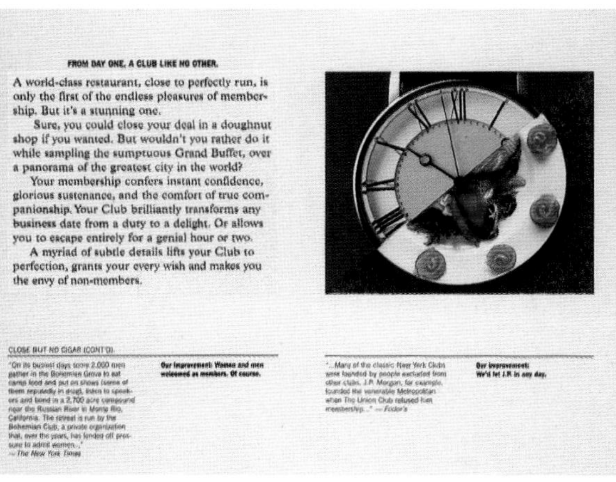

FROM DAY ONE, A CLUB LIKE NO OTHER.

A world-class restaurant, close to perfectly run, is only the first of the endless pleasures of membership. But it's a stunning one.

Sure, you could close your deal in a doughnut shop if you wanted. But wouldn't you rather do it while sampling the sumptuous Grand Buffet, over a panorama of the greatest city in the world?

Your membership confers instant confidence, glorious sustenance, and the comfort of true companionship. Your Club brilliantly transforms any business date from a duty to a delight. Or allows you to escape entirely for a genial hour or two.

A myriad of subtle details lifts your Club to perfection, grants your every wish and makes you the envy of non-members.

8

9

CLOSE BUT NO CIGAR (CONT'D).

Our improvement: Women and men welcomed as members. Of course.

"...Many of the classic New York Clubs were founded by people excluded from other clubs. J.P. Morgan, for example, founded the venerable Metropolitan when The Union Club refused him membership..." —Fodor's

Our improvement: We'd let J.P. in any day.

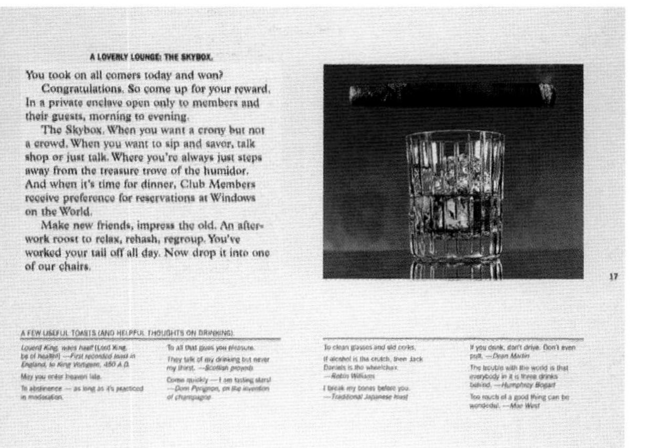

A LOVERLY LOUNGE: THE SKYBOX.

You took on all comers today and won?

Congratulations. So come up for your reward. In a private enclave open only to members and their guests, morning to evening.

The Skybox. When you want a crony but not a crowd. When you want to sip and savor, talk shop or just talk. Where you're always just steps away from the treasure trove of the humidor. And when it's time for dinner, Club Members receive preference for reservations at Windows on the World.

Make new friends, impress the old. An after-work roost to relax, rehash, regroup. You've worked your tail off all day. Now drop it into one of our chairs.

16

17

A FEW USEFUL TOASTS (AND HELPFUL THOUGHTS ON DRINKING).

May you enter heaven late.

To all that gives you pleasure.

To clean glasses and old corks.

I break my bones before you. —Traditional Japanese toast

If you drink, don't drive. Don't even putt. —Dean Martin

The trouble with the world is that everybody in it is three drinks behind. —Humphrey Bogart

Too much of a good thing can be wonderful. —Mae West

I had the idea of creating a metamorphic mural at the entry to Windows on the World that would change before your eyes. It was inspired by the idea of a theatrical scrim, which, depending on the lighting, could reveal its surface or the scene through and behind it. I assumed that a beaded curtain would function similarly and would also create a sense of sparkle and drama. For the entrance, clouds seemed an appropriate image as one stepped off the 101st floor elevator into the restaurant. I designed two overlapping images; one in reds and pinks was painted on the wall itself. The other in blues and greens was made out of beads and hung about a foot in front. Carrie Robbins, the clothing designer for the project, lead me to Eaves-Brooks Costume Company, who, among other things, designed all the trappings for the elephants at the Barnum & Bailey Circus. They did a prodigious job making the (9' x 38') curtain that took a total of 263,000 individual beads. One set of lights was to be installed between the beads and the wall mural. The other would be aimed at the front of the beaded curtain. Both sets of lights were to be on dimmers, and as one brightened the other would dim. The two cloud images would constantly replace each other with endless color variations before the viewer's eyes. At least that was the plan. After the mural was installed, I was informed that, in an effort to reduce costs, a set of lights had been eliminated, completely negating the idea behind the project.

After several years, the entry was redone and the mural was taken down without ever being seen in its intended form. It sits in boxes waiting to be installed somewhere under more favorable circumstances. You win some, you lose some.

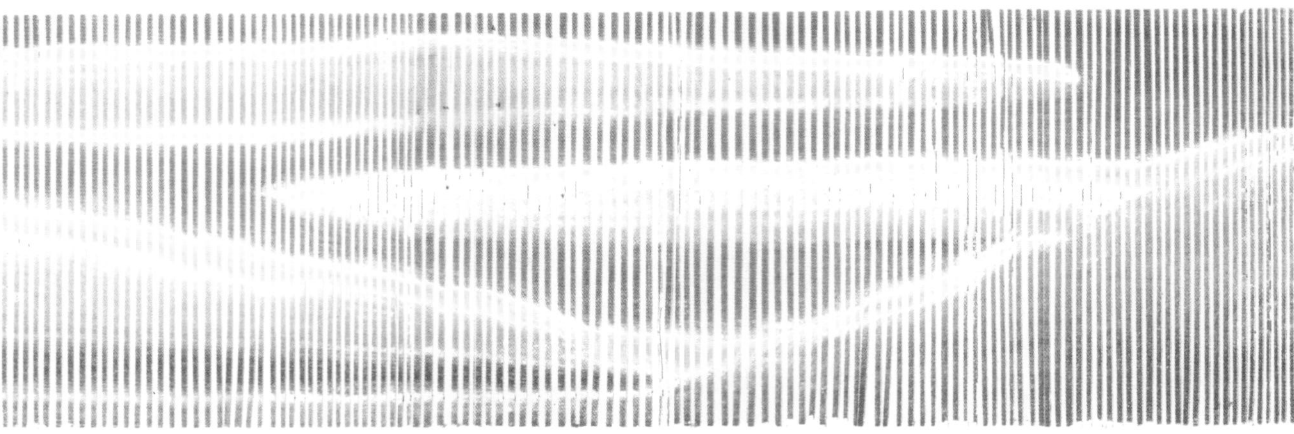

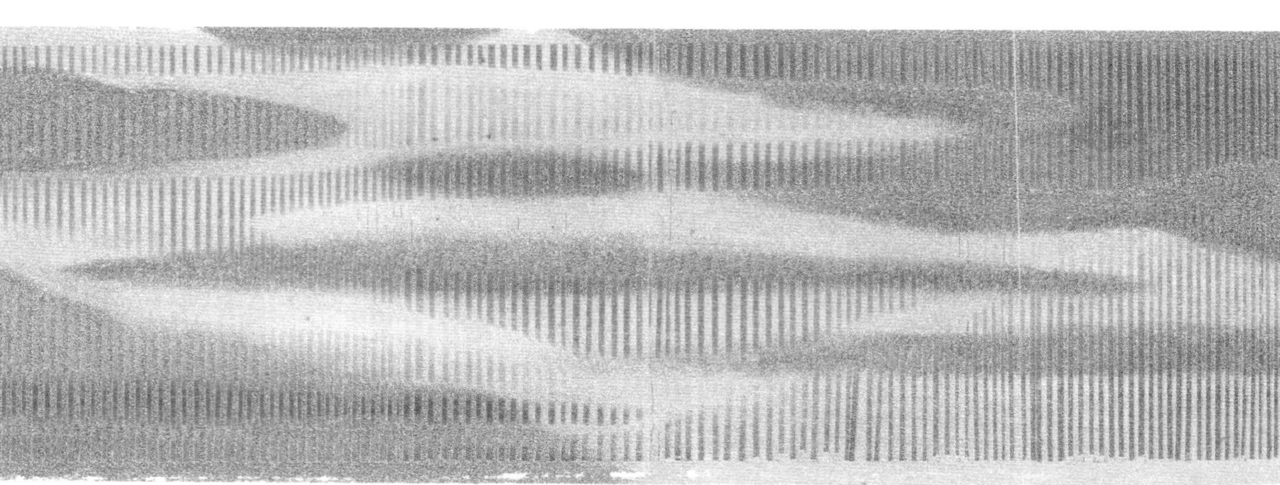

TOP Sketch of painted red clouds (back wall).

MIDDLE Sketch of blue clouds made of beads.

BOTTOM Combination of beads over back wall.

I was asked by a French ad agency to design a mural for their office that would serve as an entry and interior image. Because the agency is in the Marais, a part of Paris near the Picasso Museum, I thought the minotaur, a favorite subject of Picasso, would be a good image. The top of the minotaur is at the entry on two panels that come together and cover the door at the end of the business day. The bottom of the minotaur is on the ceiling of the reception area. If it weren't for my fee, this would have been an inexpensive and dramatic way of solving an interior design problem.

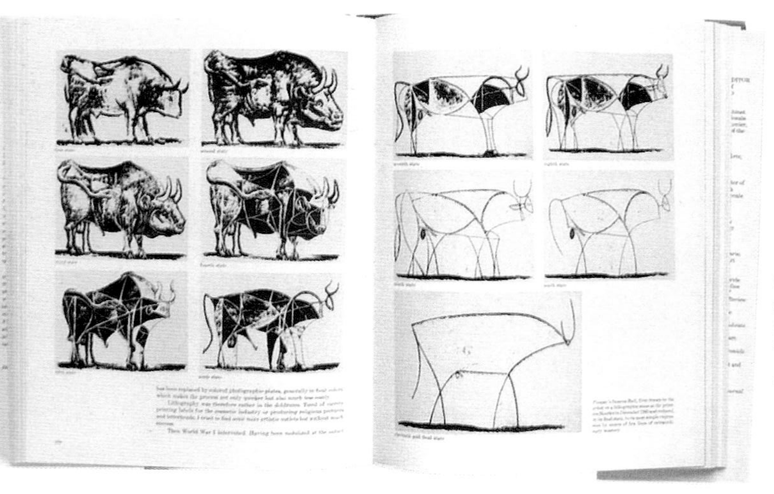

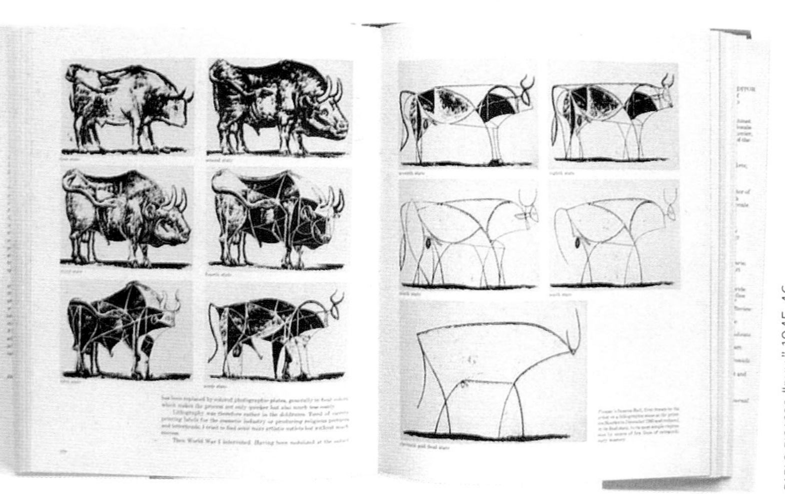

PABLO PICASSO "BULL" 1945-46

This study on a single etching plate, originally used for a story by Balzac, was one of the most important influences of my life. Here Picasso shows a bull in a series of transformations from naturalistic to reductive symbolism. Every iteration is marvelous and when I saw this series of prints I realized for the first time that style deserved no loyalty. The question is always one of quality, regardless of the stylistic assumptions.

A German manufacturer of carpeting produced enormous amounts of commercial carpeting but aspired to produce more artistic works. They initiated a series of commissions, engaging designers and painters known for their work in other areas, including David Hockney who has a wonderful flair for decorative objects, as well as Roy Lichtenstein, Arata Isozaki, Sol LeWitt, and Oswald Mathias Ungers.

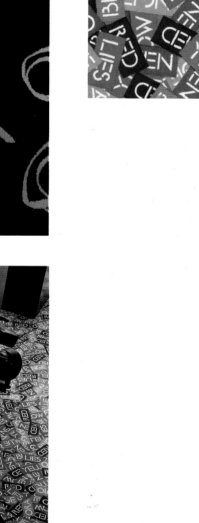

BELOW I chose to design one carpet with a narrative or joke built into the design. The carpet is a mislabeled assortment of colored rectangles. The blue label says red, the green label says yellow, the pink label says orange, and so on.... Distributed among the boxes are some containing the word "LIES," which of course refers to the mislabeled rectangles. This offers a new meaning to the phrase, "Lies like a rug."

Designed Objects

The word "design" has become misused or has changed from its original meaning. Some years ago I was having a conversation with Mario Bellini, one of the preeminent industrial designers in the world. He told me the following story. He met someone who said, "I know who you are, Mr. Bellini, you make those designer chairs." At that moment Bellini realized that the word "design" was being used as a description of a certain kind of style. In this case perhaps the kind of work produced by Milanese industrial designers in the sixties and seventies. The suggestion seemed to be that all other chairs in history have not been products of a design process and came about more or less accidentally.

RIGHT This glass was commissioned by Bombay Gin as part of a series. It was difficult to make. The idea was to create an iridescent cup within the clear outer glass. The vacuum created between the two was supposed to keep your Martini cold longer—(nobody likes a warm Martini). Although it was beautifully made by Ben Moore, all the photographs made it look simply like thick glass.

OPPOSITE PAGE A range of alternative ideas.

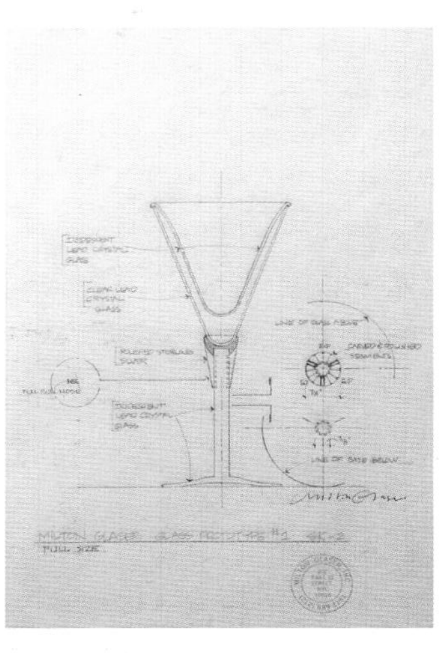

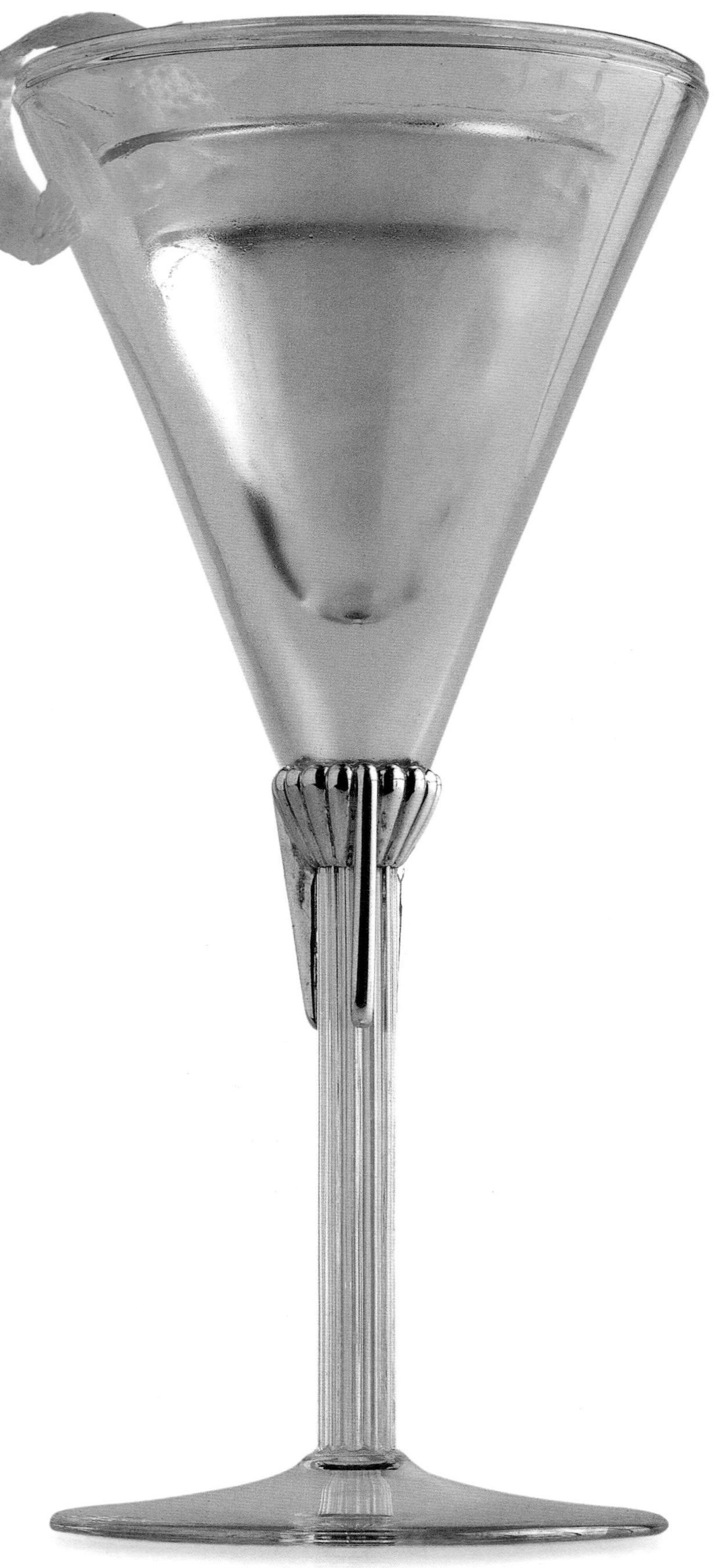

Alessi

Alessi is an Italian-based industrial company that makes home and kitchen utensils in metal, ceramic, and wood. Everything they make is distinguished by intelligence and a sense of appropriateness. Of course, we can also call this good design. Philosophically, Alberto Alessi is convinced that manufactured objects can either enrich or demean the life of the user. After being around the design field for half a century, I have found that this point of view is rare. When one encounters it, it is exhilarating.

LEFT One amusing Alessi project involved giving a basic jar shape designed by Alessandro Mendini to one hundred different designers to decorate—each piece was produced in an edition of 100. They sold out quickly. I chose to do a series of creatures that were half bird, half human.

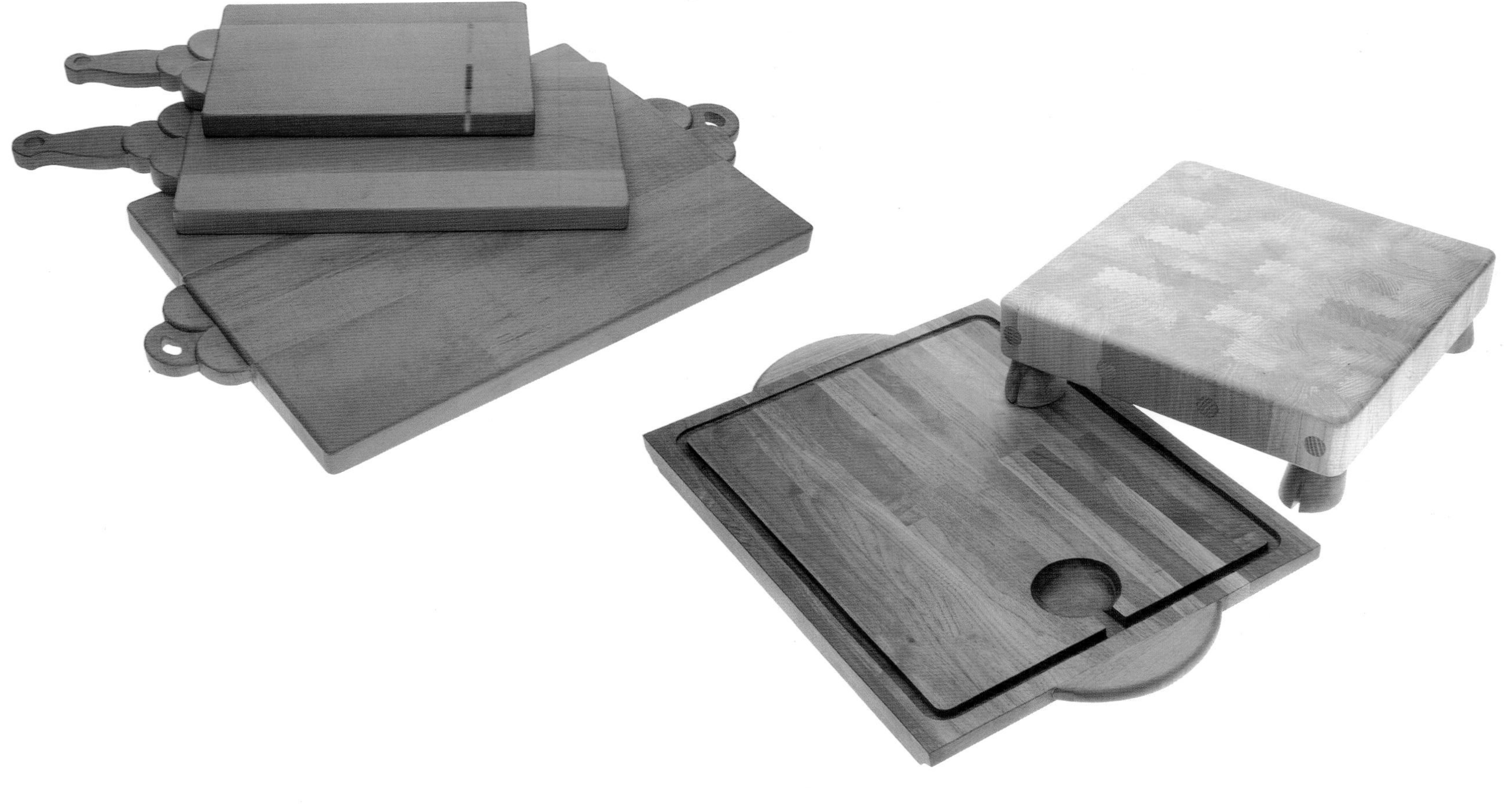

ABOVE I also designed some cutting boards for a woodworking factory that Alessi acquired in 1988. They were intended to have a rustic quality. The meat cutting board has a technological advantage in that the draining groove is a continuous incline so that all the meat juices accumulate in the circular cup rather than simply remaining in the grooves. Now, I think the chopping board with little cow's feet might be in bad taste.

LEFT Alberto Alessi asked a number of designers and architects to design things for his home—I had the assignment of designing the grill above the entry gate.

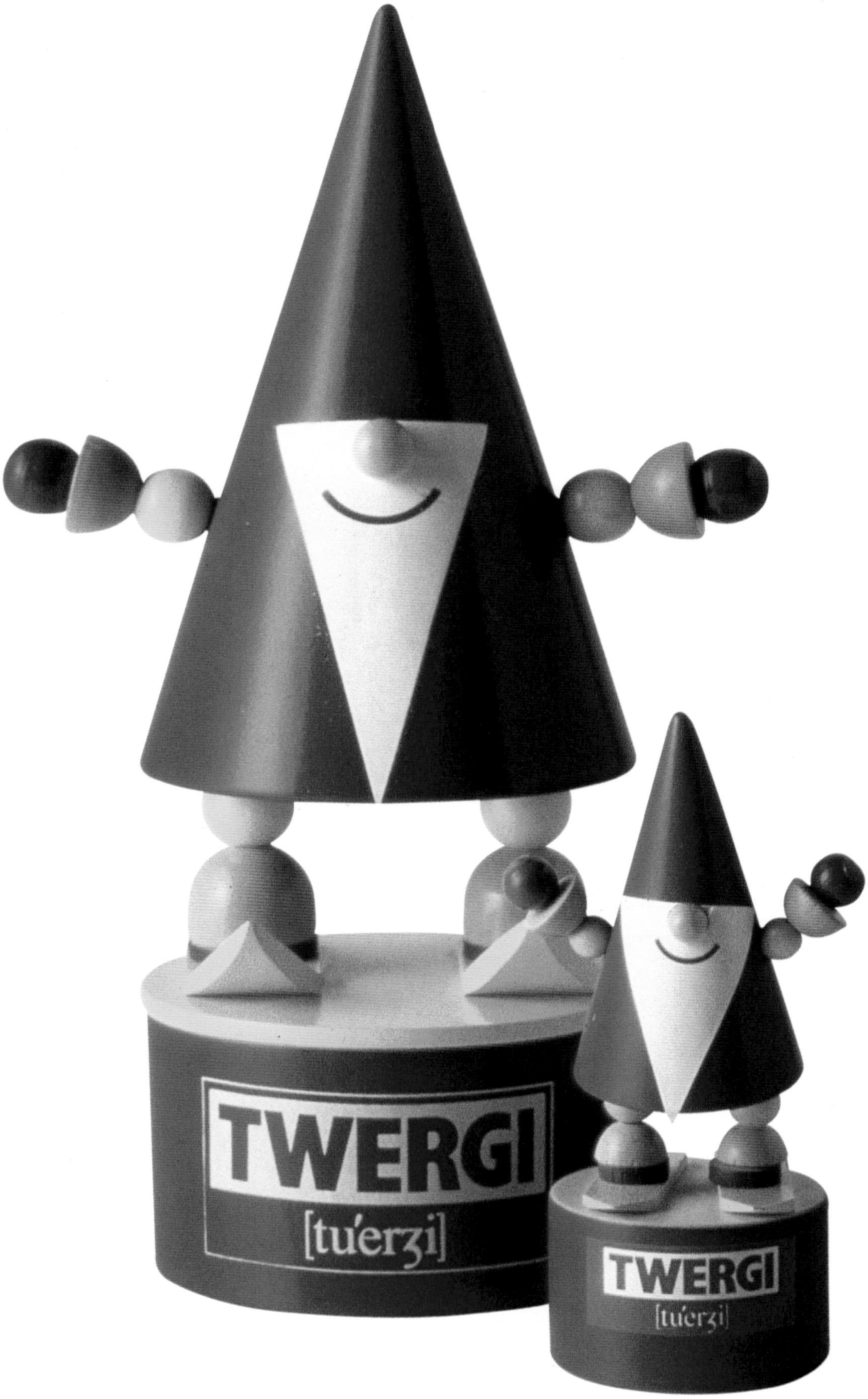

LEFT Twergi are little creatures that supposedly live in the forest around the area where the wood products factory is located. The trick was to design something that could function as a graphic mark, as well as a three dimensional object. The countryside supports a cottage industry that makes those wooden toys that collapse when you press the bottom. Alessi wanted the design to be useable for this purpose and as an alternative to the usual Disney characters.

LEFT *La Cintura di Orione* (Orion's Belt) is an ambitious book that explores the history of metallurgy—as it applies to the making of pots and pans—as well as introducing an extraordinary line of utensils designed by Richard Sapper. Alessi gave these pots and pans to some of the world's most celebrated chefs (Roger Vergé, Alain Chapel, Pierre and Michel Troisgros) who, in turn, developed recipes that were printed in the book. This very complex tome consisted of technical diagrams, historical engravings, photographs of the chefs at work in their kitchens, recipes, descriptions of the cookware, and my illustrations. It was an extremely complex project that could have become a visual nightmare.

L'usine à rêves
Alessi depuis 1921
ALBERTO ALESSI
ELECTA/ALESSI

BELOW LEFT A cover for Alessi's current catalog, "The Dream Factory."

The intersection of light and form is one of the most compelling themes in the visual arts. Light is obviously essential in creating the atmosphere of public spaces.

ABOVE A series of giant lamps and illuminated topiary forms created for the area at the base of the World Trade Center adjacent to the Big Kitchen (see page 205). The space is enormous and intimidating, and these objects represent an attempt to make it feel more friendly, much as a table lamp does in a large room.

LEFT Detail from a poster for the School of Visual Arts that was inspired by the drawings of my friend Folon and influenced the lamps that I developed for the Big Kitchen.

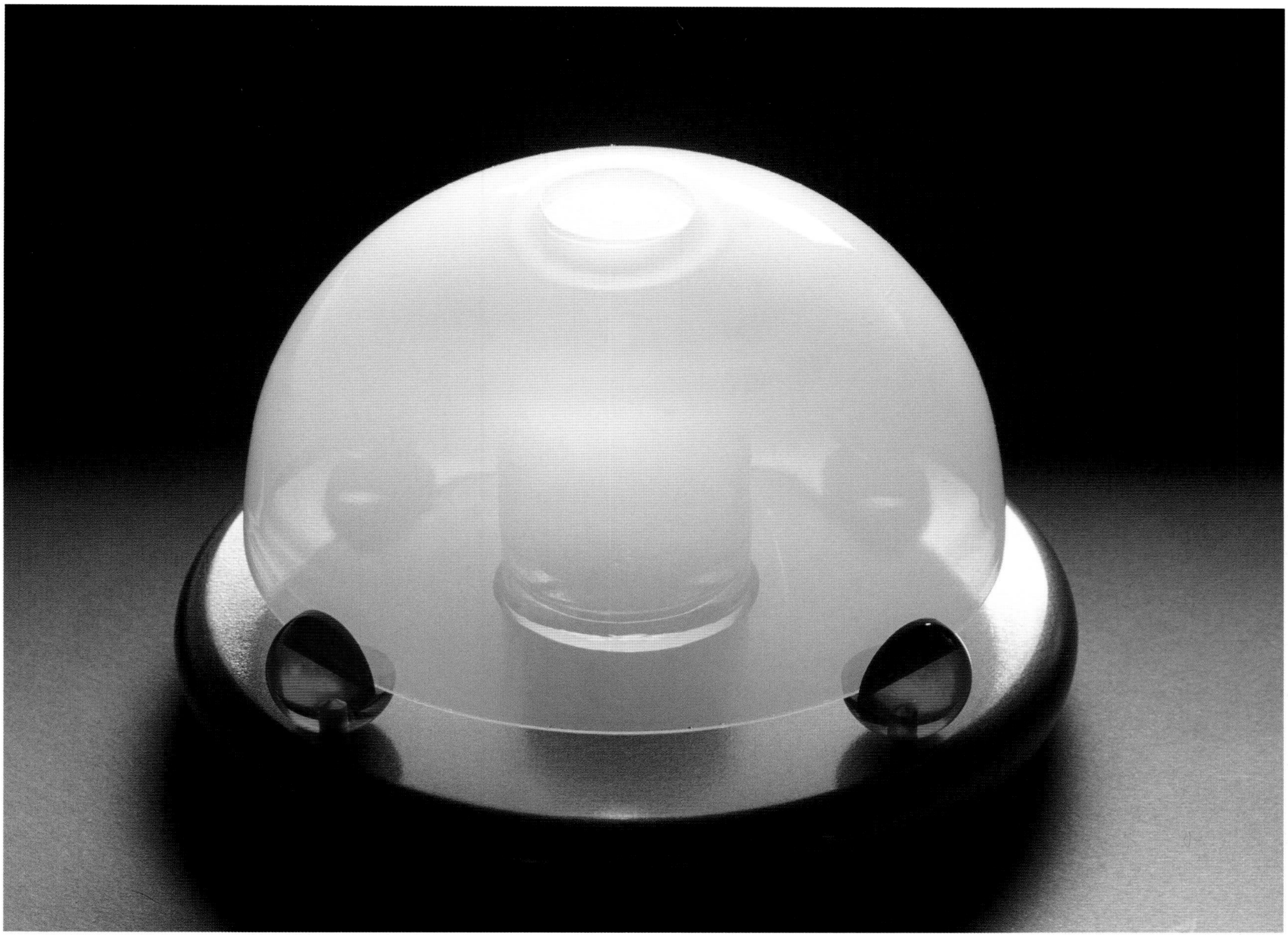

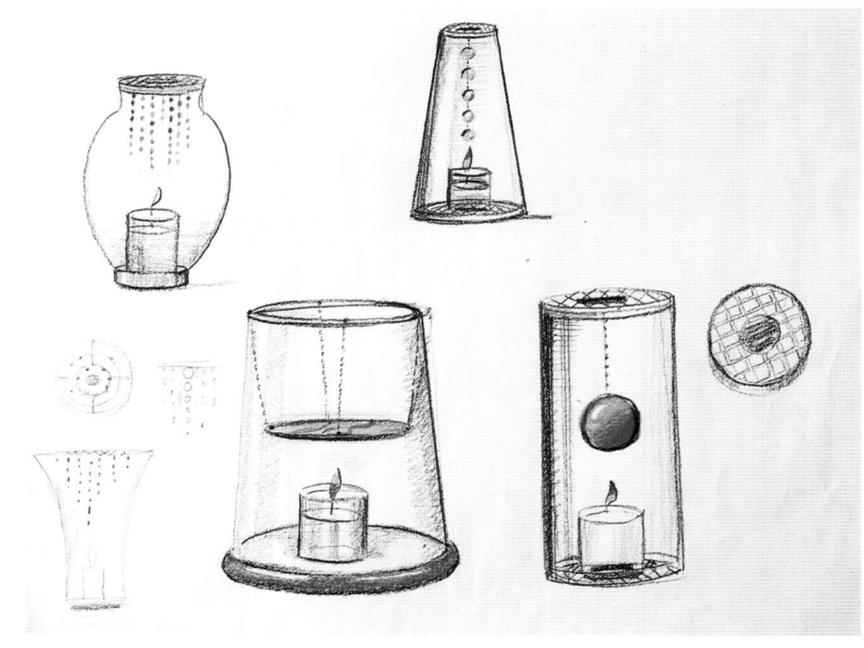

Joe Baum asked me to design a table lamp for Aurora (page 144) to relate to the spirit of the lights that illuminate the interior. For reasons I don't understand, there are very few table lights for dining that one would be willing to add to a table. This one with a votive candle inside, shielded by the partially frosted dome, gives little light, but created a nice sparkle in the room at night. Alessi later started making it in Italy, and sells it to the general public through its catalogue.

GIORGIO MORANDI

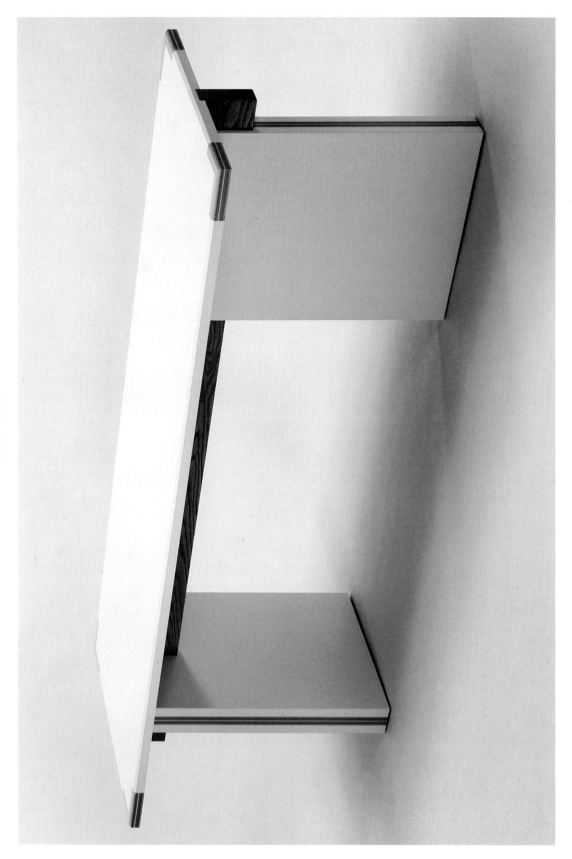

ABOVE A table I designed to show the use of a new laminate by the Formica Corp. I thought it might be interesting to combine the laminate with wood since usually these materials are kept separate from each other.

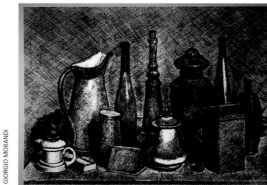

LEFT A "table lamp" that resulted from a collaboration with the celebrated interior designer Adam Tihany, to produce a series of outrageous lamps for the Italian lamp manufacturer, Foscarini of Murano. One of the lamps was an homage to Giorgio Morandi, my teacher in Bologna. I recorded the most recurring objects in his etchings and paintings (Morandi's still lifes used the same beloved bottles, vases, and pitchers continually) and sent the drawings to Luciano Vistosi, one of the preeminent glass masters in Murano. He cast them in crystal. An inventive Venetian woodworker, Livio de Marchi, carved a table to be used as the base. There is a light source beneath each object so that they can be illuminated individually or all at once. It was a very rewarding collaboration.

Incidentally, the sublime Morandi etching, ABOVE, demonstrates why I think of light when I look at Morandi.

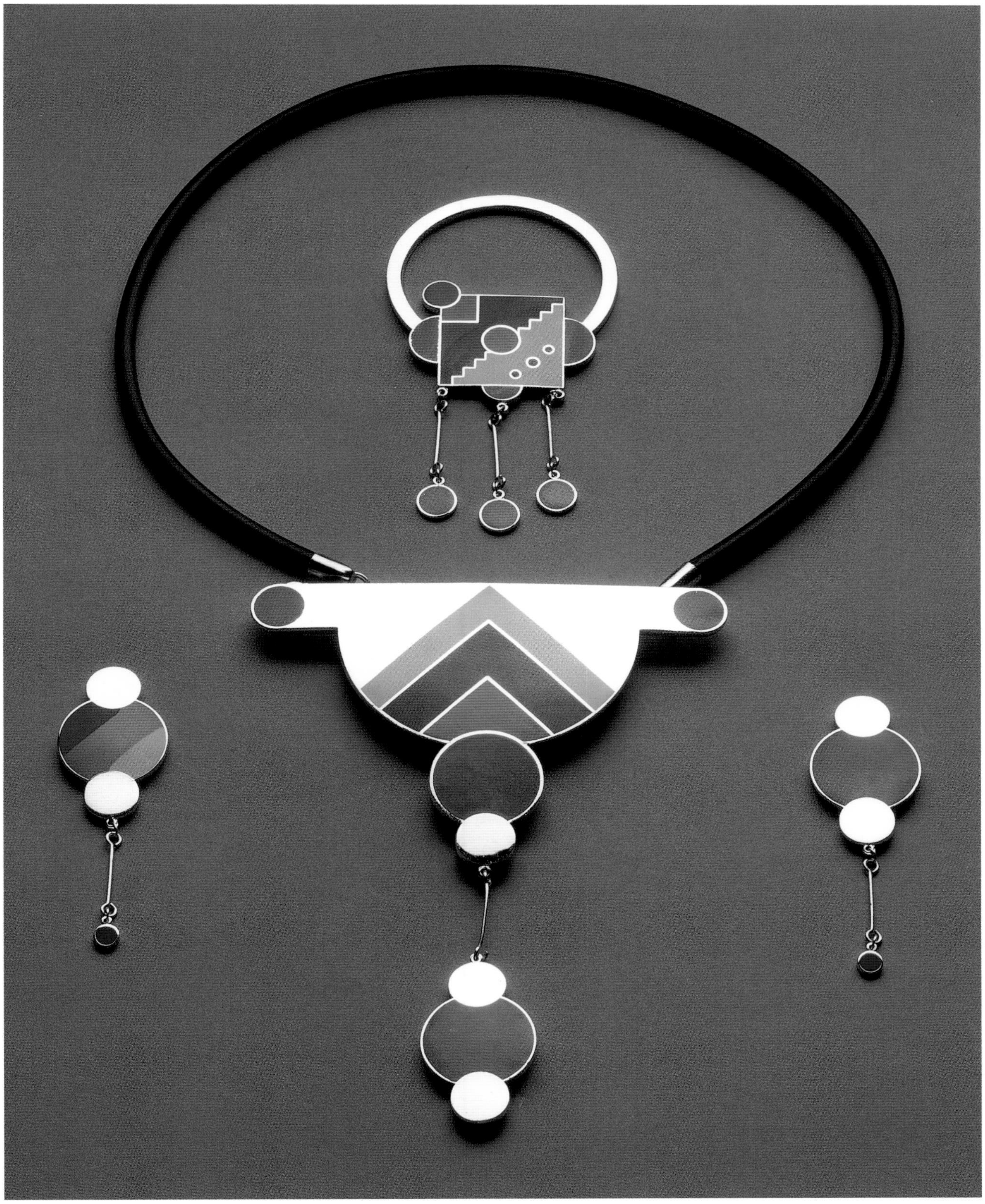

LEFT A commission from a jewelry maker who produced things in enamel resulted in this series of objects. The necklace was designed so that elements could be added to it as time went on, showing the ongoing affection of the giver.

BELOW I developed a version of the "I Love New York" logo that contains a heart within an apple. The "Big Apple," of course, refers to the city itself. A Japanese manufacturer produced a version of it as a watch, perhaps not its most appropriate use.

RIGHT A German company asked me to design a glass that would encourage children to drink milk. I could think of nothing more attractive to children—perverse little creatures that they are—than the symbol for poison. The German text reads: "Milk is good for the bones."

OPPOSITE PAGE A commission from the Heckscher Museum of Art to design a time capsule for the beginning of the millennium led to this solution. It began with a phrase I couldn't get out of my mind: "A capsule of capsules." So many of the things I do are triggered by words. This led to the idea that one could learn much about the nature of a culture by the nature of its sicknesses, psychosomatic and so on. I researched the fifty most popular over-the-counter medicines in America and had Nick Fasciano, a superb designer and craftsman, insert them in plastic tubes within a transparent box. Because of the brilliant color and transparency of the capsules, the effect is quite pleasing as well as being informative.

The Steelcase Design Partnership is involved in manufacturing a variety of office systems and environments. They wanted to produce an exhibition and a book that would convey their interest. I suggested the theme of "Work, Life, Tools," which would consist of the relationship of a variety of personalities to the tools that they used. It turned into a book and a travelling exhibition. Part of the requirement was to create an exhibition system that would be operative in any interior environment, which presumed that in some cases there would be no walls to hang things on.

We developed a simple, free-standing system that displayed a large photograph, the tool and a large quote from the personality. The photographs themselves were beautifully taken by Matthew Klein, who is responsible for almost every photograph that I've used over the last twenty-five years.

WORK, LIFE,
TOOLS.
The things we use to do the things we do

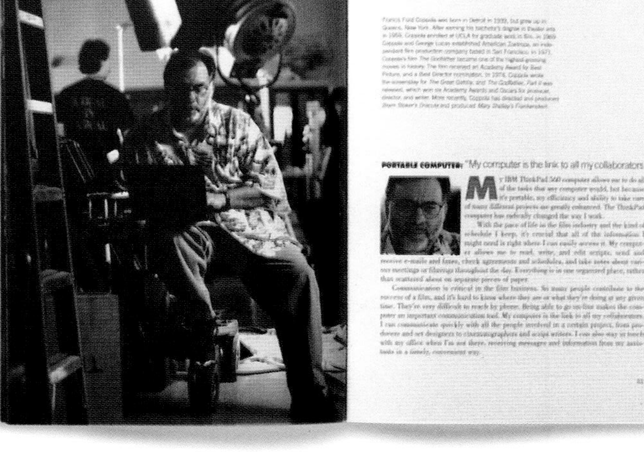

Marshal Blonsky

Duane Michels

Janette Kahn

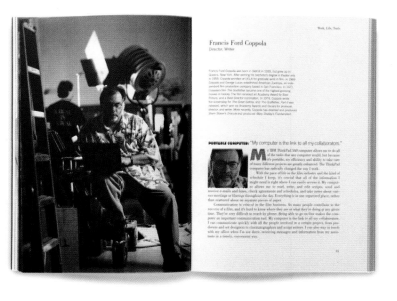

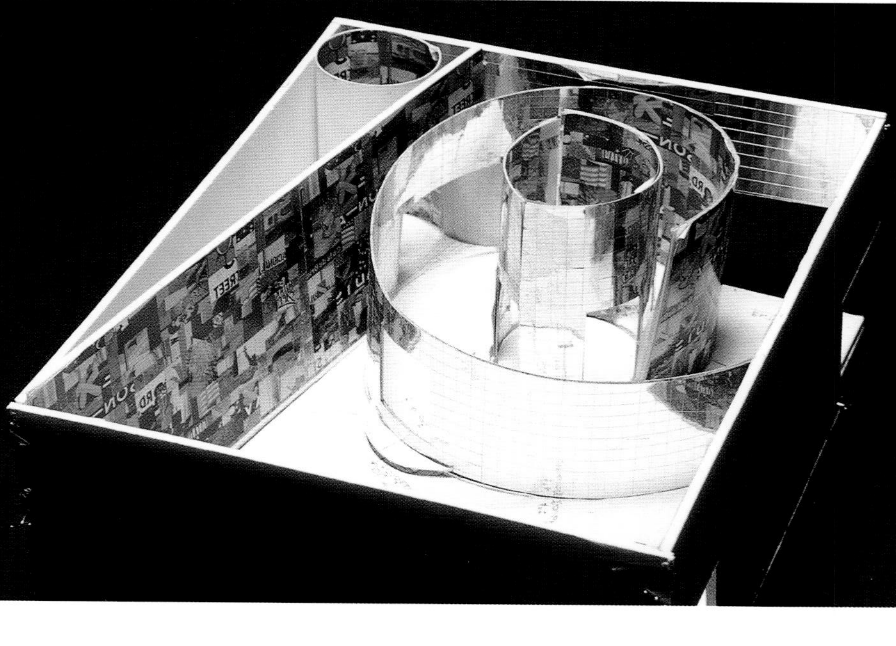

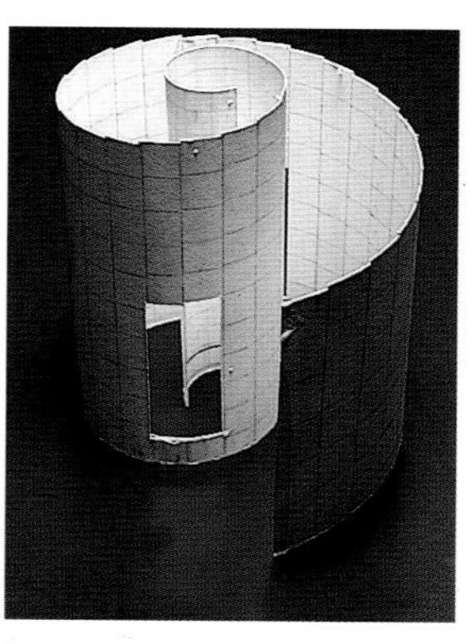

A Room at the Triennale

The city may be man's most significant creation, but as we know, living in one has its price. The endless onslaught on the senses often results in either immunity or collapse. Our interior for the Triennale attempted to recreate, on a tiny scale, the visual assault encountered daily in the city. There is something useful in removing things from their usual context in order to understand them better. The following text is a summary of our comments for the exhibition.

1. *Professional Signs.* These include the voice of government in the street signs, directional signs, and signs about what we can and cannot do. My suspicion is that the number of these signs increases in direct correspondence to the decline in the quality of life in the city. Included in this category are store signs as well as billboards and other advertising materials. Every designer I know has a collection of slides showing walls of torn posters from around the world. Their resemblance to both Schwitters's work and abstract expressionism has been duly noted. If something looks like art, but has no such intention or aspiration, what shall we call it?

2. *Non-Professional Signs.* These can be an intimate form of address that sometimes speaks to us directly from the heart. They may lack formal skill but they make up for it in vitality. Graffiti, which some scholars consider to be a new kind of folk art, can sometimes be subsumed under this heading. Tom Wolf said, "Graffiti is art... in somebody else's town." Charitably, we could say that the urge to deface and destroy the property values of the establishment reflects some of the fundamental conflicts endemic to city life.

3. *Art.* This refers to that class of objects in which the intention seems to go beyond the merely useful in trying to produce an aesthetic effect. When the effect is successful we yield to the metaphysical content. When the effect fails, we are amused or contemptuous.

4. *Inadvertent Art.* This gets back to the question raised in category 1. What is the relationship between art and intentionality? What must be observed is that on city streets we often prefer art that occurs accidentally to that which seems intentional. For those who possess visual awareness these art accidents are natural occurrences that can in fact become the subject matter for art; we also included neon, a terrible medium that produces extraordinary effects, or a wonderful medium that produces terrible effects.

5. *Reflections.* This is the central thematic and formal idea that binds this subject together. City life is an unending series of reflections. Sound and light bounce endlessly from room to room, building to building, street to street. We catch glimpses of ourselves in shop windows and the polished granite and stainless steel of office buildings. The form of our little room combines images and their reflections, including reflections of reflections, in an attempt to understand our city landscape.

BLOW-UP
AMINATE
RING THE BELL
305 CANAL ST.
№ 101
SO TO
WING MACH
HT · SOLD and S
100
AVENUE OF
THE AMERICAS
קהלת מורי׳
CONGREGATION MORYA
GRYPHON UPSTAIRS
650
№
ton
MEATS
POST NO BILLS
SAUTE TAXI INC
220 W.42 ST.
N.Y.C.
LOOK ONLY $1.00 DOZ
LIMELIGHT

SALE
CHEESE BURGER
WITH
LETTUCE-TOMATO
FRENCH FRIES
EXAS BURGER
nks & Beans
AT
&11
OMA
SUPER B
DRUG
CORP
CA 6 4151
VITAMINS
275
PPY
OVE
10% OFF with coupon
FREE ESTIMATE
BOXES DELIVERY
FIRST WARDROBE
Any Size Job
Empire
CURTAINS &
DRAPERIES
SARGE'S
RESTAURANT
SARGES
TRUCK ROUTE
LOCAL
Lincoln Tunnel
path
ONE WAY
BROADWAY COMPUTER
CORP.
SALES·SERVICE
PARTS·SUPPLIES
Hardware & Software For Your
APPLE & IBM PC
SINO
AMERICAN
TOURS
966-5866
DANNY'S
JEWELRY
PINK
GRAPEFRUIT
2 FOR 89¢
ENTRANCE
SIDE GATE
& HOUSTON STREETS

The exhibition alternated 5000 photographs taken by Matthew Klein with panels of mirror to create a complex environment in which these images were reflected and distorted in an attempt to suggest the urban visual experience.

59
Bolli
46
Rx
HARKIN GALLERY
675
712
995
JAGUAR
PORCHE
VOLVO
SUBURU
20
E
463-9000
D
A
SPECIAL
BREAKFAST
$1.07
EXPERIENCED
SALES GIRLS
WANTED
La Minita Spanish Ame
BEER SODA
HOT
COFFEE
Sandwiches
Snapple
BIG APPLE
FASTER
IN & OUT
650
148
RECORD FACTORY
Yankee
NEW

BELOW A three-dimensional "A" created from the alphabet we used for Sesame Place (p. 156)—only in this case made into a bench to sit on. We used other letters for the same purpose.

RIGHT An "A" with a drawn wing that replaces the cross bar, used as a logo together with the angel (p. 86) identifying the show "Angels in America."

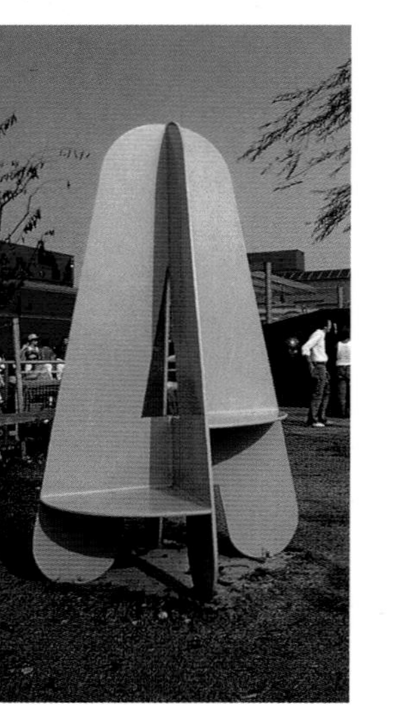

Words as Images

I think about everything the same way. I think of typography the same way I think of drawing. I think of shapes and letter forms the same way I think of the shape of three-dimensional objects. I tend to collapse everything into one idea; a kind of universality of form and shape and color where it doesn't matter whether I'm doing a drawing or a piece of sculpture or designing a typeface.

One of my best known type designs is Glaser Stencil. Part of the reason for designing it was my own needs, as these things frequently are. I like stencil typefaces and there were few acceptable stencils around that had any sort of visual coherence or quality. There was one familiar stencil typeface that replicated the form used on the sides of packing crates. It was not an attractive face in terms of its style, so I said to myself, "What the world needs is a more contemporary stencil face. Why don't I make one?"

I didn't see any necessity to reinvent the fine standards that Paul Renner, the inventor of Futura, had set. My sense of typography is based on history and the continuity of ideas in human civilization. Generally I don't see too much need for brand new typefaces.

In this particular case there seemed to be a missing element in the typographical vocabulary. Using the proportions of Futura and adding the sparkle of a stencil face, I intended it to be more contemporary-looking than existing stencil faces.

ABOVE Glaser Neo Stencil, Bold

IT'S TIME
TO TAKE
ARTHRITIS
SERIOUSLY

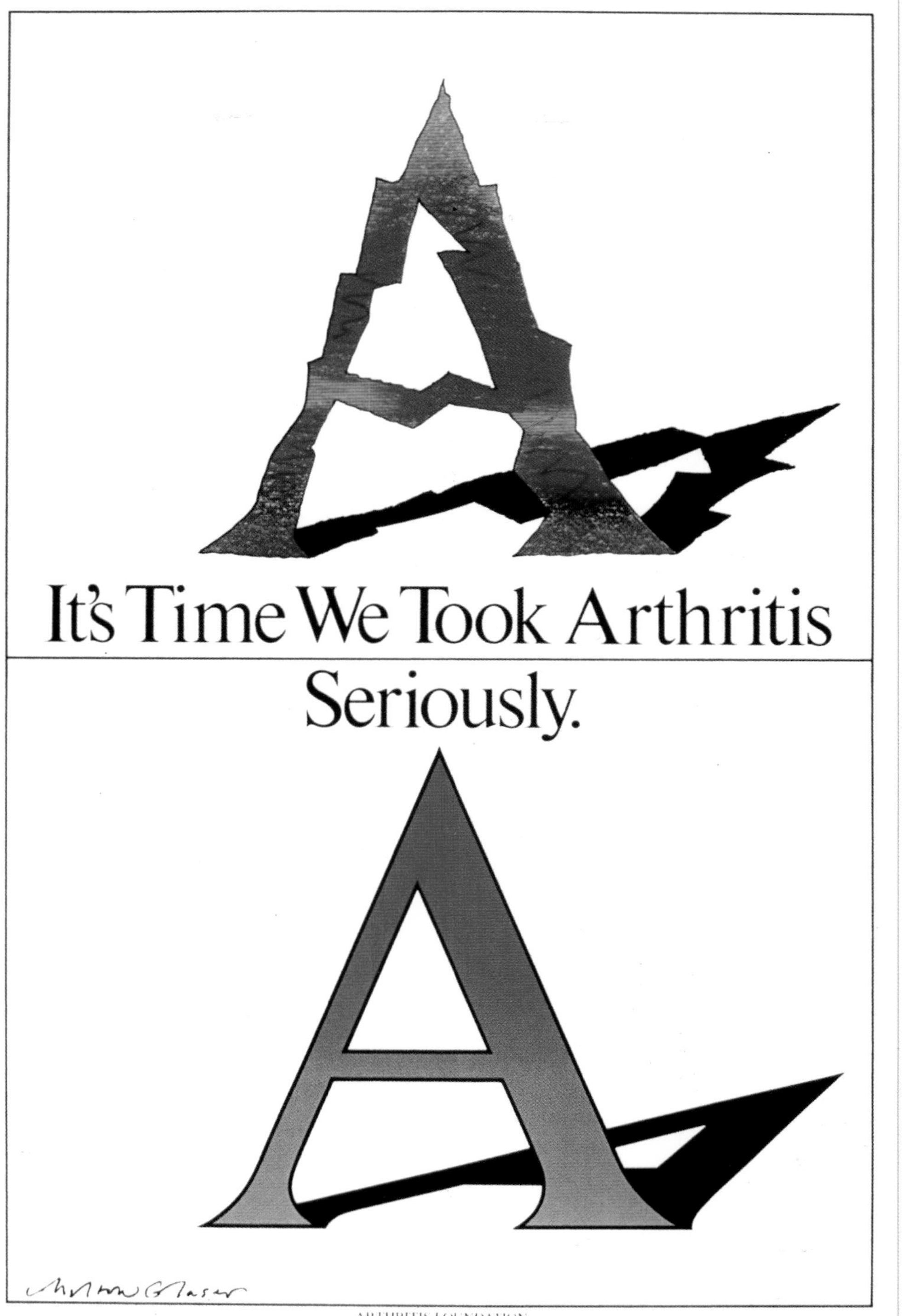
It's Time We Took Arthritis
Seriously.
ARTHRITIS FOUNDATION

LEFT The crippled "A" becomes healthy in the symbolic poster for the Arthritis Foundation.

BELOW LEFT A flight of stars begins in the "A" in a trademark for the New York Festival of the Arts.

BELOW The form of this "A" was intended to suggest the framework of a greenhouse, whose owners had the innovative idea of growing fresh herbs in a structure under the Queensboro Bridge, warmed by the exhaust heat of the Con Edison plant nearby.

NEW YORK CELEBRATES THE
ARTS
TM

ASTORIA
GREENHOUSE

RIGHT Mo Foner, an old time union organizer, asked me to design a poster that would spearhead a new organizational effort to recruit and organize membership. He suggested that the only text on the poster be the word "organize," in addition to any effective image. Because every image I tried seemed tired or melodramatic, I began to wonder whether the entire poster might be more strongly expressed by using the word itself. Without too much imagination one can see the form of the "O" as a shouting face coming forward in space. The opening of the "O" moves to the bottom of the word and transforms the letters into an exclamation mark.

RIGHT This book jacket's impact depends on limiting the amount of visual complexity. Here, the most direct presentation is to simply show the name of the author and the title of the book. The single color, red, stood out in the bookstore because it was surrounded by more complex and demanding material. The only gesture that deviated from complete simplicity was tilting the letter forms to evoke some reference to a tabloid announcement.

BELOW This jacket uses the simple idea of redundancy to create its impact. By overlaying the word "design," set in a traditional (Bodoni) typeface, with an oval that contains a sans serif (Franklin Gothic Bold Condensed), the suggestion that "new" design trumps "old" design is made.

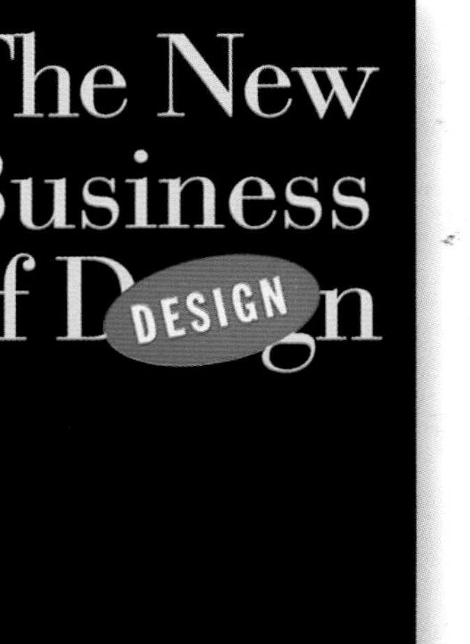

BELOW This design depends on creating a small puzzle for the viewer to solve. The "N" has to be recognized as the last letter of the word design and not as a word by itself. Since "N" isn't a word, the reader is encouraged to investigate another possibility. When the critical interval between seeing and understanding is too great, the reader abandons the effort and usually becomes irritated.

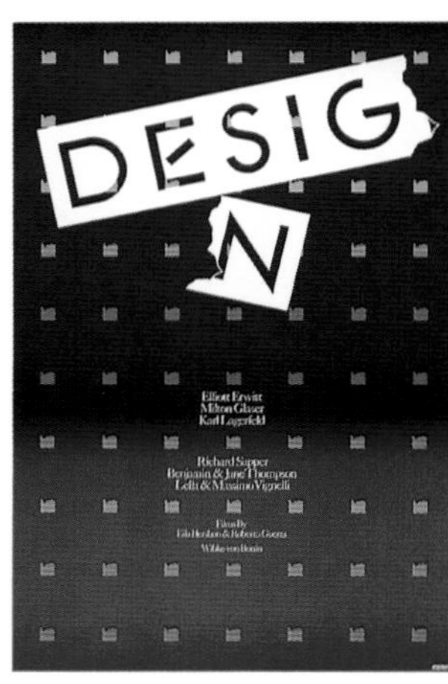

BELOW An early typographical experiment led to a solution that would have been difficult to read under most circumstances; in this case, because this is a calendar, and the preceding page reads "February," the possibility of confusion is minimized. What else would this be except "March?" The context helps understanding.

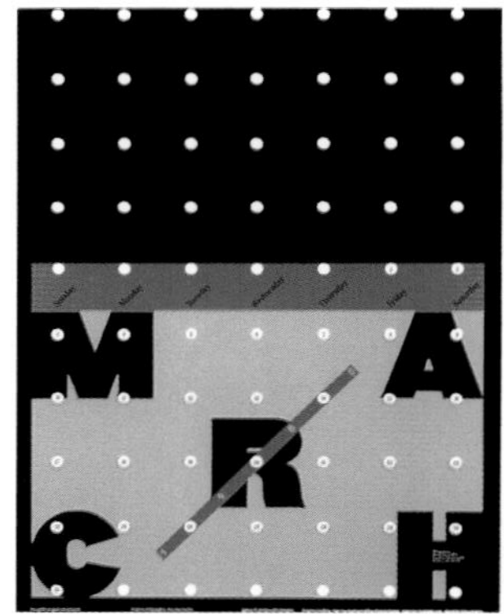

OPPOSITE PAGE Many years later, I tried a variation of the same idea for Vespa, an Italian maker of motor scooters. I had to depend on the Italian viewer's familiarity with the word and the characteristic front wheel of the scooter contained in the number fifty at the bottom of the page. Nevertheless, out of nervousness, I played it safe and put the name of the company in small type in the lower border.

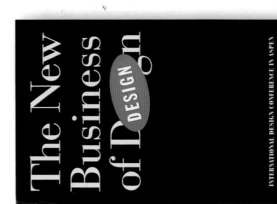

VESPA
50
50 YEARS OF VESPA

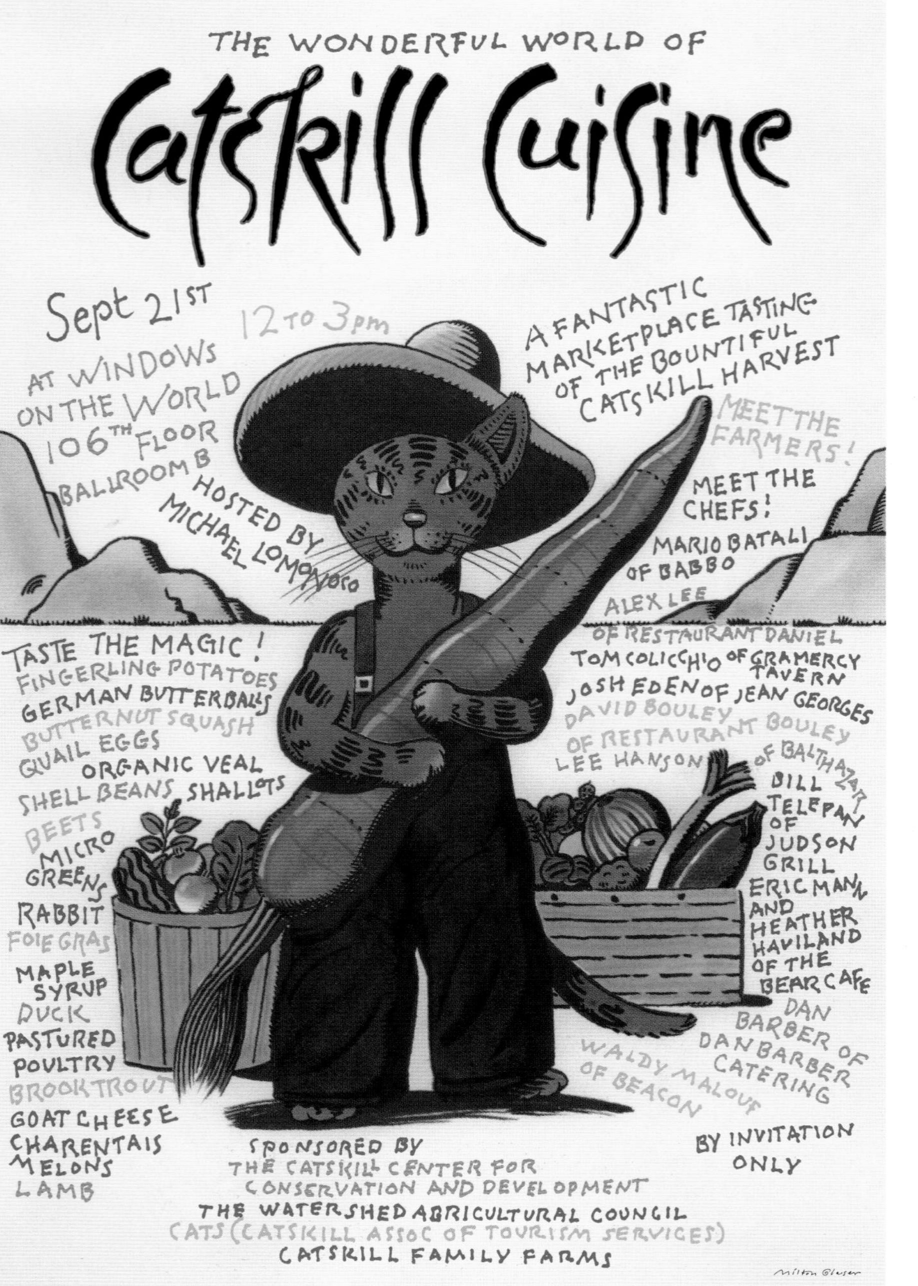

THE WONDERFUL WORLD OF
Catskill Cuisine
Sept 21ST
12 TO 3pm
AT WINDOWS ON THE WORLD 106TH FLOOR BALLROOM B
HOSTED BY MICHAEL LOMONACO
A FANTASTIC MARKETPLACE TASTING OF THE BOUNTIFUL CATSKILL HARVEST
MEET THE FARMERS!
MEET THE CHEFS!
MARIO BATALI OF BABBO
ALEX LEE OF RESTAURANT DANIEL
TOM COLICCHIO OF GRAMERCY TAVERN
JOSH EDEN OF JEAN GEORGES
DAVID BOULEY OF RESTAURANT BOULEY
LEE HANSON OF BALTHAZAR
BILL TELEPAN OF JUDSON GRILL
ERIC MANN AND HEATHER HAVILAND OF THE BEAR CAFE
DAN BARBER OF DAN BARBER CATERING
WALDY MALOUF OF BEACON
TASTE THE MAGIC!
FINGERLING POTATOES
GERMAN BUTTERBALLS
BUTTERNUT SQUASH
QUAIL EGGS
ORGANIC VEAL
SHELL BEANS SHALLOTS
BEETS
MICRO GREENS
RABBIT
FOIE GRAS
MAPLE SYRUP
DUCK
PASTURED POULTRY
BROOK TROUT
GOAT CHEESE
CHARENTAIS MELONS
LAMB
BY INVITATION ONLY
SPONSORED BY
THE CATSKILL CENTER FOR CONSERVATION AND DEVELOPMENT
THE WATERSHED AGRICULTURAL COUNCIL
CATS (CATSKILL ASSOC OF TOURISM SERVICES)
CATSKILL FAMILY FARMS

ABOVE Although there are thousands of typographic fonts available, sometimes none of them seems quite right. In this case I used my handwriting to create the visual texture that I wanted for this poster.

PP&M

LEFT Some years ago, in the sixties, I developed this logo for Peter, Paul & Mary using an Art Nouveau typeface.

BELOW Years later I designed the CD cover for an album that involved the participation of many other singers. I recreated the logo to read "Peter Paul Mary &."

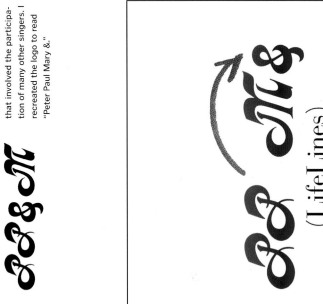

Designed by Milton Glaser

Helping.
Big Brothers Big Sisters of New York City
Since 1904, Founding Agency of the Mentoring Movement. Help us. 212.686.2042 www.bbbsny.org

RIGHT I was asked by Big Brothers Big Sisters to create an ad campaign using a new visual image for the agency. I discovered that it was impossible to create a visual image that didn't already look familiar and corny. I suggested that words would be more effective as a means of conveying their message. This solution focuses on the relationship between the words "Help" and "Helping," the first experienced as a shout of need, and the second as a response to that need.

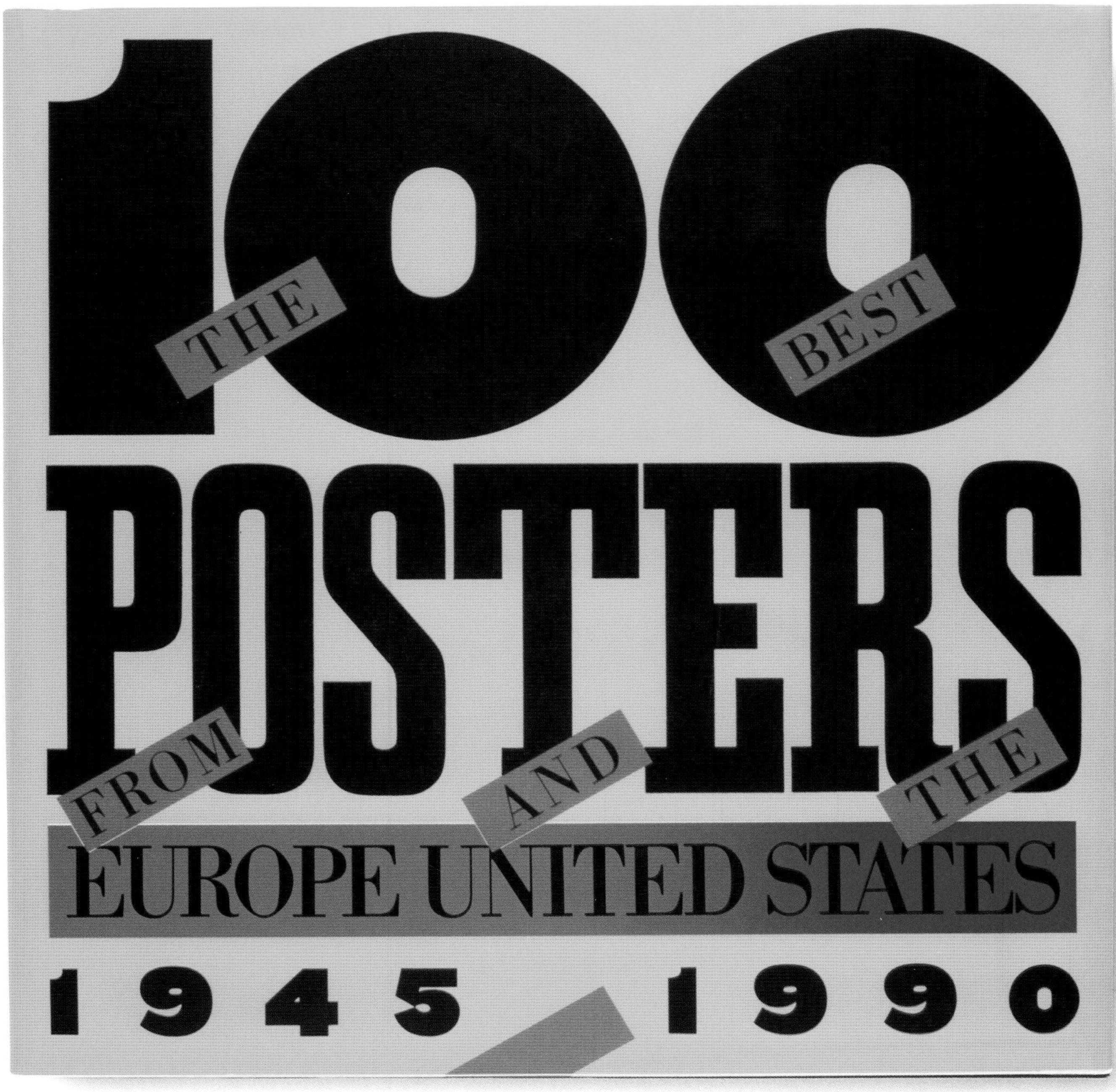

THE 100 BEST POSTERS FROM EUROPE AND THE UNITED STATES 1945 1990

ABOVE This jacket for a collection of *The Best 100 Posters of Europe and the United States* required a somewhat convoluted reading pattern, necessitated by the length of the title. By expressing the dominant ideas "100," "posters," "Europe," "United States," and "1945-1990," all the other additional supportive words became a decorative element on the surface. The presumption of visual sophistication on the part of the audience created this opportunity.

LEFT The end papers of the book used the same letter form of the "100" on the cover, this time counterpointed by a variation in diagonal movement of the supporting text.

Examples of posters for three Italian cities. Each depends to some extent on typographic playfulness.

RIGHT The first, for an effort to promote Naples, replaces the "A" in Napoli with a smoking Vesuvius. The word "Napoli" is written in a kind of old fashioned spencerian scrip rather than set in type, but for our purposes we can consider it to be a form of typography. If the viewer were not able to discern that Vesuvius was a substitute for the missing "A" the point would be lost, but since the poster was used only in Italy, and mostly in Naples, the risk seemed minimal. In the poster for Carnevale, the Tower of San Marco becomes a rocket over the Venetian Lagoon. The typography and my signature are reflected in it.

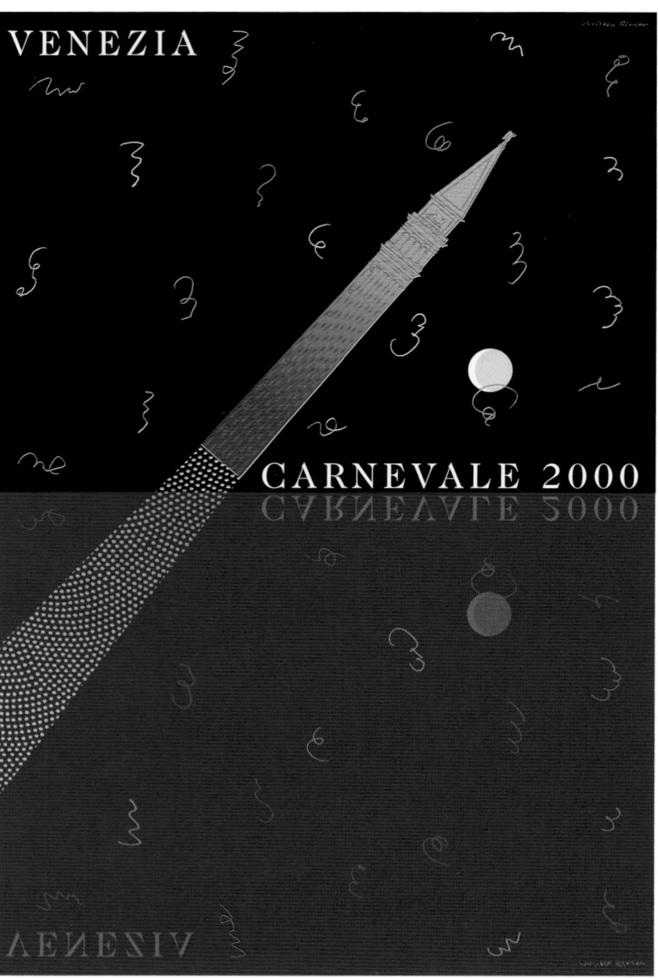

"Napoli" poster.
commissioned by the
"Napoli 99" Foundation,
as a contribution
towards the cultural
image of the city.

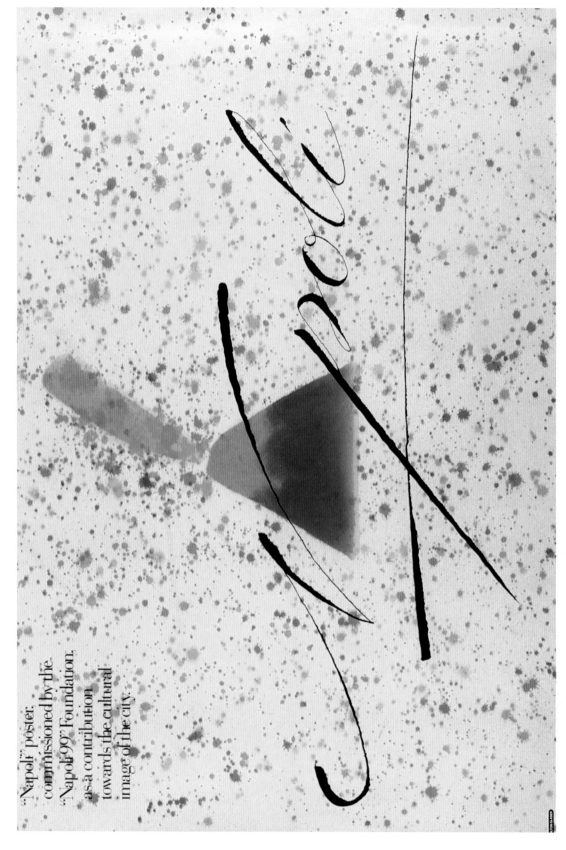

VENEZIA
CARNEVALE 2000

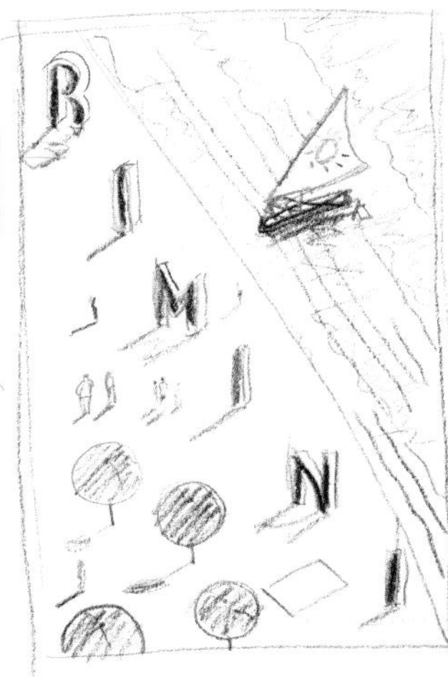

BELOW The resort city of Rimini wanted an identity program that would position it as an international destination and emphasize its historical importance. I designed a logo that incorporates the architectural form of a triumphal arch and a well-known church into its design.

RIGHT The poster uses the same letter forms but here the "M" goes for a dip in the ocean to express the idea of a seaside resort.

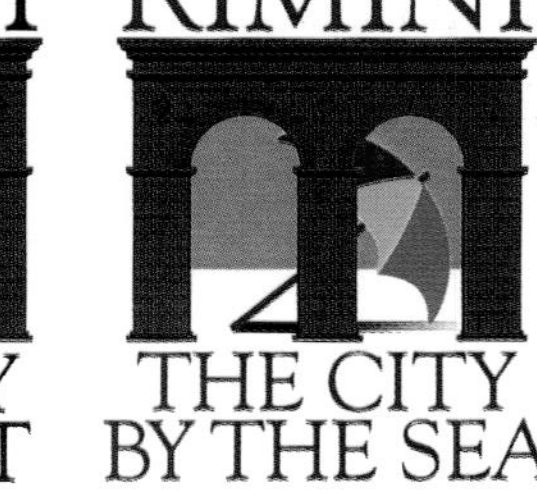

I've designed numerous alphabets, assisted by my long-time associate, George Leavitt, usually in relationship to specific assignments.

RIGHT "Kitchen" was designed for the Big Kitchen to reflect the giant letters that defined the entrance to that project (see page 205).

BELOW "Einstein Bold" was designed for the album *Einstein on the Beach*. The idea of the diagonal crossbar seemed interesting enough to build a complete alphabet around it.

CENTER The section heading for *TV Guide* shows how the letters of Einstein Bold could be used in conjunction with illustration.

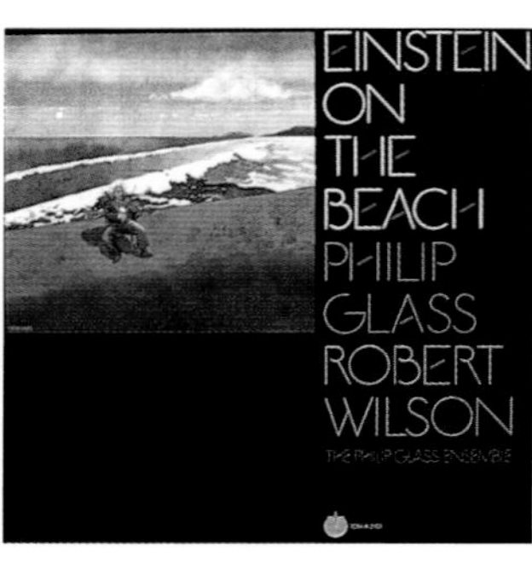

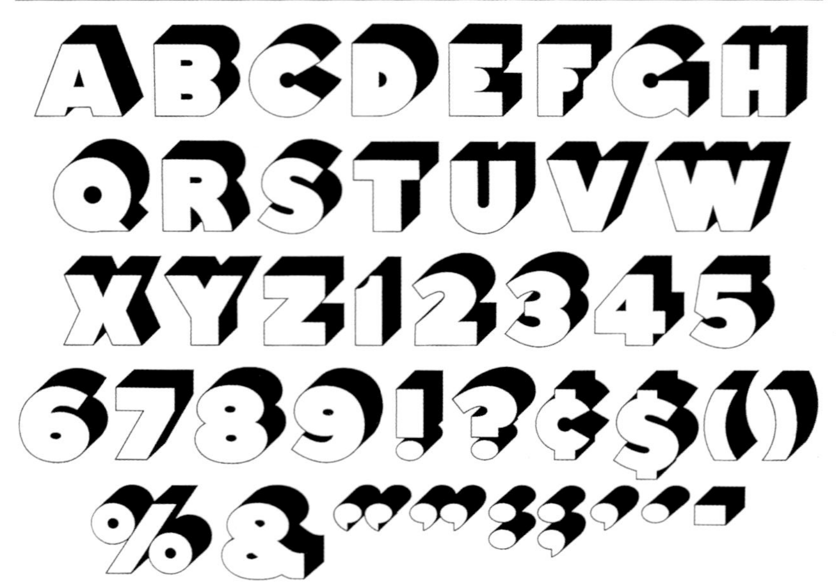

EINSTEIN BOLD

ABCDEFGHIJ
KLMNOPQR
STUVWXYZ&
8 9234575

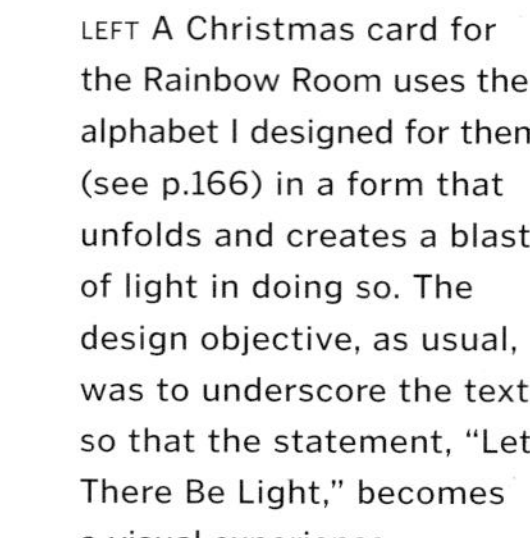

LEFT A Christmas card for the Rainbow Room uses the alphabet I designed for them (see p.166) in a form that unfolds and creates a blast of light in doing so. The design objective, as usual, was to underscore the text so that the statement, "Let There Be Light," becomes a visual experience.

L I G H T !
Every one of us wishes you a bright and shining year.
RAINBOW!
The only Rainbow that glows at night.

In 1975 Bill Doyle, then the Assistant Commissioner of Commerce for New York State, approached me with an interesting assignment. The state was about to embark on a new campaign to encourage tourism and raise residents' spirits. New York was perceived as a crime-ridden, unfriendly, if not hostile, location. The campaign using the phrase, "I Love New York" was intended to change that perception. What was needed to begin the process was a visual equivalent for the words. I produced a typographic solution, submitted it, and it was approved. A week later, I was doodling in a cab and another idea suggested itself. I called Doyle and said, "I have a better idea." "Forget it," he said. "Do you know how complicated it would be to get everybody together to approve it again?" "Let me show it to you," I implored. He came down to the office, nodded, took away the new sketch, called a meeting and had it approved.

I ♥ NY

This little item that almost didn't come into being has become my most familiar work. It has been called, with some hyperbole, the most frequently replicated piece of printed ephemera of the century. It is true that it has become so much a part of the general language that it's hard to imagine that it was actually designed by someone and did not always exist.
Why and how this ever came about is a mystery to me.

BELOW Here is something that drives me mad. Because the trademark originally was not copyrighted in order to encourage its use, anyone could do whatever they wished with it. In this example, someone decided to insert the word "love" in the center of the heart, assuming that the audience would not be clever enough to figure it out themselves. Since the entire effect depends on the viewer solving a simple puzzle—i.e., "I" is a complete word, the ❤ is a symbol for love, and NY are the initials for a place, the insertion of the word "love" destroys the effect. The spirit behind Mencken's famous line, "Nobody ever went broke underestimating the intelligence of the American public," turns out to be self-fulfilling, mischievous and responsible for a lot of the banal and patronizing work we see around us.

FAR RIGHT A series of posters designed for New York State during the same campaign to encourage tourism.

Dutch magazine, Issue #25, 2000

My favorite version of the logo.

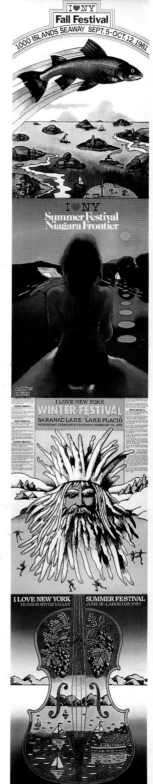

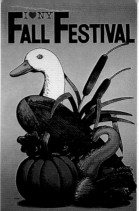

BISTROT
A CURA DI GUALTIERO MARCHESI
BRUNCH
A CURA DI GUALTIERO MARCHESI

Three parts of a Milanese restaurant

ABOVE Three divisions of a record company.

An upscale pizza joint.

Tomato, the record company.

AIDS logo

Tusk, a subsidiary of Overlook Press.

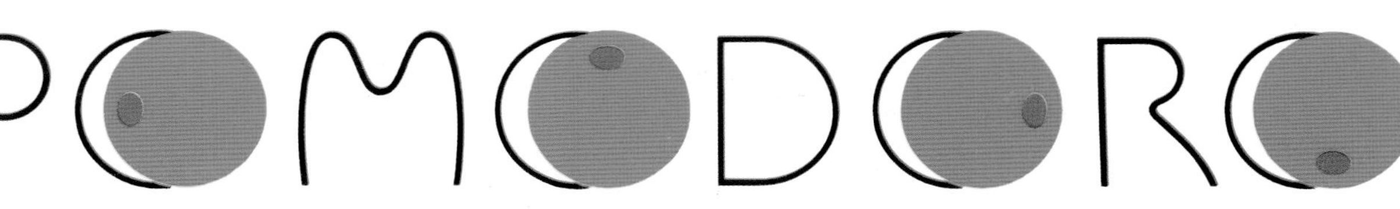

Pomodoro, a logo for a restaurant designed by Adam Tihany.

Positano, another Italian restaurant.

ZOETROPE STUDIOS

Frances Ford Copolla's film production company

A logo for a technology company.

OPPOSITE PAGE I love cooking and I have designed many cook books over the years. This one, for Zarella Martinez's *Food From My Heart* was for Mexican food.

Logo for the New York Festival of the Arts "Arts Education Week."

BELOW The DC Comics logo violates the accepted rule about logos, which is that they remain fixed in form. Here the logo becomes a "character," not unlike a super hero, and adopts the same playful animated quality. The logo is used in a variety of different positions, sometimes tumbling through space but always remaining clearly identifiable.

A label for an Italian restaurant's house wine.

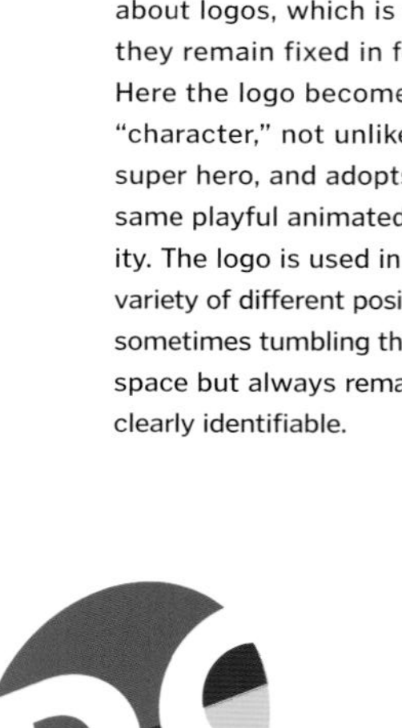

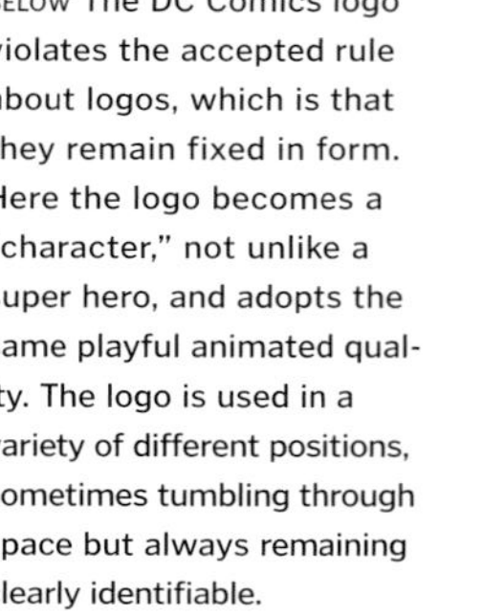

Barron's, a book publisher.

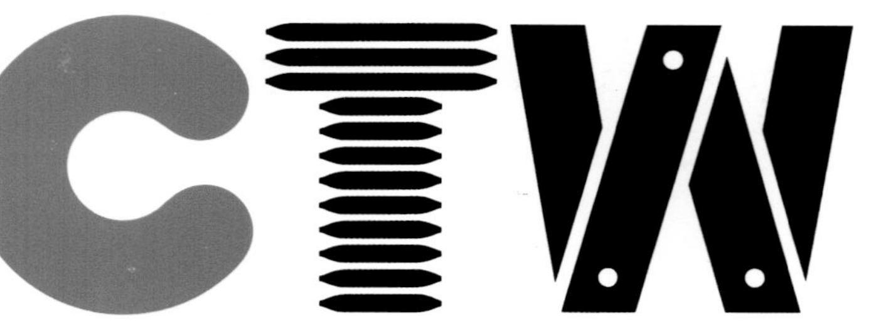

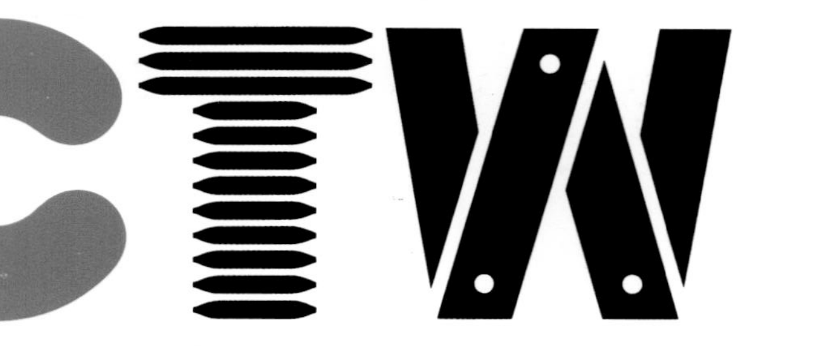

Children's Television Workshop.

The New York Beer Festival.

Zarela
MARTÍNEZ
Food
FROM MY
Heart
Cuisines of Mexico Remembered and Reimagined

ANNO 1894

GUNDEL

A dear friend, George Lang, who, together with his wife, Jennifer, runs the splendid Café Des Artistes restaurant in New York, also operate, in partnership with Ronald Lauder, Gundel, Hungary's most celebrated dining spot. The restaurant is in a turn-of-the-century landmark building next to the zoo in Budapest. Because of its Art Nouveau character and its proximity to the zoo, the solution to its identity symbol seems inevitable. The somewhat peculiar form of the lettering lent itself to a variety of uses, shown here in two posters.

ÚJRA NYÍLIK 1992 TAVASZÁN A VÁROSLIGETBEN
GUNDEL

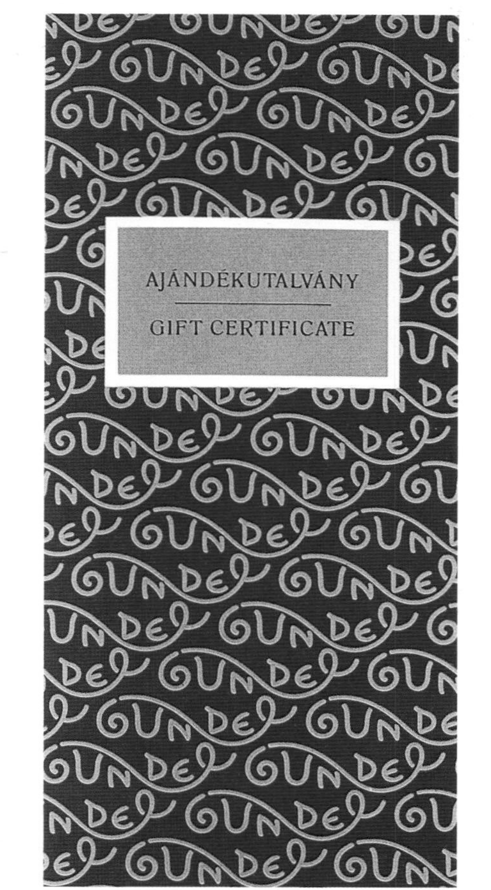
AJÁNDÉKUTALVÁNY
GIFT CERTIFICATE

When I was designing a logo for the fortieth anniversary of the School of Visual Arts, I decided to use an element of the school's facade, OPPOSITE, as a starting point. Almost inadvertently it began to look like a Frank Stella painting, which in this case was perhaps appropriate. The "4" used the vertical member of the window to define it and the "O" is inferred as it disappears behind the semicircle. All the windows were painted with this design during the anniversary year.

RIGHT The poster for the event seemed ordinary in its first iteration, where a variety of logos were combined on a flat surface. It became more interesting when I allowed them to curl and had them photographed by Matthew Klein in a way that emphasized their dimensionality. The highlights and shadows that were created help activate the surface and make the effect more illusionary.

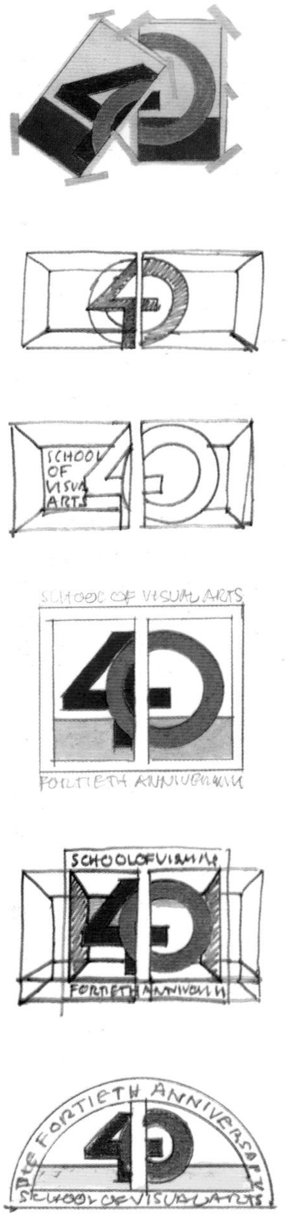

SVA - THE FIRST FORTY YEARS
(212) 689-5881

FRANK STELLA, CASTELLI GALLERY

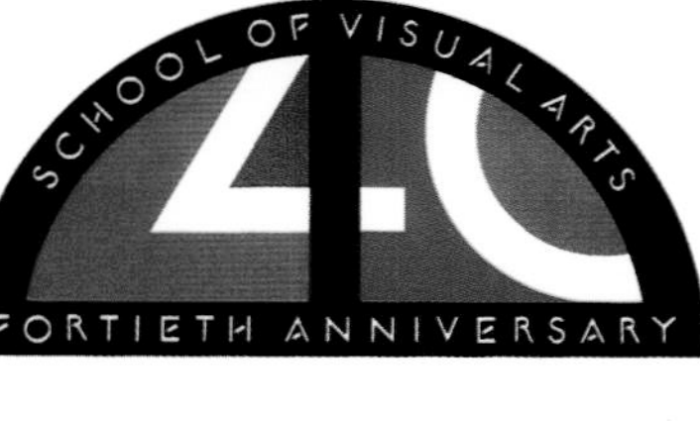

PHOTO: HAL STUCKER

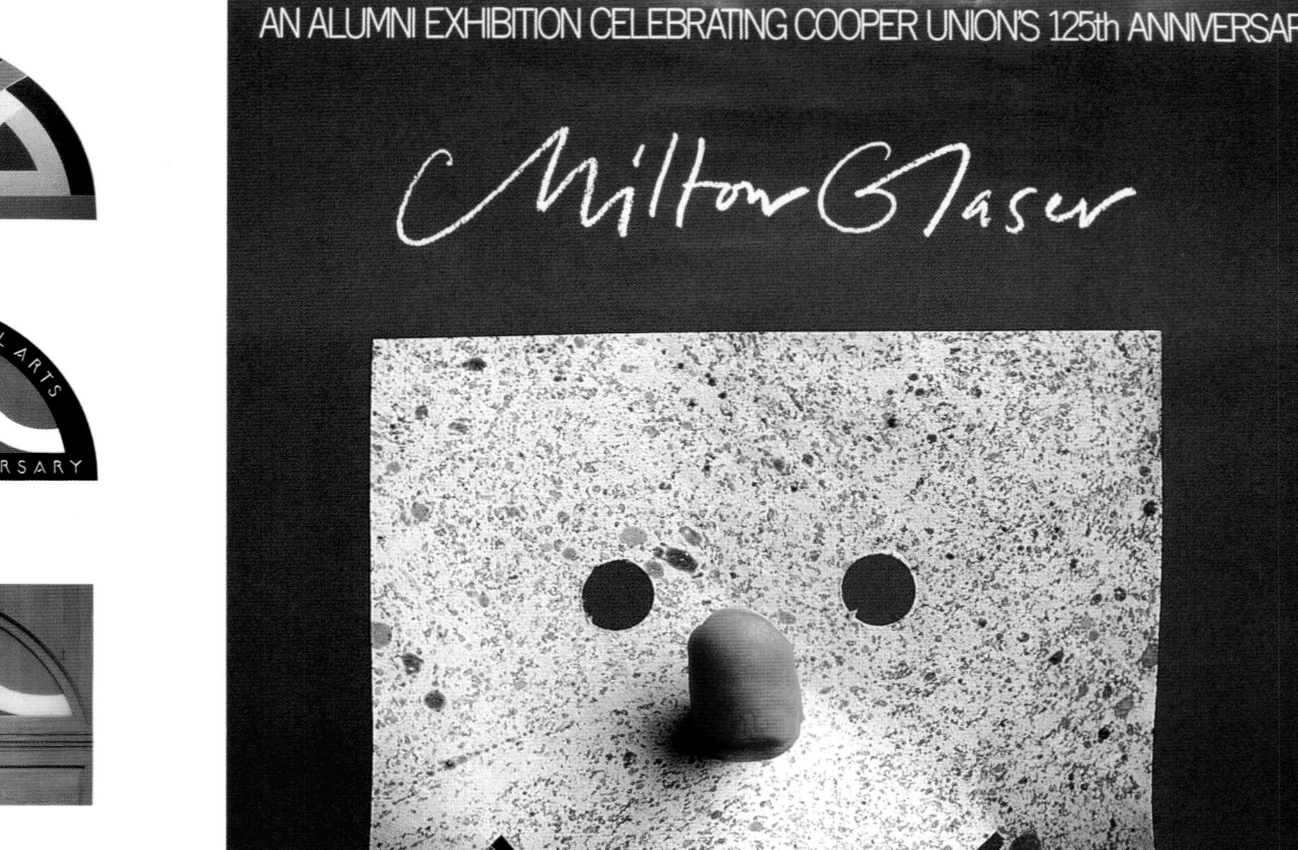

AN ALUMNI EXHIBITION CELEBRATING COOPER UNION'S 125th ANNIVERSARY
Milton Glaser
The Houghton Gallery
Cooper Union
Seven East Seventh Street
New York, NY 10003
September 6-28, 1984

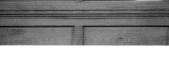

RIGHT Originally done as a cover for *Graphis* magazine, this exploration of a scrap of paper and my hand also served as an announcement for a show at Cooper Union.

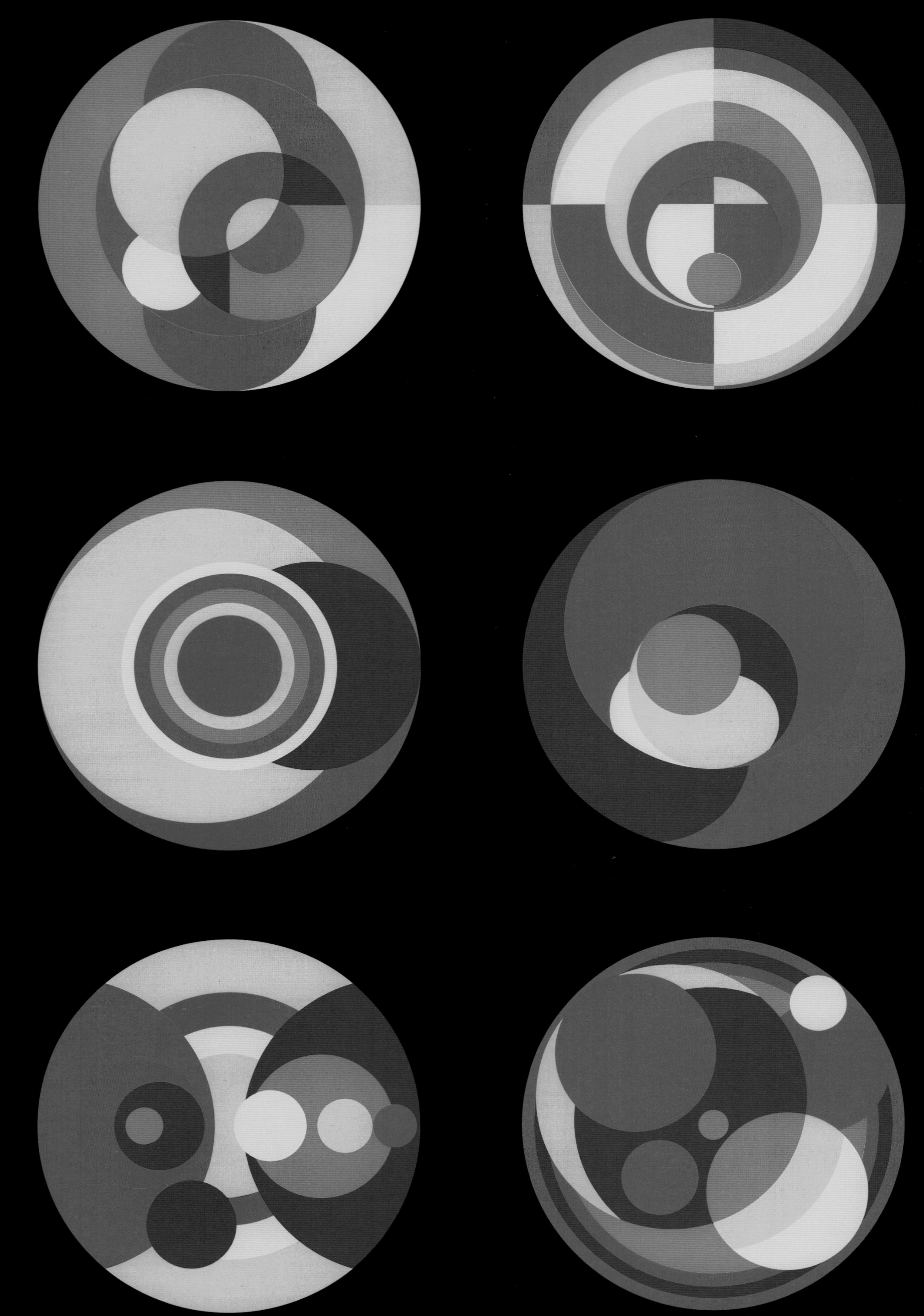

STONY BROOK

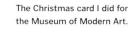

Shirley Kenny, president of Stony Brook University in New York, a remarkable educator and a wonderful friend, asked me to design a mural to enliven a narrow area in the student lounge. I thought that a series of harmonizing circular shapes could make the existing lighting look intentional. From that observation it was a small step to the idea of creating a bicycle race with moving wheels, especially since I've been obsessed with Duchamp's experimental "rotoscopes" for years. I once did a Christmas card for the Museum of Modern Art based on the observation that when circular, off-center elements were rotated, the illusion of internal motion was extraordinary. The mural is based on this fact. Every fifteen minutes a race begins, first slowly but then accelerating until the wheels become a blur. Each change of speed produces another color effect.

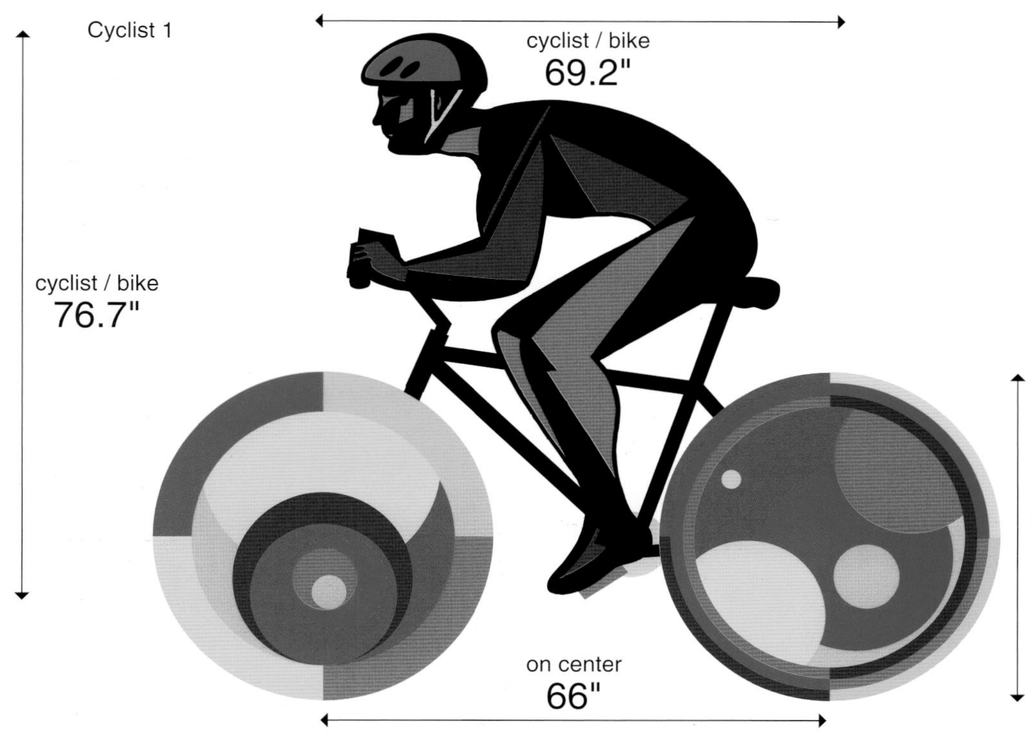

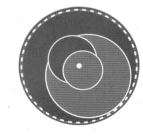

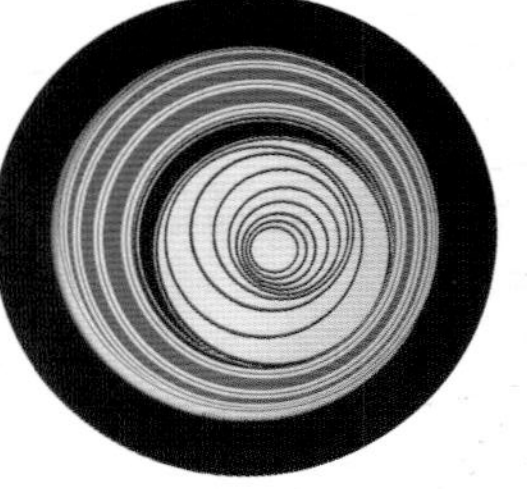
MARCEL DUCHAMP "ROTORELIEF" 1935

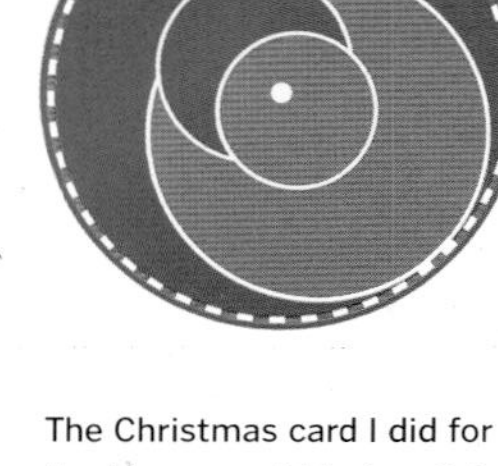
The Christmas card I did for the Museum of Modern Art.

I first started working with Shirley Kenny when she was president of Queens College in New York. When she moved to Stony Brook, I moved with her. She is a profound example of how a single person's goodwill can transform institutions. The studio does all sorts of interesting things for the university, including signage, identity, posters, awards, magazines, and anything else that enlivens campus life.

Whatever you want to do in life, we can put you on the right path. You want to study the inside of computers or combustion engines, hearts or heads? Our first-class faculty will inspire you, and our classes will ignite you (just look below at a sampling of more than 800 we offer). All at reasonable tuition—we can stretch your mind without breaking the bank.

STONY BROOK
STATE UNIVERSITY OF NEW YORK

After work, there's play, and we have plenty of that. We're moving into Division I athletics, with the best Sports Complex around. We've got clubs for every interest, from astronomy to yoga, and people from every background, from Albania to Zaire. The doors are open and the welcome is warm. Come on and add your own talents to the mix.

At Stony Brook we have harmony within diversity, many voices and many interests blending together in a single great enterprise.

DISCOVER THE EXCITEMENT OF LEARNING

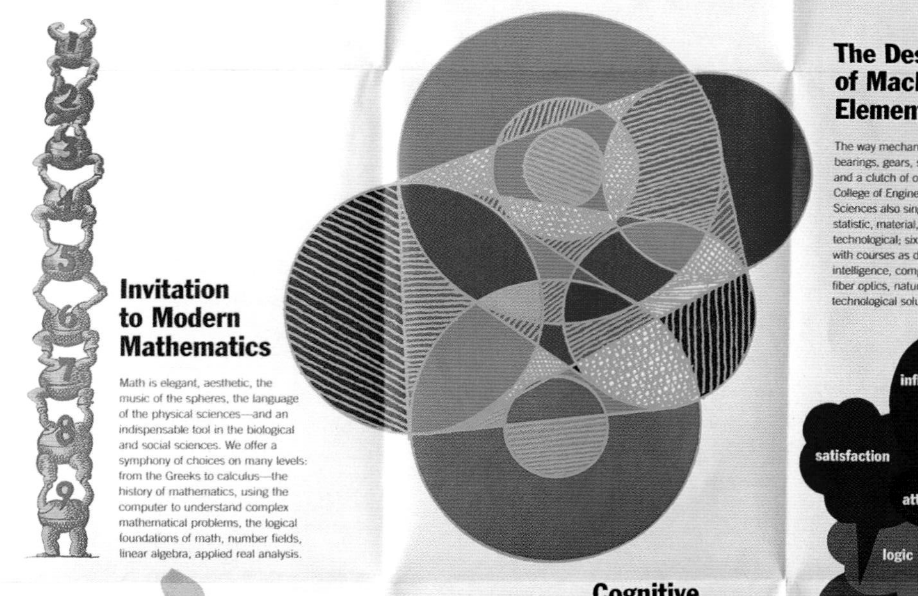

Invitation to Modern Mathematics

Math is elegant, aesthetic, the music of the spheres, the language of the physical sciences—and an indispensable tool in the biological and social sciences. We offer a symphony of choices on many levels: from the Greeks to calculus—the history of mathematics, using the computer to understand complex mathematical problems, the logical foundations of math, number fields, linear algebra, applied real analysis.

The Design of Machine Elements

The way mechanical things work—bearings, gears, shafting, fasteners, and a clutch of other things. Our College of Engineering and Applied Sciences also sings the body electric, statistic, material, computational, and technological; six different majors with courses as diverse as artificial intelligence, computer architecture, fiber optics, natural disasters, and technological solutions.

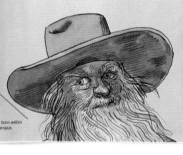

Cognitive Psychology

What happens when the mind recognizes or remembers, understands or solves problems? Gain insights through an examination of work done on human cognition. Our first-rate Psychology Department offers a wide range of compelling courses, including the psychology of eating and drinking, social psychology, theories of personality, and the psychology of work.

Botany and Biotechnology

We need plants more than they need us, for food, shelter, clothing, medicines, and industrial raw materials. Your view of the world will change once you take this course and others, including dinosaur evolution, genetics, biological clocks, marine ecology, agricultural systems, the brain and how it's a target of disease.

"Find out a lot more about Stony Brook on the other side."

Our own Walt Whitman, born within a stone's throw of the campus

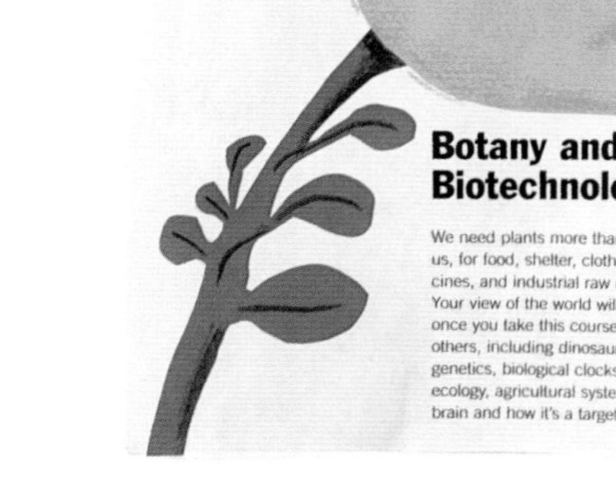

Walt Whitman, who lived near the Stony Brook campus on Long Island, is the symbol for the library that peers at you each time you open one of their letters.

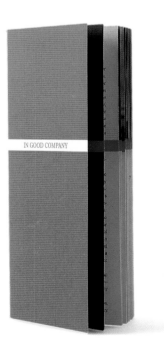

SAVE THESE APRIL 1998 DATES & CELEBRATE!
STATE UNIVERSITY OF NEW YORK
STONY BROOK
40TH
ANNIVERSARY
JOIN US!
STONY BROOK: MANY VOICES, MANY VISIONS, ONE UNIVERSITY

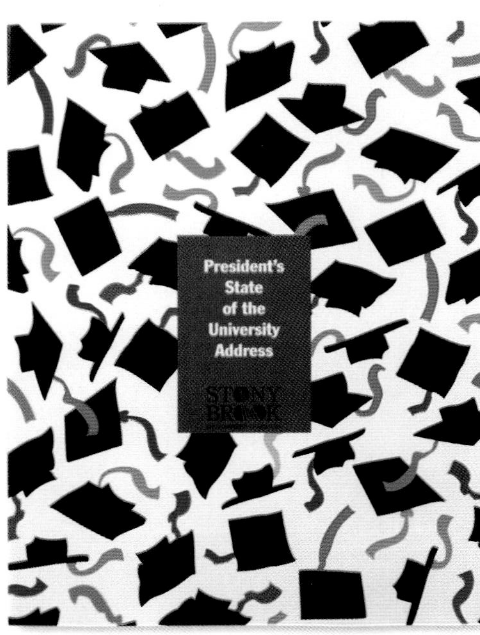

President's State of the University Address
STONY BROOK

THE ECOLOGY OF STONY BROOK

Expand your universe at a great university.

STONY BROOK

STONY BROOK
SUMMER SESSIONS 2000
UNDERGRADUATE AND GRADUATE COURSES
THE UNIVERSITY WITH A MIND OF ITS OWN.

RIGHT The kinetic "Stars of Stony Brook" award, constructed by Nicolas Fasciano.

RIGHT A bagel company approached us to do a corporate identity for their stores. We created a linkage between the idea of freshly baked bagels and time. The logo began with a clock that employed the same mechanism as the Stony Brook bicycle wheels. An illusion of dancing bagels is animated when the central disc of the clock rotates. The clock face was then translated into a flat graphic representation for use as a logo on their printed materials.

OPPOSITE PAGE A proprietary alphabet developed for the same client. Used in combination with the typeface "Gill Sans" it provided a distinctive look for all their interior signage and wall menus.

BRUGGERS REGULAR

A B C D E F G
H I J K L M N
O P Q R S T U
V W X Y Z 1 2
3 4 5 6 7 8 9
0 ' . ! ? , ; : - -- _
+ " & $ C # %
( ) [ ] / *

BRUGGERS BOLD

A B C D E F G
H I J K L M N
O P Q R S T U
V W X Y Z 1 2
3 4 5 6 7 8 9
0 ' . ! ? , ; : - - _
+ " & $ C # %
( ) [ ] / *

BRUEGGER'S

THAT WAS THEN

THIS IS NOW

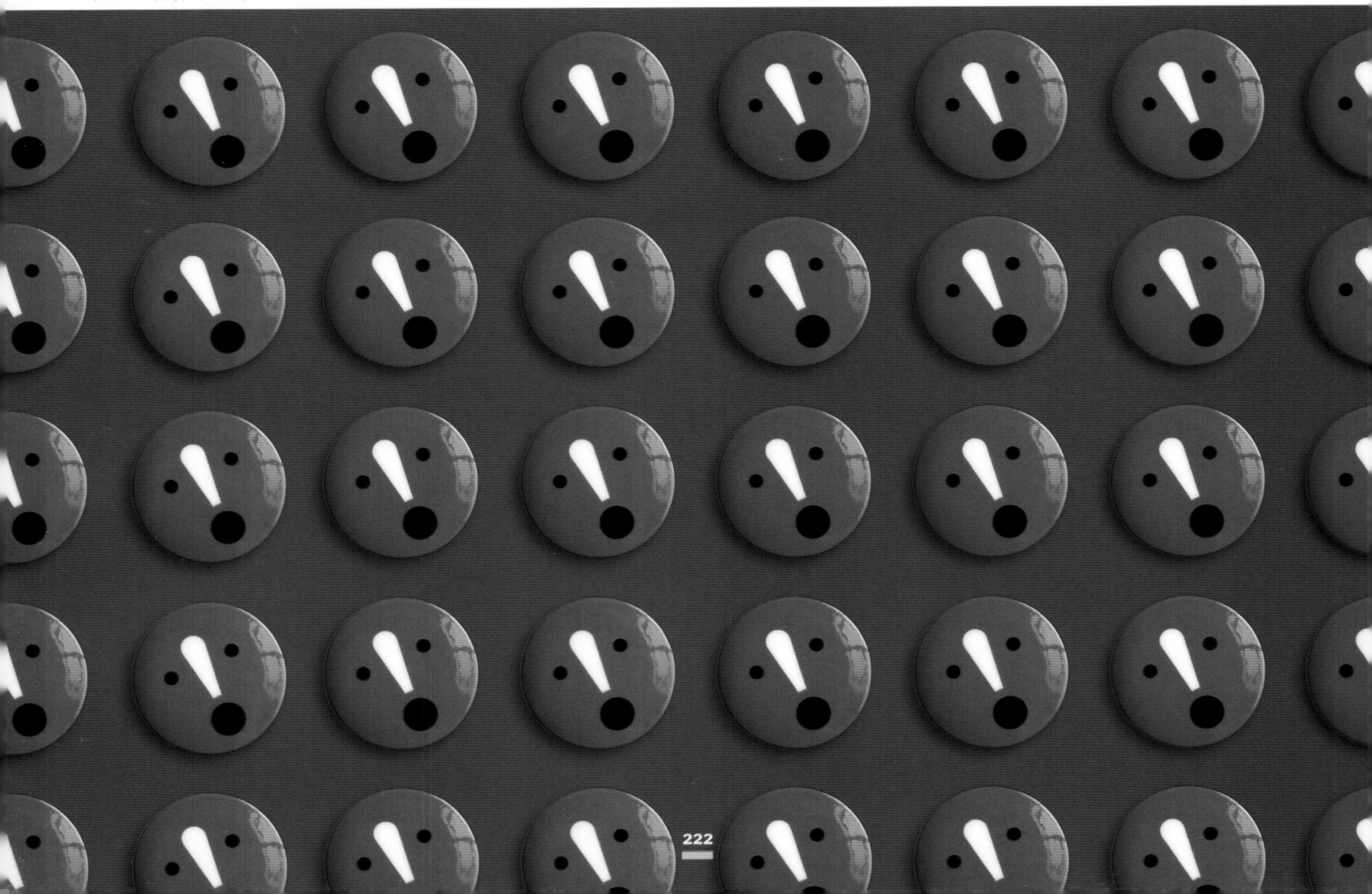

ANGELO ROGNONI, "BOMBARDAMENT A LA COTE 146, 1917

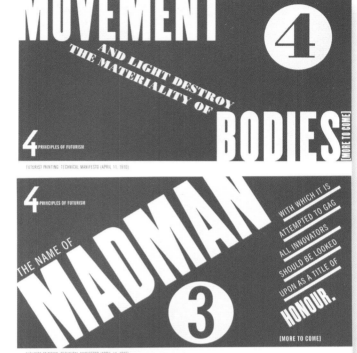

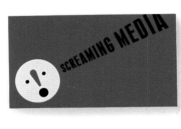

MOVEMENT
AND LIGHT DESTROY
THE MATERIALITY OF
BODIES
[MORE TO COME]
4 PRINCIPLES OF FUTURISM
THE NAME OF
MADMAN
WITH WHICH IT IS
ATTEMPTED TO GAG
ALL INNOVATORS
SHOULD BE LOOKED
UPON AS A TITLE OF
HONOUR.
[MORE TO COME]

I first met Jay Chiat in 1976 in Los Angeles, when Clay Felker and I were starting *New West Magazine*. Jay's agency, a small hot shop, was given the job of launching the magazine. The launch was successful, but the magazine faltered because Clay and I didn't really understand the difference between northern and southern California. Jay's agency, Chiat Day, grew explosively and did a lot of very good advertising, including the almost legendary Apple "1984" commercial shown *once* on a Superbowl broadcast and talked about ever since. Jay left advertising in 1995 and after a few years resurfaced as the CEO of an e-commerce business that organizes and sells custom news to web sites. When Jay asked me to design an identity for the business, I thought that the polemic language of the Futurist Manifesto would be an appropriate form of address. The idiom required some detoxification since the futurists were not only Fascists but were misogynists and racists as well. On the other hand, their call for sweeping away old thinking and pursuing what was fresh and revolutionary was very much related to Screaming Media's position in business. We developed a screaming face trade mark that proved immediately attractive, and we printed four different parts of the manifesto on the back of stationery.

RIGHT We also used various parts of the futurist text to decorate the interior of the office as an alternative to hanging pictures.

"MADMAN" WITH WHICH IT IS ATTEMPTED TO GAG ALL INNOVATORS SHOULD BE LOOKED UPON AS A TIT
WE SHALL SING THE LOVE OF
DANGER,
THE HABIT OF
ENERGY
AND BOLDNESS

OF FACTORIES SUSPENDED FROM THE CLOUDS
BY THEIR STRINGS OF SMOKE; OF BRIDGES
OF BROAD-CHESTED LOCOMOTIVES PRANCING ON THE RA

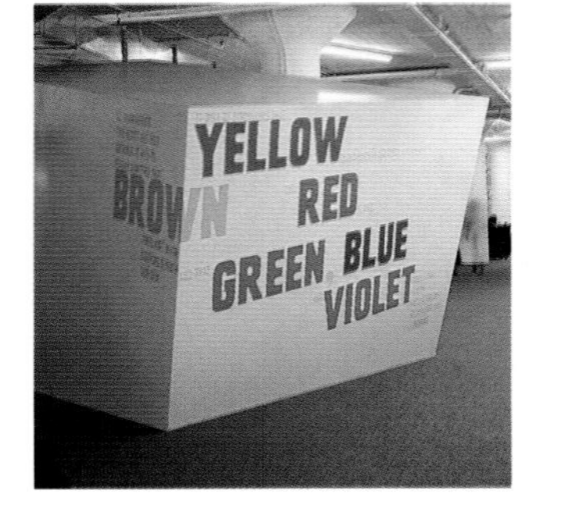

Giorgio Soavi and Olivetti

From a forthcoming book on the history of the Olivetti Corporation by Giorgio Soavi.

In most lives there are golden moments—times that pass effortlessly and happily, in which we feel we are at our best. Frequently, like the fish in water that is unaware it is in water, we become conscious of those happy times only in retrospect.

My work with Olivetti, and more precisely with Giorgio Soavi, was one of those golden periods that shed its glow over my life and influenced it in countless ways, both professionally and personally.

I remember receiving a phone call in New York during the '60s, from Milano. The voice at the other end spoke quite understandable but idiosyncratic English in a charming, one might say, seductive, tone. "I am Giorgio Soavi of Olivetti. Would you like to come to Milano? I have a project that I think might interest you."

Within days I was on a plane to Milano without ever checking on who was paying for the flight.

I don't recall whether I went to Soavi's office immediately upon arrival or after a night's sleep. As I entered his office, he looked at me and said, "You are Glaser, I am Soavi." He sounded taller on the telephone. In those days, Giorgio looked like a 7/8-scale Irish poet, only better dressed. He had light hair, a fair complexion and favored English sportcoats. One could describe him the same way today. He projected a sense of crackling energy that affected everyone who entered the room.

The space was filled with religious icons, mechanical toys, plastic food, art books, industrial prototypes, paper samples, press proofs, color swatches, printed ephemera of every imaginable kind, and dozens of projects still in the works. For anyone interested in the visual world, the room was an overwhelming buffet. The job he called about involved the design for all of Olivetti's promotional materials for the Mexican Olympics.

I returned to New York and, working with my former partner, Seymour Chwast, we developed a series of design proposals. The core idea was that everything would be round, starting with stylized Mayan masks, but going on to include stationery, note pads, address books, posters, etc. The idea was clearly absurd. Not only was it impractical, but it would add thousands of dollars to the cost of the job, not to mention the endless production headaches. Soavi was unfazed and enthusiastic. He immediately put the material into production. He was a man who thoroughly believed in Diaghilev's dictum, "astonish me," as the basis for his job as corporate design director of Olivetti.

The corporate atmosphere at Olivetti reflected its history of social concern for its employees, its enlightened commitment to design and the arts, and its generosity to the public. The history of the company, including the socialist and humanitarian impulses of the founders, has been well documented, but the consequences of those beginnings and their effects on the culture of the company are still difficult to describe.

Renzo Zorzi, Soavi's "boss" and patron in charge of marketing, was typical of the company's executives. A shy, tall, stork-like man who was primarily an academic, he passionately supported Soavi's "inventions" which made everything possible.

The atmosphere at Olivetti made it difficult to do mediocre work. Soavi had a way of selecting the perfect assignment for each of the designers he worked with, and then inspiring them to do their best work. In this regard, he was the best art director I have ever worked with (although he resists that title), perhaps because he is also a poet, novelist, critic, biographer, and maker and collector of extraordinary objects.

There were many other jobs through the years. One poster for the Sottsass Valentine typewriter replicated the intarsia decorations of the Duke of Montefeltro's library and showed the typewriter as if it were made of wood. Another showed a mournful dog at the feet of its sleeping or dead master—an image based on a painting by Piero de Cosimo—with the bright red Valentine in the background. No other company in the world would try to sell typewriters this way.

One year Soavi asked me to illustrate a series of short stories by Gogol under the heading of *Tales of St. Petersburg* (page 116). I had a marvelous time with these surreal tales, picking the stories that I found most suitable for illustration. When I presented them to Giorgio, he looked at my efforts and said, "Very nice, Glaser, but these are not the stories we are using for the book." I was distraught. "No matter," said Soavi after a moment's reflection, "I'll just run them at random through the book as an atmospheric accompaniment." Which he did. The man was fearless.

It is difficult to describe the spirit of generosity and creativity that characterized Olivetti in those days. There was a pervasive sense of optimism and pride in the company that brought out the best in people. There were many social and cultural interventions, the restoration of frescos, innumerable exhibitions of art and design, not to mention the countless gifts to friends and customers. In fact, the most significant part of his job seemed to be the invention of these gifts—diaries, superbly illustrated books by the best artists in the world, ashtrays, luggage, desk sets, all beautifully designed and given away freely.

At the time, and now in retrospect, Olivetti was the very model of corporate responsibility. The company clearly demonstrated that a corporation could operate within a framework of humanistic concern.

The world and the nature of business have changed. Economic and financial considerations drive corporate decisions, leaving little room for alternative values. Olivetti is no longer the same.

Some of the posters for Olivetti were comments on Italian art history.

ABOVE The Mourning Dog, from a Piero di Cosimo painting, remains one of my favorite animal images of all time.

RIGHT The wooden cabinet derives directly from the inlaid walls in the Duke of Urbino's study, with the unexpected addition of a wooden typewriter.

VALENTINE OLIVETTI

PEIRO DI COSIMO "MOURNING DOG"

LEFT Olivetti introduced a typewriter with a ball mechanism and wanted to emphasize that fact with a series of posters. The falling figures trail the ribbons of the available printing colors.

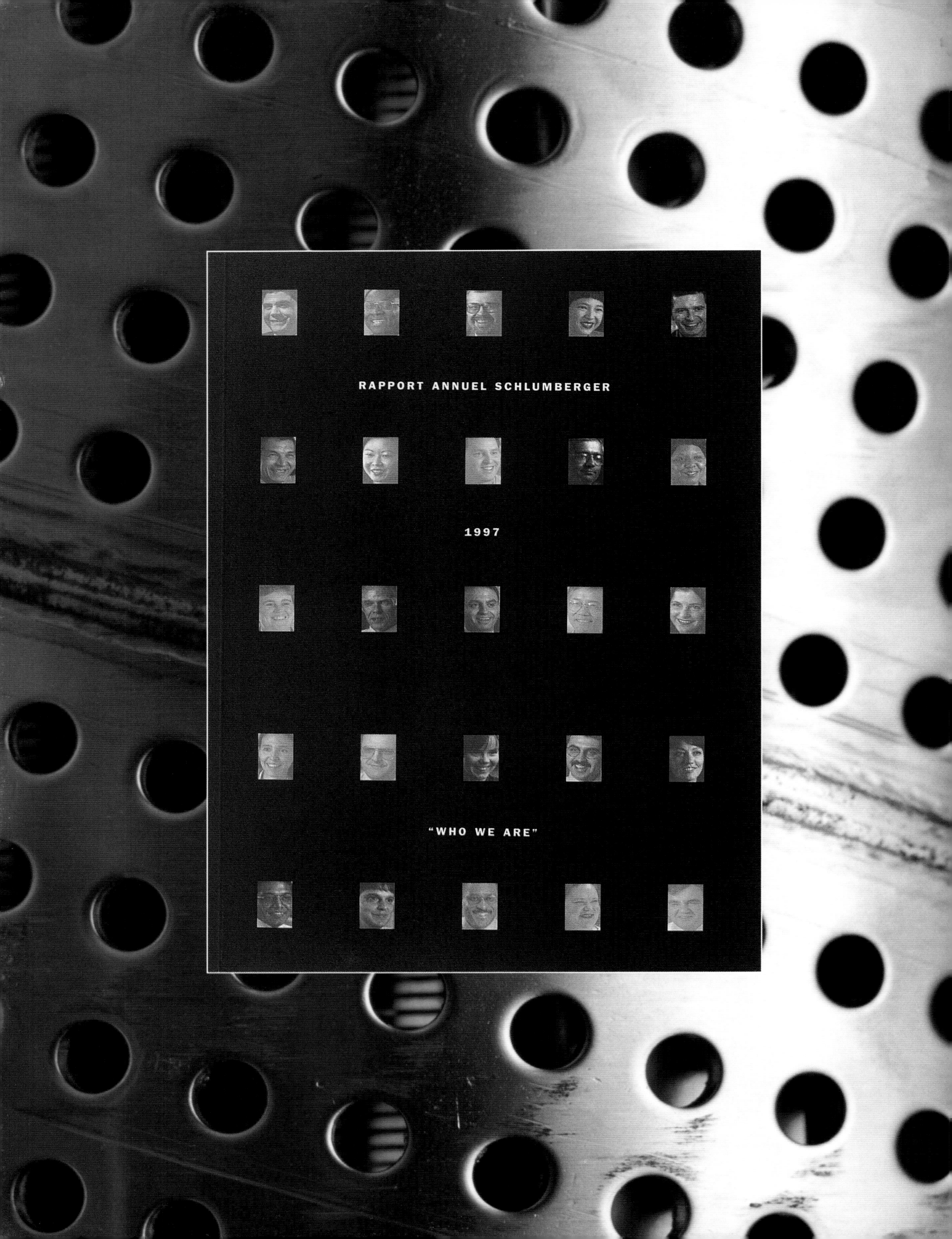
RAPPORT ANNUEL SCHLUMBERGER
1997
"WHO WE ARE"

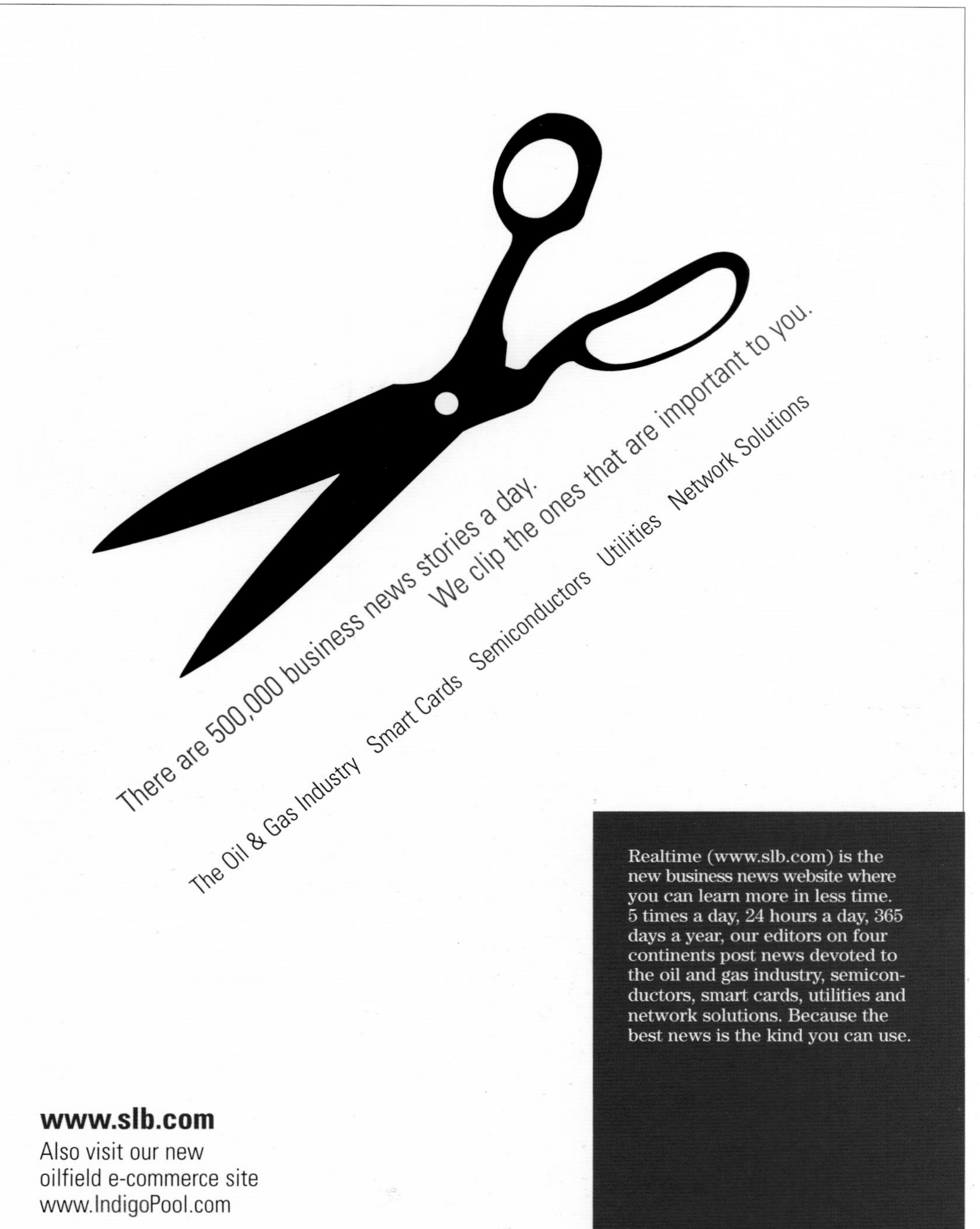

There are 500,000 business news stories a day.
We clip the ones that are important to you.
The Oil & Gas Industry Smart Cards Semiconductors Utilities Network Solutions
Realtime (www.slb.com) is the new business news website where you can learn more in less time. 5 times a day, 24 hours a day, 365 days a year, our editors on four continents post news devoted to the oil and gas industry, semiconductors, smart cards, utilities and network solutions. Because the best news is the kind you can use.
www.slb.com
Also visit our new oilfield e-commerce site www.IndigoPool.com

My relationship with Schlumberger, a global corporation that initially was in the oil field measurement business, but now is involved in many other activities, has lasted more than thirty years, through many changes of management. This is unusual in the design world since changes in management usually involve changing suppliers as well. Whatever the reason, we've been able to do a variety of projects for them, including numerous annual reports, exhibitions, brochures, identity, web site development, advertising, and so on. The design issue usually is to reconcile the inherent conservatism of an important and highly regarded company with a sense of cutting edge technology and innovative engineering—not simple.

OPPOSITE PAGE Schlumberger's annual reports have been pocket size for the last six years. This format seems to make them friendlier and easier to read. The photograph in the background is by Matthew Klein, from the current report.

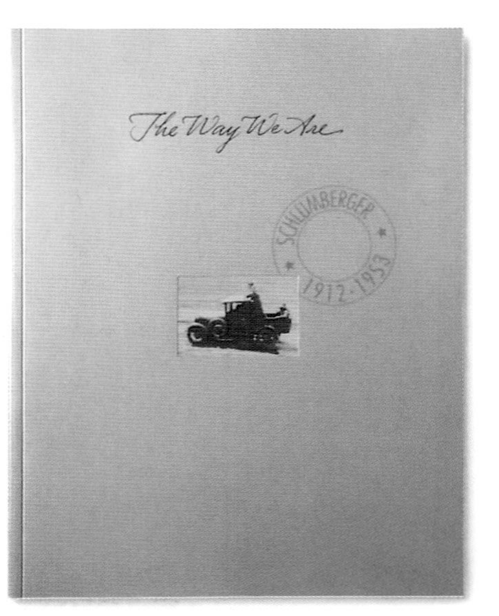

You go to the airport and just raise your hand and you call an aerotaxi like you call a cab. The only thing you had to be sure of was that the tanks were full. It was necessary to check, even to pay out of your own pocket to make sure you would have enough fuel to reach where you wanted to go.

Jean Gartner

CORREOS DE VENEZUELA
2/7/49
MARACAIBO

A book tracing the early history of Schlumberger in the form of postcards originally written by field workers to their friends and loved ones. Because the actual handwriting was incomprehensible, the messages had to be rewritten in a variety of scripts that simulated the French written hand. All of this was accomplished by Raphael Boguslav, an old high school friend and unexcelled calligrapher.

TOP RIGHT We also developed an exhibition system for this project.

ABOVE A complicated folding brochure, based on a timeline, that explains the fifty year history of Schlumberger's research facility.

SCHLUMBERGER 1983 ANNUAL REPORT

LEFT A comic strip-like cover, drawn by Jim McMullan, caused some internal controversy when it was first published. It eventually became one of the most popular covers.

It its heyday, Brooklyn had more than one hundred breweries. By the mid 1970s they had all vanished for one reason or another. In 1987 a former journalist named Steve Hindy came to see me. He and his partner, Tom Potter, wanted to create a new beer that would ultimately be brewed in Brooklyn. The name "Brooklyn" suggested, among other things, the Dodgers, the baseball team still associated with Brooklyn many years after they treacherously decamped for Los Angeles. The partners wanted their label to have a European appearance to differentiate it from popular American beers and to suggest their commitment to a more complex and interesting product. I designed a "B" that looked as though it belonged on a Dodger uniform. Actually, the lettering

on the real uniforms was quite straightforward, but through some trick of memory, most people recall it looking like this logo. The logo was applied to their packaging, promotional material, T-shirts, and trucks, and in 1996 to the front of the first brewery to be built in Brooklyn in more than thirty years. They now produce 12 kinds of beer with significant success. Nice guys, great beer.

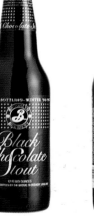

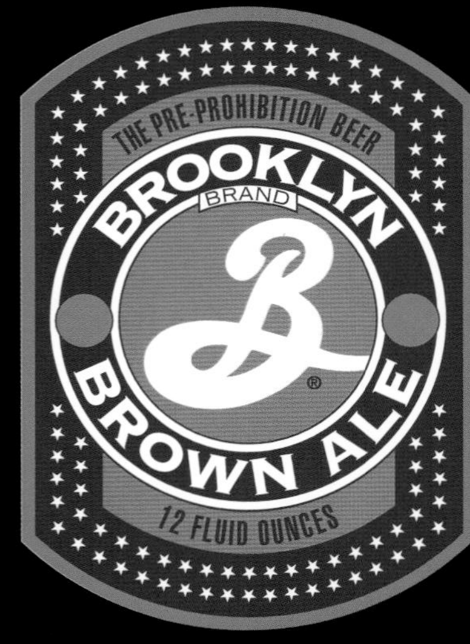

The new proposed glass bottle.

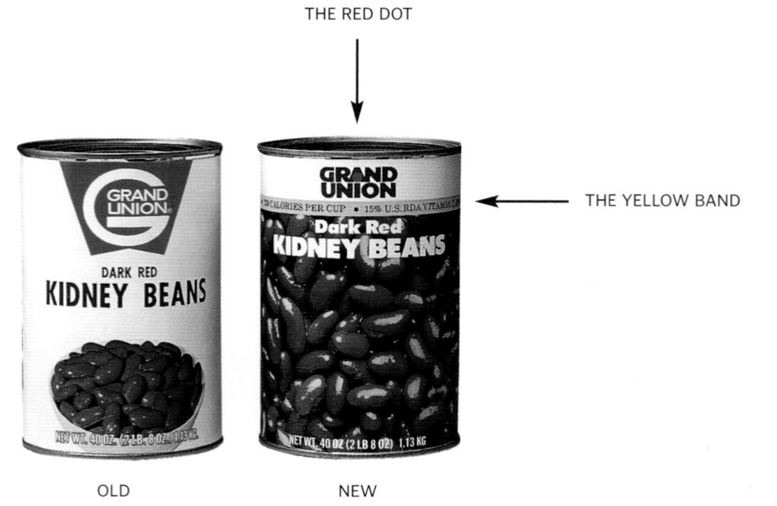

Grand Union

A chance encounter with a remarkable man led to my being involved in the design of supermarkets for more than twenty years. In 1974, my partner, Clay Felker, and I were looking for a buyer for *New York Magazine*, a publication we had started in 1968. We were introduced to Sir James Goldsmith, a controversial English entrepreneur who had, among other things, significant holdings in publications and food companies. The *New York Magazine* deal didn't work out, but Goldsmith and I developed an immediate friendship.

Six months later he called and asked whether I might like to redesign *L'Express*, the distinguished French news magazine that was one of several publications he owned. Working in New York and Paris over a period of six or seven months, I redesigned *L'Express* together with the editors and Sir James. He was considerably smarter than his editors and dominated them through charm or fear. The redesigned magazine proved to be successful, increasing its circulation and advertising pages. Four months later I received another call from Sir James: "Do you know anything about supermarkets, dear boy?" I said I did not, but it seemed not to matter.

Sir James owned Grand Union, a chain of about 500 supermarkets mostly located on the East Coast. They had been conservatively managed for many years and badly needed to be reinvented. I put a wonderful team of architects and graphic and industrial designers together and we started to work on a new prototype in Wykoff, New Jersey. Three months later we presented our ideas on how the supermarkets might be rethought. Goldsmith responded enthusiastically. Three months after that, construction began.

The new store was a great success. We had created a new identity and signage system, but more important, we changed many of the assumptions on how to present food and inform the customer about what they were buying. We introduced the "yellow band" containing useful consumer information on all the packages. The "red dot" in the logo became a signal for sale items, "Red Dot Specials," as part of a total information system. We worked with a brilliant copy writer named Julian Koenig, who came up with such lines as "When you see the dot you save a lot."

My experience as a designer of magazines helped in the process. I knew that the word "magazine," derived from the French word "magasin," meaning "storehouse," could also serve as another description of a supermarket. In any event, the overriding issue was how to make the Grand Union supermarket not merely a convenient place to shop but the customer's favorite market. To accomplish this we changed the aisle system to make the customer's path more discretionary, varied the quality of lighting throughout the store, developed new information systems, designed thousands of packages and, over the course of twenty years, helped reinvent the modern market.

The overriding idea behind the changes actually began with our work at *New York Magazine*, when the idea of being on the reader's side provided the philosophical basis for the magazine—not merely as a promotional tool, but as a matter of conviction. Goldsmith made me a member of the Grand Union board as well as giving me stock in the company. Consequently, I was deeply invested in the success of the enterprise as well as being perceived as a member of the team rather than a critical outside consultant.

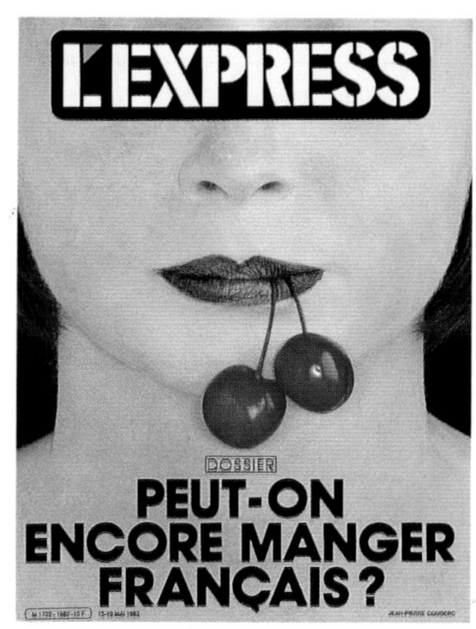

An issue of *L'Express* after the redesign.

GRAND UNION
Spanish Style TOMATO SAUCE
Diagonal Cut GREEN BEANS
BUTTER BEANS
Jumbo RIPE PITTED OLIVES
PURE GROUND BLACK PEPPER
NET WT 8 OZ 226g
JUMBO ROLL PAPER TOWELS 2-PLY
IDEAL FOR SPILLS AND CLEANING
SUGAR
GARLIC POWDER
PARSLEY FLAKES
HOMOGENIZED VITAMIN D EVAPORATED MILK
NET WT. 5.33 FL OZ 157 mL
GENTLE ENOUGH FOR BABY OR COSMETIC USE
YELLOW FACIAL TISSUES
200 2-PLY FACIAL TISSUES • EACH 8.2 IN. x 9.4 IN.
FRESH PACKED KOSHER DILL SPEARS
NET 48 FL OZ (1 QT 1 PT) 1.42 L
FRESH PACKED MILD CHERRY PEPPERS
NET 16 FL OZ (1 PT) 473 mL
FRESH PACKED HOT CHERRY PEPPERS
NET 32 FL OZ (1 QT) 946 mL
SALT
THIS SALT DOES NOT SUPPLY IODIDE, A NECESSARY NUTRIENT.
WHITE FACIAL TISSUES
LARGE FRESH EGGS
GRADE A
HALF DOZEN FRESH EGGS KEEP REFRIGERATED
SOUR CREAM
RIGATONI
MODO ITALIANO RIGATONI
ENRICHED MACARONI PRODUCT
VERMICELLI
SPAGHETTI
THIN SPAGHETTI

Experiments with partial images. The trick is that they depend on a clerk to line them up properly.

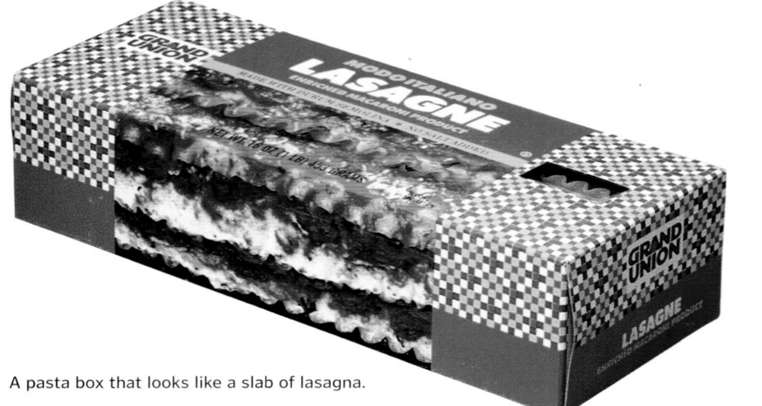

A pasta box that looks like a slab of lasagna.

We used good photography and kept the surface uncluttered so that a powerful appetite-stimulating effect was produced when the cans were seen side by side.

Jelly labels with a different kid for every flavor.

The packages inform you about which type of seed to buy.

Nuts come in many forms.

This line of kitchen essentials was designed to look good on the shelf at home.

This aluminum package for aluminum foil seemed right.

This line of imported foods was designed to look less aggressive and of higher quality than its domestic counterparts.

RIGHT We thought of the entire storefront as a sign, exemplified by this photograph of the supermarket in Paramas, New Jersey. It took three years of persuasion to get the company to remove the wall of paper signs that blocked the views into the market, even though in a mall situation the customers had already made the decision to shop at the store. The signs were disinviting and served no purpose, but the habit and tradition of using them persisted. Inside, the confusing promotional paper signs were also eliminated, providing for a more pleasant shopping environment. The chain has been bought and sold many times since the golden days of Sir James Goldsmith, and I am saddened to see all the paper signs returning once again. Change is often desirable, but sometimes it is for the worst.

BELOW The superstores were enormous, usually more than 100,000 square feet, and needed a dramatic facade. The budget was modest and the solution could not be architectural. We mounted a series of waterproofed photographic blow-ups on cut aluminum panels and positioned them slightly off the entry wall. The scale is quite dramatic.

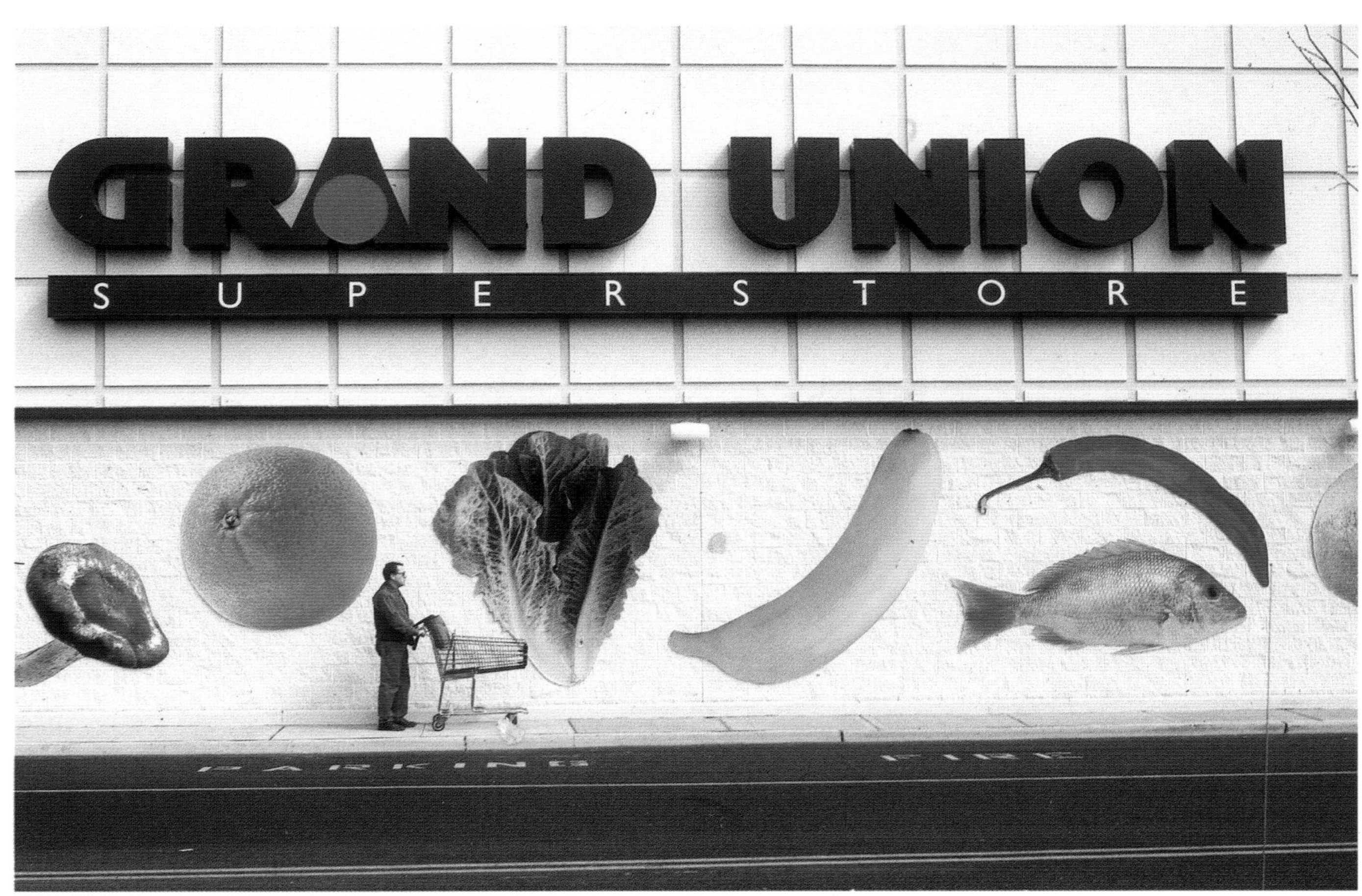

LEFT An idea I attribute to my experience designing magazines: Why not put a table of contents at the entrance to the market? The old supermarket principle was, "Make them walk through the whole store, they'll find things to buy along the way." Our principle was, "Make it easy to find everything. Customers will like the experience and come back more often."

BELOW This button involves a bit of social engineering. One of the great problems in supermarkets is the indifference of the personnel. Frequently, when one makes an inquiry, a shrugged shoulder is the response. By making employees wear this button, a disinterested response seems less appropriate. Can this make a difference? I don't know, but at the time (1975) it seemed like a good idea.

Ask Me.
I'm Here to
Help.

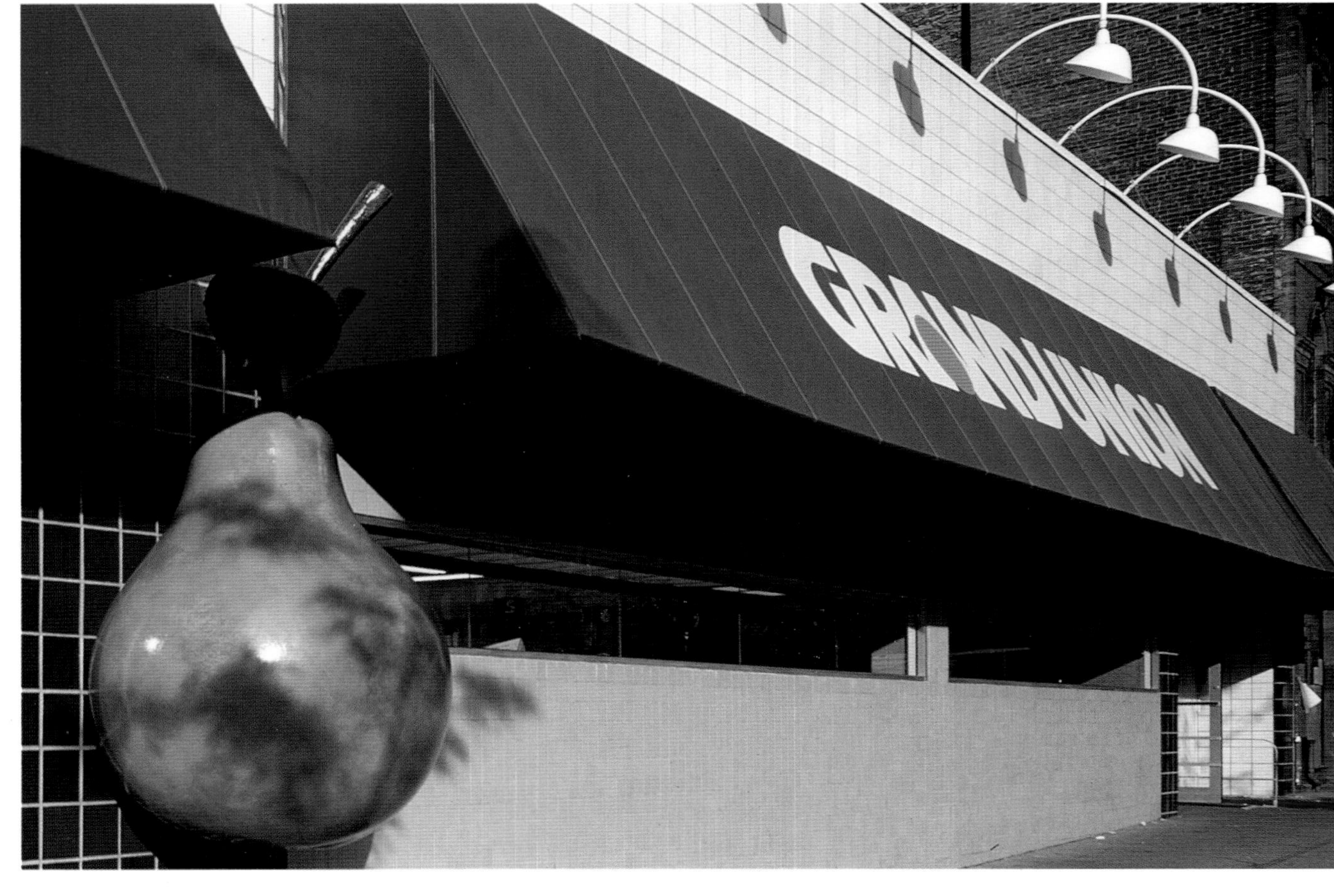

LEFT The entry area of one of the few urban stores that Grand Union operated. I proposed a friendly pear on the front to create an unexpected invitation. It was made out of fiberglass by my old friend, Jordan Steckel. It is a popular neighborhood icon that remains in place, even though the store has changed hands several times. In fact, it was so popular that it wasn't even graffitied for the first ten years.

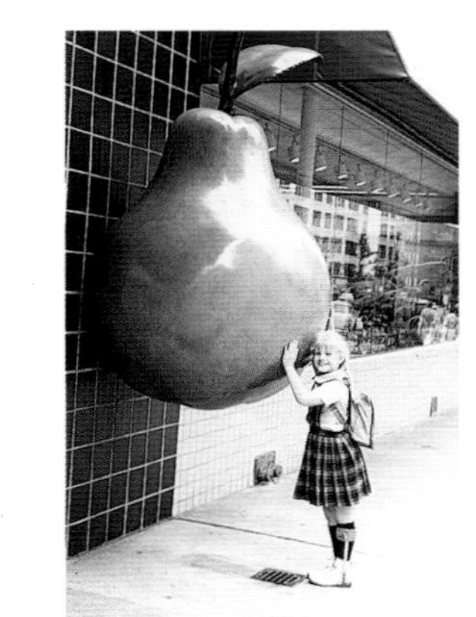

RIPENING SHELF
The produce on this shelf is not yet ripe.
If you want to purchase unripe fruits or vegetables for cooking, pickling or to ripen at home, select from this shelf.
As they ripen, they will be moved to the lower shelves and "RIPE" stickers will be put on them.

One of the obvious assumptions that drives the design of supermarkets is the lack of personnel. For instance, when you went into an old fashioned vegetable market you would ask the green grocer to pick out a nice ripe melon. After squeezing and sniffing a few, he would oblige. In the conventional supermarket, the green grocer does not exist or is never in sight when needed. I thought we could invent a simple self-service solution to the problem. Why not create a "ripening shelf?" Fruits and vegetables could be displayed on a series of shelves moving from "ripe in a week" to "ripe today." The customer then would buy produce as needed, either in advance or for use the same day. Prototypes were built and installed in a test group of stores. The idea collapsed when we discovered that employees were either incapable of telling the difference between ripe and unripe fruit or were unwilling to make the effort. For whatever reason the ripening shelves were removed from the stores and put into permanent storage.

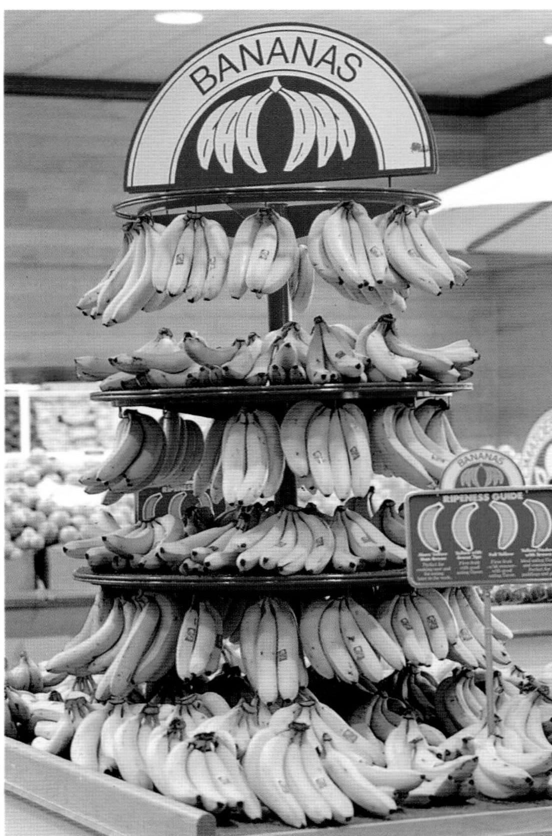

When buying food in bulk became popular, we designed parts of the market in the spirit of old fashioned grocery stores—not the most space efficient configuration, but one that created an airy experience that was a refreshing relief from the relentless compression of the aisles. As the Italians learned in the fourteenth century, narrow streets become acceptable when they lead to a piazza. Buying in bulk has become less trendy and most supermarkets have returned to their traditional space-saving forms.

RIGHT The wineshop signage helped the customer decide what to buy.

In the 70s, consumer consciousness and a sense of opportunity led some supermarkets to open discount operations that sold food for considerably less than the standard competition. This was also the moment that "generic" food gained a significant portion in the marketplace, accounting for as much as ten percent of food sales. People were aware that some part of the money they were spending for a national brand was going toward covering the enormous advertising budgets that supported those brands. This perception and the recession made discount markets and generic food popular. We were asked to design a market that would convey a plain "pipe rack" appearance to suggest bargain pricing. The floors were poured cement and we decided to use fire-treated cardboard as our basic interior and signage material. The effect was as though you had entered an enormous cardboard box. Exposed fluorescence and cardboard display units completed the effect. In the end, it probably cost as much to build as a conventional market. It ultimately failed, even though customers liked the store, because Grand Union hadn't changed its purchasing, warehousing, or distribution methods. As a result, it lost money on virtually every scale.

ABOVE AND RIGHT Study models for the Basics market.

Study model for the Basics market

The real store

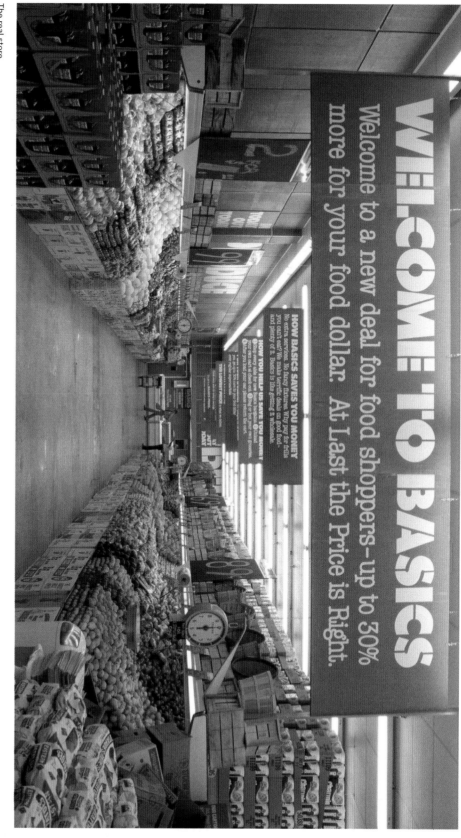

Basics generic packaging.

A significant portion of my work has been in the area of magazine and newspaper design, which essentially began when I started *New York Magazine* in 1968 with my friend and brilliant editor, Clay Felker. We had a great run until the magazine was acquired by Rupert Murdoch in 1977. Early in the game I hired Walter Bernard, who was working at *Esquire*, to assume the role of Art Director. He left *New York Magazine* at the same time Clay and I did and went on to become the art director of *Time Magazine* where he led a noteworthy redesign of that periodical. We missed working together and in 1983 created WBMG, a design office specializing in magazine and newspaper design. On the following pages are some typical examples of the work we've done together. A more complete representation would require a book in itself, which might not be a bad idea.

This page shows a variety of magazine logotypes:

1. The word "week" is integrated into the word "magazine" to give it visual distinction and to shorten the title, which permits a larger, more dramatic logo on the cover.

2. The visual idea for this muck-raking magazine was to have the logo itself peeling back the surface to reveal the reality below.

3. We moved the exclamation mark from after the word, where it might be expected, to the middle where it nicely substitutes for an "i."

4. A logo for a magazine prototype on the arts that was intended not to look like a magazine logo.

5. This logo for a french literary magazine was designed to enable it to be used over a photograph without obscuring it.

MAGA WEEK ZINE

1

BRILL'S CONTENT

2

SELL!NG

3

inspired

4

LIRE

5

LEFT This cover image came out of a simple observation. Visually "500" is expressed numerically or as the words "five hundred." By combining the two idioms a giant "5" becomes possible. This solution has become the standard cover for the last three years.

America's
Largest
Corporations
FORTUNE
DISPLAY UNTIL JUNE 9, 1997
1997
5
HUNDRED

RIGHT *Magazine Week* was a trade journal for the magazine industry and generally looked like all other indifferently designed trade journals. We convinced our client that his audience was literate and that a more dramatic and contemporary approach to the cover was appropriate. We reduced the number of messages, strengthened the logo, and clarified the typography. However, the basic problem was more resistant—there was no budget for cover art. Magazines in this category generally rely on publicity handouts or from the very sources they're writing about. When the images consist of head and product shots as in the original magazine, it doesn't matter much, but in our proposal, the cover image was significantly larger. The design strategy was to get great cover images without paying for them. The solution was disarmingly simple. Every week, throughout the United States, strong and sometimes extraordinary images are produced for magazines. We invented a competition called "Image of the Week," in which photos selected and credited to the winning magazine and photographer were run as the cover. Although I found myself slightly embarrassed by this solution, everyone involved benefited. The creators of the image were celebrated and *Magazine Week* stayed within their budget. Design problems frequently require unexpected solutions.

MAGAZINEWEEK

THE NEWSWEEKLY OF MAGAZINE PUBLISHING

Reed, Elsevier Merger Stirs Up Niche

SGD Editor Shakes Up Sporting Goods Industry; Publisher Ousted

Health Titles Flourish With Can-Do Attitude

CBW Changes Its Name To *InfoWorld Direct*

Hurricane Andrew Disrupts Mag Distribution In South Florida Area

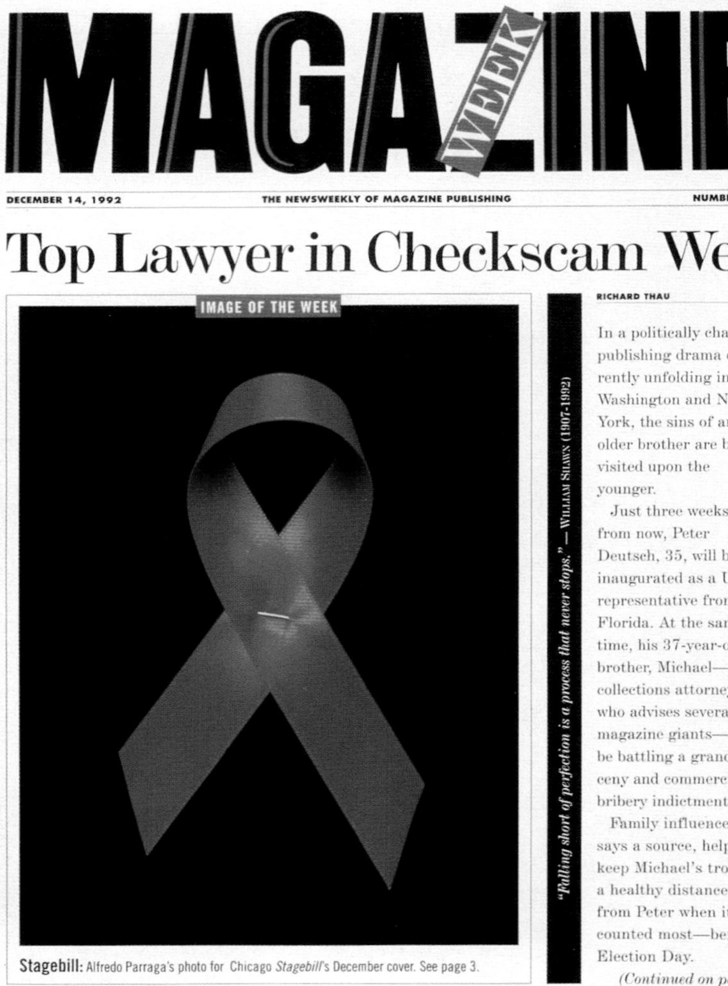

MAGAZINE WEEK

DECEMBER 14, 1992 THE NEWSWEEKLY OF MAGAZINE PUBLISHING NUMBER 241

Top Lawyer in Checkscam Web

IMAGE OF THE WEEK

"Falling short of perfection is a process that never stops." — William Shawn (1907-1992)

RICHARD THAU

In a politically charged publishing drama currently unfolding in Washington and New York, the sins of an older brother are being visited upon the younger.

Just three weeks from now, Peter Deutsch, 35, will be inaugurated as a U.S. representative from Florida. At the same time, his 37-year-old brother, Michael—a collections attorney who advises several magazine giants—will be battling a grand-larceny and commercial-bribery indictment.

Family influence, says a source, helped keep Michael's troubles a healthy distance from Peter when it counted most—before Election Day.

(Continued on page 4)

Stagebill: Alfredo Parraga's photo for Chicago *Stagebill's* December cover. See page 3.

MAGAZINE WEEK

OCTOBER 19, 1992 THE NEWSWEEKLY OF MAGAZINE PUBLISHING NUMBER 234

FIRST PICK

"A reporter is a primitive being who would go after his own mother if that was a good story." — Columnist Richard Cohen

An Old Feud Heats Up...

IRIS COHEN SELINGER

No one would ever say Steve Florio is shy. Adjacent to his handsome, very cherry wood office at *The New Yorker*, is his shrine — a private bathroom lined with photographs and framed newspaper articles of his successes. In fact, within the corridors of Conde Nast, Florio's self-promotion is sometimes jokingly compared to Don King's.

But the *New Yorker* president hardly corners the prima donna market at Conde Nast.

(Continued on page 21)

Rolling Stone October 29: The dread Sinead sans props by Albert Watson. See page 3.

Dr. Ruth talks family . . Child and Prudhomme talk food . . Trouble-free travel
Modern Maturity
Publication of AARP
December 1993–January 1994
THE NEED DECADE

OLD

November–December 1995
AARP PERSPECTIVES WHAT WILL THE FUTURE BRING?
MODERN Maturity
The Plot to Murder 'Murder, She Wrote'

NEW

Wine Spectator
The Best Nose in Napa tells All
Global Wine Marker's Split Personality
Special Reports on Nine Major International Wine Regions
The Boom in Premium Wine
Our Reader's Choice Awards

PROPOSED

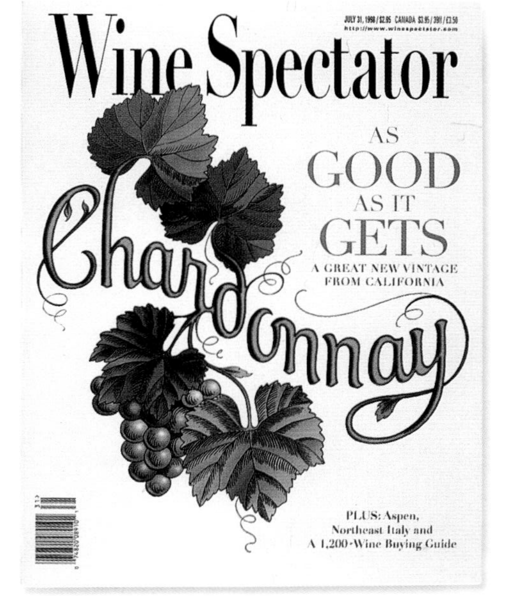

Wine Spectator
AS GOOD AS IT GETS
A GREAT NEW VINTAGE FROM CALIFORNIA
Chardonnay
PLUS: Aspen, Northeast Italy and A 1,200-Wine Buying Guide

NEW

THE·JOURNAL·OF·ART
Earthquake-proof Art
San Francisco damage puts museums on alert
Against the Grain
Artists Space vs. N.E.A.
Grant withdrawal mobilizes art community
SPECIAL REPORTS: JAPAN/EAST GERMAN ART

OLD

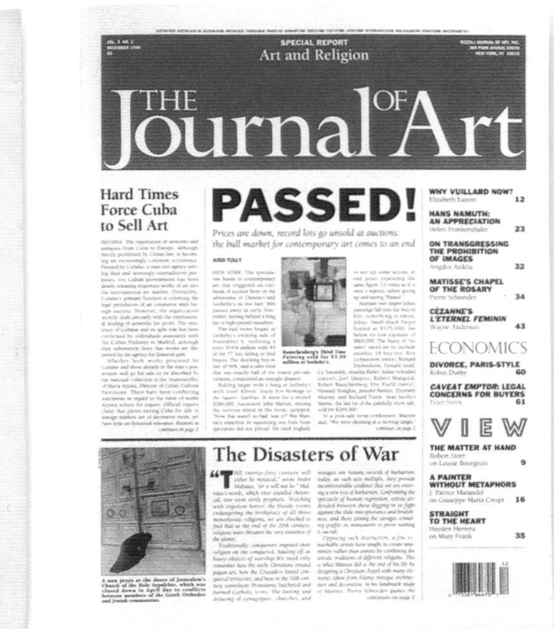

NEW

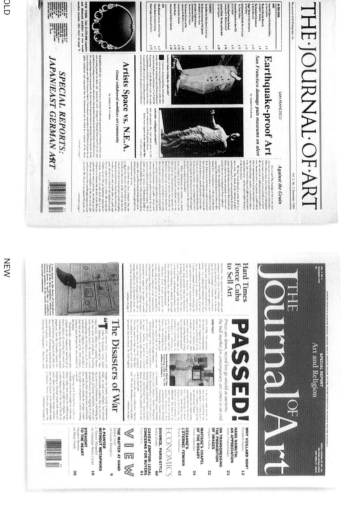

MATTHEW KLEIN

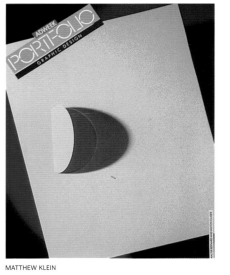

MATTHEW KLEIN

MATTHEW KLEIN

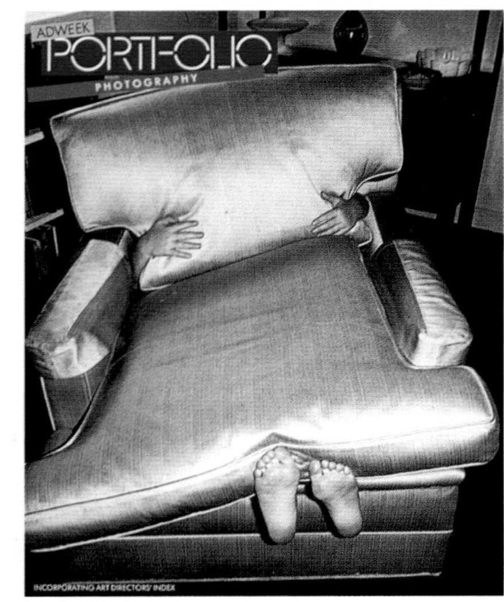

JOYCE RAULD

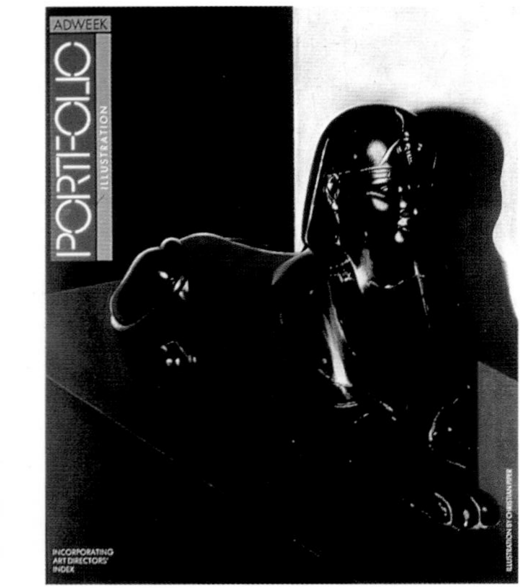

CHRISTIAN PIPER

MATTHEW KLEIN

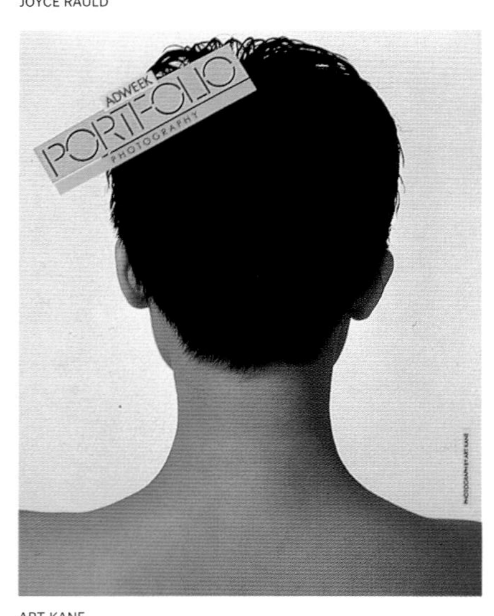

ART KANE

JIM McMULLAN

LEFT AND OPPOSITE PAGE A group of covers based on the theme of the telephone, which before e-mail was how clients and design sources communicated. We assigned the theme to a variety of illustrators and designers and were delighted by their response. You might overlook the cover in the second row on the left: all the objects displayed are skillfully made of clay by Anna V. Walker.

MATTHEW KLEIN

MATTHEW KLEIN

ELWOOD SMITH

ANNA V. WALKER

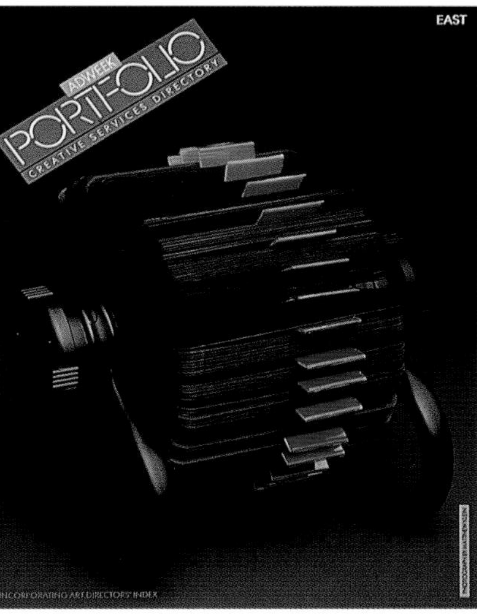

MATTHEW KLEIN

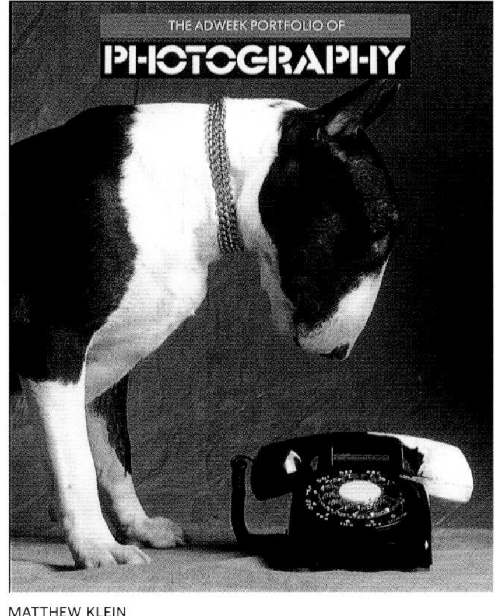

MATTHEW KLEIN

SKIP LIEPKE

JOHN CRAIG

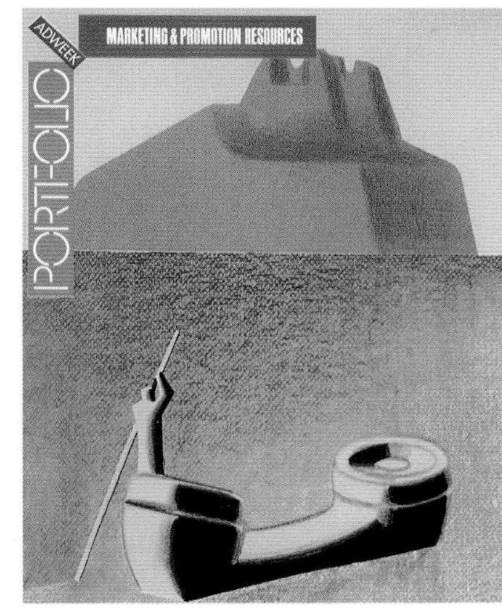

DAVID SUTER

The Steelcase Design Partnership, and their consultant George Beylarian, asked me to create a promotion piece for their furniture. I suggested a periodical that would clearly be an advertisement but which also would contain editorial material that would interest their constituents. These were largely individuals in the design business. As usual, the nature of the audience shaped the form of address. The product had to look modern. As the rest of *Art is Work* might suggest, I have no more interest in modernism than in any other style of graphic communication. I almost felt that on these pages I was consciously doing a parody of modernism. Nevertheless, the sense of reductive clarity seemed to be appreciated by the readers.

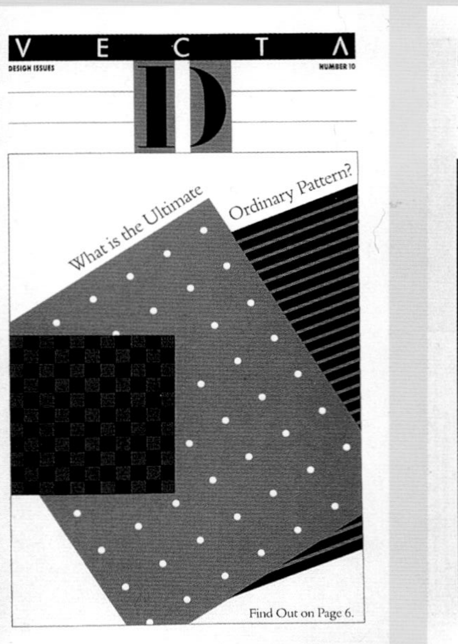

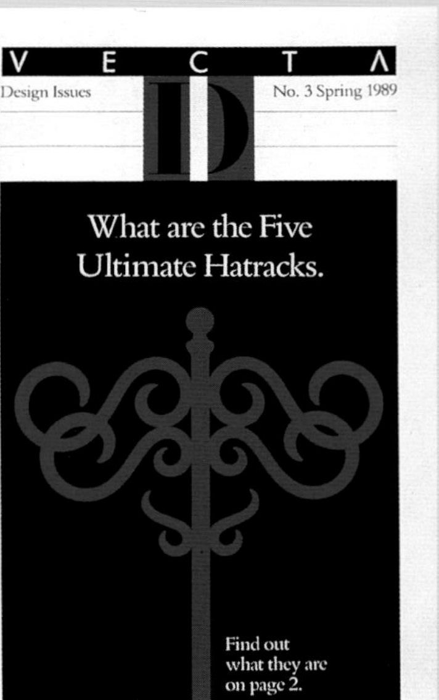

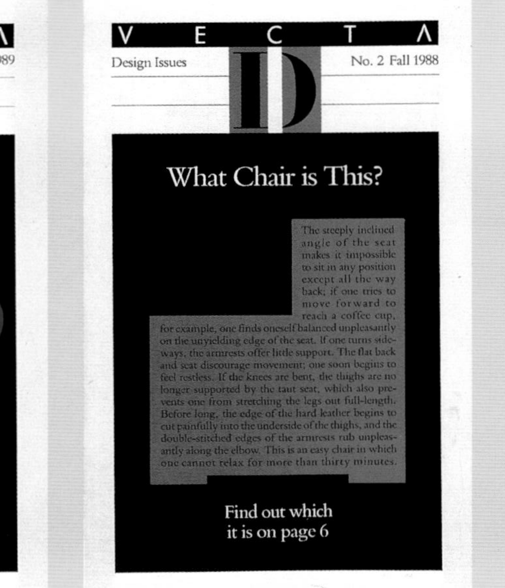

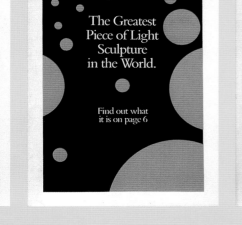

V E C T A
Design Issues
No. 1 Spring 1988
The Greatest Piece of Light Sculpture in the World.
Find out what it is on page 6

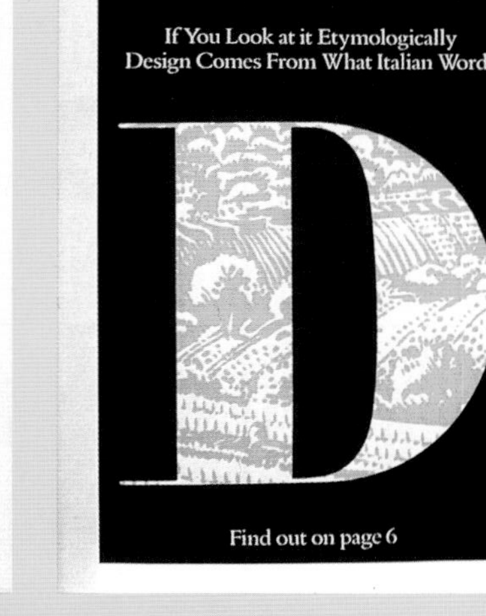
V E C T A
Design Issues
Number 4
If You Look at it Etymologically Design Comes From What Italian Word?
Find out on page 6

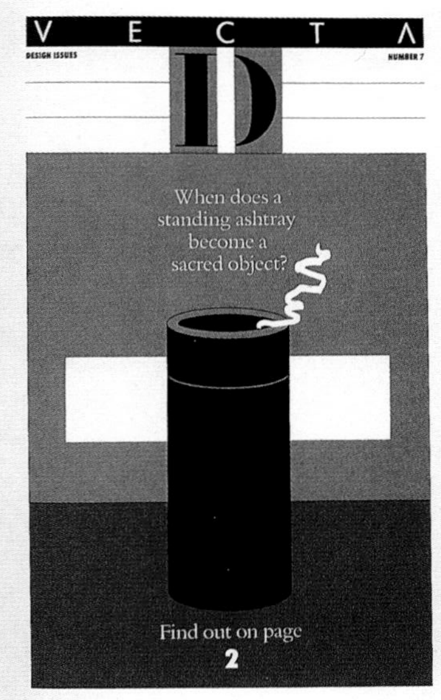
V E C T A
DESIGN ISSUES
NUMBER 7
When does a standing ashtray become a sacred object?
Find out on page
2

V E C T A
DESIGN ISSUES
NUMBER 11
What essentially American form expresses the spirit of a business-oriented culture?
Find Out on Page 2.

THOUGHTS ON THE BALLET TABLE SERIES

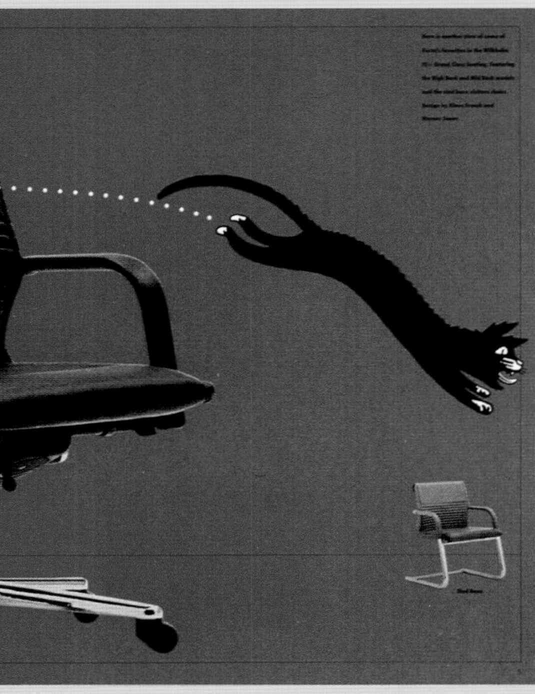

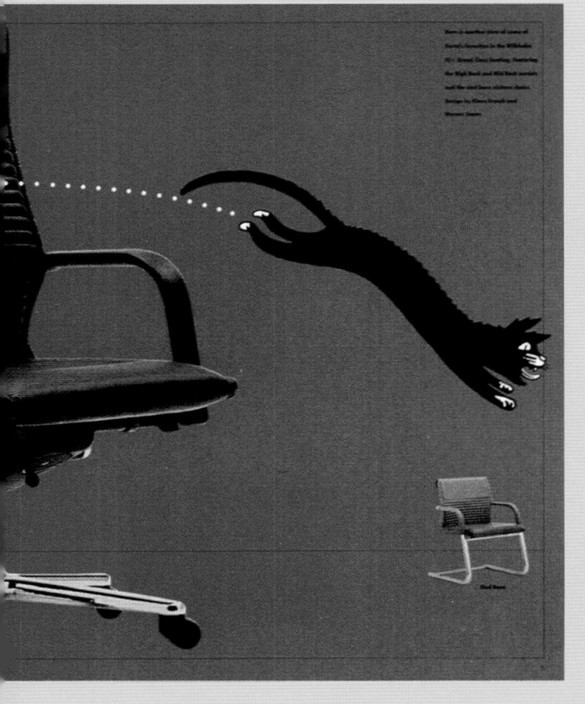

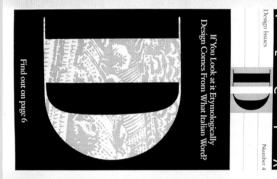

The recently deceased *U&lc* was a promotion piece for the International Typeface Corporation (ITC), started by Herb Lubalin and Ed Gottschall to sell their typefaces. It also contained a variety of editorial features to interest their readership which at one point reached 50,000.

RIGHT From time to time, designers were asked to invent an issue of the magazine. Walter and I suggested building an issue around the things that designers collect. The nature of the product encouraged more typographical playfulness than is usually acceptable. In addition to Walter and myself, our team on this project included Frank Baseman, Nancy Eising Clarendon, Sharon Okamoto and Janet Parker.

BELOW Mirko Ilić, who shares space in my building, beautifully executed an idea we had about the form of the letter "R." Since the form of the letter is composed respectively of a "column," a "bowl," and a "tail," we thought it would be charming to represent those ideas literally.

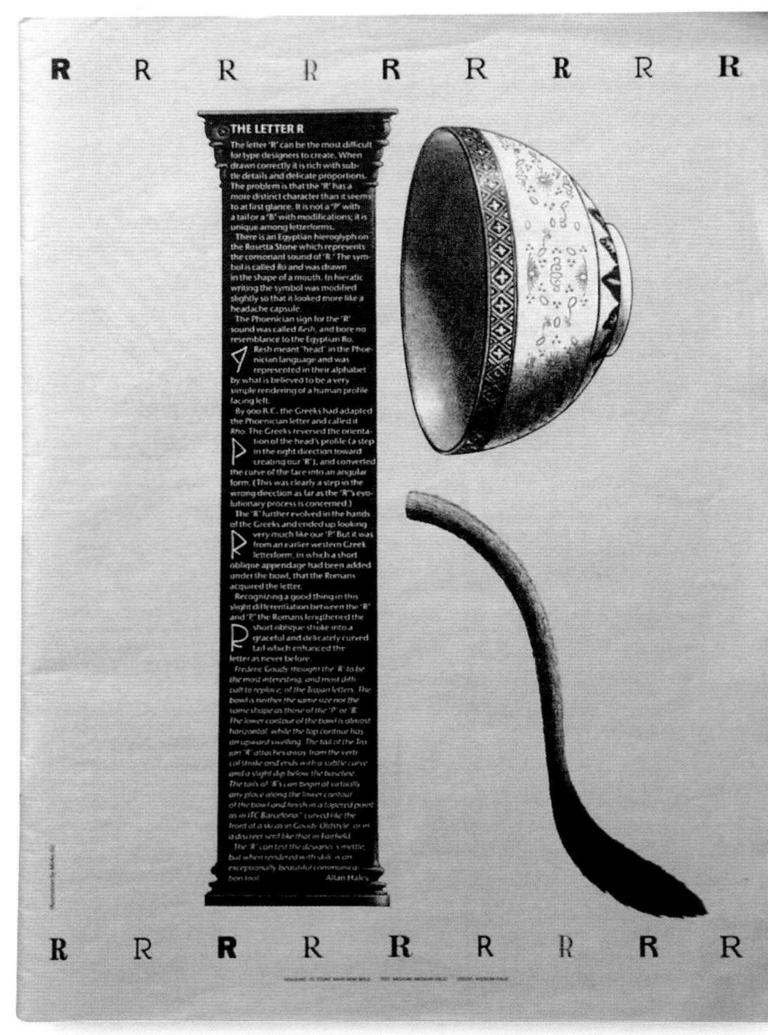

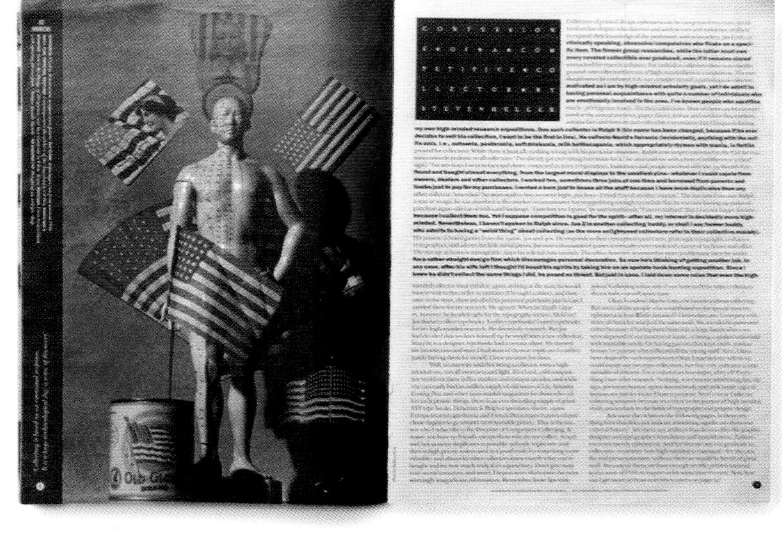

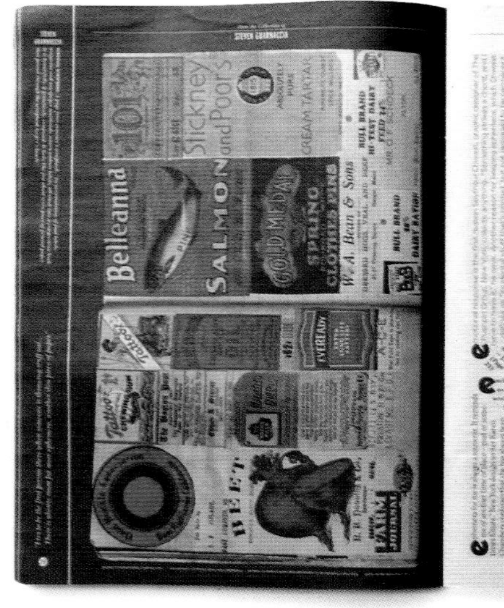

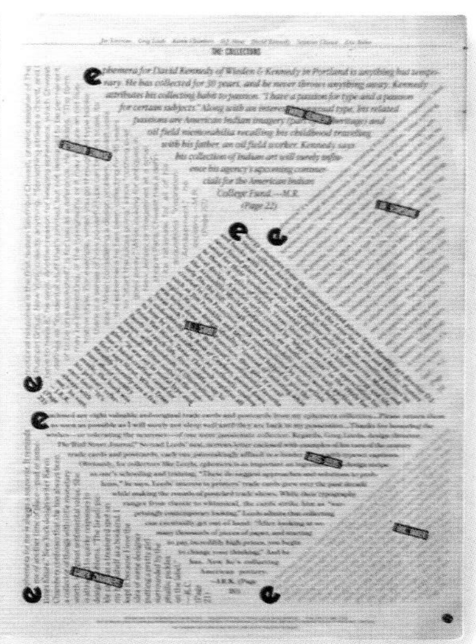

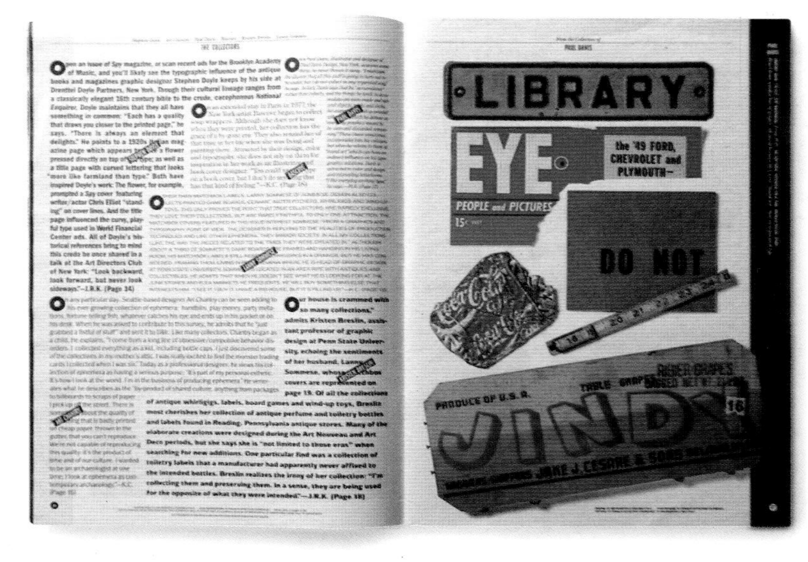

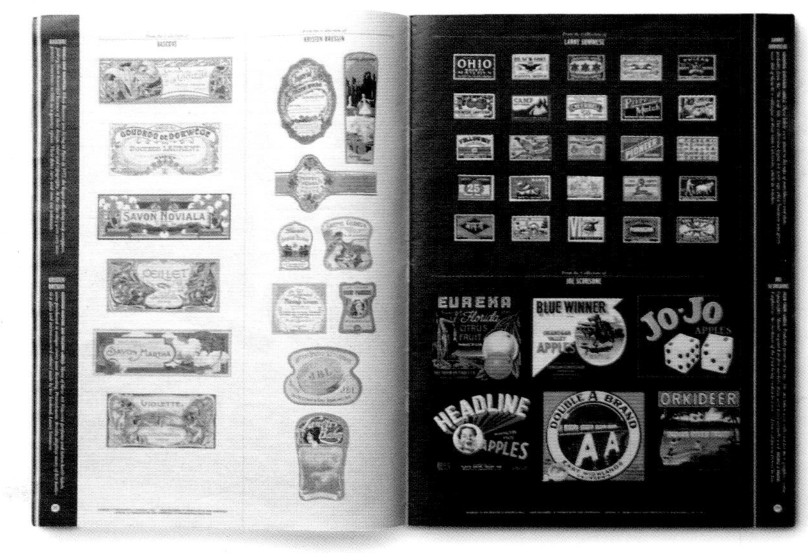

In the course of redesigning *Barron's*, an important financial newspaper, we suggested that a section called "Market Week" open with a more dramatic signal than a column of figures. Specifically, we thought that a character might be invented that would comment on the week's most dramatic stock market events. I started with a figure called "the Wizard," but the client suggested using the founder of the publication, Clarence Barron, as the spokesman for the section. It turned out to be an inspired recommendation since Barron was portly (over 300 lbs), bearded, and had flamboyant taste in clothes—all things that made him a delight to draw.

The problem was that the review of the week's events was done four hours before the newspaper went to press. Consequently, the client suggested that I arrive at the newspaper each Thursday afternoon to draw the appropriate cartoon. Not willing to spend Thursday afternoons downtown, in the financial district, I offered a counter proposal. I offered to create a series of drawings of Mr. Barron expressing a wide range of emotions: astonishment, concern, elation, suspicion, and so on. The editors could then couple a drawing that seemed right with the comment of the week. Although the drawings are repeated from time to time, readers don't seem to mind, or haven't noticed.

MARKET WEEK PULLOUT SECTION: TURN TO PAGE 28

ALAN ABELSON • 5
Whitewater rumors flood Wall Street

BOMBAY COMPANY • 17
Terrific growth story, but can it continue?

THE INTERVIEW • 24
There's life left in the bull market

BARRON'S

THE DOW JONES BUSINESS AND FINANCIAL WEEKLY

MARCH 14, 1994 $2.50

Still Going?

In all the rhapsodizing about the telecommunications revolution one fact has been sadly overlooked: Nobody has come up with a portable battery that lasts more than a few hours. For users of laptop PCs and cellular phones, when will the frustration end?
Page 29

BARRON'S
Market Week

THE TRADER
Turning On A Dime
5

INTERNATIONAL TRADER
He Does It Strictly By The Book
9

CURRENT YIELD
Bonds Pull Out of A Tailspin
10

The market greeted a new month. And what a greeting! On Wednesday the Dow suffered a major mood swing, but on the week it showed little change.

TRADING POINTS
Learning A Lesson The Hard Way
13

COMMODITIES CORNER
Inflation! Not In These Parts
14

STRIKING PRICE
A Mighty Precise Indicator
16

The most important newspaper in Catalonia has been published in Barcelona for 120 years. The owner, the Count Javier de Codó, wanted to transform it into a completely contemporary product. The entire newspaper was to be redesigned, including all supplements and magazines. The best color printing presses were purchased to ensure an entirely new level of production quality. The process took two years to complete, working alternately in New York and Barcelona. The change in the front page reflects the shift in appearance and attitude we were trying to achieve. On the right, the old front page—traditional, undramatic, gray, and old-fashioned. It does express such characteristics as authority, tradition, and seriousness, but unfortunately, these are not necessarily qualities that a new generation of readers seems to be interested in. Our plan was to try to retain the sense of authority but dramatize the stories to make them more accessible. We did this on the cover by combining two newspaper traditions, the broadsheet and the tabloid. We featured more stories than a tabloid front, but less than broadsheet. All the elements, the photos, the logo, the headlines, have been enlarged in scale to make *La Vanguardia* a more powerful presence on the newsstand. The approach was successful. The readers responded and *La Vanguardia* is now considered to be one of the best newspapers in Europe.

OPPOSITE PAGE Retaining the logo was considered essential. By simply reversing it out of a blue bar its visual meaning changed and became more assertive.

MIERCOLES, 9 SEPTIEMBRE 1987
PAG. 3

LA VANGUARDIA

Presidente: Carlos de Godó, Conde de Godó. Editor: Javier de Godó. Director: Francesc Noy

Un subteniente de la Guardia Civil, asesinado en Bilbao por un comando terrorista

El etarra Urrusolo, detectado por la policía en Madrid, donde estaría preparando un atentado

La policía asegura haber detectado al etarra Urrusolo Sistiaga en Madrid, donde podría preparar un gran atentado, temor que también se extiende a Barcelona u otras ciudades. De hecho, ayer se cometió uno en Bilbao, al ser asesinado un guardia civil al recibir un disparo en la nuca.

Una de las últimas fotos de Urrusolo (izquierda) y el guardia civil asesinado, Cristóbal Martín (derecha)

Barrionuevo, en Barcelona

Atentado en Bilbao

(Páginas 11 y 16)

Investigación judicial sobre un presunto delito ecológico en el caso del asma urbana

No hay certeza total

Alergia a la soja

(Página 15)

La coalición en el poder sufre un fuerte retroceso en las elecciones generales danesas

XAVIER BATALLA
(Página 7)

Núñez decide no asistir a las reuniones federativas

(Página 27)

Las lluvias torrenciales causan mil muertos y más de veinte mil damnificados en Venezuela

ALBERTO MÍGUEZ
(Página 24)

EN LINEA DIRECTA CON LOS ANUNCIOS ECONOMICOS

Solicite su anuncio por teléfono.
El medio más directo de contactar con La Vanguardia.

301 85 85

LA VANGUARDIA
ANUNCIOS ECONOMICOS

El Punto de Encuentro

Tribuna	5
Internacional	7
España	11
Cataluña	15
Necrologicas	20
Sociedad	24
Deportes	27
Espectaculos	31
Cartelera	33
TURISMO	35
Cultura	38
Economia	41
Anuncios Económicos	60
Tiempo	65
Pasatiempos	66
Dia a dia	67
Radio	67
Televisión	68

◀ LA POLICÍA BUSCA A DOS PIRÓMANOS FORESTALES EN CATALUÑA • PÁG. 20 ▶

www.lavanguardia.es

LA VANGUARDIA

LUNES, 31 DE JULIO DE 2000 | Fundada en 1881 por don Carlos y don Bartolomé Godó | Número 42.646 125 ptas. / 0,75 euros

Aznar: "ETA y los suyos tienen motivos para preocuparse"

▶ *Zapatero pide a Ibarretxe que reflexione y al PNV que demuestre que es demócrata*

▶ *El presidente advierte que el Gobierno no pestañeará en su lucha antiterrorista*

▶ *El alcalde nacionalista de Legorreta rompe a llorar en el homenaje a Jáuregui*

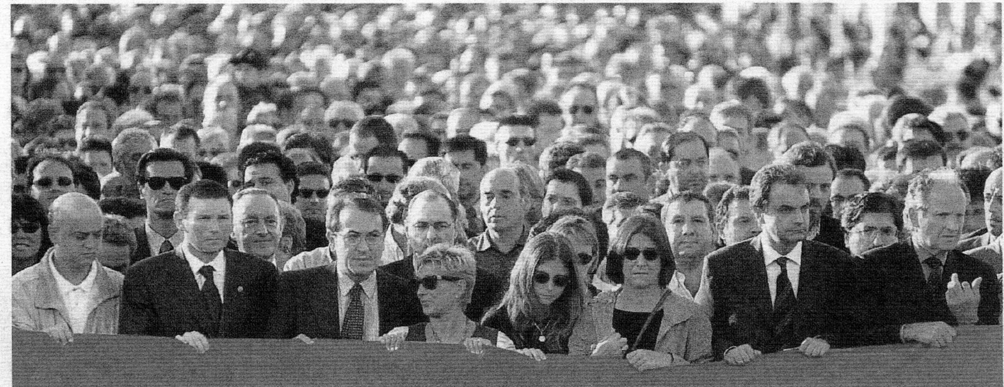

JAVIER ECHEZARRETA / EFE

TODOS CONTRA ETA. Dirigentes de todos los partidos, excepto EH, arroparon ayer a la viuda y a la hija de Juan María Jáuregui en la manifestación en la que miles de donostiarras pidieron el fin de ETA, entre ellos el lehendakari, el líder del PSOE y el alcalde de San Sebastián. **PÁGINAS 9 A 12**

Acaba el proceso de regularización

España legaliza la situación de más de 160.000 inmigrantes

BARCELONA. – Entre 160.000 y 200.000 inmigrantes lograrán legalizar su situación en España, en el proceso de regularización de extranjeros que comenzó hace cuatro meses y que termina hoy. Mientras, siguen llegando avalanchas de "sin papeles" a las costas españolas y europeas. La policía italiana interceptó ayer un barco con 418 inmigrantes de Sierra Leona, Pakistán, Afganistán y Senegal, que salió de Turquía e hizo escala en Grecia sin que nadie quisiera acogerlos. **PÁGINAS 21 Y 22**

ALEX GARCIA

Petit estrena la camiseta del Barça

PÁGINA 35

Elecciones en Venezuela

Hugo Chávez se proclama ganador antes del escrutinio

Hugo Chávez

CARACAS. – Hugo Chávez anunció ayer su victoria electoral en las presidenciales de Venezuela, antes incluso de que se cerraran los colegios electorales, animado por el resultado de las encuestas y su seguridad en un triunfo "sin golpe, sin una gota de sangre". Chávez aseguró que así se entierra "medio siglo de corrupción". **PÁGINA 3**

BERTOLUCCI QUIERE REINAR EN HOLLYWOOD ▶ Página 103

LA VANGUARDIA

CARRERAS:

La primera canción es de agradecimiento

PÁGINA 2

LA VANGUARDIA SUPLEMENTO

Cultura

Bernard-Henri Lévy entrevista al escritor peruano Mario Vargas Llosa

2

VAN GOGH

PÁGINAS 8 Y 9

Posiciones

Liquidaciones

Vibraciones

A PIE DE PÁGINA

LA VANGUARDIA

MAGAZINE

MERYL STREEP

La dama de hierro de Hollywood

Interiores

ZARAGOZA, DE RENOVAR LA UNESCO

PINTORES ESPAÑOLES HACEN LAS AMÉRICAS

BURMA: UN VIAJE POR LA FANTASÍA

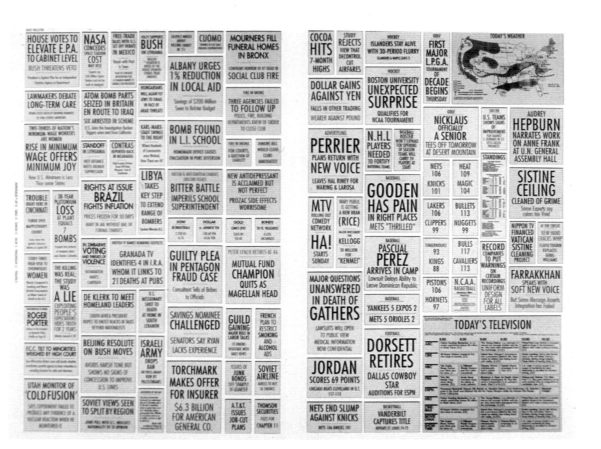

A competition on the theme of the newspaper of the future resulted in the proposals on these pages.

RIGHT First, we decided to summarize everything essential in one day's edition of *The New York Times* on two spreads. The editorial sections are signaled by the change of color. The style of typography was actually inspired by the restaurant, music, and bar advertising at the back of a *Wilkes Barre* newspaper (Shirley's hometown). For contrast and drama, we proposed that the opposite side of the sheet contain an enormous image—in this case, a detail from the Sistine Chapel before and after cleaning.

Drunk with success, we took it one step further. We would do the entire day's news on two sides of a single sheet of paper. This obviously required further compressions so we eliminated headlines and simply opened each story with the first word of the story—whether it fit or not. The other side of the sheet contains photographs occupying the exact same space as their respective texts. For the reader with little time to spare, the story can be read and the photos seen simultaneously by holding the page up to the light. One cannot overlook the opportunities for advertising, since that is how newspapers survive. So, we provided a "bellyband" that would wrap the page with a single advertiser's message.

Sadly, the Internet has made the entire effort somewhat irrelevant.

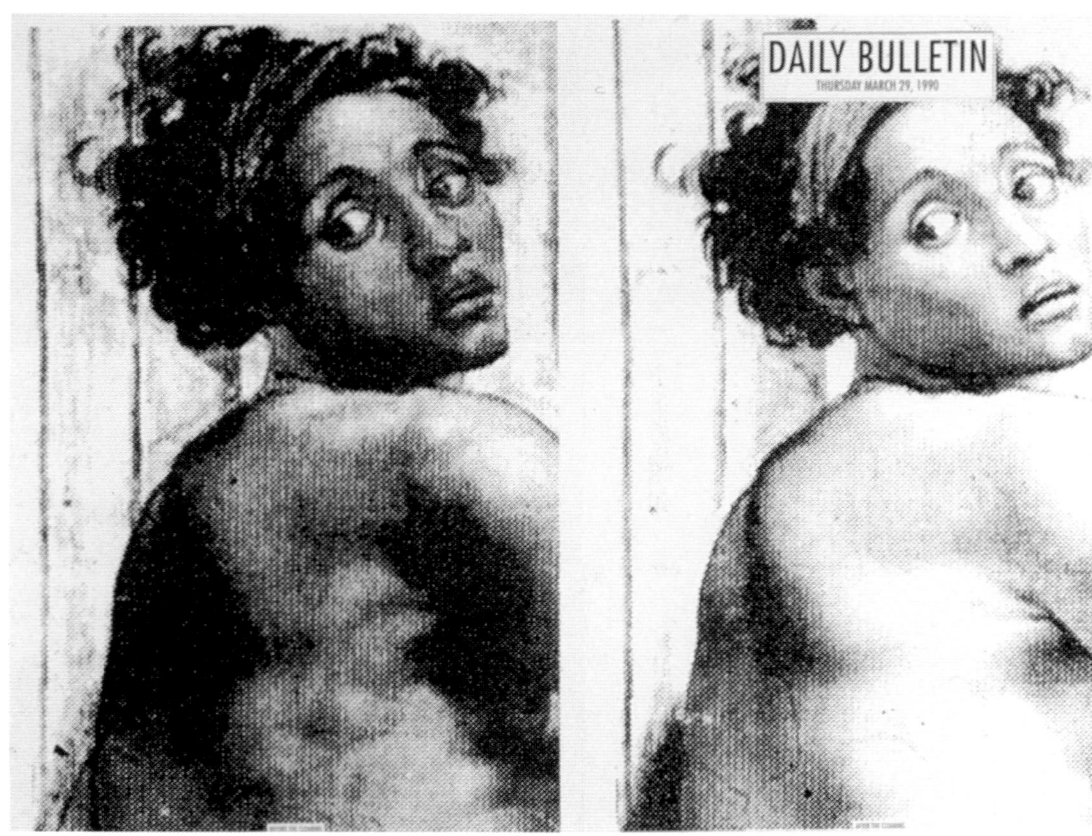

HOUSE VOTES TO ELEVATE E.P.A. TO CABINET LEVEL
BUSH THREATENS VETO

NASA CONCEDES SPACE STATION COST MAY RISE

FREE-TRADE TALKS WITH U.S. SET OFF DEBATE IN MEXICO

BUSH

CUOMO

MOURNERS FILL FUNERAL HOMES IN BRONX

SOCIAL CLUB FIRE

ALBANY URGES 1% REDUCTION IN LOCAL AID

Savings of $200 Million Seen to Bolster Budget

LAWMAKERS DEBATE LONG-TERM CARE

ATOM BOMB PARTS SEIZED IN BRITAIN EN ROUTE TO IRAQ

SIX ARRESTED IN SCHEME

THREE AGENCIES FAILED TO FOLLOW UP

BOMB FOUND IN L.I. SCHOOL

TWO-THIRDS OF NATION'S MINIMUM-WAGE WORKERS ARE WOMEN

RISE IN MINIMUM WAGE OFFERS MINIMUM JOY

STANDOFF

CONTRAS

LIBYA TAKES KEY STEP TO EXTEND RANGE OF BOMBERS

RIGHTS AT ISSUE

BRAZIL FIGHTS INFLATION

PRICES FROZEN FOR 30 DAYS

BITTER BATTLE IMPERILS SCHOOL SUPERINTENDENT

NEW ANTIDEPRESSANT IS ACCLAIMED BUT NOT PERFECT

PROZAC SIDE EFFECTS WORRISOME

TROUBLE

38-YEAR PLUTONIUM LOSS AT PLANT EQUALS 7 BOMBS

DOW

DOLLAR

GOLD

BONDS

WOMEN

THE KILLING WAS REAL; THE STUDY WAS A LIE

IN ZIMBABWE VOTING AND THREATS OF VIOLENCE

GRANADA TV IDENTIFIES 4 IN I.R.A. WHOM IT LINKS TO 21 DEATHS AT PUBS

GUILTY PLEA IN PENTAGON FRAUD CASE

PETER LYNCH RETIRES AT 46

MUTUAL FUND CHAMPION QUITS AS MAGELLAN HEAD

ROGER PORTER

EXPLOITING PEOPLE'S EXPECTATIONS

DE KLERK TO MEET HOMELAND LEADERS

SAVINGS NOMINEE CHALLENGED

SENATORS SAY RYAN LACKS EXPERIENCE

GUILD GAINING

FRENCH PLAN TO RESTRICT SMOKING AND ALCOHOL ADS

F.C.C. TILT TO MINORITIES WEIGHED BY HIGH COURT

BEIJING RESOLUTE ON BUSH MOVES

ISRAELI ARMY

TORCHMARK MAKES OFFER FOR INSURER

$6.3 BILLION FOR AMERICAN GENERAL CO.

JUNK BONDS

SOVIET AIRLINE

UTAH MONITOR OF 'COLD FUSION'

SOVIET VIEWS SEEN TO SPLIT BY REGION

A.T.&T. ISSUES JOB-CUT PLANS

THOMSON SECURITIES FILES FOR CHAPTER 11

COCOA HITS 7-MONTH HIGHS

STUDY REJECTS VIEW THAT DECONTROL CUT AIRFARES

HOCKEY

ISLANDERS STAY ALIVE WITH 3D-PERIOD FLURRY

GOLF

FIRST MAJOR L.P.G.A. TOURNAMENT OF DECADE BEGINS THURSDAY

TODAY'S WEATHER

DOLLAR GAINS AGAINST YEN

FALLS IN OTHER TRADING

WEAKER AGAINST POUND

BOSTON UNIVERSITY UNEXPECTED SURPRISE

QUALIFIES FOR NCAA TOURNAMENT

NICKLAUS OFFICIALLY A SENIOR

TEES OFF TOMORROW AT DESERT MOUNTAIN

U.S. TEAMS SHOWS SIGNS OF IMPROVEMENT

AUDREY HEPBURN NARRATES WORK ON ANNE FRANK AT U.N. GENERAL ASSEMBLY HALL

ADVERTISING

PERRIER PLANS RETURN WITH NEW VOICE

LEAVES HAL RINEY FOR WARING & LAROSA

N.H.L. PLAYERS NEEDED TO FORTIFY

NETS 106

KNICKS 101

HEAT 109

MAGIC 104

STANDINGS

SISTINE CEILING CLEANED OF GRIME

BASEBALL

GOODEN HAS PAIN IN RIGHT PLACES

METS "THRILLED"

MTV

COMEDY NETWORK

(RICE)

HA! STARTS SUNDAY

KELLOGG

"KENMEI"

LAKERS 106

CLIPPERS 99

BULLETS 113

NUGGETS 99

PASCUAL PEREZ ARRIVES IN CAMP

Lowsuit Delays Ability to Leave Dominican Republic

BULLS 117

KINGS 88

CAVALIERS 113

RECORD COMPANIES TO PUT WARNINGS ON CERTAIN RECORDINGS

NIPPON TV FINANCED VATICAN SISTINE CLEANING PROJECT

FARRAKKHAN SPEAKS WITH SOFT NEW VOICE

MAJOR QUESTIONS UNANSWERED IN DEATH OF GATHERS

YANKEES 5 EXPOS 2

METS 5 ORIOLES 2

PISTONS 106

HORNETS 97

N.C.A.A. BASKETBALL

UNIFORM DESIGN FOR ALL LABELS

TODAY'S TELEVISION

FOOTBALL

DORSETT RETIRES

DALLAS COWBOY STAR AUDITIONS FOR ESPN

JORDAN SCORES 69 POINTS

NETS END SLUMP AGAINST KNICKS

BASKETBALL

VANDERBILT CAPTURES TITLE

DAILY BULLETIN

THURSDAY MARCH 29, 1990

FIVE CENTS **mini**

Times

THURSDAY MARCH 29, 1990
VOL. CXXXIX...NO. 48,168

By BETTY JONES
Special to Mini Times

HOUS-

E VOTES BILL TO ELEVATE E.P.A. TO CABINET LEVEL

New York, March 29 - This is sample text for the mini times. It is for position only. After three weeks of tension, discord and daily pressure from Moscow, the leadership of Lithuania softened its sample text for the mini times. It is for position only.

This is sample text for the mini times it is not meant to be read. "we did not expect this and we did not count on this" the Lithuanian President said tonight. Mr. Landsbergis spoke in Vilnius, the Lithuanian capital, and his comments were reported on the Moscow television. This is sample text for the mini tmes.

By ALBERTO JONES
Special to Mini Times

LAWM

-AKERS DEBATE ON LONG-TERM CARE

New York, March 29 - This is sample text for the mini times. It is for position Mr. Landsbergis spoke in Vilnius, the Lithuanian capital, and his comments were reported on the Moscow television. This is sample text for the mini tmes. It is for position only and is not meant to be read.

By BETTY JONES
Special to Mini Times

RISE I-

N MINIMUM WAGE OFFERS MINI-MUM JOY

New York, March 29 - This is sample text for the mini times. It is for position only. After three weeks of tension, discord and daily pressure from Moscow, the leadership of Lithuania softened its 11. It may seem to some people that this amounted to a demand that power be handed over the very mext day This is sample text for the mini times.

By JONATHON SMITH
Special to Mini Times

TROU-

BLE RIGHT HERE IN CINCINNATI: FUROR OVER MAPPLETHORPE EXHIBIT

New York, March 29 - This is sample text for the mini times. It is for position only. After three weeks of tension, discord and daily pressure from Moscow, the leadership of Lithuania softened its tone today, insisting that it never expected immediate independence despite declaring itself free of Soviet rule on March 11. It may seem to some people that this amounted to a demand that power be handed over the very mext day This is sample text for the mini times. It is for position only.

This is sample text for the mini times it is not meant to be read. "we did not expect this and we did not count on this" the Lithuanian President said tonight.

By ALBERTO JONES
Special to Mini Times

38-YE-

AR PLUTONIUM LOSS AT PLANT EQUALS 7 BOMBS

New York, March 29 - This is sample text for the mini times. It is for position only. After three weeks of tension, discord and daily pressure from Moscow, the leadership of Lithuania softened its tone today, insisting that it never expected immediate independence despite declaring itself free of Soviet rule on March 11. It may seem to some people that this amounted to a demand that power be handed over the very mext day This is sample text for the mini times. It is for position only.

This is sample text for the mini times it is not meant to be read. "we did not expect this and we did not count on this" the Lithuanian President said tonight. Mr. Landsbergis spoke in Vilnius, the Lithuanian capital, and his comments were reported on the Moscow television. This is sample text for the mini tmes. It is for position only and is not meant to be read.

By JONATHON SMITH
Special to Mini Times

F.C.C. T

-ILT TO MINORITIES WEIGHED BY HIGH COURT

New York, March 29 - This is sample text for the mini times. It is for position only. After three weeks of tension, discord and daily pressure from Moscow, the leadership of Lithuania softened its tone today, insisting that it never expected immediate independence despite declaring itself free of Soviet rule on March

is not meant to be read. "we did not expect this and we did not count on this" the Lithuanian President said tonight. Mr. Landsbergis spoke in Vilnius, the text for the mini times. It is for position only. After three weeks of tension, discord and daily pressure from Moscow, the leadership of Lithuania softened its tone today, insisting that it never expected immediate independence despite declaring itself free of Soviet rule on March the Lithuanian President said tonight. Mr. Landsbergis spoke in Vilnius, the Lithuanian capital, and his comments were reported on the Moscow television. This is sample text for the mini tmes. It is for position only and is not meant to be read.

By JONATHON SMITH
Special to Mini Times

STUD-

Y REVEALS HIGH RISK TO OVERWEIGHT WOMEN

New York, March 29 - This is sample text for the mini times. It is for position only. After three weeks of tension, discord and daily pressure from Moscow, the leadership of Lithuania softened its tone today, insisting that it never expectamounted to a demand that power be handed over the very mext day This is sample text for the mini times. It is for position only.

This is sample text for the mini times it is not meant to be read. "we did not expect this and we did not count on this" the Lithuanian President said tonight. Mr. Landsbergis spoke in Vilnius, the Lithuanian capital, and his comments were reported on the Moscow television. This is sample text for the mini tmes. It is for position only and is not meant to be read.

By ALBERTO JONES
Special to Mini Times

STAN-

DOFF IN LITHUANIA

New York, March 29 - This is sample text for the mini times. It is for position only. After three weeks of tension, discord and daily pressure from Moscow, the leadership of Lithuania softened its tone today, insisting that it never expectsample text for the mini times. It is for position only.

This is sample text for the mini times it is not meant to be read. "we did not exwere reported on the Moscow television. This is sample text for the mini tmes. It is for position only and is not meant to be read.

By BETTY JONES
Special to Mini Times

RIGHT

-S AT ISSUE AS BRAZIL CONTINUES FIGHT ON INFLATION

New York, March 29 - This is sample text for the mini times. It is for position only. After three weeks of tension, discord and daily pressure from Moscow, the leadership of Lithuania softened its tone today, insisting that it never expected immediate independence despite declaring itself free of Soviet rule on March 11. It may seem to some people that this is not meant to be read. "we did not expect this and we did not count on this" the Lithuanian President said tonight. amounted to a demand that power be handed over the very mext day This is sample text for the mini times. It is for position only.

This is sample text for the mini times it is not meant to be read. "we did not expect this and we did not count on this" the Lithuanian President said tonight. Mr. Landsbergis spoke in Vilnius, the Lithuanian capital, and his comments were reported on the Moscow television. This is sample text for the mini tmes. It is for position only and is not meant to be read.

By JONATHON SMITH
Special to Mini Times

CONT-

RAS REPORTED BACK IN NICARAGUA

New York, March 29 - This is sample text for the mini times. It is for position only. After three weeks of tension, discord and daily pressure from Moscow, the leadership of Lithuania softened its tone today, insisting that it never expected immediate independence despite declaring itself free of Soviet rule on March 11. It may seem to some people

By ALBERTO JONES
Special to Mini Times

BRITI-

SH TELEVISION NAMES BOMBING SUSPECTS

New York, March 29 - This is sample text for the mini times. It is for position only. After three weeks of tension, discord and daily pressure from Moscow, the leadership of Lithuania softened its tone today, insisting that it never expected immediate independence despite declaring itself free of Soviet rule on March 11. It may seem to some people that this amounted to a demand that power be handed over the very mext day This is sample text for the mini times. It is for position only.

This is sample text for the mini times it is not meant to be read. "we did not expect this and we did not

By ALBERTO JONES
Special to Mini Times

BEIJIN

-G RESOLUTE ON MOVES BY BUSH

New York, March 29 - This is sample text for the mini times. It is for position only. After three weeks of tension, discord and daily pressure from Moscow, the leadership of Lithuania softened its tone today, insisting that it never expected immediate independence despite declaring itself free of Soviet rule on March 11. It may seem to some people that this amounted to a demand that power be handed over the very mext day This is sample text for the mini times. It is for position only.

This is sample text for the mini times it is not meant to be read. "we did not expect this and we did not count on this" the Lithuanian President said tonight. Mr. Landsbergis spoke in Vilnius, the Lithuanian capital, and his comments were reported on the Moscow television. This is sample text for the mini tmes. It is for position only and is not meant

By BETTY JONES
Special to Mini Times

SOVIE-

T VIEWS SEEN TO SPLIT BY REGION

New York, March 29 - This is sample text for the mini times. It is for position only. After three weeks of tension, discord and daily pressure from Moscow, the leadership of Lithuania softened its tone today, insisting that it never expected immediate independence despite declaring itself free of Soviet rule on March 11. It may seem to some people that this amounted to a demand that

This is sample text for the mini times it is not meant to be read. "we did not expect this and we did not count on this" the Lithuanian President said tonight. Mr. Landsbergis spoke in Vilnius, the Lithuanian capital, and his comments were reported on the Moscow television. This is sample text for the mini tmes. It is for position only and is not meant to be read.

This is sample text for the mini times it is not meant to be read. "we did not expect this and we did not count on this" the Lithuanian President said tonight. Mr. Landsbergis spoke in Vilnius, the Lithuanian capital, and his comments amounted to a demand that power be handed over the very mext day This is sample text for the mini times. It is for position only.

This is sample text for the mini times it is not meant to be read. "we did not expect this and we did not count on this" the Lithuanian President said tonight. Mr. Landsbergis spoke in Vilnius, the Lithuanian capital, and his comments were reported on the Moscow television. This is sample text for the mini tmes. It is for position only and is not meant to be read.

By JONATHON SMITH
Special to Mini Times

HUNG-

ARIANS WILL AGAIN FLY JEWS TO ISREAL UNDER ARAB THREATS

New York, March 29 - This is sample text for the mini times. It is for position only. After three weeks of tension, discord and daily pressure from Moscow, the leadership of Lithuania softened its tone today, insisting that it never expected immediate independence despite declaring itself free of Soviet rule

By BETTY JONES
Special to Mini Times

ALBA-

NY URGES 1% REDUCTION IN LOCAL AID SAVINGS OF $200 MILLION SEEN TO BOLSTER BUDGET

New York, March 29 - This is sample text for the mini times. It is for position only. After three weeks of tension, discord and daily pressure from Moscow, the leadership of Lithuania softened its tone today, insisting that it never expected immediate independence

This is sample text for the mini times it is not meant to be read. "we did not expect this and we did not count on this" the Lithuanian President said tonight. claring itself free of Soviet rule on March 11. It may seem to some people that this amounted to a demand that power be handed over the very mext day This is sample text for the mini times. It is for position only.

This is sample text for the mini times it is not meant to be read. "we did not expect this and we did not count on this" the Lithuanian President said tonight. Mr. Landsbergis spoke in Vilnius, the Lithuanian capital.

By BETTY JONES
Special to Mini Times

MOUR-

NERS FILL FUNERAL HOMES IN BRONX

New York, March 29 - This is sample text for the mini times. It is for position only. After three weeks of tension, discord and daily pressure from Moscow, the leadership of Lithuania softened its tone today, insisting that it never expected immediate independence despite declaring itself free of Soviet rule on March 11. It may seem to some people that this amounted to a demand that power be handed over the very mext day This is

By BETTY JONES
Special to Mini Times

BITTE-

R BATTLE IMPERILS SCHOOL SUPERINTENDENT

New York, March 29 - This is sample text for the mini times. It is for position only. After three weeks of tension, discord and daily pressure from Moscow, the leadership of Lithuania softened its tone today, insisting that it never expected immediate independence despite declaring itself free of Soviet rule on March sample text for the mini times. It is for position only.

By JONATHON SMITH
Special to Mini Times

FIRE I-

N BRONX

New York, March 29 - This is sample text for the mini times. It is for position only. After three weeks of tension, discord and daily pressure from Moscow, the leadership of Lithuania softened its tone today, insisting that it never expected immediate independence despite declaring itself free of Soviet rule

By ALBERTO JONES
Special to Mini Times

JORD-

AN SCORES 69 POINTS TO BEAT CLEVELAND 117-113

New York, March 29 - This is sample text for the mini times. It is for position only. After three weeks of tension, discord and daily pressure from Moscow, the leadership of Lithuania softened its tone today, insisting that it never expected immediate independence despite declaring itself free of Soviet rule on March 11. It may seem to some people that this amounted to a demand that power be handed over the very mext day This is sample text for the mini times. It is for position only.

This is sample text for the mini times it is not meant to be read. "we did not expect this and we did not count on this" the Lithuanian President said

By JONATHON SMITH
Special to Mini Times

VAND-

ERBILT CAPTURES TITLE BY DEFEATING ST. LOUIS 74-72

New York, March 29 - This is sample text for the mini times. It is for position only. After three weeks of tension, discord and daily pressure from Moscow, the leadership of Lithuania softened its tone today, insisting that it never expected immediate independence despite declaring itself free of Soviet rule on March 11. It may seem to some people that this amounted to a demand that

By ALBERTO JONES
Special to Mini Times

ISLAN

-ERS STAY ALIVE WITH 3D-PERIOD FLURRY

New York, March 29 - This is sample text for the mini times. It is for position only. After three weeks of tension, discord and daily pressure from Moscow, the leadership of Lithuania

This is sample text for the mini times it is not meant to be read. "we did not expect this and we did not count on this" the Lithuanian President said tonight. Mr. Landsbergis spoke in Vilnius handed over the very mext day This is sample text for the mini times. It is for position only.

This is sample text for the mini times it is not meant to be read. "we did not expect this and we did not count on this" the Lithuanian President said tonight. Mr. Landsbergis spoke in Vilnius, the Lithuanian capital, and his comments were reported on the Moscow television. This is sample text for the mini tmes.

By ALBERTO JONES
Special to Mini Times

PLAYE

-RS NEEDED TO FORTIFY NATIONAL HOCKEY TEAMS

New York, March 29 - This is sample text for the mini times. It is for position only. After three weeks of tension, discord and daily pressure from Moscow, the leadership of Lithuania softened its ed immediate independence despite declaring itself free of Soviet rule on March 11. It may seem to some people that this amounted to a demand that power be handed over the very mext day This is sample text for the mini times. It is for position only.

By JONATHON SMITH
Special to Mini Times

ROST-

-ER WON'T EXPAND FOR OPENING OF BASEBALL SEASON

New York, March 29 - This is sample text for the mini times. It is for position only. After three weeks of tension, discord and daily pressure from Moscow, the leadership of Lithuania softened its

is not meant to be read. "we did not expect this and we did not count on this" the Lithuanian President said tonight. Mr. Landsbergis spoke in Vilnius, the Lithuanian capital, and his comments were reported on the Moscow television. This is sample text for the mini tmes.

By ALBERTO JONES
Special to Mini Times

PASCA

-L PEREZ ARRIVES IN CAMP

New York, March 29 - This is sample text for the mini times. It is for position only. After three weeks of tension, discord and daily pressure from Moscow, the leadership of Lithuania softened its tone today, insisting that it never expected immediate independence

By BETTY JONES
Special to Mini Times

GUILT-

Y PLEA FROM CONSULTANT IN PENTAGON FRAUD CASE

New York, March 29 - This is sample text for the mini times. It is for position only. After three weeks of tension, discord and daily pressure from Moscow, the leadership of Lithuania softened its tone today, insisting that it never expected immediate independence despite declaring itself free of Soviet rule on March 11. It may seem to some people that this amounted to a demand that power be handed over the very mext day This is sample text for the mini times. It is for position only.

This is sample text for the mini times it is not meant to be read. "we did not expect this and we did not count on this" the Lithuanian President said tonight. Mr. Landsbergis spoke in Vilnius, the Lithuanian capital, and his comments were reported on the Moscow television. This is sample text for the mini tmes. It is for position only and is not meant to be read.

By ALBERTO JONES
Special to Mini Times

MUTU

-AL FUND CHAMPION QUITS MAGELLAN HEAD

New York, March 29 - This is sample text for the mini times. It is for position only. After three weeks of tension, discord and daily pressure from Moscow, the leadership of Lithuania softened its handed over the very mext day This is sample text for the mini times. It is for position only.

This is sample text for the mini times it is not meant to be read. "we did not expect this and we did not count on this" the Lithuanian President said tonight. Mr. Landsbergis spoke in Vilnius, the Lithuanian capital, and his comments were reported on the Moscow television. This is sample text for the mini tmes. It is for position only and is not meant to be read.

By BETTY JONES
Special to Mini Times

SAVIN-

GS NOMINEE CHALLENGED

New York, March 29 - This is sample text for the mini times. It is for position only. After three weeks of tension, discord and daily pressure from Moscow, the leadership of Lithuania softened its tone today, insisting that it never expected immediate independence despite declaring itself free of Soviet rule on March 11. It may seem to some people that this amounted to a demand that power be handed over the very mext day This is sample text for the mini times. It is for position only.

By ALBERTO JONES
Special to Mini Times

FREN-

CH PLAN TO RESTRICT SMOKING & ALCOHOL ADVERTISEMENTS

New York, March 29 - This is sample text for the mini times. It is for position only. After three weeks of tension, discord and daily pressure from Moscow, the leadership of Lithuania softened its tone today, insisting that it never expected immediate independence despite declaring itself free of Soviet rule on March 11. It may seem to some people that this amounted to a demand that power be handed over the very mext day

By BETTY JONES
Special to Mini Times

TORC-

HMARK MAKES $6 BILLION OFFER FOR INSURER

New York, March 29 - This is sample text for the mini times. It is for position only. After three weeks of tension, discord and daily pressure from Moscow, the leadership of Lithuania softened its tone today, insisting that it never expected immediate independence despite declaring itself free of Soviet rule on March 11. It may seem to some people that this amounted to a demand that power be handed over the very mext day This is sample text for the mini times. It is for position only.

This is sample text for the mini times it is not meant to be read.

By JONATHON SMITH
Special to Mini Times

AUDR-

EY HEPBURN NARRATES WORK ON ANNE FRANK

New York, March 29 - This is sample text for the mini times. It is for position only. After three weeks of tension, discord and daily pressure from Moscow, the leadership of Lithuania softened its tone today, insisting that it never expected immediate independence despite declaring itself free of Soviet rule on March 11. It may seem to some people that this amounted to a demand that power be handed over the very mext day This is sample text for the mini times. It is for position only.

This is sample text for the mini times it is not meant to be read. "we did not expect this and we did not count on this" the Lithuanian President said tonight. Mr. Landsbergis spoke in Vilnius, the Lithuanian capital, and his comments were reported on the Moscow television. This is sample text for the mini tmes. It is for position only and is not meant to be read.

This is sample text for the mini times it is not meant to be read. "we did not expect this and we did not count on this" the Lithuanian President said tonight. Mr. Landsbergis spoke in Vilnius, the Lithuanian capital, and his comments were reported on the Moscow television. This is sample text for the mini tmes. It is for position only and is not

By JONATHON SMITH
Special to Mini Times

AT TH-

E CIRCUS NEW OWNER FLAVIO CRACKS WHIP

New York, March 29 - This is sample text for the mini times. It is for position only. After three weeks of tension, discord and daily pressure from Moscow, the leadership of Lithuania softened its tone today, insisting that it never expected immediate independence despite declaring itself free of Soviet rule on March 11. It may seem to some people that this amounted to a demand that power be handed over the very mext day

This is sample text for the mini times it is not meant to be read. "we did not expect this and we did not count on this" the Lithuanian President said tonight

By BETTY JONES
Special to Mini Times

RECO

RD COMPANIES TO PUT WARN ON CERTAIN RECORDINGS

New York, March 29 - This is text for the mini times. It is for only. After three weeks of ten cord and daily pressure from the leadership of Lithuania s tone today, insisting that it n ed immediate independence

This is sample text for the is not meant to be read. " pect this and we did not the Lithuanian Presiden Mr. Landsbergis spoke the leadership of Lithu tone today, insisting tha ed immediate indepen claring itself free of So 11. It may seem to so amounted to a dem handed over the ve sample text for the position only.

This is sample te is not meant to b pect this and w the Lithuanian Mr. Landsber Lithuanian ca were reported on the Mo This is sample text for the mini t is for position only and is not meant to be read.

By JONATHON SMITH
Special to Mini Times

NIPPO

-N TV FINANCED VATICAN SISTINE CLEANING PROJECT

New York, March 29 - This is sample text for the mini times. It is for position only. After three weeks of tension, discord and daily pressure from Moscow, the leadership of Lithuania softened its tone today, insisting that it never expected immediate independence despite declaring itself free of Soviet rule on March 11. It may seem to some

TV HI-

GHLIGHTS

This is sample text for the mini times it is not meant to be read. "we did not expect this and we did not count on this" the Lithuanian President said tonight. Mr. Landsbergis spoke in Vilnius, the Lithuanian capital, and his

WEAT-

ER

cord and daily pressure from Moscow, the leadership of Lithuania softened its tone today, insisting that it never expected immediate independence

FIVE CENTS mini Times
THURSDAY MARCH 29, 1990
By BETTY JONES
Special to Mini Times
HOUS-
E VOTES BILL TO ELEVATE E.P.A. TO CABINET LEVEL
By BETTY JONES
Special to Mini Times
RISE I-
N MINIMUM WAGE OFFERS MINI-MUM JOY
By JONATHON SMITH
Special to Mini Times

Essays and Talks

Christmas monoprint “Dancing Fools”

ART AND WORK

Cooper Union Commencement Speech, 1997

Thank you all for the privilege of speaking to you today. I never imagined almost half a century ago, when I was waiting impatiently for this very ceremony to end, that one day I might be creating the same restlessness in a similar audience desperate to burst upon the world and reshape its form and nature. Half a century is a long time in human affairs, after all the Viennese secession only lasted twenty-five years, but truthfully, it now seems to have passed like a sweet breeze on a summer afternoon.

My wife Shirley and I lived two blocks from here for the first half of our married life, during the sixties and seventies. These were astonishing decades in which one day you would bump into W. H. Auden padding along St. Marks Place in his house slippers and the next day encounter Allen Ginsberg on his way home with a shopping bag full of groceries. When my father first arrived in America from Eastern Europe, he settled 100 yards from where Shirley and I later chose to live. His move, in the twenties, to the relative gentility of the Bronx, represented his transformation into an American citizen. He could never understand how his son ended up where he had started.

Art remains a mystery. We wonder about its significance in our lives. Why is it important? Why does it persist? When we observe the exploitation of art by the art world, the collectors, the dealers, the critics and curators, stumbling all over themselves to own, control and benefit from its production, it's easy to become cynical about its purpose.

Auden passed away some years ago but the neighborhood's restless energy is still there. Apartments no longer can be found for sixty-five dollars a month, or twenty-five if you had the fortitude to live on Avenue C. The Balloon Farm Disco is long gone but the B & H Luncheonette is still doing business at the same old location on Second Avenue. B & H, incidentally, are not the initials of the owners; they stand for "Better Health." When we were living in the neighborhood, it was our habit to have dinner at the counter of B & H before leaving for the country on Friday nights: matzoh ball soup and a tuna fish on rye with a slice of onion—enough carbohydrates to sustain a construction worker for a week. The counter man was a light skinned, white haired, ex-army guy named "Sarge," for obvious reasons. He was a short order cook (a species now in danger of extinction) who would start two orders of fried eggs, hash browns, and toast at the same time he was making a grilled cheese sandwich for someone else. This is not easy to do but Sarge managed to put your eggs in front of you, usually overcooked, but rarely burned, every time.

Sarge somehow had heard that Shirley could read palms and one evening, after putting her eggs on the counter, he asked, "Could you read my palm?" Shirley was unprepared for the request but agreed to try. She took his hand and peered at it intently. "You'll be lucky at the track," she said, with a concerned look on her face, and then went on to make some general comments that didn't strike me as being very convincing.

"**D**id you see some bad news in Sarge's palm?" I asked as we left the B & H. "No," she said, "the truth is I was stunned because Sarge doesn't have a single line on his palm. It's like a blank sheet of paper. Not only doesn't he have a past, he doesn't seem to have much of a future either." "What about being lucky at the track?" I asked. "I just made that up," Shirley said. "I knew that it was all he wanted to know."

On the other hand, all of you graduating today do have a future, and in a very significant way you are prepared to engage it, as I was forty-seven years ago. Of course, I didn't know it at the time.

One reason I was well prepared was because of an odd-looking fellow named Peter Cooper who founded this school in 1859 and had the curious conviction that making money wasn't the only significant aspiration in life. The generous spirit of this extraordinary nineteenth-century industrialist still envelopes us today because he put his money where his mouth was, right here. These days Peter Cooper might be considered a traitor to his class. He believed that life could be improved for the many, and that preparing people for life through education was the way to begin.

As I've grown older I've become more aware of how small even seemingly trivial events can change one's life. I can recall how a word of encouragement at a critical moment changed mine.

When I was in junior high school I was rather good in science and my science teacher enthusiastically encouraged me to pursue a life in that subject. At the end of the school year I told him that I had been accepted into the High School of Music and Art. I felt awkward because I knew he had other plans for me. One week later he asked me to stay after class. This was usually a bad sign. He took a small package out of his desk drawer and asked me to open it. I unwrapped it nervously and saw that it contained a box of beautiful French conte crayons. "Do good work," he said. It took me many years to understand that his real gift to me wasn't the crayons but the blessing he gave me to pursue my own passion and path in life in spite of his own interests. Without really knowing it I made an internal resolution to be worthy of his faith in me. Because he believed in me, I believed in myself. Such is the nature of the human mind. The brain is the most adaptable organ in our body. Unlike a computer, every experience we have in life is capable of changing it. In this regard it is a perfect example of Darwinian theory. My good fortune continued at Cooper Union where my mind was nourished and encouraged to change by many of my teachers. I particularly remember Nicolas Marsicano, who died recently, a man so open-minded that he would never dream of imposing his own aesthetic point of view on you. If you wanted to paint like a fifteenth-century Florentine that was okay, a synthetic cubist? that was okay too. As long as you did it well, Nicolas didn't care. In that regard, he anticipated the emerging postmodern view that style and art have very little to do with one another. This quality of open-mindedness is in short supply these days. Even though, paradoxically, our time is characterized by the dissolution of belief. Open-mindedness encourages skepticism, but cynicism is its enemy. Detached "coolness" is a poor substitute for intellectual inquiry. Personally, I can hardly wait for the arrival of Post Ironic Art. Irony was originally used as a means of intensifying experience, now it mainly serves to discredit it.

Art remains a mystery. We wonder about its significance in our lives. Why is it important? Why does it persist? When we observe the exploitation of art by the art world, the collectors, the dealers, the critics and curators, stumbling over themselves to own, control and benefit from its production, it's easy to become cynical about its purpose. Not to mention the historical examples of church and state using art as a means of propaganda and control over people's beliefs and lives.

But we may have arrived at a new historical moment that is truly unprecedented. The end of the modernist agenda and the discovery that art can no longer be defined by the way it looks. I am sure there is a comparable situation in the sciences, because art and science are twins swimming in the same zeitgeist.

A short time ago I was watching a program on television about wild life in Australia. Don't ask me why. The show was exploring the mating habits of the bower bird, a handsome creature that has a curious courting practice. The male builds a structure, a bower if you will, out of weeds and sticks, a sort of tunnel shaped like a gothic arch. The female bower birds are attracted to the place, enter the tunnel, and in a flash the male has his way with them. The most astonishing thing about this is that the female will not enter the bower unless it is well constructed and pleasing in appearance.

The male does his best to create an aesthetically pleasing structure, going so far as to pile up colorful stones adjacent to the bower. If he's an insensitive clod and builds a sloppy honeymoon suite, he's out of luck; the female won't enter and he shall be robbed of the opportunity to pass on his genes.

The story struck me with considerable force because it validated something I've felt for a long time—that art and the idea of beauty are somehow linked to our survival, not only in a cultural sense, where shared values and beliefs create the commonalties and communities that defuse hostility, but also at the most fundamental cellular level. Art is a survival mechanism. It prepares us for life.

When I was asked to deliver today's commencement, I wanted to tell you something truly useful, something like Nelson Algren's famous year-end resolutions. You may remember "never eat at a place called Mom's," "never play cards with a guy named Doc," and "never go to bed with someone who has more trouble than you do." I could only think of one thing in the same category. It was a discovery made by Fritz Perls, a gestalt therapist and behavioral guru in the sixties. Fritz said a lot of silly things but I've been guided by one of his observations for more than thirty years and it has served me well. Perls noted that every human relationship was either toxic or nourishing. That is to say, you're either being fed or poisoned. There's a simple test to determine which is happening. Spend some time with the other person. At the end of your time together observe yourself and determine whether you have more energy of less. If you have more, you've been nourished, if less, you've been poisoned. Check it out.

We are living in a momentous time in human history where the idea of democracy has possessed more of the world than ever before. The old principles of autocratic control and privilege are crumbling even as new forms of oppression arise. Whether all of you have the courage to sustain this movement toward increased human freedom remains to be seen, but you have been well prepared. Do good work.

DESIGN AND AMBIGUITY

45th Annual Convention of the New York State Art Teachers Association.

When I entitled this talk "Design and Ambiguity," it was principally because I had no idea of what I might be talking about. As things worked out, I'm going to talk about some concepts that are in fact ambiguous to me.

As I grow older, I am surprised to discover that things have not gotten any clearer. On the contrary, the simplest things seem to have become more puzzling.

I would like to talk briefly about four things: first, the relationship between art, design, and business. I'll talk about the use of light in illustration and design, followed by the mysteries of likeness, and finally a bit about ambiguity in design.

Then I'll show some slides so the evening won't be a total loss.

The instinct to create form usually occurs early. The term "artistic" is most often used to describe this tendency, although any child who draws or cuts paper has no idea of what this term means. It seems to be a fundamental drive of the human species that can be easily discouraged by life and society. In early childhood, the interest is celebrated and encouraged by parents and teachers. It is only somewhat later that this encouragement fades as questions of practicality begin. Only the most willful and possessed child is able to resist the pressure towards a more conventional path. At this point there is little distinction in a child's mind between a career as a designer and life as a painter.

These early impulses toward form have aesthetic and moral implications rooted in the idea of making objects in order to understand the world and ourselves. I was five years old when my cousin, Saul, came into the house carrying a brown paper bag. "Do you want to see a bird?" he asked. I said yes, thinking that the bag contained a bird. He took out a pencil and drew a realistic bird on the bag. I was astounded. It was the first drawing I had ever seen in the process of being made that actually resembled the object depicted. I decided at that moment to spend my life in pursuit of that kind of miracle, and I have never deviated from that course.

As I have mentioned, when the visually obsessed are younger, they are pushed toward a decision to enter either the world of commerce or the world of art. One offers the possibility of making a living, and the other, by and large, does not.

At art schools, which are usually divided between the fine arts and the applied arts, a peculiar process begins. Those students who select design as their major are perceived as having "sold out," that is, of having exchanged their higher calling for commercial reasons. They are shunned and humiliated by the fine arts faculty and students. One of the causes of this behavior undoubtedly stems from the recognition that the relentless pursuit of money does not help one's spiritual development. We all know rich men don't go to heaven. Another seems to be a materialistic society's need to separate aesthetics from utility for political reasons.

Undoubtedly, status and self-aggrandizing impulses also contribute to this separation. The fear of corruption leads to the following arguable hierarchy of roles, the exact order varies a bit, but those at the top are closest to God and inspire more respect.

Art Hierarchy

PAINTER
ARCHITECT
SCULPTOR
ARTIST-CRAFTSMAN *
CITY PLANNER
INDUSTRIAL DESIGNER
GRAPHIC DESIGNER
LANDSCAPE ARCHITECT
INTERIOR DESIGNER
BOOK DESIGNER
EDITORIAL DESIGNER
ADVERTISING DESIGNER
(ART DIRECTOR)
CRAFTSMAN
COMMERCIAL ARTIST **

* *This is an interesting new term that attempts to blur the distinction between two formerly distinct activities. It seems to have come into use because Art has somewhat undefinable value which allows it to be sold at any price; and Craft is related to labor costs which seems finite. By claiming a relationship to art, status can be enhanced and prices can be raised.*

** *It's true that many of the roles can be subsumed by the phrase commercial artist, but if you describe yourself that way, you go right to the bottom of the list.*

Lewis Hyde, in the book called "The Gift," argues persuasively that an artist's role in civilized culture is very much related to gift giving in primitive cultures. In primitive cultures, the ritual of giving insists that the gifts themselves cannot be kept for personal gain. The gift must be passed on and serves the species by establishing connections and responsibilities between giver and receiver. With an impressive leap of the imagination, Hyde suggests that artists serve this same function in civilized communities. His final point being that art is not about exchanging goods; rather, it is a gift that unifies societies and provides a basis for understanding. Shamans and magicians create the mythology and imagery of non-industrialized cultures. Artists do it for us. Picasso was the great visual mythmaker of a preceding generation. In our time, in the world of painting, the emphasis has changed from the creation of myth to the creation of merchandise.

If one of the definitions we have concerning art is that it serves its public by reflecting and explaining the world at a particular moment in history, it is hard to believe that design does not serve in a similar way. In any case, the issue has become blurred since art currently seems to be mostly about money, and designers seem to be increasingly, concerned about ethics, the environment, and their effect on the world.

All that aside, the effect of separating art and design, which occurs in the schools, and continues later in life, erodes the perception that design shares with art a responsibility to community, and an ethical center. Designers are placed somewhere between the ethos of art and the ethos of business, and this causes a lifetime of conflicting identifications.

It was interesting for me to read in a recent *New York Times* review of a show of Rembrandt drawings, that questions of Rembrandt's motivations are now being raised by a generation of revisionist critics. The suggestion is that Rembrandt was not a unique genius who was simply seeking to express his innermost thoughts, but rather, a shrewd and manipulative opportunist simply trying to accommodate the preferences of his clients—the wealthy Dutch Burgers. Could it be that even the mightiest of figures in the history of painting could have sold out and been trying to make a living by satisfying his client? What does that say about the rest of us?

If businessmen continue to believe that design is only a question of effective marketing, they misunderstand both the role of design and business, and its effect on cultural and communal values. In other words, the effect of business on culture is not about buying paintings to decorate an office, or supporting television programming on the ballet, or even being on a museum board, but rather to recognize that in their daily business life the products they make have a profound cultural effect. This daily activity is not separated from the culture we live in, but serves it and shapes it at the same time. Among other things, the well-made object enhances life. The shoddy one erodes it. Only when this perception changes that "bottom line" results are not the only way to evaluate the meaning of a business or a life, will the situation begin to change.

We seem to be in a moment in history where this change is imperative, or perhaps it has always

ART ETHOS	QUESTIONS	BUSINESS ETHOS
NO. Art must express personal values and vision. To accommodate the market place is a sell-out.	Is it appropriate to change your personal style to accommodate the marketplace?	**YES.** Business, almost by definition, must respond to the needs of the market. Not to do so would be stupid and irresponsible.
NO. Art depends on the acknowledgement and continuity if its influences. We celebrate that community.	Is it appropriate to copy someone else's idea and use it for your own purposes without acknowledging the source?	**YES.** All ideas are meant to be effectively used for specific ends. A free market depends on being able to use anyone's ideas.
YES. That is one of the roles that art has historically served.	Is one of the roles of work to illuminate the human condition?	**NO.** In business we may reflect the human condition but illuminating it is irrelevant.
YES. Artistic decisions are linked to moral decisions and cannot be separated.	Can work serve as a means of discovering what we believe in, or help us in forming our values?	**NO.** This is not a relevant concern in business- the voyage of self discovery is best pursued elsewhere.
YES. In some metaphysical way art can reach people and join them in a community of common understanding and purpose.	Can one's work help the species survive?	**YES.** Business and competition create affluence, and the exchange of ideas, goods and services benefits everyone.
NO.	Is it acceptable to work only in order to make money? 1 2 3 midpoint 5 6 7	**YES.**

seemed this way since the industrial revolution. In any case we require a shift of emphasis from the idea we all grew up with that "good design is good business," to the suggestion that both design and business should serve the common communal good.

Power and design share the same definition. Both express the ability to achieve an intended plan. Designers, like all members of the human species, often suffer from a sense of powerlessness because their power (and hence their effectiveness) is in the hands of another—the client.

It is not surprising that the client inspires awe, fear, and loathing. These are the sentiments of the powerless confronting the powerful. Designers are always asking themselves: how do I become more effective (read powerful)? Actually, the question is more usually expressed as: "how do I educate the client to see things my way?" The phrase "to educate the client," is a time-worn and mischievous cliche. It is also egotistically presumptuous. People in business, and other clients, yield power to us for a variety of reasons. The most frequent one being the perceptions that the designer has technical and intellectual skills that can be utilized to achieve the client's objectives. Another is personal affinity and friendship. I know that this is not theoretically supposed to be a professional consideration, but through the years I have observed that I have done my best work with people I have had a personal relationship with. A third reason, and one I find compelling at this moment in history, is a shared belief that design and designers can serve a high moral purpose. What purpose? Our old friend, the common communal good. Design has a long history in this regard. The idea that design has social consequences is not exactly new. Art Nouveau, the Arts and Crafts movement, and the Bauhaus to name but three; all relate the perfectibility of form to the perfectibility of the human species. In our time, it is instructive to see how we have stripped Modernist thought of both its spiritual and political dimensions, and retained only its academic and formal values.

In the United States the social impulses that characterized Bauhaus thought began to be transformed by our pragmatic objectives, such as the use of design as a marketing tool and the elevation of style and taste as the moral center of design. The primacy of individual opportunity and capitalistic efficiency replaced much of the mildly socialist impulses of the modern movement.

Modernism, which once represented a new aesthetic, linked to social objectives, has been robbed of its meaning by this reduction. In design terms, it has become a style most frequently used as an abstract representation of corporate power—just look at the endless array of mindless geometric trade marks that glut our minds and vision.

Design transforms society—it helps create our mythology and consequently shapes our future. In many ways it has replaced the role that high art once filled. It is time we all acknowledge and respect that fact.

DESIGN AND BUSINESS & THE WAR IS OVER

AIGA Journal, Volume 14–No.3, 1996

When I first came to Aspen, the mantra, "good design is good business," was the guiding assumption of our professional lives. Although it sounded beneficial to business, like all true mantras it had a secret metaphysical objective: to spiritually transform the listener. We were convinced that once business experienced "beauty" (good design), a transformation would occur. Business would be enlightened and pay us to produce well-made objects for a waiting public. That public would, in turn, be educated into a new awareness. Society would be transformed and the world would be a better place. This belief can only be looked on now as an extraordinary combination of innocence and wishful thinking.

After forty years, business now indeed believes that good design is good business. In fact, it believes in it so strongly that design has been removed from the hands of designers and put into the hands of the marketing department. In addition, the meaning of the word "good" has suffered an extraordinary redefinition. Among an ever increasing number of clients, it now only means "what yields profits."

While we might agree that all of life is an attempt to mediate between spiritual and material needs, at this moment in our work the material seems to have swept the spiritual aside. Hardball is now the name of the game, and the rules have changed. This of course is nothing new. The struggle between these issues is as old as humankind. Through the years, as the power of official religion declined, the source and receptacle of truth and morality became "the arts"—and all those who were involved in it formed a new kind of priesthood. Designers very often perceived themselves as being part of this alliance against the philistines whose lack of religiosity had to be opposed in order to produce a better world. Now this conflict seems to have resurfaced with a vengeance. One might say that what we are experiencing is merely a question of atmosphere, but the atmosphere is the air we breathe, and it has turned decidedly poisonous. Let me use a recent contract I received from a record company to illustrate this change in spirit. The contract reads, in part:

> "**Y**ou acknowledge that we shall own all right, title and interest in and to the Package and all components thereof, including, but not limited to, the worldwide copyrights in the Package. You acknowledge that the Package constitutes a work specifically ordered by us for use as a contribution to a collective work. You further acknowledge that we shall have the right to use the Package and/or any of the components thereof and reproductions thereof for any and all purposes throughout the universe, in perpetuity, including, but not limited to, album artwork, advertising, promotion, publicity, and merchandising, and that no further money shall be payable to you in connection with any such use. Finally, you acknowledge that we shall have the right to retain possession of the original artwork comprising the Package."

The first thing one notices is the punishing tone. This is not an agreement between colleagues, but the voice of the victor in a recently concluded war. It reinstates the principle of "work for hire," a concept that presumes that the client initiates and conceptualizes the work in question, and that the designer merely acts as a supplier to execute it. It destroys the relationship between payment and usage so that, although the work has been created for a specific purpose (and paid for accordingly), the client is free to use it anywhere, and forever, without further payments. This violates the most fundamental assumptions about compensation of professionals, i.e., that what something is being used for and how frequently it is used is the basis for determining how much should be paid for it. It also claims ownership of the original art, marking the reintroduction of a mean-spirited and unfair doctrine that we all assumed had been legally eliminated. The overall posture, of course, reflects what is seen in the larger culture—a kind of class warfare that occurs when societies lose their sense of common purpose. The collegial sense of being in the same boat, pulling towards a common shore, has been eroded and replaced by the sense that the rowers are below decks and the orders are coming from above.

The Aspen Conference itself was founded in 1951 by Walter Paepcke and Egbert Jacobson, his art director, to promote design as a function of management. It became, for a time, the preeminent symbol of the modern alliance of commerce and culture. They were joined in this adventure, at least spiritually, by such remarkable figures as Joseph Albers, Herbert Bayer, and Laszlo Moholy-Nagy, the last of whom was active in Chicago's new Bauhaus, a school committed to the principles of modernism and the reconciliation of art and consumer capitalism. It is not an overstatement to say that design education in America began here. It is important to remember that the Bauhaus was not simply a trade school, but represented nothing less than the transformation of the life and world of inner man, and "the building of a new concept of the world by the architects of a new civilization." Cultural reform was at the center of Bauhaus thought, as it has been in many art movements. The Arts and Crafts movement in England, as well as the Viennese Secessionalists shared this common characteristic. Modernism itself, in its earliest form, was a religious movement that rejected what it perceived to be the unfair dogma of Catholicism, and attempted to restore religion to a meaningful role in people's lives.

In America, the metaphysical objectives and the ideal of civic responsibility went underground or were swept partially away. The pressures of professional practice and bread winning left little room for theoretical inquiry into social issues. Nevertheless, the feeling that the arts in general, and design in particular, could improve the human condition persisted and informed the practice.

In the struggle between commerce and culture, commerce has triumphed, and the war is over. It occurred so swiftly that none of us were quite prepared for it, although we all sensed that all was not well in our world. Anxiety, frustration, humiliation, and despair are the feelings that are revealed when designers now talk among themselves about their work. These are the feelings of losers, or at least of loss. The two most frequent complaints concern the decline of respect for creative accomplishment and the increasing encroachment of repetitious production activity on available professional time. These are linked complaints that are the inevitable consequence of the change in mythology and status that the field has gone through. The relationship of graphic design to art and social reform has become largely irrelevant. In short, designers have been transformed from privileged members of an artistic class or priesthood into industrial workers. This analogy partially explains why the first question now asked about a designer by a client is more often not how creative or professionally competent she or he might be, but how much do they charge per hour. If someone is tightening screws on a production line, it scarcely matters that he or she might be a brilliant poet. They still only earn $15 an hour. The same assumption makes it understandable how a person with six weeks of computer training now can become a designer with significant responsibility in a corporation without having any knowledge of color, form, art history, or aesthetics in general. We once thought of these things as essential to a designer's education.

But why now? What brought us to this unhappy circumstance when there is more design interest, more graphic designers, and more schools teaching the subject than at any time in history? Overpopulation may be one of the problems, particularly when combined with the downsizing that a contracting economy and the computer have caused. Economic forces and technology have always driven aesthetics, although sometimes the relationship is not obvious. Aldus, the great Venetian printer, discovered that by setting his texts in more condensed italic letters he could reduce the length of his books by twenty percent. That observation enabled him to save an enormous amount in paper costs and sell the same text cheaper than his contemporaries could. He became the most successful printer in Venice, and the italic style of typography became dominant in books for the next hundred years.

In the past the design process seemed esoteric, highly specialized, full of internal rituals, and hard to understand from the outside. These characteristics are all typical of spiritual or artistic activity, and serve as a means of protection. The computer, with its unprecedented power to change meaning, has made the process transparent and therefore controllable; and as we know, control is the name of the game. The argument within the field about computers has been mostly concerned with whether they are an aid or a hindrance to creativity. These concerns resemble the semiconscious babblings of someone that has just been run over by a truck. The phrase, "It's only a tool," scarcely considers the fact that this tool has totally redefined the practice and recast its values, all within a decade.

Clients can now micro-manage every step of the design process, and production has become the central and most time consuming part of every design office's activity. The overriding values are efficiency and cost control.

The use of the computer encourages a subtle shift of emphasis from the invented form to the assembled one. Imagery is now obtained increasingly from existing files and sources more cheaply than they can be produced by assigning new work. Electronic clip books have become the raw material for a kind of illustration we might call computer surrealism. Magritte is spinning in his grave, and who can blame him?

The computer appears to be an empowering and democratic tool. The operator can achieve results that previously were obtainable only through the long process of study and skill development. This partially explains its addictive effect on the user. For myself, someone deeply shaped by old value systems, all expressive forms that are easily achieved are suspect. There are many more bad examples of clay modeling than stone carving; the very resistance of the stone makes one approach the act of carving thoughtfully and with sustained energy. This may also be a small and passing issue. History has shown us that technologies develop their own standards.

Within the field, the internal dissonance caused by these issues can be increasingly felt. Some older designers have resisted the changes in style and attitude that are now emerging in part from the effects of the computer, but also caused by a generational shift and the general atmosphere of nihilistic relativism that marks our time. This resistance is not always harmful since it often prevents meretricious notions from entering the culture too easily. What is most disturbing is the sour and polarizing spirit that surrounds the discourse.

A new generation of critics has emerged, and there has been more critical writing on the subject of design than ever before. To some extent, the arguments remind us of the dramatic increase in communication that occurs shortly before people decide to get a divorce. The fundamental question of what good design is, and how it functions in society, has been scrutinized from many new points of view. By and large, philosophical inquiry has been separated from professional practice, and those interested in criticism have been essentially marginalized and left to ply their wares in academia and specialized journals.

There is something else to consider that may help us understand where we are: the relationship between the victory of entrepreneurial capitalism, the fall of world communism, and the almost universal collapse of liberal ideology. Here, we can see the connection between reduced ecological and social programs, the attack on "soft-headed or subversive do-gooders" (like the NEA and public broadcasting), and our own sense of loss. Flush with success and in the midst of its validating triumph around the world, Business is in no mood for accommodation. Recent history has proven to business that unyielding toughness pays, and self inquiry is a form of weakness. Unfortunately, with the elimination of an external threat those same convictions have been turned inward. Once again the wisest phrase in the language comes to mind: Pogo's immortal words, "We have met the enemy and he is us." The tendency of unconstrained business to produce a sense of unfairness and class warfare has emerged dramatically, and most of us have been affected by it.

We may be facing the most significant design problem of our lives—how to restore the "good" in good design. Or put another way, how to create a new narrative for our work that restores its moral center, creates a new sense of community, and reestablishes the continuity of generous humanism that is our heritage.

The war is over. It is time to begin again.

DESIGN IN A CLIMATE OF CONTEMPT

[excerpt] AIGA Journal, Volume 10–No.4, 1992

Things can get disheartening in professional life....

Our office was asked if we had any interest in designing the mascot for the 1996 Olympics in Atlanta. I assumed the project was similar to the way Mariscal's dog had been used for the Barcelona Olympics. We submitted a letter of interest and a package of work related to the problem. Apparently we were successful, because the following letter arrived a month later:

"Congratulations! You have been selected as a finalist to compete for the creation and design of the official Games mascot for the 1996 Atlanta Centennial Olympic Games ó the most important peacetime event this century. This designation places you among an elite group of professional artists and designers who are being asked to submit a proposal to the Atlanta Committee for the Olympic Games (ACOG) by 5:00pm, Friday, May 1, 1992.

Guidelines for submission of proposal
1. Deadline for submission: 5 pm, Friday, May 1, 1992
2. Only one (1) mascot proposal may be submitted
3. Submission must be on 18" x 24" poster board in the format shown on the enclosed illustration
4. Proposal must be in full recommended colors
5. Include your rationale ("why this critter?") for the mascot
6. Include at least one other application (example: doing a sport)

Compensation
There will be no compensation per se for the mascot design selected. However, once the winning design has been chosen, ACOG will negotiate appropriate compensation for refinements and production of a standards manual. Designs which are not selected will be returned.
NOTE: ACOG must own all rights to the mascot which is ultimately selected to represent the 1996 Atlanta Centennial Olympic Games. For this reason, all rights to the selected mascot must be transferable to ACOG and the creator and submitter of the selected mascot will be required to assign all rights to ACOG. Please sign and return the enclosed copy of this letter to acknowledge your understanding."

I take it that the word "refinements" means client changes, which will be paid for at whatever rate the client deems "appropriate." On one hand, the work is so worthless that it will not be paid for. On the other, the client retains all rights in case it turns out to be a gold mine. If this is not an expression of contempt, what is? Sadly, I suspect that dozens of designers accepted the terms of this contract because of whatever promotional benefits might ensue to them.

What can account for this dismal proposal? It is not a case of pro bono work for an AIDS benefit. Rather, it is a significant, highly specialized problem for commercial application with enormous financial consequences. In our society we express our respect for work by paying for it. When we refuse to do so, we are expressing contempt for the work and the worker. In these difficult times, the fundamental rules of human conduct are under attack in and out of business. The only appropriate response is not to allow our own sense of values and self respect to erode in the face of that attack.

In the past the design process seemed esoteric, highly specialized, full of internal rituals and hard to understand from the outside. These characteristics are all typical of spiritual or artistic activity, and serve as a means of protection. The computer, with its unprecedented power to change meaning, has made the process transparent and therefore controllable; and as we know, control is the name of the game.

CENSORIOUS ADVERTISING

Editorial in The Nation, 1997

Some months ago, I was nominated for the annual Chrysler Award for Innovation in Design. These awards have been around for five years and represent one of the few acknowledgments outside the profession that design is worthy of attention. A nomination is no indication of whether one will win, but I was flattered nevertheless.

A short time later, a friend sent me a piece from *The Wall Street Journal* written by Bruce Knecht, a thoughtful writer who covers the media. The article documents a letter dated January 30, 1996, sent by Chrysler's advertising agency to magazines that carry Chrysler advertising. It requires those magazines to submit articles in advance for screening by Chrysler to determine whether they contain any editorial content that may be construed as provocative or offensive. If these articles offended Chrysler's sensibility, it would pull its advertising.

In response to this alarming policy, I withdrew my nomination for the design awards. My letter to Chee Pearlman and Michael Sorkin, who administer the awards, included the following paragraph:

"Advertising in the right editorial environment has always been the prerogative of advertisers, but preemptive withdrawal is a new and repellent development. It is reminiscent of the McCarthy era in the fifties where script submission to agencies and advertisers was a common practice on television. This was one of the dark moments in our recent history. Censorship of this kind that acts to curtail the exchange of unpopular ideas is unacceptable for all those who care about human freedom and a healthy democratic society."

Art remains a mystery. We wonder about its significance in our lives. Why is it important? Why does it persist? When we observe the exploitation of art by the art world, the collectors, the dealers, the critics and curators, stumbling all over themselves to own, control and benefit from its production, it's easy to become cynical about its purpose.

At the same time I urged other participants involved in the awards, including Sorkin and Pearlman, to join me in opposing Chrysler's position. They declined, but several others accepted, including Steve Heller, the art director of *The New York Times Book Review,* who was also nominated this year; Jessica Helfand, a writer and designer who was a juror this year, and Tibor Kalman, the designer and editor and who was a juror this year and recipient of the award last year. Kalman has offered to give his $10,000 award to charity or to use it to publicly fight this nasty form of censorship.

Several days later, I had lunch with Pete Hamill, editor of the *New York Daily News*; Frank Lalli, editor of *Money* magazine; and Betsy Carter, editor of *New Woman*, the present and incoming presidents of the American Society of Newspaper Editors. At that luncheon, I was informed that A.S.N.E. was preparing a response that would condemn the prepublication approval of magazine content by advertisers. The A.S.N.E. statement, released on June 23, says what would appear to be self-evident that—editors have final authority over the editorial content of their magazines. They issued a call to publishers not to bow to advertising pressure. At this date, the publishers have not responded to this appeal.

Advertising influence in the magazine world is an old story—insiders have always known about cigarette campaign requirements to have at least ten pages separating their ads from any cancer-related story, or the fact that the airlines pull their ads when crashes are in the news. Some years ago, an old friend of mine, the magazine art director Henry Wolf, took a copy of *Vogue* and attached a colored thread to every ad that related to some editorial mention within the issue. When he was done, the results looked like a small Persian rug. This sort of thing has always been characteristic of the magazine business, most notably in the fashion and shelter magazines. Even so, the Chrysler policy represents a new chilling initiative. The idea of the advertisers reading manuscripts in advance and then deciding whether to cut the economic lifeline that keeps magazines alive violates our sense of fairness and our notion of how a free press works.

Incidentally, this policy does not seem to be unique to Chrysler. In fact, they complained that they are being persecuted by stories on the subject because they are willing to acknowledge a policy that many other companies practice covertly.

It is curious that after the triumph of capitalism, American business is embracing the politburo practice of censoring ideas it deems unacceptable. What is equally curious is the fact the there seems to be more public concern about freedom of the press in Hong Kong than in our own country.

The changes in our society that make it possible for a corporation to publicly announce this sort of policy and without embarrassment are difficult to understand. Certainly, the absence of strong contravening voices has something to do with it. The disbelief in the motives of our political leaders, the decline of labor unions and the collapse of liberal activism all have contributed to a power vacuum that big business has aggressively filled. All of us, in and out of the media, have a great deal to lose if this insidious attack on the principles of a free press continues unchallenged.

NB - Several months later, perhaps realizing that they were on the wrong side of the issue, Chrysler officially changed their policy concerning advanced editorial notification of a magazine's content.

INFLUENCE, IMITATION, AND PLAGIARISM

Lecture to students at the School of Visual Arts, 1986

In April 1983 I prepared a talk to be delivered at the AGI Congress about certain pieces I had done based on Italian themes and influences. Colin Forbes thought that would be appropriate for a meeting held in Gargonza. As I put this show together it raised some questions in my mind about the issue of influences and originality.

What are the differences between influence, imitation, and plagiarism? It's obvious that in a culture that celebrates and rewards individualism and uniqueness, designers, not to mention poets, painters and composers would be concerned about being accused of stealing ideas.

We recognize and celebrate influence, since human culture and even civilization itself depends on it. Beethoven stands on Mozart's shoulders. Influence makes progress and change possible. Influence is a well-regarded way of sharing and transmitting ideas—we might look on this activity as a form of gift-giving between groups or individuals.

We are somewhat less clear about the role of imitation, although other cultures that are perhaps less concerned about the role of the individual and more interested in their society as a whole, take a different view of imitation. As you may know, in Chinese art and artifacts, imitations (when well done) are considered to have the same value as the original. In most primitive cultures, the imitation of historical models for ritual purposes demands adherence to agreed upon forms, so that the magic will not be lost. In this case imitation is highly desirable.

Imitation serves another societal need—it establishes a context or set of values for the introduction of the new. If ideas were not imitated, they would have much more difficulty entering the culture. Van Dyck imitated his mentor Rubens, and as a result we understand and value Rubens more.

It is only relatively recently, with the concept of property value, that "originality" refers to something absolutely new, without precedent. Initially the word "original" meant something that had existed from the beginning of time. This change occurred along with a change in the definition of art from something well-made to something new.

In an industrialized capitalistic society, the imitation of another's idea begins to raise questions of private property and financial rewards. It creates the condition where tiny bits of printed ephemera such as the red border on *Time* magazine or the twisted noodle under the word Coca-Cola become objects worth millions of dollars. This creates a condition where almost every major corporation employs hundreds of three hundred dollar an hour lawyers who do nothing except search relentlessly for possible trademark violations.

We seem to be clear on the value of influence, a bit ambivalent about imitation, but absolutely in agreement about plagiarism. We despise and condemn it as a form of theft. The exact boundaries between these three ideas—influence, imitation and plagiarism seem extremely difficult to fix. For people in the design and illustration business, the issue becomes very complex, since in addition to trying to create their own style, which has property value, they also have to speak the current vernacular language in order to be understood. It's a sort of mad juggling act with one eye on your contemporaries and the other on your navel. It is no wonder that many designers begin a new assignment by first riffling though last year's annual. Ultimately every practitioner develops some kind of dialectic between the side of his work that is personal and the side that is based on shared communal ideas.

Finally a few observations about the characteristics of imitation, influence, and plagiarism that may help define their differences. Imitation and influence generally acknowledge their sources, plagiarism conceals them. In both, the fact that the original idea is continued and celebrated, with or without significant modifications is a central issue. In plagiarism the intent is to cash in on the idea and use it for other reasons, usually self-aggrandizement or financial reward. The attempt to conceal sources produces work without the internal tension that original works possess. Since only surfaces are copied, plagiarized works are always characterized by a lack of energy. After acknowledging how difficult it is to clearly establish the boundaries between these ideas, a most amazing fact emerges—we all know it when we see it.

MENTORS

Speech to AIGA Meeting, 1988

Whenever I'm not too sure about a subject I'm going to speak about, I go to the dictionary to find out what it is that I'm going to speak about. In this case, I really didn't have very much of an idea of what the word "mentor" really meant. I discovered in the dictionary that it suggests someone who gives sage advice, and also a friend of Telemachus. I remember vaguely that Telemachus was a figure in *The Odyssey*, and then I looked up Telemachus and discovered that he was the son of Odysseus. Mentor was actually a person. For those of you who know your Greek mythology, you will recall that he was the friend that Odysseus left behind to take care of the household while he was gone on the Odyssey. Odysseus went away for about ten years, longer than anyone expected, and when he came back, the household was in a terrific mess. As you remember, all of the suitors were sitting around vying for the hand of Penelope, Odysseus' wife. Actually, Mentor did a very poor job of what he was entrusted to do. Mentor continues to give advice in the myth, but this time with the voice of Athena, the goddess of light, wisdom, and beauty. In short, he loses his autonomy and becomes simply a mouthpiece for the goddess. And through this advice, eventually Odysseus and his son manage to get rid of all the suitors in a very dramatic scene, and the story more or less comes to a happy ending.

It is interesting to note, however, that the voice of Mentor was in fact the voice of a pagan, feminist goddess. In 1699, the Archbishop of Cambria wrote a little novel based on the life of Telemachus in which he eliminates Athena, and Mentor becomes the source of wisdom. It is not the first time in human history where pagan, feminist wisdom is transformed into male rationality. At any rate, by the 19th Century the word had passed into the language and lost its origins, and mentor became used in the sense that we use it today.

It seems to me that mentoring is at its best when it is, to some extent, at arms length. Which is to say, that where there is no self-interest in it. Where there is neither a desire to control nor any erotic component in the relationship. Otherwise, these mentoring relationships, can turn and become a source of disappointment or generate a sense of betrayal.

I have that sense with a man who thinks he discovered me by giving me my first job. He underpaid me for many years, but would constantly remind me of the fact that he had found me. He may have thought of himself as my mentor. I thought of him as a pain in the neck. But I have had true mentors starting with my junior high school chemistry teacher who gave me a box of Conte Crayons when I graduated, to a wonderful man by the name of George Salter, who was one of the shapers of design in our times. He was a terrific calligrapher, an urbane and sophisticated man who made me understand that you didn't have to be dumb if you were a designer. He gave me my first job as a professional. It was to follow his model and do the covers for *Ellery Queen Mystery Magazine*. I did one, and then realized that I couldn't continue doing it. I knew I had to find my own path. When I told him that, he accepted it perfectly, and it did not in any way hurt our relationship.

I had another mentor in a friend named Albert Rudolf, sort of a self-invented swami. He studied in India, became Rudi, was anointed as a swami, came back and taught what is called Kundalini Yoga, which is a rather esoteric form of yoga based on the idea of releasing the serpent power at the base of the spine. I don't think I ever released my serpent power, but it was a great privilege to know him. One day we were sitting in his store, and a shipment of about 100 Tibetan bronzes arrived. They were unpacked, and Rudi took ten or twelve and put them in a case. People came in and pointed to one of them, and they'd say, "How much is that?" Rudi answered, "$1,400." They'd point to another one and Rudi would say, "$800." Someone else would come in and ask how much something was, and Rudi would say, "$1,200." At the end of the day I turned to Rudi and said, "Hey look, where are these prices coming from? You bought 100 pieces. You paid for them collectively. You don't have any idea how much each piece costs. You don't even know very much about Tibetan bronzes. You don't know what year they're from or how scarce they are. Where are these prices coming from?" "Look, stupid," he explained, "every work of art is a vehicle for the creator's energy. That energy lasts forever. I'm an expert on energy. I see how much energy is coming out of the piece, multiply it by five, and that's where the price comes from."

At the time, I thought that was truly absurd. And now I think he's exactly right. There is no other way to ascertain the value of a work of art.

Perhaps the most profound mentor I have ever had is a man by the name of Giorgio Morandi, who was a teacher and painter/etcher, who very much changed my perception of what it meant to be in the world. He was a man of the most extraordinary modesty. Some years ago, I had a show with Giorgio Morandi at the Museum of Modern Art in Bologna. This is from the introduction to the catalog:

REFLECTIONS ON MORANDI AND BOLOGNA

When I was growing up in the Bronx the world was divided into two species, Jews and Italians. The Jews came from Eastern Europe, worked in the garment trade, lived in cramped three or four room apartments, and inspired their children to seek a better life through education. The Italians came from Sicily or Naples, lived communally in two family attached homes, made their own wine and were usually the poorest and most belligerent students in the public schools. They also pursued me relentlessly and beat me up regularly for having killed Christ, a crime I knew I was innocent of, but unaccountably felt guilty about any how. In 1951, I received my Fulbright Grant to study etching at the Academia di Belle Arti in Bologna. I was twenty-one and I had never been away from home before. I was understandably apprehensive about entering the homeland of my enemy. On my second day in Rome, I was sitting on a bench near the Stazione Termini, which seemed strangely familiar because of all the neo-realistic films I had seen where it served as a tumultuous background. I was drawing in my sketchbook and after a few moments I noticed a short dark man, whose head was capped with dark, curly hair observing me at a distance. I was not yet accustomed to the unflinching, aggressive stare that is characteristically Roman. I felt him approach and heard him say in strongly accented English, "Would you like to buy a Parker 51, cheap?" After the war Parker 51 fountain pens, bought by American service men at one Px and then resold on the street, had become a desirable black; market status item — inevitably, a flood of counterfeit pens entered the market at the same time. "I make you a good price," he continued, "thirty-five dollars." "I have a pen," I responded, hoping to discourage him. "Twenty dollars," he persisted. "I have a pen," I repeated. "Fifteen dollars," he offered, undeterred. "Look, I have a pen, I don't want a pen, I don't need a pen." "Alright, alright," he said, "make me an offer." I couldn't believe his doggedness and hoping to rid myself of this tormenter, I said, "I'll give you 400 lira." (In those days, the equivalent of 80 cents.) I can still clearly remember the momentary look of surprise that crossed his face as he cocked an eyebrow, drew a breath, and said, "O.K." He pocketed the money and walked off. After a moment he turned back and approached me again. "Are you Jewish?" All my history of early humiliations came to the surface as I stood up (I was at least 8 inches taller than he was), determined to even the score right then and there. "Yes I am," I said through clenched teeth. "Me too," he offered with a smile, "would you like to visit the ghetto?" I was so thoroughly unprepared for this question that I could only nod in astonishment and proceeded to follow him passively through a series of winding streets that led away from the station. It was only the beginning. After a while we came to what appeared to be a typically poor and time worn Roman quarter. We walked down the middle of a sunny street lined with a disorderly assortment of wooden tables and chairs. It was close to lunch and men in undershirts and women dressed in black shapeless dresses were sitting down drinking red wine and eating bread, cheese, and fruit. As we approached each group, they would raise their hand and shout, "Shalom! Shalom!" As this was happening the earth seemed to shift beneath my feet. My companion said, "Would you like to see the temple (Synagogue)?" I nodded, incapable of speech, and we continued walking for a short distance. We stopped at a large Romanesque structure of an impressive size; we had arrived at the synagogue, but it had no relationship to the modest red brick building I remember from the Bronx. Attached to the side of the building was a large marble slab inscribed with hundreds of Italian names. "Whose names are these?" I asked. "Those were Jews killed by Mussolini." They were not the Eastern European names I had always assumed indicated a Jew. These were all Italian like Luzzatti and Ottolenghi. At that moment I felt my innocence slipping away, and I knew I would never see the world in the same way again. Two weeks later I enrolled at the Academia di Belle Arti in Bologna to study etching with Giorgio Morandi. I had originally proposed to study the iconography of 15th-century Florence and Venetian painting (a proposal that from the beginning had little chance of being realized). My Fulbright adviser suggested that I might study at the Academia in Bologna, a city conveniently located between Florence and

It seems to me that mentoring is at its best when it is, to some extent, at arms length. Which is to say, that where there is no self-interest in it. Where there is neither a desire to control nor any erotic component in the relationship. Otherwise, these mentoring relationships can turn and become a source of disappointment or generate a sense of betrayal.

Venice, which geographically might help facilitate my project. And so I found myself in a cold dreary room at the academy together with ten or twelve teenage high school students awaiting the arrival of the teacher, Giorgio Morandi. He entered the room, a tall, trim, slightly stooped man already in his sixties with his white hair combed over his forehead not unlike Laurence Olivier in the movie, "Hamlet." He projected a sense of modesty and calm that was immediately reassuring. In all of my time at the Academia we only spoke about art on one occasion. We were standing by the sink where the etching plates were cleaned. There was a small reproduction of an etching of shells by Rembrandt pinned on the wall above the sink. Morandi leaned over my shoulder and in a conspiratorial voice said, "It's impossible to make black as black as Rembrandt did. I believe he might have used Dutch mordant and let the plate etch in it for many days." With those words he turned and never mentioned anything about art or etching to me again, except for his legendary "coraggio!" as one was about to plunge the copper plate into the acid bath. What I learned from Morandi was conveyed by the very essence of his being. He appeared to be free from the pull of money or desire of almost any kind. He only taught hard ground etching, an unforgiving technique where a multitude of precisely overlaying lines could produce the illusion of tonality. It's instructive that Morandi, the most tonal of all 20th-century painters, would chose this medium to produce some of his most significant masterpieces. His life seemed to me then as it does today, the ideal life of a true artist. Lucidity and balance are the words that come to mind when I think of Morandi. He lived silently and produced monuments.

In those days, the idea of ever having a show with Morandi was inconceivable. It still is. The grace of Morandi's work is in the spiritual dimension. The nature, of my work has always been in the world of commerce. Morandi is all about transcendence. The subject of all meaningful works of art is about moving people to action or influencing their perception about things or events. In my time, there has been more concern than ever in history about keeping these two discreet activities clearly separated. This is especially true since art has increasingly begun to replace religion as something to believe in. There is a profound desire to keep art pure and uncorrupted by worldly considerations. Curiously, the erosion of art does not come from the encroachment of the implied or commercial arts, but rather from the cynical and conspiratorial efforts of collectors, dealers, periodicals, and museums to manipulate art as a commodity. For me, this exhibition is not about the question of art versus commerce, but rather how the trajectory of someone's life can be changed by even a brief contact with a remarkable person or a special place. Finally, it is an act of closure and gratitude for the privileged time, almost forty years ago, spent in Bologna with Giorgio Morandi.

For years, I have struggled with the question of whether designers, by virtue of their positions as communicators, should have more ethical responsibility than the average good citizen. Perhaps a better question would be "Should they have less?"

I've actually had two artistic models in my life. One was Pablo Picasso, the man who wanted everything—all the money, all the fame, all the women. I like a quote about Picasso: "No idea was safe when Picasso was in the room." Morandi, on the other hand, wanted nothing. If you wanted to buy a painting from Morandi, he would take $200 from you and sign your name and address on the back of a canvas. Some years later, when he finished a painting, he'd turn it over, find out who it belonged to, and send it to you in the mail. This was at a time when his paintings were selling for $10,000 to $15,000. He wanted no power, except the most significant power, the power over his own life.

THE MANY ITALIAN CUISINES

Speech given at the Aspen Design Conference, 1984

Thank you. I, like Professor Zeri, am also very interested in the relationship between food and culture and find myself reading cookbooks all the time as well. In fact I have to confess I've read considerably more cookbooks than I have novels in my life. I'm also interested in cooking as an extension of ideas about design because in many ways there are analogies between the act of cooking and the act of design. Perhaps not even the most obvious ones like the consideration of texture and form and color and sequence and so on, all of which are issues that we're concerned with as designers and recipients of design. But also the more interesting aspect of the relationship between familiarity and novelty or as Paolo Portugese(?) mentioned last night in speaking of architecture in context, the relationship between permanence and innovation. I hate innovative food. I truly despise food innovation. I remember being in a restaurant in New York owned by a client of mine, a kind of pseudo-Italian restaurant as it turns out, when I ordered spaghetti a la matriciana, and the dish came to the table and there were two big chicken breasts on it. I said, "I ordered spaghetti a la matriciana." He said, "That's right." I said, "It doesn't come with chicken breasts." He said, "We don't charge you more for it!" When I order spaghetti a la matriciana, what I want is a classical dish prepared in the same way so that I can compare the dish to my memory of it, to the model I hold in my mind. I don't want it to be improved upon. There are many things that should not be improved upon. This is a very tough idea to present to the design community sometimes but there are a lot of things that should be left alone. Spaghetti a la matriciana only being one of them. Anyhow, last night I had dinner and I approached it with some apprehension because the dinner was supposed—it was told to me—was going to be a dinner of innovative food. And occasionally innovation in the hand of an extraordinarily gifted talent can actually be interesting or amusing or extraordinary but that doesn't happen too often. In any case, Fabio Picchi and his wife, Bendetta—Bendetta Vitale—had prepared this meal. I'll tell you what we had. We had a pudding of cauliflower. Then a Brunelleschi Dome of string beans encircled by a mousse of tuna fish. And then we had a very traditional Tuscan pate served with little toast rounds. And then a kind of souffle of leeks and ricotta cheese, presented as though it were a tropical island on a coral reef sort of surrounded by a sauce made of zucchini. And then we had a zuppa di pepperoni, which was this extraordinary soup made out of yellow peppers and potatoes, sort of Kodak yellow, luminous Kodak yellow with a river of golden olive oil flowing through the middle of it. Absolutely extraordinary dish. And then we had a very traditional Tuscan dish which sounds terrible. Its made out of stale bread and tomatoes. It's called pappa di pomodoro. Its a kind of dish that's fed to the very old and the very young. A kind of pap of tomatoes and bread and it's absolutely fantastic. And this was one of the very best I had ever had. And then we had anitra ripiena which was a duck stuffed with forcemeat served with Italian eggplant and pignoli nuts. Then we had a salad made out of diced beets, potatoes, zucchini, string beans and carrots. Sublime. And then we had some dessert, a rasberry tart and an incredibly thick chocolate mousse that you could just barely swallow. Well, I found the meal absolutely extraordinary and not because it was innovative but because the relationship between innovation and familiarity was in the right place. All the dishes it seemed to me came out of a sublime understanding of the history of people who had eaten that kind of food before and the references contained within it just maintains the continuity of form. So the old provides the context for the new. I think that's the kind of thing that designers are always concerned about. To be truly innovative in design you basically lose contact with your audience because the new is incomprehensible. And here the relationship between what was old, what was familiar and what was novel was exquisitely felt. We often hear the description of the design process as an activity that shapes events in order to produce a desired effect. Well last night the desired effect was the delight and the satisfaction of the audience, which was achieved. And in those terms by that definition I would have to say that Fabio and Bendetta are two of the greatest designers in Italy.

THE TRUTH

Essay for AIGA Journal, 2000

I went to Las Vegas for the first time to participate in the AIGA conference. I was booked at the Venetian—a hotel whose vast vistas of painted, cloud-filled skies had required the skills of more mural painters than existed in Venice during the entire fifteenth century.

On my first day at the hotel, I noticed a sign that said "Grand Canal." I asked the concierge at the reception desk where it was. "One flight up", she said. The earth reeled beneath my feet. A canal one flight up; what a concept.

The canal was, in fact, upstairs, complete with gondola and gondolier who would cheerfully take you around a bend to the Piazza San Marco. Later that same day, the hotel's plumbing broke down, and suddenly the entire ground floor began to smell like Venice on a warm day. I actually found myself wondering whether the hotel had planned it. Is there such a thing as virtual smell?

On the Dallas leg of the flight from Las Vegas after the AIGA conference, the hostess entered the aisle with a vigorously steaming tray of hot towels. I noticed that a wine glass filled with water was the source of the steam.

"**W**hat is that?" I asked the hostess, pointing to the glass.

"Dry ice and water," she replied.

"Is that for drama?" I asked.

"Yes," she replied.

Even to a dormant mind, a trip to Las Vegas inevitably raises the question of "What is real?" and, by inference, "What is truth?" It actually provided the subtext for the conference itself, notably in Kurt Anderson's talk on whether real is better than fake and Denise Caruso's concern about who to trust on the Net.

Obviously, the question of "What is the truth?" is one of humankind's most persistent questions, but it seems ever more insistent at this moment than at any other time. What can it mean when a freezing glass of dry ice is used to simulate a steaming towel on a plane trip? Can this modest deception benefit either the airline or its passengers? Where was the decision made to do it? In the boardroom? In the advertising agency? On the flight itself? Does the airline believe that the drama of the steaming towels will suggest a policy of concerned service? What happens to the customer in the last row of the plane when he is handed a cold towel while the tray above his head is steaming madly? Does he doubt his own nervous system? What makes me uncomfortable with all of this? Why do I believe that harm is being done? All of which leads us in a convoluted way to the question of professional ethics.

"How can we tell the truth?" can be thought of as two separate questions. The first part asks why we believe what we believe; the second, where ethical questions begin, involves our responsibility to others.

One must start with the presumption that telling the truth is important for human survival, but at this moment of relativism and virtuality, I'm not sure how many would agree on what truth is or how important it is in our private and professional lives.

But we must begin somewhere. The question becomes a professional one, because as designers or *communicators* (the preferred current description), we are constantly informing the public, transmitting information, and affecting the beliefs and values of others. Should telling the truth be a fundamental requirement of this role? Is there a difference between telling the truth to your wife and family and telling the truth to a general public? What is that difference?

As a profession that defines itself by effectively persuading others, it's impossible to consider our work outside the context of advertising, an activity that is so fundamental to our economy and so pervasively influential that it may have informed our idea of what truth is, more than any other single thing.

We drown in the sea of relentless persuasion that we help create as well as receive. There are now ads under our feet in supermarkets. I opened a fortune cookie the other night and found that an advertisement for an e-commerce company had replaced my fortune. (I am not kidding!) And some weeks ago, we were informed that the pauses in Rush Limbaugh's talk show had been electronically eliminated to gain six more advertising messages per hour. All of these messages intend to sell rather than inform, and tend to distend or modify the truth in ways that we can no longer see. Our brains and sense of truth cannot be unaffected by this onslaught.

For years, I have struggled with the question of whether designers, by virtue of their positions as communicators, should have more ethical responsibility than the average good citizen. Perhaps a better question would be "Should they have less?"

A QUESTIONNAIRE

I had the pleasure of illustrating Dante's *Purgatory* this year for an Italian publisher. I was impressed by the fact that the difference between those unfortunates in Hell and those in Purgatory was that the former had no idea of how they had sinned. Those in Hell were there forever. Those in Purgatory knew what they had done and were waiting it out, with at least the possibility of redemption, thus establishing the difference between despair and hope.

Of course, Dante's metaphors are all about the life we now lead, and I assume the distinction between Hell and Purgatory is the distinction between awareness and denial.

In regard to professional ethics, acknowledging what it is we do is a beginning. A journey cannot be started without understanding where you are. It is clear that in our profession, the question of misrepresenting the truth arises almost immediately. So much of what we do can be seen as a distortion of the truth. Put another way, "He who enters the bath, sweats."

Finally, all questions of ethics become personal, and to establish your own level of discomfort with bending the truth, read the following chart to determine how far down on the road to Hell you are willing to go.

The Road to Hell

1 Designing a package to look larger on the shelf

2 Doing an ad for a slow-moving, boring film to make it seem like a lighthearted comedy

3 Designing a crest for a new vineyard to suggest that it's been in business for a long time

4 Designing a jacket for a book whose sexual content you find personally repellent

5 Participating in a design award program whose sponsor was known to demand advance knowledge of the editorial content of magazines in order to determine whether it would withdraw its advertising

6 Designing a package for a cereal aimed at children which has low nutritional value and high sugar content

7 Designing a line of T-shirts for a manufacturer who employs child labor

8 Designing a promotion for a diet product that you know doesn't work

9 Designing an ad for a political candidate whose policies you believe would be harmful to the general public

10 Designing a brochure piece for an automobile whose gas tanks were known to occasionally explode

11 Designing an ad for a product whose continued use might cause the user's death

Content Facts

	% Of Content
Quantifiable Facts	20%
Deliberate Falsehoods	12%
Inadvertent Errors	.05%
Filler (Organic)	38%
Sugars	3%
Harmful By Products	3%
Superficial Images	28%
Questionable Values	33%
Pure Bullshit	20%
Good Intentions	10%
Trendy Graphics	28%
Stolen Ideas	22%

Milton Glaser, Inc.
207 East 32nd Street
New York NY 10016
www.miltonglaser.com
www.miltonglaserposters.com

Nice Baby, 1996

The primary typefaces used throughout *Art Is Work* are
Poynter OldStyle and Poynter Gothic,
supplied by The Font House, Inc. in Boston.